Personal Finance For Dummie$® For Canadians, 2nd Edition

by Eric Tyson and Tony Ma~~rtin~~

Quick Reference Card

Eric and Tony's Keys to Personal Financial Success

- **Take charge of your finances.** Procrastinating is detrimental to your long-term financial health. Don't wait for a crisis or major life event to get your act together. Read this book and start implementing now!

- **Never buy items that depreciate on credit.** Cars, clothing, vacations, and so on lose value over time. Use debt only to make investments in things that gain value, such as real estate, a business, or an education.

- **Use credit cards only for convenience, not for carrying debt.** If you have a tendency to run up credit card debt, get rid of your cards and use only cash, cheques, and debit cards.

- **Live within your means and don't try to keep up with the Joneses.** Many who engage in conspicuous consumption are borrowing against their futures; some end up bankrupt.

- **Save and invest at least 5 to 10 percent of your income.** Preferably, invest through an RRSP or other retirement savings plan to reduce your taxes and ensure your future financial independence.

- **Understand and use your employee benefits.** If self-employed, find out the best investment and insurance options available to you, and use them.

- **Research financial products or services before you buy.** Never purchase a financial product on the basis of an advertisement or salesperson's solicitation.

- **Avoid financial products that carry high commissions and expenses.** Companies that sell their products through aggressive sales techniques generally have the worst financial products and the highest commissions.

- **Don't buy any financial product that you don't understand.** Ask questions and compare what you're offered to the best sources recommended in this book.

- **Invest the majority of your long-term money in ownership vehicles that have appreciation potential, such as stocks, real estate, and your own business.** When you invest in bonds or bank accounts, you simply lend your money to others; only bankers get wealthy lending their money to others.

...For Dummies: Bestselling Book Series for Beginners

Personal Finance For Dummie$® For Canadians, 2nd Edition

Quick Reference Card

by Eric Tyson and Tony Martin

Avoid making emotionally-based financial decisions. For example, investors who panic and sell their stock holdings after a major market correction miss a buying opportunity. Be especially careful in making important financial decisions after a major life change such as a divorce, job loss, or death in your family.

Make investing decisions based upon your needs and the long-term fundamentals of what you're buying. Ignore the predictive advice offered by financial prognosticators. Never make decisions based on news headlines. Nobody has a working crystal ball.

Own your home. In the long run, owning is more cost-effective than renting, unless you have a terrific rent-control deal. Don't buy until you can stay put for a number of years.

Purchase broad insurance coverage to protect against financial catastrophes. Eliminate insurance for small potential losses.

If you're married, make time to discuss joint goals, issues, and concerns. Be accepting of your partner's money personality; learn to compromise and manage as a team.

Prepare for life changes. The better you are at living within your means and anticipating life changes, the better off you will be financially and emotionally.

Read publications that have high quality standards and that aren't afraid to take a stand and recommend what's in your best interests.

Prioritize your financial goals and start working toward them. Be patient. Focus on your accomplishments and learn from your past mistakes.

Hire yourself first. You're the best financial person that you can hire. If you need help making a major decision, hire conflict-free advisors who charge fees for their time. Work in partnership with advisors. Never abdicate control.

Invest in yourself. Invest in your education, in your health, and in your relationships with family and friends. Having a lot of money isn't worth much if you don't have your health and people with whom to share your life.

IDG BOOKS WORLDWIDE

Copyright © 1998 Eric Tyson and Tony Martin. All rights reserved.

Cheat Sheet $2.95 value. Item 5123-X.

For more information about IDG Books, call 1-800-762-2974.

...For Dummies: Bestselling Book Series for Beginners

Praise for Eric Tyson, Tony Martin, and This Book

"Worth getting. Scores of all-purpose money-management books reach bookstores every year, but only once every couple of years does a standout personal finance primer come along. *Personal Finance For Dummies*...provides detailed, action-oriented advice on everyday financial questions..."

> — Kristin Davis, *Kiplinger's Personal Finance Magazine*

"Eric Tyson is doing something important—namely, helping people at all income levels to take control of their financial futures. This book is a natural outgrowth of Tyson's vision that he has nurtured for years...I am enthusiastic about his efforts and see this book as yet one more step down the path of turning his vision into practical reality."

> — James C. Collins, co-author of the bestseller *Built to Last* and *Beyond Entrepreneurship*, Lecturer in Business, Stanford Graduate School of Business

"Smart advice for dummies...skip the tomes...and buy *Personal Finance For Dummies*, which rewards your candor with advice and comfort."

> — Temma Ehrenfeld, *Newsweek*

"Best new personal finance book."

> — Michael Pellechia, Syndicated Columnist

"Tony Martin has a great gift for making complex material clear, relevant—and a pleasure to read."

> — Penny Williams, Magazine Editor

"Breaking down complicated personal financial concepts and strategies into plain, understandable English is no easy task, but you can count on Tony Martin to do it. He's able to take the dustiest, driest, most difficult financial terms and topics and make them intelligible, interesting, and, well, even entertaining!"

> — David T. Holmes, Partner, Holmes Creative Communications

"*Personal Finance For Dummies*…is an absolute necessity for all Canadians in these economic times. The book clearly and concisely presents essential personal finance information and advice in an engaging, straightforward style. Every bookshelf should have a copy."
— Colleen Mooney, M.B.A., Hospital Administrator

"For those named in the title, such as myself, *Personal Finance For Dummies* is a godsend. It's bright, funny, and it can save you money, too."
— Jerome Crowe, reporter, *L.A. Times*

"…presents complicated issues with simplicity, clarity and a touch of humor."
— *The Times-Picayune,* New Orleans, LA

"*Personal Finance For Dummies* is a sane and useful guide that will be of benefit to anyone seeking a careful and prudent method of managing their financial world."
— John Robbins, founder of EarthSave and author of *May All Be Fed*

"If you're wondering where to start in becoming financially literate, may I recommend *Personal Finance For Dummies*…"
— Peter McWilliams, *Worcester Telegram & Gazette,* Worcester, MA

"Comprehensive, well-organized information in an easy-to-read format."
— Dianne L. Zimmerman, Rockville, MD

"Simple and straightforward explanations. This book helped me sort through all the hype and advertising out there and helped me increase my net worth!"
— Bryan Hailey, Fairbanks, AK

"Layout of [the] information made it easy to find exactly what I needed."
— Charles St. Clair, Rosedale, IN

"Fun to read, informative. I wish all financial magazines and prospectuses were as fun to read."
— Mike Mendiola, Whittier, CA

PERSONAL FINANCE

FOR

DUMMIE$®

FOR CANADIANS, 2ND EDITION

PERSONAL FINANCE FOR DUMMIE$®

FOR CANADIANS. 2ND EDITION

by Eric Tyson and Tony Martin

IDG Books Worldwide, Inc.
An International Data Group Company

Foster City, CA ♦ Chicago, IL ♦ Indianapolis, IN ♦ New York, NY

Personal Finance For Dummies® For Canadians, 2nd Edition

Published by
IDG Books Worldwide, Inc.
An International Data Group Company
919 E. Hillsdale Blvd.
Suite 400
Foster City, CA 94404
www.idgbooks.com (IDG Books Worldwide Web site)
www.dummies.com (Dummies Press Web site)

Library of Congress Catalog Card No.: 98-87436

ISBN: 0-7645-5123-X

Printed in the United States of America

10 9 8 7 6 5 4 3 2 1

2O/RU/QZ/ZY/IN

Distributed in the United States by IDG Books Worldwide, Inc.

Distributed by Macmillan Canada for Canada; by Transworld Publishers Limited in the United Kingdom; by IDG Norge Books for Norway; by IDG Sweden Books for Sweden; by Woodslane Pty. Ltd. for Australia; by Woodslane (NZ) Ltd. for New Zealand; by Addison Wesley Longman Singapore Pte Ltd. for Singapore, Malaysia, Thailand, Indonesia and Korea; by Norma Comunicaciones S.A. for Colombia; by Intersoft for South Africa; by International Thomson Publishing for Germany, Austria and Switzerland; by Toppan Company Ltd. for Japan; by Distribuidora Cuspide for Argentina; by Livraria Cultura for Brazil; by Ediciencia S.A. for Ecuador; by Ediciones ZETA S.C.R. Ltda. for Peru; by WS Computer Publishing Corporation, Inc., for the Philippines; by Unalis Corporation for Taiwan; by Contemporanea de Ediciones for Venezuela; by Computer Book & Magazine Store for Puerto Rico; by Express Computer Distributors for the Caribbean and West Indies. Authorized Sales Agent: Anthony Rudkin Associates for the Middle East and North Africa.

For general information on IDG Books Worldwide's books in the U.S., please call our Consumer Customer Service department at 800-762-2974. For reseller information, including discounts and premium sales, please call our Reseller Customer Service department at 800-434-3422.

For information on where to purchase IDG Books Worldwide's books outside the U.S., please contact our International Sales department at 650-655-3200 or fax 650-655-3297.

For information on foreign language translations, please contact our Foreign & Subsidiary Rights department at 650-655-3021 or fax 650-655-3281.

For sales inquiries and special prices for bulk quantities, please contact our Sales department at 650-655-3200 or write to the address above.

For information on using IDG Books Worldwide's books in the classroom or for ordering examination copies, please contact our Educational Sales department at 800-434-2086 or fax 317-596-5499.

For press review copies, author interviews, or other publicity information, please contact our Public Relations department at 650-655-3000 or fax 650-655-3299.

For authorization to photocopy items for corporate, personal, or educational use, please contact Copyright Clearance Center, 222 Rosewood Drive, Danvers, MA 01923, or fax 978-750-4470.

is a trademark under exclusive license to IDG Books Worldwide, Inc., from International Data Group, Inc.

About the Authors

Eric Tyson first became interested in money matters more than two decades ago. After his father was laid off during the 1973 recession and received some retirement money from Philco-Ford, Eric worked with his dad to make investing decisions with the money.

Today, Eric is a nationally recognized personal financial counsellor, writer, and lecturer. He has taught thousands of people from all income levels, so he knows the financial concerns and questions of real folks just like you. Despite being handicapped by an M.B.A. from Stanford, and a B.S. in Economics and Biology from Yale, Eric remains a master at "keeping it simple."

An accomplished freelance personal finance writer, his Investor's Guide syndicated column, distributed by King Features, is read by millions nationally.

He is author of national best-selling financial books in the *...For Dummies* series on personal finance, investing, and mutual funds, and co-authored best-selling books on home buying and taxes. His work has been featured and quoted in numerous local and national publications including *Newsweek, The Wall Street Journal, Los Angeles Times, Chicago Tribune, Forbes, Kiplinger's Personal Finance Magazine, Parenting, Money, Bottom Line/Personal,* as well as on the NBC *Today Show,* ABC, CNBC, PBS Nightly Business Report, CNN, and FOX-TV, and on CBS national radio, NPR *Sound Money,* Bloomberg Business Radio, and Business Radio Network.

Tony Martin, after graduating from Queen's University with a business degree, set off to see the world. (Best buy? A two-day "cruise" from Jakarta to Singapore for $8, including a place to unroll a sleeping bag on deck, and fish and rice three times a day.) He then joined CBC radio and, from then on, has been involved in many media helping people understand the world of money and get control of their finances.

Tony's work has appeared in many leading publications, including *The Globe And Mail,* the *Report on Business* magazine, *IEMoney, The Financial Post, The Ottawa Citizen,* and *Readers' Digest.* He also is the editor for the personal finance Web site at `www.imoney.com`'s Knowledge base. He produced and wrote for the popular personal finance television series, Money$Worth, and his work has also been aired on Business Week, a nationally syndicated television program. He frequently comments on personal finance matters, and has appeared on CBC's Midday, CityLine, and numerous other radio and television stations.

Tony is also the author of *Me and My Money,* based on his popular column profiling the investing techniques of individual Canadians from the weekend Investing section of *The Globe And Mail*'s Report on Business.

ABOUT IDG BOOKS WORLDWIDE

Welcome to the world of IDG Books Worldwide.

IDG Books Worldwide, Inc., is a subsidiary of International Data Group, the world's largest publisher of computer-related information and the leading global provider of information services on information technology. IDG was founded more than 25 years ago and now employs more than 8,500 people worldwide. IDG publishes more than 275 computer publications in over 75 countries (see listing below). More than 90 million people read one or more IDG publications each month.

Launched in 1990, IDG Books Worldwide is today the #1 publisher of best-selling computer books in the United States. We are proud to have received eight awards from the Computer Press Association in recognition of editorial excellence and three from *Computer Currents'* First Annual Readers' Choice Awards. Our best-selling ...*For Dummies*® series has more than 50 million copies in print with translations in 38 languages. IDG Books Worldwide, through a joint venture with IDG's Hi-Tech Beijing, became the first U.S. publisher to publish a computer book in the People's Republic of China. In record time, IDG Books Worldwide has become the first choice for millions of readers around the world who want to learn how to better manage their businesses.

Our mission is simple: Every one of our books is designed to bring extra value and skill-building instructions to the reader. Our books are written by experts who understand and care about our readers. The knowledge base of our editorial staff comes from years of experience in publishing, education, and journalism — experience we use to produce books for the '90s. In short, we care about books, so we attract the best people. We devote special attention to details such as audience, interior design, use of icons, and illustrations. And because we use an efficient process of authoring, editing, and desktop publishing our books electronically, we can spend more time ensuring superior content and spend less time on the technicalities of making books.

You can count on our commitment to deliver high-quality books at competitive prices on topics you want to read about. At IDG Books Worldwide, we continue in the IDG tradition of delivering quality for more than 25 years. You'll find no better book on a subject than one from IDG Books Worldwide.

John Kilcullen
CEO
IDG Books Worldwide, Inc.

Steven Berkowitz
President and Publisher
IDG Books Worldwide, Inc.

Eighth Annual
Computer Press
Awards ≥1992

Ninth Annual
Computer Press
Awards ≥1993

Tenth Annual
Computer Press
Awards ≥1994

Eleventh Annual
Computer Press
Awards ≥1995

Dedication

This book is hereby and irrevocably dedicated to our families and friends, as well as clients and customers, who ultimately have taught us everything that we know about how to explain financial terms and strategies so that all of us may benefit.

Authors' Acknowledgments

Being an entrepreneur involves endless challenges, and without the support and input of good friends and mentors Peter Mazonson, Jim Collins, and my best friend and wife, Judy, I couldn't have accomplished what I have.

I hold many people accountable for my perverse and maniacal interest in figuring out the financial services industry and money matters, but most of the blame falls on my loving parents, Charles and Paulina, who taught me most of what I know that's been of use in the real world.

I'd also like to thank Maggie McCall, David Ish, Paul Kozak, Chris Treadway, Sally St. Lawrence, K.T. Rabin, Will Hearst III, Ray Brown, Susan Wolf, Rich Caramella, Lisa Baker, Renn Vera, Maureen Taylor, Jerry Jacob, Robert Crum, Duc Nguyen, and Maria Carmicino and all the good folks at King Features for believing in and supporting my writing and teaching.

— *Eric*

There is no such thing as working on one's own, as the support, good humour, and advice of many are essential to success, and I owe many thanks to my good friend Geoff Rockburn and my wife, Jane Howard, who have both been endlessly supportive and helpful over the years. I'm as grateful as always to my parents, Ruth and John, for teaching me so much about what really matters.

There are also many people in the personal finance industry who have kindly offered their help in assisting me in penetrating, understanding, and explaining money matters. Many thanks to everybody who has generously shared their insights and expertise over the years, including Peter Volpe, Gena Katz, Sandra McLeod, Anthony Layton, Paul Hickey, Jim Bullock, Alisa Dunbar, Alan Silverstein, and Janet Freedman.

In addition, I'd like to thank Peggy Wente, Douglas Goold, Dave Pyette, Karen Benzing, Don Hendry, Trish Wilson, Michael Lee, David Chilton, and Carmela DiLalla for their support and encouragement over the years.

— *Tony*

Many thanks to all the people who provided insightful comments on this book, especially tax and financial planner extraordinaire Barton Francis, financial planner par excellence Warren Baldwin, and Mike van den Akker, Gretchen Morgensen, Craig Litman, Gerri Detweiler, Mark White, Alan Bush, Nancy Coolidge, and Chris Jensen.

And thanks to all the wonderful people at IDG Books on the front line and behind the scenes, especially John Kilcullen, who had the vision, foresight, and courage to do this book, Kathy Welton, and Diane Steele. We'd especially like to thank our ever capable and talented project editor Kathy Cox and Wendy Hatch, our careful copy editor, as well as Cindy Phipps and her team in Production who made a book out of these manuscript pages. We'd also like to thank Justin Wells and Judy Lee for other thoughtful suggestions and willingness to help meet difficult deadlines.

Publisher's Acknowledgments

We're proud of this book; please register your comments through our IDG Books Worldwide Online Registration Form located at http://my2cents.dummies.com.

Some of the people who helped bring this book to market include the following:

Acquisitions, Development, and Editorial

Project Editor: Kathleen M. Cox

Acquisitions Editor: Mark Butler

Copy Editor: Wendy Hatch

Technical Editor: Warren Baldwin, B.A., C.F.P., R.F.P., Regional Vice-President, T.E. Financial Consultants Ltd., Toronto

Editorial Manager: Colleen Rainsberger

Editorial Coordinator: Maureen Kelly

Editorial Assistant: Paul Kuzmic

Production

Project Coordinator: Cindy L. Phipps

Layout and Graphics: Lou Boudreau, Linda M. Boyer, J. Tyler Connor, Maridee V. Ennis, Angela F. Hunckler, Jane E. Martin, Drew R. Moore, Heather N. Pearson, Brent Savage, Kate Snell

Proofreaders: Christine Berman, Kelli Botta, Melissa D. Buddendeck, Michelle Croninger, Rachel Garvey, Rebecca Senninger

Indexer: Mary Mortensen

Special Help

Jonathan Malysiak

General and Administrative

IDG Books Worldwide, Inc.: John Kilcullen, CEO; Steven Berkowitz, President and Publisher

IDG Books Technology Publishing: Brenda McLaughlin, Senior Vice President and Group Publisher

Dummies Technology Press and Dummies Editorial: Diane Graves Steele, Vice President and Associate Publisher; Mary Bednarek, Director of Acquisitions and Product Development; Kristin A. Cocks, Editorial Director

Dummies Trade Press: Kathleen A. Welton, Vice President and Publisher; Kevin Thornton, Acquisitions Manager

IDG Books Production for Dummies Press: Michael R. Britton, Vice President of Production and Creative Services; Beth Jenkins Roberts, Production Director; Cindy L. Phipps, Manager of Project Coordination, Production Proofreading, and Indexing; Kathie S. Schutte, Supervisor of Page Layout; Shelley Lea, Supervisor of Graphics and Design; Debbie J. Gates, Production Systems Specialist; Robert Springer, Supervisor of Proofreading; Debbie Stailey, Special Projects Coordinator; Tony Augsburger, Supervisor of Reprints and Bluelines

Dummies Packaging and Book Design: Robin Seaman, Creative Director; Jocelyn Kelaita, Product Packaging Coordinator; Kavish + Kavish, Cover Design

◆

The publisher would like to give special thanks to Patrick J. McGovern, without whom this book would not have been possible.

◆

Contents at a Glance

Cartoons at a Glance

By Rich Tennant

page 317

page 175

page 361

page 53

page 7

Fax: 978-546-7747 • **E-mail:** the5wave@tiac.net

Table of Contents

Introduction

Welcome to *Personal Finance For Dummies For Canadians,* 2nd Edition. For a number of years, we both dreamed of writing a personal finance book that would be different. The book would describe in plain, readable English the most important concepts that you need to know in order to manage your personal finances. It would give specific answers to financial questions where it could, and where it couldn't give the answers, it would suggest the best resources to turn to.

As fate would have it, our paths crossed that of IDG Books Worldwide, Inc. As computer dummies, we were overjoyed to finally find computer books that offered clear explanations and practical advice. The *...For Dummies* approach is how we both had conceived a personal finance book; we just didn't know it at the time! Eric got the folks at IDG to buy into the idea of a book on personal finance, and soon after, they agreed with Tony that Canadians, darn it, needed their own *....For Dummies* guide to personal finance.

As you can see from the quotes in the front of this edition, readers and reviewers alike were pretty pleased with the first edition. However, we and the good folks at IDG don't rest on our laurels. So what you hold in your hands reflects more hard work to bring you the freshest material to address your personal financial quandaries.

Why This Book

Many Canadians are financially illiterate. If you are, it's probably not your fault. Personal Finance 101 is not offered in our schools — not in high school, not even in the best universities, colleges, and graduate schools. It should be. (Of course, if it were, we wouldn't be able to write fun and useful books such as this — or maybe instructors would use this book in the course!)

There are some common financial problems and mistakes, and different people keep making those same mistakes over and over. This book, like a good friend, can whop you upside the head to keep you from falling into the same traps:

✔ **Not planning.** Human beings were born to procrastinate. That's why there are deadlines and extensions. With your finances, unfortunately, you have no deadlines, and you think you have unlimited extensions! You can leave your money sitting in lousy investments for years. You can end up paying higher taxes, having gaps in your retirement and insurance coverage, and overpaying for financial products. Of course, planning your finances isn't as much fun as planning a vacation, but doing the former will help you take more of the latter.

✔ **Overspending.** The average Canadian saves about 9 percent of his or her after-tax income. Although we sure do a better job than Americans, who manage to put away less than 5 percent, contrast that with the French who save about 12 percent, the Germans who save 14 percent, and the Japanese who save 15 percent. It's simple arithmetic to determine that savings is the difference between what you earn minus what you spend (assuming you're not spending more than you're earning!). To increase your savings, you either have to work more (yuck!), know a wealthy family who wants to leave its fortune to you, or simply learn to spend less. For most of us, the thrifty approach is the key to building savings and wealth.

✔ **Buying on credit.** Even with the benefit of today's lower interest rates, carrying a balance month to month on your credit card or buying a car on credit means that even more of your future earnings are earmarked for debt repayment. Buying on credit encourages you to spend more than you can really afford.

✔ **Not saving soon enough for retirement.** Most people say they want to retire by their mid-60s or sooner. But in order to accomplish this financially, you need to save a reasonable chunk (around 10 percent) of your income starting sooner rather than later. The longer you wait to start saving for retirement, the harder it is to reach your goal. And you pay much more in taxes to boot if you don't take advantage of the tax benefits of investing through particular retirement plans.

✔ **Falling prey to financial sales pitches.** Great deals that can't wait for a little reflection or a second opinion are often disasters waiting to happen. A sucker may be born every minute, but a slick salesperson is born every second! Steer clear of those who pressure you to make decisions, promise high investment returns, and lack the proper training and experience to help you.

✔ **Not doing your homework.** To get the best financial deal, you need to shop around, read reviews, and get advice from disinterested, objective third parties. You need to check references and track records so you don't hire incompetent, self-serving, or fraudulent financial advisors. But with all the different financial products available, making informed financial decisions has become an overwhelming task. We've done a lot of the homework for you with the investment, insurance, credit, and other products we recommend in this book. Where we're not able to give precise advice, we explain what additional research you need to do and how to go about doing it.

- **Making decisions based on emotion.** You're most vulnerable to making the wrong moves financially after a major life change (such as a job loss or divorce) or when you feel under pressure. Maybe your investments have plunged in value. Or a recent divorce has you fearing that you won't be able to afford to retire when you had planned, so you pour thousands of dollars into some newfangled financial product. Take your time and keep your emotions out of the picture. In Chapter 21, we discuss how to approach major life changes with an eye to determining what changes may need to be made in your financial picture.

- **Not separating the wheat from the chaff.** In any field in which you're not an expert, you run the danger of following the advice of someone who you think is an expert but really isn't. This book teaches you to separate the financial fluff from the financial facts. If you look in the mirror, you'll see the person who is best able to manage your personal finances. Educate that person and trust that person.

- **Exposure to catastrophic risk.** You're vulnerable if you or your family don't have insurance to pay for financially devastating losses. People without a savings reserve and support network can end up homeless. Many people lack sufficient insurance coverage to replace their income. Don't wait for a tragedy to strike to learn whether you have the right kind of insurance coverage.

- **Focusing too much on money.** Too much emphasis on making and saving money can warp your perspective on what's important in life. Money is not the first or even second priority in happy people's lives. Your health, your relationships with family and friends, career satisfaction, and fulfilling interests are all more important.

Unfair as it seems, many of these traps await you when you're actually seeking help. The world is filled with biased and bad financial advice; we see and hear about the consequences of this bad advice every day. Of course, every profession has some bad apples, but too many people calling themselves "financial planners" have conflicts of interest.

All too often, financial advice today ignores the big picture and focuses narrowly on investing. You need to broaden your understanding of personal finance to include all areas of your financial life: spending, taxes, saving, insurance, and planning for major goals like education, buying a home, and retirement. Because money is not an end in itself but part of your whole life, this book helps connect your financial goals and problems to the rest of your life.

Even if you understand the financial basics, thinking about your finances in a holistic way can be difficult. Sometimes you're too close to the situation to be objective. Like the organization of your desk or files (or disorganization, as the case may be), your finances may reflect the history of your life more than they reflect a comprehensive plan for your future.

You're likely a busy person and don't have enough hours in your day to get things done. Thus, you want to know how to diagnose your financial situation quickly (and painlessly) and determine what you should do from there. Unfortunately, after figuring out which financial strategies make sense for you, choosing specific financial products in the marketplace can be a nightmare. You have literally thousands of investment, insurance, and loan options to choose from. Talk about information overload!

To complicate matters, you probably hear about most products through advertising that can be misleading if not downright false. Of course, some very ethical and useful firms advertise, but so do those that are more interested in converting your hard-earned income and savings into their profits. And they may not be here tomorrow when you need them.

You want to know the best places to go for your circumstances. As a result of these concerns, we've filled this book with specific, tried-and-proven product recommendations.

Uses for This Book

You can use this book in one of three ways:

- ✔ If you want to find out about a specific area, such as getting out of high-interest consumer debt or investing in mutual funds, you can flip to that section and get your answers quickly.

- ✔ If you want a crash course in personal finance, read it cover to cover. Reading the whole book helps to solidify major financial concepts and gets you thinking about your finances in a more comprehensive way.

- ✔ As a paperweight!

Seriously, though, this book is basic enough for a novice to get his or her arms around the thorniest of financial issues. But advanced readers will be challenged as well to think about their finances in a new way and identify areas for improvement. Check out the Table of Contents for a chapter-by-chapter rundown of what's in this book. You can also look up a specific topic in the Index and then flip to the page it lists. Or you can turn the page and start at the beginning: Chapter 1.

The Big Picture

This book is divided into five parts, each covering a major area of your personal finances. The chapters within each part cover specific topics in detail. You can read each chapter and part without having to read what comes before it, which is useful if you have better things to do with your free time. This book also makes for great reading anywhere you might be sitting for a length of time (perhaps the bathroom). You may be referred occasionally to somewhere else in the book for more detail on a particular subject. Here's a summary of what you find in each part.

Part I: Before You Begin Your Journey

This part reveals common causes of missing links in personal finance knowledge and explains how to diagnose your current financial health. You may want to hire someone to help, so in this part you learn more than you ever wanted to know about finding the right person and avoiding a lemon.

Part II: Saving for a Purpose

Most people don't have gobs of extra cash. Therefore, this part shows you how to figure out where all your dollars are going and how to reduce your spending. Chapter 5 is solely devoted to solving the problem of getting out from under the burden of high-interest consumer debt, such as credit card debt. We also provide specifics for reducing your tax burden and figuring out how much you should save for retirement or some other purpose.

Part III: Investing What You Save

Earning and saving money is hard work. So you want to be careful when it comes to investing what you worked so hard to save (or waited so long to inherit!). Learning investment basics helps you pick investments wisely and understand investment risks, returns, and a whole lot more. We explain all the major and best types of investment options, including how to hire your own professional money manager through a mutual fund (don't worry if you don't have much to invest). We recommend specific strategies and investments for both inside and outside of tax-sheltered retirement plans. We also discuss buying, selling, and investing in real estate as well as other wealth-building investments.

Part IV: Protecting What You've Got

Insurance is an important part of your financial life; unfortunately, for most people, it's a thoroughly overwhelming and dreadfully boring topic. But perhaps we can pique your interest in this topic when we tell you that you probably pay more than you should for insurance and don't have the right coverages for your situation. This part tells you all you ever wanted to know (okay, fine, all you never wanted to know but probably should know anyway) about how to buy the right insurance at the best price.

Part V: The Part of Tens

We guess we're still not sure whether IDG or David Letterman first came up with top ten lists. Although Dave's are just a bit funnier (only because he has a team of professional joke writers), these lists of tens can help you manage major life changes or keep you from getting into a jam when picking a financial advisor. In this part, you can also find our recommendations for top software to dazzle and delight your friends.

Icons Used in This Book

This nerdy guy (who is rumored to bear some resemblance to a senior official at IDG Books!) appears beside discussions that aren't critical if you just want to learn basic concepts and get answers to your financial questions. You can safely ignore these sections, but reading them will deepen and enhance your personal financial knowledge. This stuff can also come in handy if you're ever on a game show or find yourself stuck on an elevator with a financial geek.

This target flags strategy recommendations for making the most of your money (for example, paying off your credit card with your lottery winnings).

This icon highlights the best financial products in investment, insurance, and so on to implement strategy recommendations (for example, call The Really Nice Bank for low-interest loans).

This icon is a friendly reminder of information discussed elsewhere in the book or stuff you definitely want to remember.

This icon marks things to avoid and common mistakes people make in managing their finances.

This icon alerts you to scams and scoundrels that prey on the unsuspecting.

This icon highlights when you should consider doing some additional research. Don't worry, we explain what to look for and look out for.

Part I

Before You Begin Your Journey

The 5th Wave   By Rich Tennant

"That reminds me – I have to figure out how to save for retirement _and_ send these two to college."

In this part . . .

You see the basic concepts that underlie sensible management of personal finances. You also find out why you didn't know these concepts before now (and whom to blame). Here, you undergo a (gentle) financial physical exam to diagnose your current economic health. You may discover that you need help, so we try to steer you toward those who can truly assist you and away from those who may have something else in mind.

Chapter 1

Potholes on the Road to Personal Financial Success

. . . .

In This Chapter

▶ Financial illiteracy and its causes

▶ Believing what you read, see, and hear

▶ Managing your very own personal finances

. . . .

"*I*'ve made just about every financial mistake there is to make" is a fairly common lament of people of all ages and stages. The admission is usually accompanied by an anxious yet depressed look, and often seems to be a request for forgiveness.

As grown-up children — referred to as adults — we aren't really allowed to make mistakes. If you mangle your car in an accident because you weren't paying attention or get fired from a job because of poor attendance and performance, you sure don't feel very good, and others around you are seldom encouraging.

With financial matters, however, the fact that you've made a mistake may not be as obvious as twisted metal or a pink slip and no more pay cheque. Some mistakes take months, years, or even decades to manifest themselves. Even then, some people don't realize the foolishness of their ways.

If you're young, congratulations for being so forward thinking as to realize the immense value of investing now in your personal financial education. You'll reap the rewards for many decades to come. But even if you're not so young, you surely have many years to make the most of what money you currently have and will earn (and may even inherit!) in the future.

Throughout this book, we hope to challenge and even change the way you think about money, about making important personal financial decisions, and heck — sometimes even about the meaning of life. No, we're not philosophers, but we do know that money, for better but more often for worse, is connected to many other parts of our lives.

Few people like to be made to feel stupid or told that they're doing something wrong. And what you do with your money is a quite personal and confidential matter. We've endeavoured not to be paternalistic in this book but to provide guidance and advice that's in your best interest. You don't have to take it all — pick what works best for you and understand the pros and cons of your options. But from this day forward, please don't make the easily avoidable mistakes that we document in this chapter and throughout this book.

What You Don't Know CAN Hurt You

No, you're not a dummy. We're barely acquainted, but we do know that you're not dumb. Real dummies don't read and educate themselves. And real dummies don't understand the value of investing in their education. Real dummies also can't deflate their egos enough to admit that they need help and guidance.

Here's what dumb is: Dumb is the man who walked into a Circle-K convenience store, put a $20 bill on the counter, and asked for change. When the cashier opened the register, the man pulled a gun and demanded all the cash. The crook took the loot — $15 — and fled, leaving his $20 bill on the counter.

So you most definitely aren't dumb! But you may be financially illiterate. Sadly, most Canadians don't know how to manage their personal finances because in most cases they were never taught how to do so. Nearly 100 percent of our high schools and universities offer not a single course to teach this vital, lifelong-needed skill.

For the handful of schools that do offer a course remotely related to a personal finance class, the class is typically an economics course and an elective at that. "Archaic theory is being taught, and it doesn't do anything for the students as far as preparing them for the real world," says one high school principal. Having taken more than our fair share of economics courses in university, we wholeheartedly agree.

Lucky people learn the financial keys to success at home or from knowledgeable friends. Others never learn or learn the hard way: by making lots of costly mistakes. Lack of proficiency in personal financial management causes not only tremendous anxiety but also serious problems. Consider the following sobering statistics:

✔ Approximately 80,000 personal bankruptcies are filed in Canada each year. That's about 1 in every 100 households. So in the next ten years, nearly one in every ten households in Canada — one of the most affluent countries in the world — will file for bankruptcy.

✔ One in two marriages ends in divorce. Studies show that financial disagreement is one of the leading causes of marital discord. In a survey conducted by *Worth* magazine and the market research firm of Roper/Starch, couples admitted fighting about money more than anything else and more than three times more often than they fight about their sex lives. And a staggering 57 percent of those surveyed agreed with the statement, "In every marriage, money eventually becomes the most important concern."

✔ Almost half of all Canadians believe that the interest on a home mortgage is deductible (it isn't!) and that putting their savings in Canadian-only investments reduces the amount of risk (it doesn't!). In one survey, almost 80 percent of respondents said that they believe it's best to put retirement savings in the lowest-risk investments (you're catching on . . . it usually isn't!).

✔ In a Princeton Survey Research Associates investing-basics test, approximately a third of those quizzed answered fewer than 50 percent of the questions correctly. These results are all the more stunning when you consider that all the questions only offered two or three multiple-choice answers as options.

✔ Nearly 80 percent of consumers don't know how the grace period on a credit card works. An even greater percentage don't understand that interest starts accumulating *immediately* for new purchases on credit cards with outstanding debts.

The overall costs of personal financial illiteracy to our society are huge. The high rate of spending and low rate of saving in Canada lead to lower long-term economic growth and higher interest rates. Annually, billions of dollars are wasted in North America through the purchase of inferior and inefficient financial products.

Uh-oh. Now we've *really* depressed you. You were probably feeling bad enough about your own financial situation, and here you are taking responsibility for the country's economic problems, too!

Teaching personal finance in schools

As part of her fifth-grade math class, Nancy Donovan teaches personal finance as a way to illustrate how math can be used in the real world. "Students choose a career, find jobs, and figure out what their taxes and take-home paycheques will be. They also have to rent apartments and figure out a monthly budget," says Donovan, adding, "Students like it, and parents have commented to me how surprised they are with how much financial knowledge their kids can handle." Donovan also has her students invest $10,000 (play money) and track the performance of their investments.

To urge that our schools teach the basics of personal finance is just common sense. We should be teaching our children how to manage a household budget, about the importance of saving money for future goals, and about the consequences and dangers of overspending. Unfortunately, few schools offer classes like Nancy Donovan's. In most cases, the financial basics aren't taught at all.

Some people argue that it's the parents' job to teach their children the financial basics. However, this well-meant sentiment is what we rely on now, and, for all too many, it isn't working. In some families, financial illiteracy is passed on from generation to generation.

Some education professionals agree that schools should teach financial basics. If people aren't taught financial basics in schools, where do they learn them? But others say that schools would have to cut something vital out of the curriculum to make room for such a course.

Giving due respect to schoolteachers who work hard and often don't earn the pay or respect of other professions, we believe that personal finance should *at a minimum* replace the least important subject that schools are teaching now. (Of course, the hard part would be getting people to agree on the least important subject.)

We must recognize that education takes place in the home, on the streets, *and* in the schools. Therefore, schools must bear some responsibility for teaching this very important life skill. And with more students holding down after-school jobs, teaching money management know-how through the schools makes even more sense.

Lobby your schools! Make sure that financial basics are taught in schools at all levels. If you think you're powerless to change the situation, you're mistaken. Many changes to our education system have started at the grass-roots level.

Talking money at home

If you were fortunate, your parents taught and instilled in you the importance of personal financial management. Many parents who didn't have the benefit of a university education or who struggled all their lives to support their families still had a deep understanding of money: how to earn it, how to spend it properly, how to save more, and how to plan for emergencies and the future.

Among the useful things your folks may have taught you are sound principles of earning, spending, and saving money. Your parents may have had to know how to do these things because they were raising a family of several children on (usually) one modest income. They knew the importance of making the most of what you have and passing on that vital skill to the kids.

In many families, however, *money* is a taboo subject — parents don't level with their kids about the limitations, realities, and details of their budgets. Some parents we talk with believe that dealing with money is an adult issue that kids should be insulated from so that the kids can better enjoy being kids. Some studies have even shown that parents today are more likely to talk with their kids about sex than about financial matters! And you know how comfortable many parents feel when talking to their kids about sex, so you can imagine how few talk about money.

In many families, kids may hear about money *only* when disagreements and financial crises bubble to the surface. Thus begins the harmful cycle of children having negative associations with money and financial management.

In some cases, parents, with the best of intentions, *do* pass on their money management habits. Unfortunately, some of those habits are, of course, *bad* habits. Now, we're not saying that you shouldn't listen to your parents. (You know how well we listened to ours!) But in personal finance, as in any other area, family advice can be problematic. Think about where your parents learned about money management and consider whether they had the time, energy, or inclination to research choices before making their decisions. For example, your parents may think that banks are the best places to invest money. Banks are **not** the best places to invest money — you can find where the better places are in Part III of this book.

In still other cases, Mom and Dad have the right approach, but the kids go to the other extreme out of rebellion. For example, if your parents spent money carefully and thoughtfully, you may tend to do the opposite, such as buying yourself gifts the moment any extra money comes your way.

Although we can't change what the educational system and your parents did or didn't teach you about personal finances, you have the ability to find out now what you need to know to manage your finances. And if you have children of your own, we're sure you'll agree that kids really are amazing. Don't underestimate their potential or send them out into the world without the skills they need to be productive and happy adults.

Illiteracy and conflicts in publishing and advising

Okay, you're smart enough to realize that you're probably not a financial genius. So you set out to take control of your finances by reading or consulting a financial advisor. Because the pitfalls are so numerous and the challenges are so mighty in choosing an advisor, we devote all of Chapter 3 to the financial planning business and what you need to know to avoid being fooled.

Reading is good. Reading is fundamental. But reading to learn about managing your money can be dangerous if you're a novice. Surprisingly, written misinformation can come from popular and seemingly reliable information sources.

Won't gurus make me rich?

One formerly best-selling personal finance book (*Wealth Without Risk* by Charles Givens) advises you to "Buy disability insurance only if you are in poor health or accident prone." Putting aside the minor detail that *no* insurance company (that's interested in making a profit) would issue you a disability policy *after* you fall into poor health, how do you know when you'll be accident prone? Because health problems and auto accidents cause many disabilities, unless you have a working crystal ball, you can't see them coming until it's too late!

That same book also purports to describe how to send your kids to university "free." A few months before your child begins university, you're supposed to buy a four-bedroom property a few miles from campus. Then you're advised to rent out the house to students. The idea is that while your kid completes a four-year degree, the value of your rental property appreciates dramatically because of the shortage of off-campus housing in almost every college campus area.

You realize, we're sure, that university students will give your property the same love and attention that people give to rental cars. And, on the financial side, a modestly priced property would need to *increase by 25 to 50 percent in value over a four-year period* for this university-financing scheme to work. This is about as common as triplets (yes, it happens, but rarely).

Furthermore, this risky strategy is more likely to cost you money than to pay for university. Many real estate markets *drop* in value over a four-year time period, and if that were to happen, your already substantial university costs would be added to, not paid off. Then you need to factor in the hassles and expenses of locating, buying, and selling the property. And another minor detail: How many parents paying tuition bills also have piles of extra cash lying around available for the down payment on a property?

Don't the media act as watchdogs?

You may be asking how Charles Givens became so popular despite the obvious flaws in his advice. His success was thanks to his talent for working the media and great self-promotion through seminars. One of the problems of the mass media is that hucksters like Givens can get good coverage and publicity. Many members of the media are also financially illiterate. And they love a good story. So Givens got all sorts of free publicity, being quoted in the press and invited on a number of programs such as *The Today Show, Oprah, Donahue,* and *Larry King Live.*

Thousands of people went to seminars conducted by Givens, partly because of the credibility Givens built through media appearances. As has now been well documented by some of those same media, many unsuspecting investors were sold commission-laden products, including risky limited partnerships, through his organization.

Don't assume that someone with something to sell who is getting good press will take care of you. That "guru" could just be good at press relations and self-promotion. Certainly, talk shows and the media at large can and do provide useful information on a variety of topics, but be aware that sometimes bad eggs turn up on them. And the bad eggs don't always smell up front. Follow up on the news reports you receive to check their accuracy, and pay more attention to those with the best track record.

Just as at the circus, oddities sell

Over recent years, we've done some work with different parts of the media and observed how and what the media follows and ignores. As anyone who followed the O.J. Simpson trial knows, some members of the media love to hype an unusual story. The financial media, when at its worst, is no different than the news media that fawned all over the O.J. trial. The more bizarre and novel something is, the more attention it gets — never mind if it's good for the readers and viewers.

With financial "guru" Charles Givens, the appeal was that people believed they could get rich without taking risks. Recent years have seen a flood of "We Can Beat the Market" investing books written by a 17-year-old high school student, an investment club, and others. One such book was written by a couple of Generation Xers who, despite failing at publishing a print newsletter, soared to fame by claiming that, using the online world to research stocks, anybody can easily and with low risk make 25 to 35+ percent per year. As you see in Part III, such returns are unrealistic, but they play well with some members of the media.

Don't financial media know what's going to happen next?

Scores of widely read financial publications offer predictive advice and commentary about investment markets. But such commentary can often be wrong or misguided.

For example, on October 16, 1987, just three days before the U.S. stock market crashed, one of the most widely read daily business papers had this to say about the prior day's stock market decline: "But it is not yet time to pry the rubber seals out of the office windows . . . On September 22nd, it should be remembered, the market had a record 75-point one-day rise. The underlying economic news is mostly good, not bad."

On the next trading day — Monday, October 19 — the stock market plunged 508 points — nearly 23 percent!

Although most financial publications shy away from making predictions, many love to quote predictions made by the "experts." The monthly, weekly, and daily barrage of conflicting crystal ball visions causes many investors — perhaps even you — to be paralyzed and fearful. As you can clearly see in Part III of this book, you don't need a working crystal ball or a guru telling you when to buy and sell. The best investments for growth are not only easy to identify but, once bought, are generally best held for the long haul.

Don't writers know what they're writing about?

Writers are people too. Some are good, some are bad; some are full of hot tips, some are full of hot air. During the 1980s, one of the most widely read personal finance magazines ran a piece that purported to tell you where to get "safe, high yields." In addition to utility stocks and junk bonds, the article recommended real estate and oil and gas *limited partnerships* (LPs) sold through brokers. Such LPs aren't safe investments, as we explain in Chapter 3. Over the past decade, most people who bought these problematic investment vehicles lost huge portions of their money.

Another popular business magazine ran an article that touted life insurance as one of the best investments. The piece advocated the purchase of *cash-value insurance* — which contains an investment account as well as life insurance protection. The article went on to claim that life insurance should be the first consideration in most responsible investment programs. As you see in Parts III and IV of this book, this advice is *wrong, wrong, wrong* for the vast majority of working people who need life insurance. (They should buy *term insurance,* which is pure life insurance protection.) Any number of investment options would make a better first consideration than buying cash-value insurance, but you wouldn't have learned that from reading the article.

More than a few writers and talk-show hosts claim to be personal finance experts but hardly ever address spending and debt issues. Instead, they focus almost exclusively on investments. For example, they may make you feel like an undisciplined failure for not saving through your employer's retirement savings program to reduce your taxes when other considerations may also apply.

Saving through your employer's retirement plan is all well and good, but the truth is, many people live pay cheque to pay cheque. So unless you *first* learn how to reduce spending and get out from under high-cost consumer debt, the "experts" can talk until they're blue in the face about terrific investment strategies. If you don't have anything to invest in the first place, then the experts really aren't helping you.

There are good writers and smart writers at most financial publications. But there are also some people who would have been better off covering politics. Come to think of it, some of them *do* also cover politics, and therein lies part of the problem — you get financial advice from people who don't focus on the field, have little if any training in it, and have no experience as a practitioner working with people like you.

Don't book publishers exercise due diligence?

Book publishers are businesses first, and like most businesses, their business practices vary. Some have a reputation for care and quality; some just want to push a product out the door with maximum hype and minimum effort.

For example, you may think that book publishers check out an author before they sign him or her to write an entire book. Well, you may be surprised to learn that some publishers don't do their homework.

What most publishers care about first is how marketable an author is. Some authors are marketable because of their well-earned reputation for sound advice. Others are marketable because of stellar promotional campaigns built on smoke and mirrors. Still others may have the potential for marketability if a publisher takes a chance on them, but most publishers like a sure thing.

Even more troubling, in the many advice guides on the market, few publishers require that the books be technically reviewed for accuracy by an expert in the field other than the author, who sometimes may not be an expert. You're expected to be your own technical reviewer, but do you have the expertise to do that? (Don't worry, this book has been checked for accuracy.)

We know that financial ideas and strategies can differ considerably. Different is not necessarily wrong. But when a reviewer looks at our text and tells us that another, better way is out there, we take a second look. Maybe we even see things a new way. That's not possible if we're the only experts who see our book before publication. How do you know if a book's been technically reviewed? Check the credits page or the author's acknowledgements.

Warning signs of pandering to advertisers

Newspapers, magazines, online services, radio, television — you name it — thousands of publications and media outlets today dole out personal financial advice and perspectives. Although many of these "service providers" collect revenue from you, the subscriber, virtually all are dependent — in some cases, fully dependent — on advertising dollars.

Although advertising is a necessary part of capitalism, unfortunately and sadly, advertisers can taint and, in some cases, dictate the content of what you read, listen to, and view.

So how can you separate the good from the advertiser-biased publications?

We've developed some ideas on the subject from having written and worked for a number of publications and from observing the workings of even more.

First, consider how dependent a publication or media outlet is on advertising. We see the most conflicts of interest that involve pandering to advertisers done by "free" publications and radio and television, which derive all their revenue from advertising. Much of what's on the Internet is advertiser-driven as well.

Next, as you read various publications, watch TV, or listen to radio, note how consumer-oriented these media are. For example, if lots of auto manufacturers advertise, does the media outlet ever tell you how to save money when shopping for a car and the importance of buying a car within your means?

Do you get the feeling that your interests are being protected? Or do you feel that the media outlet is primarily creating an advertiser-friendly broadcast or publication?

Authors write books for many reasons other than to teach and educate. For example, some investment books are written by investment newsletter sellers. Rather than teaching you how to make good investments, the author makes the investment world sound complicated so that you'll feel the need to subscribe to his ongoing newsletter. The most common reason financial book authors write books is to further their own business interests. That may not always be a bad thing, but it's not the best thing for you when trying to educate yourself and better manage your own finances.

You Can and You Must Just Do It!

Once you learn the basic concepts and where to buy the best financial products when you need to buy them, you'll soon see that managing your personal finances isn't much harder than other things you do regularly, like tying your shoelaces and getting to and from work each day.

We're only human

Perhaps you know that you should be living within your means, buying and holding sound investments for the long term, and securing proper insurance coverage. However, you can't bring yourself to do these things. Everywhere you turn lurks temptation to spend money. Ads show attractive and popular people enjoying the fruits of their labours — a new car, exotic vacation, and lavish home.

Maybe you felt deprived as a youngster by your tightwad parents, or you're bored with life and like the adventure of buying new things. If only you can hit it big on one or two investments, you think, you could get rich quick and do what you really want with your life. As for disasters and catastrophes, well, those things happen to other people, don't they? Not to you. Besides, you'll probably have advance warning of pending problems and can prepare accordingly.

Your emotions and temptations can get the better of you. Certainly part of successfully managing your finances involves coming to terms with your shortcomings and the consequences of your behaviors. If you don't, you may end up enslaved to a dead-end job to keep feeding your spending addiction. Or you can spend more time with your investments than you do with your family, risking divorce. And catastrophes can happen to anyone, even you, without warning or time to prepare.

Knowing the right answers isn't enough. You need to practise good financial habits just as you practise other habits, such as brushing your teeth. Don't be overwhelmed. As you read this book, make a short list of your financial marching orders and then start chipping away. We also highlight ways to overcome temptations and keep control of your money rather than letting your emotions and money rule you.

Regardless of your income, you can make your dollars stretch further if you learn good financial habits and avoid mistakes. In fact, the lower your income, the more important it is that you make the most of your income and savings (because you don't have the luxury of falling back on your next fat pay cheque or dividends cheque to bail you out).

More and more industries are subject to global competition, and you need to be on your financial toes now more than ever. Job security is on the wane. Layoffs and retraining for new jobs are on the increase. Putting in 20 or 30 years for one company and retiring with the gold watch and lifetime pension are becoming as rare as never having computer problems.

Speaking of company pensions, odds are increasing that you work for an employer that has you save toward your own retirement. Not only do you need to save the money, you must also decide how to invest it.

Managing your personal finances involves much more than just managing and investing money. It also includes making all the pieces of your financial life fit together. It means lifting yourself out of financial illiteracy. Like planning a vacation, managing your personal finances means formulating a plan to make the best use of your limited time and dollars.

Here are a few areas you likely need to tackle:

- ✔ **Tracking and reducing spending.** If, like most people, you aren't saving sufficiently to meet your future financial goals, then sound financial management also involves tracking and reducing your spending. See Part II.

- ✔ **Investing what you save.** Investing your savings is, of course, an important part of your financial puzzle. So, too, are understanding and making the best use of tax incentives, tax breaks, and your employer's benefits.

- ✔ **Making informed real estate and insurance purchases.** You need to ensure that you invest in real estate intelligently, that you have the right types of insurance coverage, and that you don't pay more than necessary.

Intelligent personal financial strategies have little to do with your gender, ethnicity, or marital status. We *all* need to manage our finances. Some aspects of financial management become more or less important at different points in your life, but for the most part, the principles remain the same for all of us. Before you can take control, though, you first have to take stock. Turn to the next chapter to begin your financial physical exam. (Don't worry, we don't use rubber gloves or needles.)

Chapter 2

Measuring Your Financial Health

*L*ike many medical problems, financial problems are best detected early (clean living doesn't hurt either). Most problems can be fixed over time and with changes in your behavior. That's what the rest of the book is all about.

This chapter puts you through a *financial physical* to help you detect problems with your current financial health. But don't get depressed and dwell on your problems. View them for what they are: opportunities to improve your financial situation. In fact, the more areas for improvement you can identify, the greater the potential you have to build real wealth and accomplish your financial and personal goals.

Your Financial Net Worth

Your financial net worth is an important barometer of your financial health. It indicates your capacity to accomplish major financial goals such as buying a home, retiring, and withstanding unexpected expenses or loss of income.

Before we crunch any numbers here, before you experience the thrill of bigness or the agony of nothingness or negativity, let's get one thing perfectly clear. Sit down. Take a deep breath. And repeat after us:

"My financial net worth has absolutely, positively *no* relationship to my worth as a human being."

This is not a test. You don't have to compare your number with your neighbour's. It's not the scorecard of life. So do we have an understanding? Good! We hate to see people get depressed about unimportant things that they have the power and ability to change.

Your *net worth* is your financial assets minus your financial liabilities.

Financial Assets – Financial Liabilities = Net Worth

Financial assets

A *financial asset* is worth real money or is something that you plan to convert to hard dollars that you can use to buy things now or in the future.

Financial assets generally include money in bank accounts, stocks, bonds, and mutual fund accounts (see Part III, which deals with investments). Also included is money that you have in retirement accounts, including those with your employer. You should also include the value of any businesses or real estate that you own.

We generally recommend that you exclude your personal residence. Include your home *only* if you expect to someday sell it or otherwise live off the money you now have tied up in it. If you plan on selling or downsizing your home, add that portion of the money from the sale that you expect to realize and use to your list of assets.

Assets also include your future expected government benefits and pension payments if your employer has such a plan. These are usually quoted in dollars per month rather than in a lump sum value. We show you in a moment how to account for these monthly benefits when tallying your financial assets.

Personal property such as your car, clothing, stereo, wine glasses, and straight teeth do *not* count as financial assets. We know adding these things to your assets makes your assets *look* larger (and some financial software packages and publications encourage you to list these items as assets), but you can't live off them unless you hock them at a pawn shop or otherwise sell them to meet your financial goals. (Technically, your smile might be able to charm others, so your teeth may actually have some value, but you shouldn't count on it.)

Financial liabilities

Your *financial liabilities* must be subtracted from your assets to arrive at your financial net worth.

Liabilities include loans and debts outstanding, like credit card and auto loan debts. Include money you've borrowed from family and friends (unless you're not gonna pay it back — we won't tell). Include mortgage debt on your home as a liability *only* if you include the value of your home in your asset list. Be sure to include debt owed on other real estate no matter what.

Your net worth calculation

Ready? Table 2-1 provides a place for you to figure your financial assets. Go ahead and write in the spaces provided, unless you plan to lend this book to someone and you don't want to put your money situation on display. *Note:* See Table 8-1 in Chapter 8 to estimate your government benefits.

Table 2-1	Your Financial Assets
Account	*Value*
Savings and investment accounts (including retirement accounts)	
Example: Bank savings account	$ 5,000
_____	$ _____
_____	$ _____
_____	$ _____
_____	$ _____
_____	$ _____
_____	$ _____
Total =	$ _____
Benefits earned that pay a monthly retirement income	
Employer's pensions	$ _____ / month
Government benefits	$ _____ / month
	x 240*
Total =	$ _____
Total Financial Assets =	$ _____

* In Table 2-1, to convert benefits that will be paid to you monthly into a total dollar amount, we assume that you'll live 20 years in retirement. (Ah, think of two decades of lollygagging around!) As a shortcut, multiply the benefits that you'll collect monthly in retirement by 240 (12 months in a year times 20 years). Inflation may reduce the value of your employer's pension if it doesn't contain a cost-of-living increase each year in the same way that government benefits do. Don't sweat this now — we'll take care of it in the section on planning for retirement (see Chapter 8). If your pension doesn't have inflation protection, cut the number you've arrived at for your pension benefits in half if you are near retirement, and by ²/₃ if you're in your early 40s or younger.

Now comes the potentially depressing part — your debts and loans in Table 2-2:

Table 2-2	Your Financial Liabilities
Loan	*Balance*
Example: Gouge 'Em Bank Credit Card	$ 4,000
_____	$ _____
_____	$ _____
_____	$ _____
_____	$ _____
_____	$ _____
_____	$ _____
Total Financial Liabilities =	$ _____

Now subtract your liabilities from your assets to figure your net worth in Table 2-3:

Table 2-3	Your Net Worth
Find	*Write It Here*
Total Financial Assets (from Table 2-1)	$ _____
Minus	–
Total Financial Liabilities (from Table 2-2)	$ _____
Net Worth =	$ _____

Interpreting your net worth results

Your net worth is important and useful only to you and your unique situation and goals. What is a lot of money to a person with a simple lifestyle and minimal expectations may seem like very little to another with desires for an opulent lifestyle and high expectations.

In Chapter 8, you need to crunch some more numbers to determine your financial status more precisely for such goals as retirement planning. In the meantime, here's a quick way to evaluate the health of your net worth:

✔ **Your net worth is less than half your annual income or even negative.** You've got lots of company. If you're in your 20s and just starting to work, this is less concerning. It's most important to get rid of your debts, the highest-interest ones first. Then you need to build a safety reserve equal to three to six months of living expenses. You should definitely learn more about getting out of debt, reducing your spending, and developing tax-wise ways to save and invest your future earnings.

✔ **Your net worth is more than half your annual income but less than a few years' annual income.** If you're younger than 40, and especially if you own a home, consider yourself in good shape at this point. If you're older and still renting, you may be in okay shape, but you probably need to reduce your spending and accelerate your savings if you want to buy a home and retire by your 60s.

✔ **Your net worth is more than a few years' annual income.** You're probably on track to meet reasonable financial goals and may actually be ahead of the game, especially if you haven't reached your 40s yet.

Bad Debt versus Good Debt

Why do you borrow money? Usually, it's because you don't have enough money to buy something you want or need — such as a college education. If you want to buy a four-year college education, you can easily spend $40,000 or more. Not too many people have that kind of spare cash. So borrowing money to finance part of that cost enables you to buy the education.

How about a new car? A trip to your friendly local car dealer shows you that a new set of wheels will set you back around $15,000 or more. Although more people have the money to pay for that than, say, the college education, what if you don't? Should you finance the car the way you'd finance the education?

The auto dealers and bankers eager to make you an auto loan say you deserve to — and can afford to — drive a nice, new car, so borrow away.

We say, *NO! NO! NO!* to auto loans.

Why do we disagree with the auto dealers and lenders? For starters, we're not trying to sell you a car or loan from which we derive a profit! More importantly, there's a *big* difference between borrowing for something that represents a long-term investment and borrowing for consumption.

Borrowing: Not for consumer consumption

Take a vacation (no, we don't mean right now). If you spend, say, $1,500 on a vacation, the money is gone. Poof! You may have fond memories and even some Kodak moments, but you have no financial value to show for it. "But," you say, "vacations replenish my soul and make me more productive when I return. In fact, the vacation more than pays for itself!"

Great. We're not saying don't take a vacation. By all means, take one, two, three, or as many as you can afford yearly. But that's the point — *what you can afford.* If you had to borrow money to take the vacation in the form of an outstanding balance on your credit card for many months, then you *could not afford* the vacation you took.

We refer to debt incurred for consumption as *bad debt.* Don't get us wrong — you're not a bad person for having the debt, but the debt is bad for your long-term financial health. Borrowing to purchase a car or clothing also impairs your long-term financial health. This is bad debt, too.

You'll be able to take many more vacations during your lifetime if you save in advance to afford them. If you get into the habit of borrowing and paying all that interest for vacations, cars, clothing, and other consumer items, you'll spend more of your future income paying back the debt and interest. So you'll have *less* money available for vacations and all your other goals.

One of the reasons you'll have less money using bad debt is because of the relatively high interest rates banks and other lenders charge for such debt. Money borrowed on credit cards, auto loans, and through other types of consumer loans not only collects a relatively high interest rate but is also generally not tax-deductible. Good debt, such as for real estate and business, is available at lower interest rates and is often tax-deductible. Thus, bad debt not only is bad for your long-term financial health but is also much *more expensive* than good debt.

We're not saying never borrow money or that all debt is bad. To the contrary, borrowing to pay for educational expenses can make sense. Education is generally a good long-term investment. It should increase your earning potential. This is *good debt.* Likewise, taking on a reasonable amount of debt to buy or start a business or to purchase real estate can be good debt. If properly and smartly managed, these investments should also increase in value.

How much bad debt is too much?

A useful but perhaps painful way to size up your debt load is to calculate how much debt you have relative to your annual income. Ignore, for now, good debt — the loans you may owe on real estate, a business, an education, and so on. We're focusing on bad debt, the higher-interest stuff used to buy items that depreciate in value.

For example, suppose that you earn $30,000 per year. Between your credit cards and an auto loan, you have $15,000 of debt. In this case, your bad debt represents 50 percent of your annual income.

$$\frac{\text{debt}}{\text{annual income}} = \text{debt danger ratio}$$

The financially healthy amount of bad debt is zero.

When your *debt danger ratio* starts to push beyond 25 percent of your income, that can spell real trouble. High-interest debt on credit cards and auto loans is like cancer when it gets to those levels. As with cancer, the growth of the debt can snowball out of control unless something significant intervenes. If you have this much debt, turn to Chapter 5 to find out how to get rid of it.

How much good debt is acceptable? The answer varies. The key question is, are you able to save sufficiently to accomplish your goals? Later in this chapter, we help you figure how much you're actually saving, and Chapter 8 assists you in determining what you should be saving to accomplish your goals. Also see Chapter 16 for a discussion of deciding how much mortgage debt is appropriate to take on when buying a home.

Avoid borrowing money for consumption (bad debt) — for spending on things like cars, clothing, vacations, and so on that decrease in value and eventually become financially worthless. Borrow money only for investments (good debt) — for purchasing things that retain and hopefully increase in value over the long term, such as education, real estate, or your own business.

Playing the float

We authors have credit cards, and we use them — but we try to always pay our balances in full each month by the due date. Besides the convenience that credit cards offer us in not having to carry around extra cash and cheques, we get another benefit: We have free use of the bank's money extended to us through our credit card charges.

When you charge on a credit card that doesn't have an outstanding balance carried over from the prior month, you typically have several weeks, known as the *grace period,* from the date of the charge to when you must pay your bill. Financial types call this *playing the float.* Had you paid for this purchase by cash or cheque, you would have had to shell out the money sooner.

If you have difficulty saving money, and plastic tends to burn holes through your budget, forget the float game. You're better off not using your credit cards. The same applies for those who pay their bills in full but who spend more because it's so easy to do so with a piece of plastic.

Savings Analysis

In the past year, how much money have you actually saved? By savings we mean the amount of new money you've added to your nest egg, stash, or whatever you like to call it.

Most people don't know or have only a vague idea of the rate at which they save money. The answer may sober, terrify, or pleasantly surprise you. In order to calculate your savings over the past year, you need to calculate your net worth as of today *and* as of one year ago.

The amount you actually saved over the past year is equal to the change in your net worth over the past year — in other words, your net worth today minus your net worth from one year ago. We know it may be a pain to find statements showing what your savings and investments were worth a year ago, but bear with us. It's a useful exercise.

If you own your home, ignore this in the calculations. And don't include personal property such as a car, computer, clothing, and so on with your assets.

Okay, now that you have your two figures, go ahead and plug them into Step 1 of Table 2-4. You may be anticipating the exercise and are already subtracting your net worth of a year ago from what it is today in order to determine your rate of savings. Your instincts are correct, but the exercise is not quite that simple. We must ask you to do a few more calculations in Step 2 of Table 2-4. Why? Well, counting the appreciation of investments you owned over the past year as savings wouldn't be fair. Suppose that you bought 100 shares of a stock a year ago at $17/share and now the value is at $34/share. Your investment increased in value during the past year by $1,700. Although you would be the envy of your friends at the next party if you casually mentioned your investments, the $1,700 of increased value of your investment is not really savings. Instead, it represents appreciation on your investments, so you must remove this appreciation from the calculations.

Note: Just so you know, we're not unfairly penalizing you for your shrewd investments — you also get to add back the decline in value of your less-successful investments.

If all this gives you a headache or you got stuck or if you just hate crunching numbers, try the intuitive, seat-of-the-pants approach: Do you save a regular portion of your monthly income? You may save it in a separate savings account, an RRSP (Registered Retirement Savings Plan), or other retirement account, and so on.

Table 2-4	Your Savings Rate over the Past Year	
Today	*One Year Ago*	
Step 1: Figuring your savings.		
Savings & investments $ _____	Savings & investments $ _____	
− Loans & debts $ _____	− Loans & debts $ _____	
= Net worth today $ _____	= Net worth 1 year ago $ _____	
Step 2: Correcting for changes in value of investments you owned during the year.		
Net worth today $ _____		
− Net worth 1 year ago $ _____		
− Appreciation of investments (over past year) $ _____		
+ Depreciation of investments (over past year) $ _____		
= Savings rate $ _____		

How much do you save in a typical month? Get out your statements for accounts that you contribute to or save money in monthly. It doesn't matter if it's an RRSP that you can't access. Money is money. Savings is savings.

Note: If you're able to save, say, $200 per month for a few months but then spend it all on auto repairs, you're not saving. If you contributed $2,000 to an RRSP, for example, but depleted money that you had from long ago (in other words, it wasn't saved during the past year), you should not count the $2,000 as savings.

As you'll see later, you very likely should be saving at least 5 to 10 percent of your annual income for longer-term financial goals such as retirement. If you're not, be sure to read Chapter 6 on how to reduce your spending so that you can increase your savings.

How Are You at Investing?

Congratulations! You've completed the hardest part of your financial physical. The physical is a whole lot easier from here on in!

Regardless of how much or how little money you have invested in bank, mutual fund, or other types of accounts, you, of course, want your money invested in the wisest way possible.

Knowing the rights and wrongs of investing is vital to your long-term financial well-being. Few people have so much extra money that they can afford major or frequent investing mistakes. The following questions help you size up how much time you need to spend with Part III of this book, which focuses on investing.

Note: Answer each of the following questions with Yes or No. The more *No* answers you reluctantly scribble, the more you need to learn about investing, and the faster you should turn to Part III.

_____ Do you understand the investments you're currently in?

_____ Is the money that you would need to tap in a short-term emergency placed in an investment whose principal doesn't fluctuate in value?

_____ Do you know what income tax bracket you're in, and do you factor that into which investments you choose?

_____ For money outside of RRSPs and retirement plans, do you understand how those investments produce income, dividends, and gains, and whether those investments make the most sense from the standpoint of taxes?

_____ Do you have your money in different, diversified investments that aren't dependent on one or a few securities or one type of investment (that is, bonds, stocks, and so on)?

_____ Is the money that you'll need for a major expenditure in the next few years invested conservatively rather than in riskier investments such as stocks, real estate, or pork bellies?

_____ Is the money that you've earmarked for longer-term purposes (more than five years) invested to keep you well ahead of inflation?

_____ Is the bulk of your long-term money invested inside RRSPs and retirement plans, and have you exhausted possibilities for directing more money into these tax-sheltered accounts?

_____ Is your longer-term money, particularly what's inside of RRSPs, invested in quality, growth-oriented investments rather than preservation-of-principal-oriented investments?

_____ If you work with a financial advisor, is that person compensated in a way that eliminates potential conflicts of interest in the strategies and investments he or she recommends?

Making and saving money is not a guarantee of financial success but rather a prerequisite. If you don't know how to choose quality investments that meet your needs, you'll more than likely throw money away, which leads to the same end result as never having earned and saved it in the first place. Worse still, you won't have derived any enjoyment from spending the lost money on items that you needed or wanted. Learn the best ways to invest; otherwise, you'll just be spinning your wheels working and saving.

How's Your Insurance Intelligence?

Now we're in the home stretch of your financial physical. Last but not least, you must deal with the prickly subject of protecting your assets and yourself with *insurance*. If you're like most people, reviewing your insurance policies and coverages is about as much fun as a root canal. Open wide!

Answer each of the following questions with Yes or No.

_____ On each policy that you have, do you understand the individual coverages and protection types and amounts?

_____ Does your current insurance protection make sense given your current financial situation (as opposed to when you bought the policies)?

_____ If you couldn't make it financially without your income, do you have adequate long-term disability insurance coverage?

_____ If you have family members who are dependent on your continued income, do you have adequate life insurance coverage to replace that income should you die?

_____ If you bought life insurance (and have a net worth of less than $2 million to $3 million), did you buy term insurance?

_____ Do you carry enough liability insurance on your home, car (including umbrella/excess liability), and business to protect all your assets?

_____ Did you recently (in the last year or two) shop around for the best price on your insurance policies?

_____ Do you know whether your insurance companies have good track records regarding paying claims and keeping their customers satisfied?

That wasn't so bad, was it? If you answered *No* more than once or twice, don't feel dumb — more than nine out of ten people make major mistakes when buying insurance. See Part IV for your salvation. If you answered *Yes* to all the preceding questions, you can be spared from reading Part IV, but bear in mind that most people need help in this area as much as they do in other areas of personal finance.

Well, you survived your financial physical! Just like health exams, financial physicals can make you feel a little uncomfortable. The good news is that you now you know more about your current financial health. Reading the rest of this book will help you to improve on it!

Chapter 3

Hiring Financial Help: Truths and Consequences

*I*f you've recovered from your financial physical, you may be considering hiring help to whip you back into shape. Hiring help may seem like a practical choice if you're busy or if you'd simply rather spend time on other things.

Hiring a competent, ethical, and unbiased financial planner or advisor to help you make and implement financial decisions *can* be money well spent. But if you pick a poor advisor or someone who really isn't a financial planner but a salesperson in disguise, things could get worse instead of better. So before we talk about the different types of help to hire, let's take a little journey with Alice to give you an idea of what you're up against in the land of financial planners.

Alice in Financial Planner Land

This is the real-life tale of one person's search for sound financial advice. Alice (note how her name allowed us to come up with a catchy title for this section!) struck out the first four times she sought financial help. Her story illustrates many of the pitfalls in finding a good financial planner.

Alice's adventures

First, on the recommendation of her accountant, Alice called a *financial consultant* who was a *certified financial planner* (CFP) at a well-known brokerage firm. Although Alice explained that she wanted a conservative investment, the broker sold her a mutual fund that, unbeknownst to Alice, primarily held *aggressive growth* (volatile) stocks.

After buying the fund and getting her first account statement a few days later, Alice noticed that there were several thousand dollars less in the fund than she had invested. The broker had told her he earned a 4 percent commission but assured her that she need not concern herself with it because the fund paid him and it wouldn't affect her investment.

After a little investigation, Alice discovered that the fund had, in fact, paid the broker out of her investment — a hefty 6.5 percent commission. Thus, the broker had not only lied about where the commission dollars came from (all such commissions come from the investors' money), but he had also understated the size of his commission.

Understandably steamed, Alice called the regulating agency, and after she jumped through many hoops, the brokerage firm coughed up nearly $2,000 for the broker's lie about the commission amount.

Thinking that perhaps men and women simply don't communicate well, Alice next turned to a female financial planner on the recommendation of a friend. The planner told Alice: "Women need to stick together." Then she promptly tried to sell Alice a limited partnership that, the planner said, was *sure* to return upward of 20 to 40 percent per year.

Alice took a gander at the *prospectus* — a delightfully long document written by lawyers — and saw in black and white on page 2 that the partnership paid the selling broker a 10 percent sales commission (which, she now knew, would be deducted from her investment).

Because Alice is a conscientious investor, she did more research and learned that limited partnerships are also handicapped by high, ongoing management fees. Alice did not return the dozen or so follow-up calls ("to see how you are doing") from her "sister" financial planner and fortunately passed on the partnership.

Wanting to learn more before her next attempt to get help, Alice enrolled in an "adult education class" at a local college. Alice, a student eager to learn, attended all the classes but soon felt only more confused. The world of finance and investments, her teacher said, is *very, very complicated.* Unless, of course, you're a financial expert.

The teacher, a "certified financial planner," told the class that he was just such an expert. He offered a free, one-hour consultation to all his students at the end of his "course." During her free session, Alice was told that she should invest in an *annuity*. Investigation, however, revealed (you guessed it) high sales commissions and management fees.

Alice was also uncomfortable because planner number three hadn't inquired about other aspects of her situation and seemed intent only on selling her an annuity. Annuities didn't make sense for her, she later learned, because she was nearly retired and was in a low tax bracket.

At this point, most people probably would have bought a good financial book or put their money in a mattress or the next best place — their local bank — but Alice really wanted to talk to someone about her money issues and ideas.

After listening to a financial planner on a radio call-in program, Alice had the planner mail his background materials to her. In addition to a certified financial-planning credential, *this* planner had a seemingly endless list of other, lofty-sounding credentials, such as RIA, BSCE, LLB, and MBA.

Quite wary of sales commissions by now, Alice also liked the sound of the planner's fee: $350 for his time to help with her investment decisions and to discuss her other financial questions. Part way through their two-hour, $350 consultation, however, planner number four tried to persuade Alice that what she really needed was to hire him as an ongoing manager of her money. For just $2,000 per year for the service (commissions and manage- ment fees were extra), he would trade her in and out of investments based on his economic analyses and expert prognostications.

That seemed like a lot of money to Alice, who had $150,000 to invest, and she didn't like the thought of turning over her money to someone who could move it among various investments without her approval. Besides, she was interested in learning more about finance, and this "planner" kept telling her how complicated it is to make investing and other financial decisions. Alice therefore declined planner number four's sales pitch for managing her investments, whereupon the moody planner stormed out of her house, complaining that she had wasted his time (for which he had his $350 cheque in hand for a mere two hours of his time!).

Lessons learned from Alice's trip to Financial Planner Land

Alice's case highlights four major problems that people often encounter when hiring financial help:

✔ First, you absolutely, positively *must* do your homework before hiring any financial advisor. Just look at Alice: Despite enthusiastic recommendations from her accountant and another from a friend, Alice ended up with bad advice from biased advisors.

✔ Second, the financial planning and brokerage fields are mine fields for consumers. The fundamental problem is the enormous conflict of interest that's created when "advisors" sell products that earn them sales commissions to people who believe they're getting unbiased advice. Selling ongoing money management services, as Alice learned from the last "advisor," creates conflicts of interest as well.

As an analogy, imagine that you have flu symptoms. Would you be comfortable seeing a physician who didn't charge for office visits but made money only by selling you drugs? Maybe you don't *need* the drugs — or at least not so many expensive ones. Maybe what you really need is Mom's chicken soup and 16 hours of sleep.

In a review of the financial planning industry, *Consumer Reports* said, "Financial planners often end up being wolves in sheep's clothing with hidden agendas to sell mutual funds, for example, or life insurance." Respected financial columnist Jane Bryant Quinn of *Newsweek* has said, "Planners are supposed to pull apart your finances and suggest better ways of meeting your goals. They purport to be objective. But they can't be if they work for brokerage firms or insurance companies or if their income depends on sales commissions from the products they sell."

✔ Third, financial advisors often like to make things far more complicated than need be, and they're often not interested in educating you. As others have observed, financial planning is hardly the only occupation guilty of this. As author George Bernard Shaw put it, "All professions are conspiracies against the laity."

The more you know and the more you realize that investing and other financial decisions needn't be complicated, the more you'll realise that you don't need to spend gobs of money — or any money at all — on financial planners and advisors. If you look in the mirror, you see the person who is most qualified to be your best financial advisor and who has your best interests at heart.

✔ Fourth, don't place a whole lot of faith in credentials, especially the Certified Financial Planner (CFP) moniker, which *Forbes* magazine columnist Gretchen Morgensen called a "meaningless label," adding, "When picking a financial planner, pay a lot of attention to how the planner is compensated. Pay no attention to CFPs. . . ."

What's truly amazing about Alice's situation is that none of the so-called financial "planners" ever bothered to ask about her insurance and debt situation. As it turns out, Alice not only lacked adequate homeowner's insurance, but she also had no health insurance!

Alice also had some relatively high-interest consumer debt that none of the "planners" ever asked about, probably because paying off her debt would have diminished the funds that Alice would have available for investment. Alice could afford both the insurance and debt payoff. In short, no one had taken the time to explain to Alice the costs and risks of not getting her financial house in order.

Finally, in case you're wondering, Alice did happily invest her money in a nice portfolio of commission-free mutual funds (see Chapter 12), which have been performing just swimmingly for her over the years.

The Frustrations of Finding Good Financial Planners

Overwhelmed and undereducated consumers like Alice, especially those in low- and middle-income brackets, have few attractive options if they want to hire financial help. The great majority of people who call themselves *financial planners* and *financial consultants* sell products and work on commission, which, as Alice found, creates enormous conflicts of interest. Those conflicts of interest stem from the fact that the broker has an incentive to recommend strategies and sell products that pay generous commissions and to ignore strategies and products that pay no or low commissions.

Of the few financial advisors who are *fee-only,* some make a good portion of their fees from money-management services. (*Fee-only* or *fee-based* means that the advisors' fees are paid by their clients, not by companies whose products the advisors recommend.) Thus, some fee-based advisors tend to focus on those who have already accumulated significant wealth. Fee-based advisors may also have conflicts of interest in that they gravitate toward strategies and recommendations that involve their ongoing management of your money and tend to ignore or dismiss tactics that diminish the pool of investment money that they can manage for an ongoing fee.

Regulatory problems

A pretty basic problem of oversight afflicts the financial planning field. Regulatory oversight is minimal *at best.* In all provinces except Quebec, anyone can hang out a shingle and call him- or herself a financial planner.

The credentialization of Canada: What credentials qualify a financial advisor?

It seems that everywhere you turn today, more and more people carry credentials after their names. We have certified lactation consultants, certified foot reflexologists, and registered dietitians.

Among salespeople, especially in the financial services industry, the use of dubious credentials and self-anointed and misleading titles is on the increase. Stockbrokers are no longer called stockbrokers — they are "financial consultants" and "financial advisors." Some life insurance agents now call themselves "estate planning specialists." Next thing you know, when you visit an auto dealer, you'll speak with a certified transportation consultant, and when you buy your next home, it will be through a certified housing consultant rather than a real estate agent. It seems that everything today is *certified* — even the once "used car" is now referred to by some dealers as "certified pre-owned!"

Speaking of "certified," tens of thousands of people, mostly in Canada and the United States, have earned the Certified Financial Planning credential. This is basically a home-study course that, unlike gaining entrance into medical, law, or business school, virtually anyone can undertake. The test itself isn't difficult to pass — an astounding 74 percent of people recently enrolled in the College for Financial Planning passed the CFP test. Gaining admission to a top professional school and becoming an architect, attorney, or doctor is exponentially more difficult and demanding.

The CFP Board of Standards, which licenses the CFP credential, claims that the combination of passing a test and meeting continuing education requirements ensures that the profession is doing the best that it can. To that, we and others who often see CFP incompetence and conflicts of interest politely say, "Bunk!" Here's why:

- ✔ The CFP tests nothing of a planner's business ethics or how the planner earns income.

- ✔ The CFP exam covers arcane financial details, which are rarely encountered by consumer-oriented planners and could easily be contained in a handy reference book.

- ✔ The CFP curriculum has little practical information on the important topics of asset allocation and mutual fund selection.

- ✔ The few individuals who don't pass the CFP exam on the first try are told what answers they got wrong so that they can focus their time memorizing the trivial details and pass the exam on the second try.

When *The Boston Globe* columnist Charles Jaffe took the CFP exam, he concluded that "... financial planning is a long way from qualifying as a profession."

Unfortunately, the vast majority of people with CFPs work on commission and are employed by securities and insurance brokerage firms, so they're not really financial planners so much as salespeople with "credentials." Most of the rest sell ongoing money management services.

Meeting the CFP continuing education requirements is a sham. CFPs can attend what amounts to sales presentations by companies pitching financial products to earn continuing education credit hours. Another method is for CFPs to read financial planning journals, which have multiple-choice and true-false questions in the back. The planner can take the test on his or her own time and even refer to the relevant articles to find the answers!

If you're interested in hiring financial help, be sure to read Chapter 20, which details the ten questions you should ask before hiring a financial advisor, including how to make sense of all the credential gobbledygook.

Financial planners *should* have to disclose in writing, prior to working with clients, how they are compensated. This would make it easier for people to know how the planner earns a living. And it would eliminate much of the need for more formal government regulation. However, it's unlikely that we'll see any sort of legislation on this, at least in the foreseeable future. The public doesn't get up in arms about it, and the financial industry is much keener on policing itself, so there's not a lot of reason for politicians to make this the issue of the day.

Financial planners' top conflicts of interest

All professions have conflicts of interest. Some fields have more than others, and the financial planning field is one of those fields. Knowing where some of the land mines lie can certainly help. Here, then, are the most common reasons that planners may not have 20/20 vision when giving financial directions.

Selling and pushing products that pay commissions

If a financial planner doesn't charge you a fee for his time, you can rest assured that he earns commissions on the products he tries to sell you. In order to sell financial products, this planner must be licensed to deal in those products. A person who sells financial products and earns commissions from those products is a salesperson, *not* a financial planner. Financial planning involves taking an objective, holistic look at your personal financial puzzle to find the pieces that fit it well — something that most brokers are neither trained nor financially motivated to do.

To make it even harder for you to discern planners' agendas, you can *not* assume that planners who do charge fees for their time don't also earn commissions selling products. Sadly for people seeking financial advice, compensation *double-dipping* is becoming more and more common.

Selling products that provide a commission tends to skew a planner's recommendations. Products that carry commissions mean that you have fewer of your dollars working in the investments and insurance you buy. Because a commission is earned only when a product is sold, such a product or service is inevitably more attractive in the planner's eyes than any other option. For example, if the planner sells disability insurance that you could obtain at a lower cost through your employer or a group trade association (see Chapter 18), he may overlook or criticize your most attractive option (buying through your employer) and focus on *his* most attractive option — selling you a higher cost disability policy on which he derives a commission.

Another danger of trusting the recommendation of a commission-based planner is that she may steer you toward the products that have the biggest payback for her. These products are among the *worst* for you because they siphon off even more of your money up front to pay the commission. They also tend to be among the costliest and riskiest financial products available.

Commission-greedy planners may also try to *churn* your investments. They encourage you to buy and sell at the drop of a hat, attributing the need to changes in the economy or the companies you've invested in. More trading means — big surprise — more commissions for the broker.

Taking a narrow view

Because of the way they earn their money, many planners are biased in favor of certain strategies and products. As a result, they don't typically keep your overall financial needs in mind. For example, if you have a problem with accumulated credit card debts, some planners may never know (or care) because they're focused on selling you an investment product. Likewise, a planner who sells a lot of life insurance tends to develop recommendations that require its purchase.

Not recommending saving through your employer's retirement plan

One of your best financial options is to take advantage of saving through your employer's retirement savings plan. Although this method of saving may not be as exciting as risking your money in cattle futures, it's not as dull as watching paint dry — and, most importantly, it's tax-deductible. Planners are sometimes reluctant to recommend taking full advantage of this option: It doesn't leave as much money for the purchase of their commission-laden investment products.

"Financial planning" in banks

Over the past couple of decades, banks have witnessed a gradual erosion of the money in their coffers and vaults. The reason is simple: Increasing numbers of investors realized that banks are generally lousy places to build wealth. The highest-yielding bank savings accounts and *GICs* (guaranteed investment certificates) barely keep an investor ahead of inflation. If you factor in both inflation and taxes, these bank "investments" provide no real growth on your investment dollars.

Increasingly, banks have "financial representatives" and "investment specialists" sitting in their branches waiting to pounce on bank customers with big balances. In many financial institutions, these "financial planners" are simply out to sell that bank's or trust company's particular products.

Many of the reps in banks are inexperienced and don't understand what they are selling and what's suitable for particular customers. Furthermore, these reps often have little knowledge about competing products in the marketplace and usually are restricted to selling only their in-house offerings.

Selling ongoing money-management services

Many financial planners/advisors who don't work on commission make their money by managing your money for an ongoing fee percentage (typically 1 to 3 percent annually of your investment). Although this removes the incentive to *churn* your account (buy and sell repeatedly and rapidly) to run up more commissions, it's a service that you're unlikely to need.

An ongoing fee percentage still creates a conflict of interest; the financial planner will tend to steer you away from beneficial financial strategies that reduce the asset pool from which he derives his percentage. Maximizing contributions to your employer's pension plan, paying off debts like your mortgage, investing in real estate or small business, and so on — these financial strategies may make the most sense for you but are rarely recommended by an advisor who works on a percentage of assets under management basis.

The latest rage, particularly among brokerage firms, is the *wrap account* (also known as the *managed account*). Wrap accounts can cost you around 2.5 percent of your assets annually. As we explain in Part III, you can hire *professional money managers* for under 2 percent per year or less.

Ignoring debts

Sometimes, your best investment is to pay off outstanding loans, whether credit card, auto, or even mortgage debts. But most financial planners don't recommend this strategy because paying down debts depletes the capital with which you could otherwise buy investments — the investments that the broker may be trying to sell you to earn a commission or the advisor would like to manage for an ongoing fee.

Not recommending real estate and small business investments

Like paying off debts, investing in real estate and small business takes away from your interest and ability to invest elsewhere. Most planners won't help with these choices. They may even tell you tales of real-estate and small-business-investing disasters to give you cold feet.

Sure, the value of real estate can go down just like any other investment. But over the long haul, owning a home makes good financial sense for most people. With small business, the risks are higher, but so are the potential returns. Don't let a financial planner convince you that these options are foolish — in fact, if you do your homework and know what you're doing, you can make higher rates of returns investing in real estate and small business than you can in traditional securities such as stocks and bonds. See Part III to read more about your investing options.

Selling legal services

More and more planners are getting into the business of drawing up *trusts* and providing other estate-planning services for their clients. Although these and other legal documents may be right for you, you may be able to draw them up yourself at far lower cost if your situation isn't complicated (see Chapter 19).

If you want advice on whether you need these legal documents, do a little investigating: Do some additional reading or consult an advisor who won't actually perform the work. Legal matters are complex enough that the competence of someone who doesn't specialize in it full time should be carefully scrutinized. If you do ultimately hire someone to perform estate-planning services for you, hire someone who specializes and works at it full-time. Read Chapter 19 to learn more about estate planning.

Scaring you unnecessarily

Some planners put together nifty computer-generated projections showing that you will need millions of dollars by the time you retire to maintain your standard of living. Or that tuition will cost hundreds of thousands of dollars by the time your 2-year-old is ready for university.

Waking up a client to the realities of his or her financial situation is an important and difficult job for a good financial planner. But some unscrupulous planners take this task to an extreme, deliberately scaring you into buying what they're selling. They paint a bleak picture and imply that you can fix your problems only if you do what they say. Don't let them scare you — you've got *Personal Finance For Dummie$ For Canadians,* with Eric Tyson and Tony Martin on your side! Don't worry; instead, read this book and get your financial life in order.

Creating dependency

Another conflict of interest issue: Financial planners have a tendency to create dependency, making things seem so complicated that their clients feel as though they could never manage their finances on their own. If your advisor is reluctant to tell you how you can educate yourself about personal finance, or if he advises you that your time would be better spent learning yoga, you've probably found a *self-perpetuating consultant.*

Financial Management Options

Everyone has three basic choices about how to approach managing money: You can do nothing, you can do it yourself, or you can hire someone to help you.

Doing nothing

The *do nothing* approach has a large following (and you thought you were the only one!). People who fall into this category may be leading terribly exciting, interesting lives and are therefore too busy to attend to something so mundane as dealing with their personal finances. Or they may be leading terribly mundane lives but are too busy fantasizing about more appealing ways to spend their time. For both types, everything from a major UFO sighting to taking out the garbage captures the imagination more than thinking about financial management.

But the dangers of doing nothing are many. Problem areas, left to themselves, get worse. Putting off saving for retirement or ignoring your buildup of debt eventually comes back to haunt you. Not carrying adequate insurance can be devastating when an accident occurs. In the last several years, fires, flooding, and ice storms all have shown how precariously we live in paradise.

Even if you've followed the do nothing approach all your life, you're now officially promoted out of it! You bought this book to learn more about personal finance and to make changes in your money matters, right? So take control and keep reading!

Doing it yourself

Do-it-yourselfers learn enough about financial topics to make informed decisions on their own. Doing anything yourself, of course, requires you to invest some of your time to learn the basic concepts and keep up with changes. For some, personal financial management becomes a challenging and absorbing interest. Others focus on what they need to do to get the job done quickly and efficiently.

It's a myth that, if you self-direct your finances and make your own decisions, you will spend endless hours doing so. The harder part for most people is catching up to where they should be and correcting past mistakes. After you get things in order — which you can easily do with this book as your companion — you shouldn't need to spend more than an hour or two every few months on your personal finances (unless a major issue, like a real estate purchase, comes up).

Some in the financial advisory business like to make things seem so complicated that they compare what they do to brain surgery! Their argument goes, "You wouldn't perform brain surgery on yourself, so why would you manage your money yourself?" Well, to this we say, personal financial management *ain't* brain surgery — not even close. You can manage on your own and, in fact, you can do better than what most advisors can do for you. Why? Because you're not subject to conflicts of interest, and you care the most about your money.

Hiring financial help

Realizing that you need to hire someone to help you make and implement financial decisions can be a valuable insight. Spending a few hours and several hundred dollars to hire a competent professional can be a good investment, even if you have a modest income or assets. But you need to know what your money is buying.

Financial planners or advisors make money in one of three ways:

- ✔ They earn commissions based on sales of financial products.
- ✔ They charge a percentage of the assets that they invest for you.
- ✔ They charge by the hour.

If you followed Alice's journey into this area at the beginning of the chapter, you can tell that hiring financial assistance can be anything but a tea party.

Planners paid a commission

Commission-based planners aren't really planners, advisors, or counsellors at all — they are salespeople. Many *stock brokers* and *insurance brokers* of the 1970s and 1980s are now called *financial consultants* or *financial service representatives* in order to glamorize the profession and obscure how the planners are compensated. Ditto for insurance salespeople calling themselves *estate planning specialists*.

That's like a Honda dealer calling himself a *transportation consultant*. A Honda dealer is a salesperson who makes a living selling Hondas, period. He's definitely not going to tell you nice things about Ford, Chrysler, or Toyota cars — unless, of course, he happens to sell those, too. He also has no interest in educating you about money-saving public transit possibilities.

As we discuss earlier in this chapter, salespeople and brokers masquerading as planners can have enormous self-interest when they push certain products, particularly those products paying generous commissions. Table 3-1 gives you an idea of the commissions that a financial planner/salesperson can earn through selling particular financial products.

Table 3-1	Financial Product Commissions
Product	*Commission*
Life Insurance ($250,000, age 45):	
Term Life	$150 to $650
Universal/Whole Life	$1,020 to $2,580

Product	Commission
Disability Insurance:	
($4,000/month benefit, age 35)	$345 to $1,200
Investments ($20,000):	
Mutual Funds	$200 to $1,200
Limited Partnerships	$1,400 to $2,000
Annuities	$1,000 to $1,800

Advisors paid a percentage of assets under management

A generally better choice than a commission-based planner is a financial advisor who charges a percentage of the assets that are managed or invested. This compensation system removes the incentives to sell you products with high commissions and to churn your assets with lots of transactions to generate more of those commissions.

Although it's an improvement over product-pushers working on commission, the fee-based system has flaws, too. First off, suppose that you're trying to decide whether to invest in stocks, bonds, or real estate. A planner who earns her living managing your money likely won't recommend real estate because that would deplete your investment capital.

Fee-based planners are also only interested in managing money for those who have already accumulated a fair amount of it — which rules out most people.

If what you really do need is someone to manage your money (you lucky dog), mutual funds or private money managers (discussed in Chapter 11) are what you should look for, not a financial planner who also tries to manage money.

Advisors paid an hourly fee

Your best bet for professional help with your personal finances is an advisor who charges for his time. Because he doesn't sell any financial products, his objectivity is maintained. He doesn't perform money management, so he can help you make comprehensive financial decisions dealing with loans, retirement planning, and selecting good investments, including real estate, mutual funds, and small business.

The primary risk in selecting an hourly based planner is incompetence. You can address this by checking references and learning enough yourself to discern between good and bad financial advice. Another risk comes from not clearly defining the work to be done and the approximate total cost before you begin. You also should review some of the other key questions outlined in Chapter 20.

A drawback of an entirely different kind occurs when you don't follow through on the recommendations of your advisor. You paid for her work but didn't act on it, so you didn't capture its value. If part of the reason that you hired the planner in the first place was that you're too busy or not interested enough to make changes to your financial situation, then you should look for this support in the services you buy from the planner.

If you just need someone as a sounding board for ideas or to recommend a specific strategy or product, you can hire an hourly based planner for one or two sessions of advice. You save money doing the legwork and implementation on your own. Just make sure that the planner is willing to give you specific-enough advice that you can implement on your own.

Should You Hire a Financial Planner?

Most people reading this book don't need to hire financial planners. But just because you're financially savvy, you shouldn't be too quick to write off the value of hiring help.

Good reasons for hiring a financial planner can be the same reasons for hiring someone to clean your home or do your taxes. If you're too busy or don't enjoy doing it, that's a fine reason to hire help. If you're uncomfortable making decisions on your own, using a planner for a second opinion makes good sense. And if you shy away from numbers and bristle at the thought of long division, a good planner can help you.

How a good financial planner can help

The following gives you a rundown of some of the important things a competent financial planner can help you do.

Identifying problems and goals

Many otherwise-intelligent people have a hard time being objective about their financial problems. They may ignore their debts or have unrealistic goals and expectations given their financial situations and behaviours. And many are so busy with other aspects of their lives that they never take the time to think about what their financial goals are. A good financial planner can give you the objective look you need.

Surprisingly, some people are in better financial position than they thought in relation to their goals. Good counsellors really enjoy this aspect of their jobs — good news is easier and much more fun to deliver.

Identifying strategies to reach your financial goals

If your mind is like our minds, it's a jumble of various plans, ideas, and concerns, along with a cobweb or two. A good counsellor can help you sort out and straighten your thoughts and can propose alternative strategies for you to consider in accomplishing your financial goals.

Setting priorities

You could be doing dozens of things to improve your financial situation, but making a few key changes could have the greatest value. Equally important is identifying the changes that fit your overall situation and that won't keep you awake at night fretting about them. Good planners help you prioritize.

Saving research time and hassle

Even if you know what major financial decisions are most important to you, doing the research can be time-consuming and frustrating if you don't know where to turn for good information and advice. A good planner does research to match your needs to the best available strategies and products. So much lousy information is out there on various financial topics that you can easily get lost, discouraged, sidetracked, or swindled. A good advisor can keep you from making a bad decision based on poor or insufficient information. Your free time is precious. (Does your car license plate holder say I'D RATHER BE . . .? If so, you may be a good candidate to hire a financial planner — unless, of course, it says I'D RATHER BE MANAGING MY OWN MONEY.)

Purchasing commission-free financial products

If you hire a planner who charges for her time, you can easily save hundreds or thousands of dollars by avoiding the cost of commissions in the financial products you buy. This commission-free situation is especially valuable when it comes to purchasing investments and insurance.

Avoiding lousy financial products and strategies

A good counsellor can keep you from doing something really dumb — particularly if a commission-based salesperson is giving you the *hard sell*. A conflict-free planner can recommend what's in your best interest.

Providing an objective voice for major decisions

Deciding when to retire, how much to spend on a home purchase, and where to invest your money are big decisions. Getting swept up in the emotional upheaval of these issues can cloud your perspective and objectivity. A competent and sensitive advisor can cut through this cloud to raise issues and provide sound counsel.

Helping you to just DO it

Deciding what you need to do is not enough — you have to actually do it, too. And although you can use a planner for advice and make all the changes on your own, a good counsellor can also help you follow through with your plan. After all, part of the reason you hired the counsellor in the first place may be that you're too busy or uninterested to manage your finances. If the counsellor merely produces a nice-looking report of recommendations and doesn't encourage you to implement them, all you're left with is part of a dead tree!

Mediating

If you have a spouse or partner, financial decisions can produce real fireworks, particularly with financial decisions involving the extended family. Although a counsellor can't be a therapist, a good one can be sensitive to the different needs and concerns of each party and can try to find middle ground on the financial issues you grapple with.

Making you money and allowing you peace of mind

The whole point of professional financial planning is to help you make the most of your money and help you plan for and attain your financial and personal goals. In the process, the financial planner should show you how to enhance your investment returns; reduce your spending, taxes, and insurance costs; increase your savings; improve your catastrophic insurance coverage; and achieve your financial independence goals. And last but not least: Putting your financial house in order should take some weight off your mind — like that clean, light-headed feeling after a haircut.

Not for everyone

Although some people can benefit from the advice of a knowledgeable and ethical financial planner, you should consider your personality type before you decide to hire help. Our experience has been that some people (believe it or not) enjoy the research and number-crunching. If this is you or if you're not really comfortable taking advice, you're better off doing your own homework and creating your own plan.

Likewise, if you have a specific tax or legal matter, you're better off hiring a good professional who specializes in that field rather than a financial planner.

How to find a good financial planner

Locating a good financial planner who is willing to work with the not-yet-rich-and-famous and who doesn't have conflicts of interest can be like finding a needle in a haystack. Two methods that can serve as good starting points are personal referrals and associations.

Personal referrals

One of the best ways to find a good financial planner is to get a personal referral from a satisfied customer who is someone you trust. A referral from an accountant or an attorney whose judgement you've trusted can help as well.

Word-of-mouth is how the best financial planners continue to build their practices. Satisfied customers are any professional's best and least-costly marketers.

However, never *ever* take a recommendation from anyone as gospel. We don't care *who* makes the referral — even if it's your mother or the Pope. You must do your homework: Ask the planner the ten questions in Chapter 20. We've seen people get into real trouble because of blindly accepting someone else's recommendation. ***Remember:*** The person making the recommendation is (probably) not a personal finance expert. He or she could be just as bewildered as you are.

You may get referred to a planner or broker who returns the favour by sending business to the tax, legal, or real estate person who referred you. On more than a few occasions, professionals in other fields have made it clear to Eric, a financial counsellor, that they would refer business to him if he referred business to them. He refused, of course. Good professionals don't do tit for tat. Hire professionals who make referrals to others based on their competence and ethics.

Associations

Associations of financial planners are more than happy to refer you to planners in your area. But as we discuss earlier in this chapter, the major trade associations are composed of planners who sell products and work on commission.

A good place to start is:

> **Canadian Association of Financial Planners (CAFP)**
> **439 University Ave., Suite 1710**
> **Toronto, Ontario**
> **M5G 1Y8**
> **(Phone 416-593-6592 / 800-346-2237)**
> www.CAFP.com

The CAFP controls the Registered Financial Planner designation (RFP). To be an RFP, planners must meet certain educational requirements, pass a national six-hour exam, maintain liability insurance, and do at least 30 hours of professional development a year. Members agree to abide by a code of ethics, which includes telling their clients up front how they are compensated. Also, accredited RFP practitioners must carry professional errors and omissions insurance. After all, everybody makes mistakes at times.

Write or call the CAFP and ask for a directory of its members, called The Consumer Guide to Financial Planning. Beyond phone numbers and addresses, you'll also find information on each planner's qualifications, areas of expertise, and, importantly, how he or she is paid.

Caution: Savings at Risk

You have no interest in becoming a financial planner (presumably), so why waste your time reading about the ways that planners of dubious distinction often cultivate their clients? Simple: The channel through which you hear of a planner may provide clues to a planner's integrity and way of doing business.

- **Cold calling.** You've just come home after a hard day. No sooner has your posterior hit the recliner to settle in for the night when the phone rings. It's Joe the financial planner, and he wants to help you achieve all your financial dreams. *Cold calling* (the salesperson calls you, without an appointment) is the most inefficient way a planner can get new clients. It's also intrusive and is typically used by aggressive salespeople working on commission.

- **Adult education classes.** Here's what often happens at adult education classes given at local universities: You pay a reasonable fee for the course. You go to class giddy at the prospect of learning how to manage your finances. And then the instructor ends up being a broker or financial planner hungry for clients. He confuses more than he conveys. He's short on specifics. But he'll be more than happy to show you the way if you contact (and hire) him outside of class.

Instructors for these courses are usually paid to teach. If they are, then they don't need to solicit clients in class — in fact, it's unethical for them to do so. We should note, however, that part of the problem is that some universities take advantage of the fact that they know such "teachers" want to solicit business. So the universities set the pay at a low level, thinking, erroneously, that they'll save money. Our advice: *Never* assume that someone who teaches a financial-planning course at a local university is ethical, competent, or looking out for your best interests. Although we may sound cynical by saying this, assume that these people are none of the above until they clearly prove otherwise.

Ethical instructors who are there to teach do *not* solicit clients and may actively discourage students from hiring them. Smart universities pay their instructors well and weed out the instructors who are more interested in building up their client base than teaching.

✔ **"Free" seminars.** This is a case of "you get what you pay for." Because you don't pay a fee to attend "free seminars" and the "teachers" don't get paid either, these events tend to be more clear-cut sales pitches. The "instructor" may share some information, but smart seminar leaders know that the goal of a successful seminar is to establish themselves as experts and to whet the prospects' appetites.

Note: Be *especially* wary of seminars targeted at selected groups, such as special seminars for people who have received retirement plan distributions or those touting "Financial Planning for Women." Basic financial planning is not specific to gender, ethnicity, or marital status.

Don't assume that the financial planner giving a presentation at your employer's office is the right planner for you, either. It's surprising how little some corporate benefits departments investigate the people they let in. In most cases, planners are accepted simply because they don't charge. One organization gave preference to planners who, in addition to doing free presentations, also brought in a catered lunch! Guess what — this attracted lots of the brokers who sell commission-based products.

Part II
Saving for a Purpose

The 5th Wave   By Rich Tennant

"I've been working over 80 hours a week for the past two years preparing for retirement, and it hasn't bothered me OR my wife, whats-her-name."

In this part . . .

We show you how to identify where your hard-earned dollars are going. We pinpoint numerous ways to make those dollars go toward helping you build up your savings instead of going to wasteful spending. What? You're buried in debt with little to show for it? Well, it's never too late to start digging out. Here you find out how to reduce your taxes and credit card burden, how to save for retirement, how to get the best deal on a mortgage, and lots more.

Chapter 4

Your Money: Where Did It Go?

These little proverbs have been around for a long time; they offer good, common-sense advice:

> *Pay yourself first.*
> *It's not what you make, it's what you keep.*
> *A penny saved is a penny earned.*

Although we certainly can't hope to compete with the eloquence of these nuggets of wisdom, allow us to add a little advice of our own: In order to accomplish your financial goals, you must live within your means.

To live within your means involves three steps:

1. **Spend less than you earn.**

2. **Save what you do not spend.**

3. **Invest what you save.**

For those of you who have a hard time living within your means, the first step is usually the hardest: spending less than you earn. Many folks earn just enough to make ends meet. And some can't even do that; they simply spend more than they make. The result of such spending habits is, of course, accumulation of debt — witness the Canadian government and its more than half a trillion dollars worth of debt accumulation.

Whatever your financial dreams, you need to save and invest (unless you plan on winning the lottery or gaining a large inheritance). To put yourself in a position that allows you to start saving, you first need to take a close look at your spending habits.

Why You Overspend

Canada has become a spending disaster. In 1996, for example, Canadians on average managed to put aside less than 5 percent of their after-tax income. Why? Simply because most of the influences on you in society are encouraging you to spend, and because credit is so widely and easily available.

You're just a consumption machine

Think about it: In the media and in the hallowed halls of our government, more often than not, you're referred to as a *consumer*.

Not a person, not a citizen, not a human being — but a c-o-n-s-u-m-e-r.

In fact, some people feel unpatriotic or inadequate if they don't spend enough. "Saving too much and not spending enough could hurt the economy," they say. "People could be thrown out of work, and it could be a friend or family member. My favorite politician might not get reelected if I don't single-handedly prop up the economy by spending. I wouldn't be doing my part if I didn't consume by spending as much as possible."

Balderdash! Ultimately, you're the one who suffers the consequences of spending more than you can afford.

Access to credit

As you probably already know, spending your money is very easy to do. Thanks to innovations in technology like bank machines and credit cards, your money is always available for spending, 24 hours a day, 365 days a year (except during leap years, when your money is available 366 days a year). Every little outlet in the mall is pitching its own credit card, including the gas station across the street and the convenience store down the road. It certainly won't surprise us when kids on every block start taking credit cards at their lemonade stands. We can hear it now: "We take Visa, but we don't take American Express."

Sometimes, it may seem as though lenders are trying to give away money by making credit so easily available. But this is a dangerous illusion. When it comes to consumer debt (credit cards, auto loans, and the like), lenders aren't giving away anything except the opportunity for you to get in over your head, rack up high interest charges, and delay your progress toward your financial and personal goals.

Credit is most dangerous when you make consumption purchases that you couldn't afford in the first place.

Ten leading causes of overspending

Many people are tempted to live beyond their means. In Canada, the total amount of outstanding consumer installment debt that is on credit cards, auto loans, and other monthly lines of credit exceeds a quarter of consumers' after-tax income.

Here are some of the adversaries you're up against as you attempt to control your spending. (In Chapter 5, we explain detailed strategies for getting out of debt.)

Using credit cards

The modern-day bank credit card was invented by Bank of America near the tail end of the baby boom. The credit industry has been booming along with the boomers ever since.

If you pay your bill in full every month, credit cards offer a convenient way to buy things with an interest-free, short-term loan. But if you carry your debt from one month to the next at high interest rates, credit cards encourage you to live beyond your means. Credit cards make spending money that you don't have easy and tempting.

If you have a knack for charging up a storm and spending more than you should with those little pieces of plastic, only one solution exists: Get rid of them. Put scissors to the plastic. Go cold turkey. You *can* function without them (see the next chapter for details if you think you can't live without credit cards).

Making minimum monthly payments

You'll *never* get your credit card debt paid off if you keep charging on your card and make only the minimum monthly payment. Interest continues to pile up on your outstanding debt. Paying only the minimum monthly payment is like using a Dixie cup to bail water from a sinking boat that has a basketball-sized hole in the bottom.

Taking out car loans

It's too easy to walk onto a car lot and go home with a new car that you could never afford if you had to pay cash. The dealer gets you thinking in terms of monthly payments that sound very small compared to what that four-wheeler is *really* gonna cost you. Auto loans and leases are easy for just about anyone to get (except maybe a recently paroled felon).

Suppose that you're tired of driving around in the old clunker. The car is battle-scarred and boring, and you don't like to be seen in it. Plus, the car is likely to only need more and more repairs in the months ahead. So off you go to your friendly local car dealer.

You start looking around at all the shiny new cars and then — like the feeling you experience when spotting a water fountain on a scorching hot day — there it is: the replacement for your old clunker. It's sleek and clean and — oooh, look! — it has A/C, a CD player, and power everything.

Before you have an opportunity to read the fine print on the sticker page on the side window, the salesperson moseys on up next to you. He gets you talking about how nice the car is, the weather — anything but the price of that car.

"How," you begin to think to yourself, "can this guy afford to spend time with me without knowing if I can afford this thing?" After taking you out for a test drive and talking more about the car, the weather, and your love life, or lack thereof, comes your moment of truth.

The salesperson, it seems, doesn't care about how much money you have. If, in fact, you have lots of money, that doesn't matter either. Either way, it's no problem!

The car is only $299 a month.

That's not bad, you think. Heck, you were expecting to hear that the car cost at least 15 to 20 grand. Before you know it, the dealer runs a credit report on you, has you sign a few papers, and minutes later you're driving home — the proud owner of a spanking new car.

See, the dealer wants you to think in terms of monthly payments because the cost *sounds* so cheap: $299 for a car. But, of course, that's $299 per month, every month, for many, many months. You're gonna be payin' forever — after all, you just bought a car that cost a huge chunk (perhaps 100 percent or more) of your yearly take-home income!

But it gets worse. What does the total sticker price come to when interest charges are added in? And how about insurance and registration and maintenance over the seven or so years that you'll own it? Now you're probably up to more than a *year's* worth of your income. Ouch! See Chapter 6 for how to spend what you afford on a car.

Bending to peer pressure

You go out with the guys or the gals (or both) to dinner, a movie, and then club-hopping. Try to remember the last time one of you said, "Let's go someplace cheaper. I can't afford to spend this much."

On the one hand, you don't want to be a stick in the mud. But on the other hand, some of your friends have more money than you do — and the ones who don't may be running up debt even faster than you are.

Spending to feel good

Life is full of stress, obligations, and demands. "I work hard," you say. "And darn it, I deserve to indulge!" Especially after your boss took the credit for your last great idea or blamed you for his last major screwup. So you buy something expensive or go to a fancy restaurant. Feel better? You won't when the bill arrives. And the more you spend, the less you save, and the longer you'll be stuck working and working for jerks like that!

Becoming addicted to spending

Just as people can become addicted to alcohol, tobacco, TV, and even love, some become addicted to the high they get from spending. A number of psychological causes can be identified for spending addiction, some of them dating back to how your family handled money and spending. (And you thought you'd identified all the problems you can blame on Mom and Dad!)

If your spending and debt problems are chronic, Debtors Anonymous, a 12-step support group program patterned after Alcoholics Anonymous, can help. See Chapter 5 for more information.

Trying to keep current

You just have to see the latest hit movie or wear the latest designer clothes or get the new, superimproved, oversized tennis racquet with shock-absorbers, double-wishbone suspension, polyxylitol handgrips, and what not. All your friends are getting one, so you'd better get one, too. Right?

Wrong. Besides, many new technologies or products don't live up to their billing. Be smug and wait until a product is proven and until you can afford it. By then, you may also find it's on sale.

Ignoring your financial goals when buying

When was the last time you heard someone say that he decided to forego a purchase because he was saving toward retirement or a home purchase? Doesn't happen very often does it? Just dealing with the here-and-now and forgetting your long-term needs and goals are very tempting. That's why people toil away for too many years in jobs they dislike.

Living for today has its virtues: Tomorrow *may* not come. But odds are very high that it will. Will you still feel the same way tomorrow about today's spending decisions? Or will you feel guilty that you again failed to stick to your goals?

Of course, this assumes that you have financial goals to stick to. Most people haven't yet set goals and don't know how much they should be saving to accomplish them. Chapter 8 helps you to kick-start that process.

Wanting only the best for your children

For children, many of the best things in life are free, just as they are for you. Junior *can* live without the latest $100 sneakers. Later on in life, your children will thank you: It's better to have sound judgement and wise thriftiness than the worship of material goods.

Education can cost good money, we know. However, education experts are the first to dissuade you of the assumption that you're doing the best for your children if you spend lots of money to live in a town with a supposedly top-of-the-line school district or to fund the tuition of a private school education from preschool through high school if you can't be home enough to take care of your children's other wants and needs.

Education begins in and is best done in the home. Some parents we see spend so much time running around working, working, working to afford all the supposedly best things for their kids that they neglect to spend *time* with their kids — the most important ingredient to their children's long-term happiness and success.

Thinking that money can buy happiness

Recall the handful of moments in your life that you wouldn't trade for anything. Odds are, those moments don't include the time you bought a car or found a sweater that you liked for 50 percent off at your favorite retailer. The old saying is true: The most enjoyable and precious things of value in your life can't be bought.

What we're about to say should go without saying, but we must say it because many people act as if it weren't so: Money can't buy happiness. It is tempting to think that if you could make only 10 or 20 percent more money, you'd be happier and less stressed out over your bills. You'd have more money to travel, eat out, and buy that new car you've been eyeing, right? Not so fast. A great deal of thoughtful research suggests that little relationship exists between money and happiness.

"Wealth is like health: Although its absence can breed misery, having it is no guarantee of happiness," summarizes Dr. David Myers, professor of psychology at Michigan's Hope College, in his book, published by Avon, *The Pursuit of Happiness: Discovering the Pathway to Fulfillment, Well-Being, and Enduring Personal Joy.* (This guy has it good! Imagine studying happiness for a living.)

Despite cheap air travel, VCRs, compact discs, microwaves, computers, voice mail, and all the other stuff that's supposed to make our lives easier and more enjoyable, many of us aren't any happier than we were three decades ago. According to research conducted by the National Opinion Research Center, 35 percent of people in 1957 said that they were "very happy," whereas in the 1990s, fewer said the same. These unexpected results occurred even though incomes, after adjusting for inflation, more than doubled during that time.

Being happy with what you have

Canadians — even those who have not had "easy" lives — should be able to come up with things to be happy about and grateful for: Families who love them; friends who laugh at their stupid jokes; the freedom to catch a movie or play or read a good book; great singing voices, senses of humour, or full heads of hair; the fact that they live in a country not at war with any other country.

And financially speaking, Canadians are pretty spoiled. Two-thirds of the people in the world have a standard of living that is a mere 20 percent of the Canadian average. Think about that. In other words, the average Canadian is five times better off financially than two out of every three people in the world.

Be happy with what you have and content with the things that you can't change. We know financially wealthy people who have all the material goods they want yet are emotionally poor. Likewise, we know people who are struggling financially and are quite happy, contented, and emotionally wealthy.

As Dr. Myers observes of U.S. statistics in *The Pursuit of Happiness*, ". . . if anything, to judge by soaring rates of depression, the quintupling of the violent crime rate since 1960, the doubling of the divorce rate, and the tripling of the teen suicide rate, we're richer and less happy."

Spending Analysis

Washing your face, brushing your teeth, and exercising regularly are good habits. The financial equivalents of these habits are spending less than you earn and saving enough to meet your future financial objectives.

Despite relatively high incomes compared with the rest of the world, most Canadians have a hard time saving a good percentage of their incomes compared with the rest of the world. Why? We spend too much — often far more than is necessary.

The first step to saving more of the income that you work so hard for is to figure out where that income typically gets spent; that's what the spending analysis in the next section helps you determine.

You should do the spending analysis if any of the following apply to you:

- ✔ You aren't saving enough money to meet your financial goals.
- ✔ You feel as if your spending is out of control or you don't really know where all your income goes.

> ✔ You're anticipating a significant life change (for example, marriage, leaving your job to start a business, having children, retiring, and so on).

If you're a good saver already, you may not need to complete the spending analysis. If you're saving enough to accomplish your goals (see Chapter 8), we don't see much value in continually tracking your spending. You've already established the good habit — saving. The good habit is *not* month after month of keeping track of exactly where you spend your money. As long as you're saving enough and simply spending what's left over, we say, who cares where the money is being spent!

The immediate goal of a spending analysis is to figure out what you typically spend your money on. The long-range goal is to establish a good habit: to maintain a regular, automatic savings routine.

Notice the first four letters in the word *analysis*. (You may never have noticed, but we felt the need to bring it to your attention.) Knowing where your money is going each month is very useful. It's terrific to make changes in your spending and to cut out the fat so that you can save more money and meet your financial goals. But you'll perhaps make yourself and those around you into very unhappy campers if you try to be anal-retentive about documenting precisely where you're spending every single dollar and cent.

Remember: What matters is that you save what you want and need to achieve your goals.

Tracking your spending on paper

Unless you keep meticulous records that detail every dollar you spend, you won't have perfect information. Don't sweat it! You have a number of available sources that should allow you to reconstruct where you've been spending the bulk of your money.

Doing your spending analysis is a little bit like being a detective. Your goal is to reconstruct the crime of *spending*. You probably have some major clues at your fingertips or piled somewhere on your desk or on the table where you plop yourself down to pay bills.

Get out your

> ✔ Recent pay stubs
>
> ✔ Tax returns
>
> ✔ Chequebook register or canceled cheques
>
> ✔ Credit and charge card bills

Ideally, you should assemble the documents needed to track one year's (12 months') spending. But, if your spending patterns don't fluctuate greatly from month to month (or if your dog ate some of the old bills), you can reduce your data gathering to one six-month period or to every other or every third month for the past year. If you take a major vacation or spend a large amount on gifts during certain times of the year, make sure to include these months in your analysis.

The hardest transactions to track are cash transactions because they don't leave a paper trail. Over the course of a week or perhaps even a month, you *could* keep track of everything you buy with cash. Tracking cash can be an enlightening exercise — it can also be a hassle. If you're lazy like we sometimes are or lack the time and patience, try *estimating*. Think about a typical week or month — how often do you buy things with cash? For example, if you eat lunch out four days a week at work, paying around $5 a shot, that's about $80 a month.

Try to separate your expenditures into as many useful and detailed categories as possible. Table 4-1 gives you a suggested format. You can tailor it to fit your needs. Remember, if you lump too much of your spending into broad, meaningless categories like *Other,* you'll end up where you started: wondering where all the money went.

Table 4-1	Detail Your Spending	
Category	*Monthly Average ($)*	*Percent of Total Gross Income (%)*
Taxes, taxes, taxes (income)		_____
Income tax	_____	
Canada/Quebec Pension Plan	_____	
Employment Insurance Premiums	_____	
The roof over your head		_____
Rent	_____	
Mortgage	_____	
Property taxes	_____	
Heating	_____	
Hydro	_____	
Water/garbage	_____	
Phone	_____	
Cable TV	_____	
Furniture/appliances	_____	
Maintenance/repairs	_____	

(continued)

Table 4-1 *(continued)*

Category	Monthly Average ($)	Percent of Total Gross Income (%)
Food, glorious food		_____
Supermarket	_____	
Restaurants and takeout	_____	
Getting around		_____
Gasoline	_____	
Maintenance/repairs	_____	
License fees	_____	
Tolls and parking	_____	
Bus or subway fares	_____	
Style		_____
Clothing	_____	
Shoes	_____	
Jewelry (watches, earrings)	_____	
Dry cleaning	_____	
Debt repayments		_____
Credit/charge cards	_____	
Car loans	_____	
Student loans	_____	
Other	_____	
Fun stuff		_____
Entertainment (movies, concerts)	_____	
Vacation and travel	_____	
Gifts	_____	
Hobbies	_____	
Pets	_____	
Other	_____	
Personal care		_____
Haircuts	_____	
Health club or gym	_____	
Makeup	_____	
Other	_____	

Category	Monthly Average ($)	Percent of Total Gross Income (%)
Personal business		_____
Accountant/lawyer/ financial advisor	_____	
Other	_____	
Health care		_____
Physicians and hospitals	_____	
Drugs	_____	
Dental and eyecare	_____	
Therapy	_____	
Insurance		_____
Homeowner's/renter's	_____	
Auto	_____	
Health	_____	
Life	_____	
Disability	_____	
Educational expenses		_____
Courses	_____	
Books	_____	
Supplies	_____	
Children		_____
Day care	_____	
Toys	_____	
Child support	_____	
Charitable donations	_____	_____
Other	_____	_____
_____	_____	
_____	_____	
_____	_____	
_____	_____	
_____	_____	
_____	_____	

Tracking your spending on the computer

More and more software packages are being developed and improved to help you pay bills and track your spending. The main advantage of these software packages is that they continually track your spending as long as you keep entering the information. And, after you learn how to use these packages (not always an easy thing to do), they can speed the process of writing cheques.

But you don't need a computer and fancy software packages to figure out where you're spending money and to pay your bills. More than a few software purchasers give up entering the data after a few months. If tracking your spending is what you're after, you're likely to have only the information in the software from bills you pay by cheque. Expenses you pay by credit card and cash need to be entered specially into the software if you want to capture that data, too.

Like home exercise equipment and exotic kitchen appliances, some software ends up in the consumer graveyard.

Paper, pencil, and a calculator work just fine.

If you do want to try computerizing your bill payments and expense tracking, the best software packages currently available are recommended in Chapter 22.

Spending less: The secret to growing rich on your income

Some people bring in tiny incomes, some earn hundreds of thousands of dollars or more, and others make something in between. At every income level, people fall into one of the following three categories:

- ✓ People who spend more than they earn (accumulate debt)
- ✓ People who spend all that they earn (save nothing)
- ✓ People who save 2, 5, 10, even 20 percent (or more!)

We've seen $30,000 earners save 20 percent of their income ($6,000), $60,000 earners save just 5 percent ($3,000), and people earning well into six figures annually who save nothing or are accumulating debt.

Suppose that you currently earn $30,000 per year and spend all of it. You wonder: "How can I save money?"

Good question!

Don't waste your time on financial administration

Tom is the model of financial organization. All his financial documents are neatly organized into color-coded folders. Every month, he enters all his spending information into his computer. He even carries a notebook to detail his cash spending so that every penny is accounted for.

Tom also balances his chequebook, "to make sure that everything is in order." He can't remember the last time his bank made a mistake, but he knows a friend who once found a $50 error.

If you spend seven hours per month as Tom does balancing your chequebook and detailing all your spending, you may be wasting nearly two weeks' worth of time per year — the equivalent of two-thirds of your vacation time if you take three weeks annually.

Suppose that you're "lucky" enough, every other year, to find a $100 error the bank makes in its favor. If you spend just three hours per month tracking your spending and balancing your chequebook to discover this glitch, you'll spend 72 hours over two years to find a $100 mistake. Your hourly pay: $1.39 per hour. You could make more flipping burgers at a burger joint if you wanted to moonlight. (**Note:** If you make significant-size deposits into or out of your account, be sure that those are captured on your statement.)

To add insult to injury, after working a full week and doing all your financial and other chores, you may not have the desire and energy left to do the more important stuff. Looking at your big personal financial picture — establishing goals, choosing wise investments, ensuring proper insurance coverage — may continue to be shoved to the back burner. As a result, you may lose thousands of dollars annually. Over the course of your adult life, this could translate into tens or even hundreds of thousands of lost dollars.

Tom, for example, didn't know how much he should be saving to meet his retirement goals. He hadn't reviewed his employer's benefit materials to understand his insurance and retirement plan options. He knows he pays a lot in taxes, but he hasn't educated himself about how to reduce his taxes.

You want to make the most of your money. Unless you truly enjoy dealing with money, you need to prioritize the money activities that you work on. Time is limited, and life is short. Working harder on financial administration doesn't earn you bonus points. The more time you spend dealing with your personal finances, the less time is available to gab with friends, watch a good movie, read a good novel, and do other things you really enjoy.

Don't get us wrong — nothing is inherently wrong with balancing your chequebook. In fact, if you regularly bounce cheques because you don't know how low your balance is, the exercise might save you a lot in returned cheque fees. However, if you keep enough money in your chequing account so that your balance rarely drops to $0.00, balancing your chequebook is probably a waste of your valuable time, even if your hourly wages aren't lofty.

If you're busy, consider ways to reduce the amount of time spent on financially mundane tasks like paying bills. Increasing numbers of companies, for example, allow you to have your monthly bills paid to them electronically via your bank chequing account or charged on your credit card (only do this if you pay your credit card bill in full each month). The fewer bills you have to pay, the fewer separate cheques and envelopes you must process each month. That translates into more free time for you and fewer paper cuts!

Rather than knocking yourself out at a second job or hustling for that next promotion, you could try living below your income. In other words, spend less than you earn. (We know spending less than you earn is hard to imagine, but you can do it.) Consider that for every discontented person earning and spending $30,000 per year, someone else is out there making do on $27,000.

A great many people live on less than you make. If you spent as they do, you could save and invest the difference.

As Dr. David Myers (read about him in the section, "Ten leading causes of overspending," earlier in this chapter) says: "Satisfaction isn't so much getting what you want as wanting what you have. There are two ways to be rich: one is to have great wealth, the other is to have few wants."

Chapter 5

Dealing with Debt and Credit Problems

In This Chapter

▶ Using your savings to reduce your debt

▶ Getting out of debt when you don't have savings

▶ The pros and cons of filing for bankruptcy

▶ Dealing with credit problems

*B*orrowing money has a lot in common with eating. You need to eat to live, but some foods are better for you than others. And it's tempting to eat too many of the bad foods.

So it is with debt: Some debt is good, and some is bad. When debt is used for investing in your future, we call it *good debt*. Borrowing money to afford an education, buy real estate, or invest in a small business is like eating foods rich in calcium for strong bones or eating fruits and vegetables for their vitamins.

But accumulating *bad debt* (consumer debt) is like living on a diet of sugar and caffeine: a quick fix with no long-term nutritional value. Borrowing on your credit card to afford that vacation to Fiji is costly and detrimental to your long-term financial health.

In this chapter, we help you battle the increasing problem of consumer debt. Getting rid of your bad debts may be even more difficult for you than giving up the sugar-laden foods you love. But in the long run, you'll be glad you did; you'll be financially healthier and emotionally happier. And once you get rid of your debts, practice the best way to deal with credit problems: **Don't borrow.**

To decide which debt reduction strategies make sense for you, you first must consider your overall financial situation and calculate your total debts relative to your income.

Using Savings to Reduce Your Debt

Many people have built up a psychological brick wall between their savings and investment accounts and their debt accounts. Failing to view their finances holistically, they have simply gotten into the habit of looking at these accounts individually. The thought of putting a door in that big brick wall has never occurred to them.

Money you may be overlooking

Have you ever reached into the pocket of an old winter parka and found a rolled-up twenty dollar bill you forgot you had? Stumbling across some forgotten funds is always a pleasant experience. But before you root through all your closets in search of stray cash to help you pay down that nagging credit card debt, check out some of these financial jacket pockets that you may have overlooked:

✔ **Borrow against your cash-value life insurance policy.** If you were approached by a life insurance agent, odds are good that this is the type of policy you were sold because it pays high commissions to its agents. Or perhaps your parents bought one for you when you were a little gremlin. Borrow against the cash value to pay down your debts. Also, be sure to check whether any of the loan "proceeds" will be taxable. (*Note:* Continuing with such a policy may not be the best thing to do — see Chapter 18 for more details.)

✔ **Sell investments held outside of RRSPs.** Maybe you have some shares of stock or a Canada Savings Bond gathering dust in your safety deposit box. Consider cashing in these investments to pay down your loan balances. Just be sure to consider the tax consequences of selling, and if possible, only sell those investments that won't generate a big tax bill.

✔ **Borrow against the equity in your home.** If you're a homeowner, you may be able to tap into your home's *equity,* which is the difference between the property's market value and outstanding loan balance. You can generally borrow against real estate at a lower interest rate.

✔ **Borrow from (friends and) family.** They know you, love you, realize your shortcomings, and — heck — probably won't be as cold-hearted as some bankers we know. Money borrowed from family members can have strings attached, of course. Treating the obligation seriously is important. It's also best to write up a simple agreement listing the terms and conditions of your loan to avoid misunderstandings. Unless your family members are like the worst bankers we know, you'll probably get a fair interest rate, and your family will have the satisfaction of helping you out — just don't forget to pay them back.

Using savings to pay down debts may seem like you're losing money, but you aren't losing, you're gaining. Remember that the growth of your money is determined by your *net worth* — the difference between your assets and your liabilities (see Chapter 2). Hopefully, your savings and investments are earning a decent return, but if you have consumer debts, odds are that the interest on those debts is high.

If you have loans at, say, 8 percent, paying them off is like finding an investment with a guaranteed return of 8 percent — *tax free*. If you're in a 41 percent tax bracket, for example, you would actually need an income-earning investment that yielded even more — around 13 percent — to net 8 percent after paying taxes in order to justify not paying off your 8 percent loans. The higher your tax bracket (see Chapter 7), the higher the return you need on your investments to justify keeping high-interest consumer debt.

If you have the savings to pay off high-interest credit card and auto loans, do it. You diminish your savings, true, but you also reduce your debts. You benefit financially because the interest on your savings is far less than the interest your debt accrues. Make sure to pay off the loans with the highest interest rates first.

Even if you think you're an investment genius and can earn more on your investments, swallow your ego and pay down the debts anyway. In order to chase that higher potential return from investments, you need to take substantial risk. You *may* earn more investing in that hot stock tip or that bargain real estate located on a toxic waste site, but more than likely, you won't.

If you use your accessible savings to pay down debts, be careful to leave yourself enough of an emergency cushion. You want to be in a position to withstand an unexpected large expense or temporary loss of income. On the other hand, if you use savings to pay down credit card debt, unless your card gets cancelled, you can run your credit card balances back up in a financial pinch (or turn to a family member or wealthy friend for a low-interest loan).

Decreasing Debt When You Lack Savings

"I don't have savings, you nincompoops," you exclaim, "that's why I have all this debt!"

If you read the preceding section, thank you for patiently waiting. We just wanted to make sure that you didn't have any money that you forgot about. (The number of people with consumer debt who can pay it down with savings but haven't done so always surprises us.)

But on to your quandary: You lack savings to pay off your high-interest consumer debt. Well, not surprisingly, you have some work to do. If you currently spend all your income (and more!), you need to figure out how you can decrease your spending (see Chapter 6 for lots of great ideas) and/or increase your income. In the meantime, you need to slow the growth of your debt. Read the rest of this chapter to learn how.

Investigate lower interest rate credit cards

Different credit cards charge different interest rates. Why in the world should you pay 14, 16, 18 percent or more when you can pay less? For years, the average credit card interest rate has hovered around 18 percent. The credit card business has become quite competitive. Gone are the days when all banks charged 18 percent or more for VISA and MasterCard.

Here's one of the few times in your life when you should want to be below average! Until you get your debt paid off, make it more difficult for your debt to grow. You may be able to accomplish this slowing process by reducing the interest rate you pay on your debt.

If you earn a decent income, are not *too* burdened with debt, and have a clean credit record, qualifying for lower-rate cards is relatively painless. Some persistence (and clean-up work) may be required if you have nicks in your credit report or have income and debt problems. After you're approved for a new, lower-interest rate credit card, you can simply transfer your outstanding balance from your higher-rate card.

 Something that you might want to try is simply calling the bank that issued your current high interest-rate credit card and saying that you want to cancel your card because you found a competitor that offers no annual fee and a lower interest rate. Your bank may choose to match the terms of the "competitor" rather than lose you as a customer.

 Table 5-1 lists some of the consistently low interest-rate credit cards. Please note that these cards charge interest rates that are variable and are offered by banks that are somewhat picky about whom they accept for a low-rate card. But you have nothing to lose if you apply.

 While you're paying down your credit card balance(s), stop making new charges on cards that have outstanding balances. Many people don't realize that interest starts to accumulate *immediately* when they carry a balance. *You have no grace period* — the 20-odd days you normally have to pay your balance in full without incurring interest charges — if you carry a credit card balance month-to-month.

Table 5-1	Low-Interest Rate Credit Cards		
Institution	*Card Name*	*Interest Rate*	*Annual Fee*
Bank of Montreal 800-263-2263	Low Rate MasterCard	12.9%	$15
Canada Trust 800-281-8014	Gold MasterCard	11.9%	$39
CIBC 800-465-4653	Select VISA	9.9%	$29
Royal Bank 800-668-9700	Low Option Rate VISA	9.5%	$25
Scotiabank 800-387-6466	Value VISA	9.25%	$29
Toronto-Dominion 800-268-9460	TD Emerald	9.25%	$12

Cut 'em up, cut 'em all up

If you have a pattern of living beyond your means by buying on credit, get rid of the culprit — the credit card, that is. To kick the habit, a smoker needs to toss the cigarettes, and an alcoholic needs to get rid of the booze. Cut up your credit cards and call the issuers of the cards to cancel your accounts. And when you buy consumer items such as cars and furniture, do not apply for E-Z credit.

The world worked fine back in the years *B.C.* (Before Credit). Think about it: Just a couple of generations ago, credit cards didn't even exist. People paid with cash and cheques — imagine that! You *can* function in our increasingly high-tech world without buying anything on a credit card. In certain cases, you may need a card as collateral — like when you rent a car. When you bring back the rental car, however, you can pay with cash or cheque. Leave the card in a safety deposit box, at home in the back of your sock drawer, or in your freezer and pull (thaw) it out only for the occasional car rental.

If you can trust yourself, keep a separate credit card *only* for new purchases that you absolutely can pay in full each month. Be careful, though — you may be tempted to let that balance roll over for a month or two, and you'll start running up your debt again. Better yet, consider getting a debit card (see the next section) while you pay off your credit cards.

Debit cards: The best of both worlds

Credit cards are the main reason that today's consumers consume more than they can afford. So logic would say that one way you can keep your spending in check is to not use your credit cards. But in a society used to flashing the widely accepted VISA and MasterCard plastic for purchases, changing habits is hard. And you may be legitimately concerned that carrying your chequebook or cash can be a hassle or costly if you're mugged.

Well, *debit cards* truly offer the best of both worlds. The beauty of the debit card is that it offers you the convenience of making purchases with a piece of plastic without the temptation and ability to run up credit card debt. Debit cards keep you from spending money you don't have and help you live within your means.

If you've ever used an Automatic Banking Machine (ABM), you already have a debit card. Through the miracle of modern technology, your bank card is already programmed to also function as a debit card. You can also have a traditional credit card set up to do double duty as a debit card.

If you have a card that doubles as a credit card and a bank machine card, you won't be able to use it as a debit card. Visit your financial institution and request that they issue another bank card that isn't hooked up to your credit card account.

The big difference from credit cards is that, as with cheques you write, debit card purchase amounts are deducted electronically from your chequing account as soon as your transaction is approved. The debit card system is often referred to as the Direct Payment system.

Using the cards to make a purchase is very similar to using them at an ABM. After your purchases are totalled, you're asked to swipe your card through an electronic reader. You'll then be asked to okay the amount, designate whether you want the money to be taken out of your savings or chequing account, and enter your PIN (personal identification number). Once approved, the money is deducted from your account within seconds.

If you keep your chequing account balance low and don't ordinarily balance your chequebook, you may need to start balancing your chequebook if you switch over to a debit card. Otherwise, you could face unnecessary bounced cheque charges.

The following financial institutions are now hooked up to the Direct Payment system. If you have a banking card (but not a banking/credit card) from any of them, it now also doubles as a debit card.

- Alberta Treasury Branches
- AMEX Bank of Canada
- Banco Commerciale of Canada
- Bank of Montreal
- Caisses Populaires Desjardin
- Canada Trust
- Canadian Western Bank
- CDSL Canada Ltd.
- CIBC
- Citibank of Canada
- Credit Union Central of Canada
- CS Coop
- DUCA Community Credit Union
- Global Payment Systems of Canada Ltd.
- Hepcoe Credit Union Ltd.
- Hong Kong Bank
- ING Trust of Canada
- L'Alliance des Caisse Populaires de l'Ontario
- Laurentian Bank
- Montreal Trust
- National Bank of Greece (Canada)
- Ontario Civil Service Credit Union
- Peace Hills Trust Co.
- Royal Bank
- Royal Trust
- St. Stanislaus-Casimir's Polish Parishes Credit Union
- Shared Network Services, Inc.
- Scotiabank
- TD Bank

You should also know about other differences between debit and credit cards:

- If you pay your credit card bill in full and on time each month, charging on your credit card gives you free use of the money you owe until it's time to pay the bill; debit cards take the money out of your chequing account almost immediately. (Some cards now charge a fee even if you pay off your balance in full. You didn't think the banks would let you use the float forever, did you?)

- Credit cards more easily allow you to dispute charges for problematic merchandise through the issuing bank. Most banks allow you to dispute charges for up to 60 days after purchase and will credit the disputed amount back to your account pending resolution. Most debit cards offer a much shorter window, typically less than one week, to dispute charges.

Resisting the credit temptation

Getting out of debt is not an easy thing to do, but we know you can do it with this book by your side. Once you're out of debt, most, but not all, of the battle is won. Following are some additional tactics you can use to limit the influence credit cards hold over your life in the future:

✔ **Get rid of your extra credit cards.** You don't need three, five, or ten credit cards! You can live with one (and actually none), given the wide acceptance of most cards. Count 'em up, including retail store and gas cards, and get rid of 'em. Retailers, such as department stores and gas stations, just love to give you one of their cards. Not only do these cards charge outrageously high interest rates, they duplicate VISA and MasterCard. Virtually all retailers that accept credit cards accept VISA and MasterCard. More credit lines mean more temptation to spend what you can't afford.

✔ **Reduce your credit limit.** Just because your bank keeps raising your credit limit to reward you for being such a profitable customer doesn't mean that you have to accept the increase. Call your credit-card service's 800 number and *lower* your credit limit to a level you're comfortable with.

✔ **Replace your credit cards with a charge card.** A *charge card* (such as the original American Express Card) requires you to pay your balance in full each billing period. You have no credit line or interest charges. Of course, spending more than you can afford to pay when the bill comes due is possible. But, you're much less likely to overspend if you know you have to pay in full monthly.

✔ **Never buy on credit anything that depreciates.** Meals out, cars, clothing, and shoes all depreciate in value. Never buy these things on credit. Borrow money only for investments — education, real estate, or your own business, for example.

✔ **Think in terms of total cost.** Everything sounds cheaper in terms of monthly payments — that's how salespeople lure you into buying things you don't have the money to afford. Take a calculator along if necessary to tally up the sticker price, interest charges, and upkeep. The total cost will scare you. *It should.*

✔ **Stop the junk mail avalanche.** Look at your daily mail — we bet half of it is solicitations and mail-order catalogues. Save some trees and your time sorting junk mail by removing yourself from most mailing lists. Write to the Canadian Direct Marketing Association, 1 Concord Gate, Suite 607, Don Mills, Ontario, M3C 3N6.

✔ **Limit what you can spend.** Go shopping with a small amount of cash and no plastic or cheques. That way you can only spend what little cash you have with you!

Filing for Bankruptcy

For consumers in over their heads, the realisation that their monthly income is increasingly exceeded by their bill payments is usually a painful one. In many cases, years can pass before drastic measures like bankruptcy are considered. Both financial and emotional issues come into play in one of the most difficult, painful, yet potentially beneficial decisions.

When Helen, a mother of two and a sales representative, contacted bankruptcy attorney Harry Orr earlier this year, her total credit card debt of about $20,000 equalled her annual gross income of $20,000. Due to the crushing debt load, she couldn't meet her minimum monthly credit card payments. Rent and food gobbled up most of her earnings. What little was left over went to the squeakiest wheel.

Creditors were breathing down Helen's back. "I started getting calls from collection departments at home and work — it was embarrassing," relates Helen. Helen's case is typical in that credit card debt was the prime cause of her bankruptcy. "If credit card debt didn't exist, I wouldn't have a job," says Orr.

Helen's case is typical in other regards. Her debt accumulated over a number of years. A former homeowner with a master's degree from a prestigious university, Helen had good credit until a couple of years before. After divorcing, Helen rented an apartment with her two children while holding down a job. Unfortunately, she was laid off when her employer encountered tough times.

At first, bills to her dentist and doctor went unpaid. Then when Helen went into business for herself, she used her credit cards to purchase office furniture and pay other start-up expenses. "I would have done more corner cutting, but the credit cards were easily available cash and allowed me to think in terms of monthly payments," says Helen.

As the debt load grew, partly exacerbated by the double-digit interest rates on the cards, more and more purchases got charged — from the kids' clothing to repairs for the car. Finally, out of cash, she had to take a large cash advance on her credit cards to pay for rent and food.

Despite trying to work out lower monthly payments to keep everyone happy, most of the banks to which Helen owed money were inflexible. "When I asked one bank's VISA department if it preferred that I declare bankruptcy because it was unwilling to lower my monthly payment, the representative said yes," Helen says. Out of options, Helen filed for personal bankruptcy.

Bankruptcy benefits

Every year, more than 50,000 Canadian households (that's about 1 in every 200 households) file for personal bankruptcy.

The value or benefit of bankruptcy is that certain types of debts can be completely eliminated or *discharged*. Debts that typically can be discharged include credit card, medical, auto, utilities, rent, taxes, and student loans. Debts that may not be cancelled include child support, alimony, and court-ordered fines and penalties (for example, traffic tickets). Helen was an ideal candidate for bankruptcy because her debts (credit cards) were dischargeable.

Helen also met another important criterion: Her level of high-interest consumer debt relative to her annual income was high. When this ratio exceeds more than 25 percent, filing for bankruptcy may be your best option.

Eliminating your debt also allows you to start working toward your financial goals. Depending on the amount of debt you have outstanding relative to your income, you may need a decade or more to pay it all off. In Helen's case, at the age of 48, she had no money saved for retirement to supplement government benefits, and she was increasingly unable to spend money on her children.

In addition to the financial benefits are the emotional benefits in filing for bankruptcy. "I was horrified at filing, but it is good to be rid of the debts and collection calls — I should have filed six months earlier. I was constantly worried. When I saw homeless families come to the soup kitchen where I sometimes volunteer, I thought that someday that could be me and my kids," she said.

Bankruptcy drawbacks

Filing for bankruptcy, needless to say, has a number of drawbacks. First, bankruptcy appears on your credit report for seven years, so you will have difficulty obtaining credit, especially in the years immediately following your filing.

If you already have problems on your credit report, however, because of late payments or failure to pay previous debts, damage has already been done. And, without savings, you probably won't make major purchases, such as a home, in the next several years anyway.

If you do file for bankruptcy, getting credit in the future is not impossible. You'll probably be able to obtain a *secured credit card,* which requires you to deposit money in a bank account equal to the credit limit on your credit card. If you can hold down a stable job, most creditors are willing to give you loans within a few years of your filing for bankruptcy. Almost all lenders ignore bankruptcy after five to seven years.

Another bankruptcy drawback is that it costs money. We know this seems terribly unfair. You're already in financial trouble — that's why you're filing for bankruptcy! Nevertheless, filing for bankruptcy will probably set you back from several hundred dollars up to several thousand in court filing and legal fees.

Finally, most people find that filing for bankruptcy causes emotional stress. Admitting that your personal income can't keep pace with your debt obligations is a painful thing to do. Although filing for bankruptcy clears the decks of debt and gives you a fresh financial start, feeling a profound sense of failure is only human. Despite the increasing frequency of bankruptcy, bankruptcy filers are reluctant to talk about it with others, including family and friends.

Another part of the emotional side of filing bankruptcy is that you must open your personal financial affairs to court scrutiny and court control during the several months it takes to administer a bankruptcy. A court-appointed bankruptcy trustee oversees your case and tries to recover as much of your property as possible to satisfy the *creditors* — those to whom you owe money.

Some people also feel that they're shirking responsibility by filing for bankruptcy. One client Eric worked with who should have filed couldn't bring herself to do it. She said, "I spent that money, and it's my responsibility to pay it back."

Most banks make gobs and gobs of money from their credit card businesses. We can tell you that credit cards are one of the most profitable lines of business for banks. If you don't believe us, consider that, at a banking conference sponsored by the investment bank Salomon Brothers, CEO John Reed referred to the credit card business for banks as a "high-return, low-risk" business. Now you know why your mailbox is always filled with solicitations for more cards even though you're already up to your eyeballs in solicitations.

So if you file for bankruptcy, don't feel too bad about not paying back the bank. The nice merchants where you bought the merchandise have already been paid. *Charge-offs* — the banker's term for taking the loss on debt that you discharge through bankruptcy — are part of the business. This is another reason why the interest rate is so high on credit cards and why you shouldn't borrow on credit cards.

What you can keep if you file for bankruptcy

In every province, you can retain certain property and assets, even though you're filing for bankruptcy. In most cases, you're allowed to keep around $2,000 of furniture and $1,000 worth of personal effects. If they're necessary for you to earn a living, you likely will also be able to keep a few thousand dollars' worth of the tools of your trade.

"Light" and "full" bankruptcy

You can file one of two forms of personal bankruptcy:

- ✓ **A consumer proposal** allows you to try to work out a deal with your creditors without having to go the route of actually filing for bankruptcy. A trustee assists you in assessing your assets and income, organises a budget for you, and provides a few counselling sessions. Your trustee then presents a detailed plan to your creditors detailing how much and when you'll pay them, to which the creditors have 30 days to respond. If your plan is accepted, you'll still have to teach yourself to live on a lot less.

  In order to take the consumer proposal option, your debts must total less than $75,000, excluding your mortgage. In addition, alimony, child support, and legal fines aren't covered by the proposal. They remain payable in full. This is often a sensible route to take, especially if you have a lot of assets and a regular income. In a regular bankruptcy, almost all your assets are sold. Under a consumer proposal, that may not be necessary if your creditors are willing to settle for a piece of your pay cheque.

- ✓ **Full bankruptcy** is your only other alternative if your consumer proposal is turned down or if your debts are too high to allow you to try the proposal route. The trustee takes control of your assets, sells them, and distributes the proceeds to your creditors. After the paperwork is filed, you're officially "bankrupt" for nine months.

Bankruptcy advice

Be very careful where you get advice about whether to file for bankruptcy. Many people make the mistake of turning to and solely trusting bankruptcy lawyers or Consumer Credit Counselling Services (CCCS).

Lawyers who earn a legal fee from doing bankruptcy filings have a conflict of interest. All things being equal, their bias is to — you guessed it — *recommend bankruptcy,* which generates their fees.

CCCS faces the opposite conflict. CCCS offices say they provide a nonprofit, educational service to help consumers who are in debt. Although it's true that CCCS offices have some well-intentioned employees, it's also true that CCCS offices are in general largely funded by credit card issuers. Thus, CCCS counsellors may be disinclined to recommend bankruptcy. (See the sidebar "Potentially biased advice at CCCS" for more about how CCCS may skew your options in the wrong direction.)

Potentially biased advice at CCCS

Every year, hundreds of debt-burdened consumers seek "counselling" from the many Consumer Credit Counselling Service offices across the country. Unfortunately, the service does not always work the way it's pitched.

CCCS offices market themselves as a "non-profit community service." In some cases, though, a more appropriate name for them would be the Credit Card Collection Agency.

Unbeknownst to most people who use CCCS is the fact that the great majority of the funding for most offices comes from fees that creditors pay to CCCS.

CCCS's strategy is to place those who come in for help onto their "debt management program." Under this program, counsellees agree to pay a certain amount per month to CCCS, which in turn parcels out the money to the various creditors. The debt management program may ignore other non-credit card debts that the counsellees may have, such as a mortgage and outstanding medical bills. And CCCS counsellors may be disinclined to discuss the bankruptcy option, because that means the credit card companies end up with nothing. Also, with provincial funding for CCCS cut back or cut off completely, many CCCS offices now turn to their clients to help raise revenue. Some offices, for example, take a percentage of the money clients give them to distribute to creditors as a fee.

If you want to learn more about the pros, cons, and details of filing for bankruptcy, pick up a copy of *Buy Now, Pay Later? What You Should Know about Credit, Debt, and Bankruptcy: A Legal Guide* by Allan A. Parker (published by Self-Counsel Press).

If you're comfortable with your decision to file, an intermediate approach would be to hire a paralegal typing service to prepare the forms, which can be a cost-effective way to get help with the process if you don't need heavy-duty legal advice. Look in your local Yellow Pages under Paralegals.

Regardless of how you deal with paying off your debt, you're in real danger of falling back into old habits. Backsliding happens not only to people who file bankruptcy but also to those who use savings or home equity to eliminate their debt. If history has shown that you're likely to fall into this trap, the best and only solution is to go cold turkey. Eliminate your access to credit and pay for everything with cash, cheques, and debit cards.

Ending the Debt-and-Spend Cycle

As hard as they try to break the habit, some people become addicted to spending and borrowing. It becomes a chronic problem that starts to interfere with other aspects of their lives. Financial problems can lead to problems at work and with family and even friends.

Officially started in 1976, Debtors Anonymous (DA) is a nonprofit organization that provides support, primarily through group meetings, to people trying to break their debting and spending habits. DA is modelled after the 12-step Alcoholics Anonymous program.

Like AA, Debtors Anonymous works with people from all walks of life and socioeconomic backgrounds. It's typical to find people who are financially on the edge, $100,000-plus income earners, and everybody in between, at a DA meeting. Even former millionaires join the program.

DA has a simple questionnaire to help determine whether you're a problem debtor. If you answer *yes* to at least 8 of the following 15 questions, you may be developing or already have a compulsive borrowing habit:

1. **Are your debts making your home life unhappy?**

2. **Does the pressure of your debts distract you from your daily work?**

3. **Are your debts affecting your reputation?**

4. **Do your debts cause you to think less of yourself?**

5. **Have you ever given false information in order to obtain credit?**

6. **Have you ever made unrealistic promises to your creditors?**

7. **Does the pressure of your debts make you careless of the welfare of your family?**

8. **Do you ever fear that your employer, family, or friends will learn the extent of your total indebtedness?**

9. **When faced with a difficult financial situation, does the prospect of borrowing give you an inordinate feeling of relief?**

10. **Does the pressure of your debts cause you to have difficulty sleeping?**

11. **Has the pressure of your debts ever caused you to consider getting drunk?**

12. **Have you ever borrowed money without giving adequate consideration to the rate of interest you are required to pay?**

13. **Do you usually expect a negative response when you are subject to a credit investigation?**

14. **Have you ever developed a strict regimen for paying off your debts, only to break it under pressure?**

15. **Do you justify your debts by telling yourself that you are superior to the "other" people, and when you get your "break," you'll be out of debt?**

To find a Debtors Anonymous support group in your area, check your local phone directory (in the Business section). Or write to DA's U.S.

headquarters for meeting locations in your area and a literature order form at the following address: Debtors Anonymous, P.O. Box 400, Grand Central Station, New York, NY 10163-0400, U.S.A.

Dealing with Credit Mistakes

You may not know (or care), but you probably have a personal credit report. Creditors that are considering lending you money generally examine your credit report before granting you a loan or credit line.

Many people don't realize that they have a blemish on their credit report until they're turned down for a loan or questioned by the creditor about the glitch. For example, when Eric applied for his first mortgage, he discovered a minor wart on his own credit report.

Dealing with credit report problems, while taking up some of your time, needn't be difficult if you know what and what not to do.

Obtain a copy of your credit report

If you're turned down for rental housing, employment, or a loan because of derogatory information on your credit report, get a copy of the report. To get a copy of your credit rating, contact the following credit bureaus. You'll need to send them signed photocopies of two pieces of identification along with your name, address, and SIN number.

- ✔ Equifax Canada Inc
  Box 190
  Jean-Talon Station
  Montreal P.Q.
  HIS 2Z2
  1-800-465-7166
  (Equifax will fax you an application to obtain your report.)

- ✔ Trans Union Consumer Relations Centre
  P.O. Box 338, LCp1
  Hamilton, Ontario
  L8L7W2
  1-905-575-4420

Reading a credit report is a challenge, given all the abbreviations and jargon, so we recommend that, in addition to getting the report, you ask the lender what specific information on the report led to the denial of credit.

Get others to correct their mistakes

If you obtain your credit report and find a boo-boo on it that you don't recognize as being your mistake or fault, do *not* assume that the information is correct and is simply another indicator of your faulty memory. Credit reporting bureaus and the creditors who report credit information to these bureaus make many mistakes.

You would hope and expect that, if a credit bureau has negative and incorrect information in your credit report and you phone them to bring the error to their attention, they would graciously and expeditiously fix the mistake. If you believe that, then you're the world's greatest optimist; perhaps you also believe that you won't have to wait in line at the department of motor vehicles, post office, or your local bank around noon on paydays.

Odds are you're going to have to make more phone calls or write a letter or two to fix the problems. Here's how most errors that aren't your fault are corrected:

- ✔ **It's someone else's credit problem.** A surprising number of personal credit report glitches are the result of someone else's negative information getting on your credit report. If the bad information on your report is completely foreign-looking to you, tell the credit bureau and also explain that you need more information because you don't recognise the creditor.

- ✔ **It's the creditor's mistake.** Creditors make mistakes, too. You need to write or call the creditor to have it correct the erroneous information that it sent to the credit bureau. Phoning first usually works best (the credit bureau should be able to tell you how to reach the creditor if you don't know how). If necessary, follow up with a letter.

Whether you speak with a credit bureau or an actual lender, make notes of your conversations. If representatives say they can fix the problem, get their names and extensions and follow up with them if they don't deliver as promised. If you're ensnared in bureaucratic red tape, escalate the situation by speaking with a department manager.

Tell your side of the story

With a minor credit infraction, some lenders may simply ask for an explanation. Eric had a credit report glitch that was the result of being away for several weeks and missing the payment due date for a couple of small bills. When his proposed mortgage lender saw his late payments, all Eric had to do was provide a written explanation. You and a creditor may not see eye-to-eye on a problem, and the creditor may refuse to budge.

Chapter 6

Reducing Your Spending

. . . .

In This Chapter

▶ The keys to successful spending

▶ Reducing your spending category by category

. . . .

Telling people how and where to spend their money is a risky undertaking because most people like to spend money, and most people hate to be told what to do.

You'll be glad to hear that we're *not* going to tell you exactly where you must cut spending. We're simply going to give you strategies that have worked for other people. The final decision for what to cut rests solely with you. Only you can decide what's important to you and what's dispensable — should you cut out your weekly poker games or cut back on your shoe collection?

We assume throughout these recommendations that you value your time. Therefore, we're not going to tell you to scrimp and save by doing things like cutting open a tube of toothpaste so that you can use every last bit of it. And we won't tell you to have your spouse do your ironing to reduce your dry-cleaning bills (no point in having money in the bank if you lose your significant other).

Probably, part of the reason you spend money the way you do is that you're busy. Therefore, the recommendations in this chapter focus on methods that don't involve a lot of time but that produce big savings. In other words, these strategies provide a lot of bang for the buck. We believe in saving wherever possible, but small change is awfully heavy to cart around — better to save the big bucks.

Four Keys to Successful Spending

For most people, spending money is a whole lot easier and more fun than earning it. Far be it from us to tell you to stop having fun and to turn into a penny-pinching, stay-at-home miser. Of course you can spend money. But there's a world of difference between spending money *carelessly* and spending money *wisely*.

Spending too much and not spending wisely or efficiently puts pressure on a limited income. Savings dwindle, debts accumulate, and you can't achieve your financial goals.

Sometimes, when you dive into details too quickly, you miss the big picture. So before we jump into the specific areas where you can trim your budget, here are the four overall keys to successful spending. These four principles run through most of the recommendations coming up in this chapter.

Living within your means

Spending too much is a *relative* problem. Two people can each spend $30,000 per year yet have drastically different financial circumstances. How? Suppose that one of them earns $40,000 after-tax annually, and the other makes just $25,000. The $40,000 income earner saves $10,000 each year. The $25,000 earner accumulates $5,000 of new debt (or spends that amount from prior savings). Spend within your means.

Don't let others and their spending habits dictate yours. Certain people — you know who they are — bring out the big spender in you. Do something else with them besides shopping. If you can't find any other activity to share with them, try shopping with limited cash and no credit cards. That way you can't overspend on impulse.

How much you can safely spend while still working toward your financial goals depends on what your goals are and where you are financially. Chapter 8 assists you with figuring how much you should be saving and, therefore, what you can afford to spend to accomplish your financial goals.

Finding the best value

You can find high quality and low cost in the same product. Conversely, paying a high price is no guarantee that you're getting high quality. Cars are a good example. Whether you buy a subcompact, sports car, or luxury four-door sedan, some cars are more fuel efficient and cost less to maintain than rivals that carry the same sticker price.

And when you evaluate the cost of a product or service, you need to think in terms of total long-term costs. Suppose that you're comparing the purchase of two used cars: the Solid Sedan, which costs $10,000, and the Clunker Convertible, which weighs in at $8,000. On the surface, the Convertible appears cheaper. However, the price that you pay for a car is but a small portion of what a car ultimately costs you. If the Clunker Convertible is more costly to operate, maintain, and insure over the years, it could end up costing you much more. Sometimes paying more up front for a higher-quality product or service ends up saving you more in the long run.

Those who sell particular products and services may initially appear to have your best interests at heart if they steer you toward buying something that isn't costly. However, you may be in for a rude awakening after you discover the ongoing service, maintenance, and other fees you'll face in the years ahead. For example, consider the case of a neighbour who is delighted that a gardener installed her backyard garden so inexpensively. The main reason for the low cost, she soon finds, is that many of the plantings require high maintenance and frequent replacement, which — surprise, surprise — the gardener is willing to do for a fee.

Eliminating fat

If you want to reduce your overall spending by, say, 10 percent, you could just cut all of your current expenditures by 10 percent. Or you can reach your 10 percent goal by cutting some categories a lot and others not at all. You need to set priorities and make choices about what you can and can't live without.

What you spend your money on is sometimes a matter of habit rather than what you really want or value. For example, some people shop at whatever stores are closest because they know where the stores are; they never bother to look elsewhere.

Don't waste money on brand names

Be suspicious of companies that spend gobs on image-oriented advertising. Why? Heavy advertising costs many dollars, and as a consumer of those companies' products and services, you pay for all that advertising.

All successful companies do some advertising — advertising is cost-effective and good business if it brings in enough new business. But consider the products and services and the claims that companies make.

Does a cola beverage really taste better if "It's the real thing" or "The choice of a new generation?" Consider all the silly labels and fluffy marketing of beers. Blind taste testing demonstrates little if any difference between the heavily marketed brands.

Now, if you can't live without your Coca-Cola or Pepsi and think that these products are head and shoulders above the rest, drink them to your heart's content. But question the importance of the name and image in the products you buy. Companies spend a lot of money creating and cultivating an image, which has zero real impact on how their products taste or perform.

Don't compromise on quality, especially where the quality is important to you. But don't be snookered into believing that brand-name products or products hawked by superstars are better or worth a substantially higher price.

Renting-to-own is the most expensive way to buy

$12.95 for a VCR? Talk about cheap!

Well, there's a big hitch: That's $12.95 per week, for many weeks. When all is said and done and paid, buying a $200 VCR through a rent-to-own store ends up costing a typical buyer more than $750!

Welcome to the world of rent-to-own stores, which offer cash-poor consumers the ability to lease consumer items and, at the end of the lease, an option to buy. Many items can be bought on this basis. Although this may be more of a troubling sign of the times, increasing numbers of stores are reported to offer rent-to-own engagement rings! One rent-to-own store manager said, "We do get some people with cold feet."

If you think paying an 18 percent interest rate on a credit card is expensive, imagine what you'll think of renting-to-own when we tell you that the effective interest rate charged on many purchases exceeds 100 percent and in some cases 200 percent or more! Renting-to-own makes buying on a credit card look like a deal.

We're not sharing this information with you to encourage your buying on credit cards but to point out what a rip-off renting-to-own is. Such stores prey on cashless consumers who either can't get credit cards or don't understand how expensive renting-to-own really is.

Avoid buying on credit

As we discuss in Chapters 4 and 5, buying items on credit that depreciate — such as cars, clothing, and vacations — is hazardous to your long-term financial health. Buy today only what you can afford today. If you'll be forced to carry a debt for months or years on end, then you can't really afford what you buy on credit today. Consumer credit is expensive and reinforces a bad habit: spending more than you can afford.

Strategies for Reducing Your Spending

Please keep in mind as you read through the following ideas that some of these strategies will make sense for you, and some of them won't. Start your spending reduction plan with the ones that come easily. Work your way through them. Keep a list of the options that are more challenging for you — those that require more of a sacrifice but that you can make work if necessary to achieve your spending and savings goals.

No matter which of the ideas in this chapter you choose for yourself, rest assured that keeping your budget lean and mean pays enormous dividends.

After you implement a spending reduction strategy, you'll reap the benefits for years to come. For example, suppose you're in a 41 percent tax bracket. For every $1,000 that you can shave from your annual spending (that's just $83 per month), look how much more money you'll have down the road if you can save that money in a tax-favoured RRSP or retirement plan and also put in the annual tax savings of $410 that your contribution earns you (see Chapter 9). The chart in Figure 6-1 assumes that you earn 10 percent on your investments, which we show you how to do in Part III.

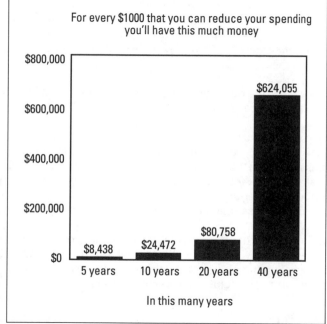

For every $1000 that you can reduce your spending you'll have this much money

Figure 6-1: The impact of cutting your spending and saving the difference.

In this many years

Food

One way to reduce your food expenditures is to stop eating. However, this tends to make you weak and dizzy, so it's probably not a viable long-term strategy. The following culinary strategies will keep you on your feet — and perhaps even improve your health — for less money.

Join a wholesale superstore

Superstores such as Costco enable you to buy groceries in bulk at wholesale prices. And, contrary to popular perception, you *don't* have to buy 1,000 rolls of toilet paper at once — just 24.

We've done price comparisons between these kinds of stores and retail grocery stores and found that wholesalers often charge 30 to 40 percent less for the exact same stuff — all without the hassle of clipping coupons or hunting for which store has the best price this month on crackers.

In addition to saving you money, you'll find that buying in bulk means that you make fewer shopping trips. You'll have more supplies around your humble abode, so you'll have less need to eat out (which is costly) or make trips to the local grocer.

Perishables run the risk of living up to their name, so don't buy what you can't use. Repackage bulk packs into smaller quantities for the freezer if possible. If you're single, shop with a friend or two and split the order. Try not to make impulse purchases, and be especially careful when you have kids in tow.

Check your local phone directory for superstores. Costco has a toll-free number to help you locate a store nearest you (800-463-3783).

Most of these stores charge a small membership fee and are, frankly, somewhat of a hassle to join. Costco, for example, charges $40 per year ($35 for small business owners) and asks for proof that you're a small-business owner or that you work for a nonprofit health-care organization, utility, bank, trust company, airline, the government, or the media. You can also join if you hold a professional license or are a member of a credit union.

The reality, though, is that if you really want to join, you can. A small-business owner whom you know well can sponsor you, for example. Or shop with a friend who's a member. Don't give up — the savings you can reap make joining a warehouse club well worth the hassle.

Eat out more frugally

Eating meals out or getting takeout can be a time-saver but can rack up big bills if done too often and lavishly. Eating out is a luxury — think of it as hiring someone to shop, cook, and clean up for you. Of course, some people hate to cook or don't have the time, space, or energy to do much in the kitchen. If this is you, choose restaurants carefully and order from the menu selectively. Here are a couple of tips:

- ✔ **Avoid beverages, especially alcohol.** Most restaurants make big profits on beverages. Drink water instead. (Water is healthful and reduces the likelihood of your wanting a nap after a big meal.)

- ✔ **Order vegetarian.** Vegetarian dishes, including pasta and rice dishes, generally cost less than meat-based entrees (and are better for you).

Budgeting to save more money

When most people hear the word *budgeting*, they usually think unpleasant thoughts — and, like dieting, rightfully so. But budgeting can help you move from knowing how much you spend on various things to successfully reducing your spending to successfully cutting your spending.

The first step in the process of budgeting, or planning your future spending, is to analyze where your current spending is going (refer to Chapter 4). After you've done that, calculate how much more you'd like to be saving per month. Then comes the harder part: deciding where to make cuts in your spending.

Suppose that you currently aren't saving any of your monthly income and you want to save 10 percent. If you can save and invest money through a tax-sheltered retirement plan such as an RRSP, you don't actually need to cut your spending by 10 percent to reach a savings goal of 10 percent (of your gross income).

When money is contributed to a tax-deductible RRSP or other retirement plan, you reduce your federal and provincial taxes. If you're a moderate income earner who's paying, say, 40 percent in federal and provincial taxes on your marginal income, you actually only need to reduce your spending by 6 percent to save 10 percent. The "other" 4 percent of savings comes from the lowering of your taxes. (The higher your tax bracket, the less you need to cut your spending to reach a particular savings goal.)

So to boost your savings rate to 10 percent, go through your current spending, category by category, until you come up with enough proposed cuts to reduce your spending by 6 percent. Make your cuts in those areas that will be least painful and where you're getting the least value from your current level of spending. Even if you don't have access to a tax-deductible retirement plan, budgeting still involves the same process.

Rather than examining your current expenses and making cuts from that starting point, another method of budgeting involves starting completely from scratch. Ask yourself how much you'd like to be spending on different categories. The advantage of this approach is that it doesn't allow your current spending levels to constrain your thinking. You'll most likely be amazed at the discrepancies between what you think you should be spending and what you actually are spending in certain categories.

We don't want to be killjoys. We're not saying that you should live on bread and water. You can have dessert — heck, have some wine, too! But perhaps not every time. Try eating appetizers and dessert at home, where they're a lot less expensive (especially if you follow our advice on shopping for food).

Shelter

Housing and all the costs associated with it (utilities, furniture, appliances, and, if you're a homeowner, maintenance and repairs) can gobble a large chunk of your monthly income. We're not suggesting that you live in an ice cave or tent (even though they're probably less costly and more energy efficient), but people often overlook common opportunities to save money in this category.

Don't take rent for granted

Rent can take up a sizable chunk of your monthly take-home pay. Many people consider rent to be a fixed and an inflexible part of their expenses. It's not. Here are some things you can do to cut it down in size:

- ✔ **Move to a lower-cost rental.** Of course, a lower-cost rental may not be as nice — it may be smaller or lack a private parking spot or be in a less-popular locale. Make the tradeoff and shave $50 to $100 or more off your monthly rent. Don't forget: The less you spend renting, the more you can save toward buying your own place. Just be sure to factor in all the costs of a new location, including possibly higher commuting costs.

- ✔ **Share a rental.** Living alone has some benefits, but financially speaking, it's a luxury. Rent a larger place with roommates. Your rental costs should go way down, and you'll get more home for your rental dollars. You have to be in a sharing mood, though. Roommates can be a hassle at times but can also be a plus — you meet all sorts of new people and have someone else to blame if the kitchen's a mess.

- ✔ **Negotiate your rental increases.** Every year, like clockwork, your landlord bumps up your rent a certain percentage. If your local rental market is soft or your living quarters are deteriorating, stand up for yourself! You have more leverage and power than you probably realize.

  If you pay your rent on time and are otherwise a good tenant, a smart landlord won't want to lose you. Filling vacancies takes time and money. State your case: You've been a responsible tenant, and your research shows comparable rentals going for less. Crying poor may help, too. At the very least, if you can't stave off the rent increase, maybe you can wrangle some improvements to the place.

- ✔ **Buy rather than rent.** No, we haven't lost our minds. Purchasing your own place can be costly, yes, but in the long run, owning should be cheaper than renting, and you'll have something to show for it in the end. If you purchase real estate with a 25-year mortgage, your mortgage payment (which is your biggest ownership expense) won't steadily rise with the cost of living. Only your property taxes, maintenance, and insurance costs are exposed to the vagaries of inflation.

  As a renter, your entire monthly housing cost can rise with increases in the cost of living (unless you are a beneficiary of rent controls).

  See Chapter 16 to find out about buying real estate, even if you're short on cash.

Saving on your phone bill

Telephone expenses are a good example of not needing to reduce your usage to save money. Just adjust the timing of your calls. In most areas, the most expensive time to place local toll or long-distance calls is weekdays between 8 a.m. and 6 p.m. From 6 p.m. to 11 p.m. is cheaper, and the cheapest time to call is late at night (usually 11 p.m. to 8 a.m.), which can save you 50–60 percent (and as a bonus, you may get the thrill of waking up the other party). This bargain rate is also available all weekend, usually beginning after 11 p.m. Friday night and ending Monday at 8 a.m.

Check with your long-distance provider to make sure that you're on the lowest-cost calling program given the patterns of your calls. You may also be able to save money on your toll calls by switching companies. Quality is virtually the same from company to company.

Some to consider are ACC (800-387-0005), AT&T (800-670-2266), Fonorola (888-399-3666), and Sprint (800-980-5464). Depending on where you live, you may also find that smaller companies, while not providing a completely national service, offer significant savings on calls between certain areas. For example, London Telecom (800-363-3528) serves most major centres and offers several bargain flat monthly rate plans, depending on how much you call long distance.

Sometimes sending a thoughtful letter is cheaper, more appreciated, and longer lasting than placing a phone call. Just block out an hour, grab pen and paper, and rediscover the lost art of letter writing. Formulating your thoughts on paper can be clarifying and therapeutic to boot. Computer users may find that they save money as well by sending e-mail.

Save on homeowner expenses

As every homeowner knows, houses suck money. You should be especially careful to watch your money in this area of your budget.

✔ **Don't overspend.** If you're on the verge of buying your first home or trading up to a more costly property, crunch some realistic numbers before you jump. The most common mistake people make is overstretching when buying a home. If too little money is left over for other needs — such as taking trips, eating out, enjoying hobbies, or saving for retirement — your new dream house may become a financial prison.

Calculate how much you can afford to spend monthly on a home by figuring your other needs first. (Doing the exercises in Chapter 4 about where you're spending your money and in Chapter 8 about saving for retirement will help.)

Although real estate can be a good long-term investment, a great deal of your discretionary dollars can end up being poured into your home. In addition to decorating and remodeling, some people feel the need to trade up to a bigger home every few years. Of course, after they're in their new home, the remodeling and renovation cycle simply begins again, which costs even more money. Be happy with what you have. The world will always have people with bigger, nicer houses and more toys than you have.

✔ **Rent out a room.** If you already own your place, selling it and buying a less-expensive place can be a big hassle. Have you considered taking in a tenant to reduce your housing expenses? Check out the renter thoroughly: Get references, run a credit report (or arrange to have your bank do it for you), and talk about ground rules and expectations before sharing your space. Don't forget to check with your insurance company to see whether your homeowner's policy needs adjustments to cover potential liability from renting.

✔ **Refinance your mortgage.** This step may seem like common sense, but surprisingly, many people don't keep up to date on mortgage rates. If interest rates are lower than when you obtained your current mortgage, you may be able to save money by refinancing (see Chapter 16 for more information).

✔ **Appeal your property-tax assessment.** In many areas of the country, housing prices have gone down in recent years. If you're still paying property taxes based on a higher valuation, you may be able to save money by appealing your assessment. Check with your local assessor's office for the procedure to follow. You may need to prove that your property is worth less today, and you can prove that by using the sale prices of comparable homes in your area. An appraiser's recent evaluation of your property would do — you may already have one if you refinanced your mortgage recently.

✔ **Reduce utility costs.** Sometimes you have to spend money to save money. Old refrigerators, for example, can waste a lot of electricity. Insulate an attic to save on heating and air-conditioning bills. Install water flow regulators in shower heads and toilet tanks. Even if you don't live in an area susceptible to droughts, why waste water unnecessarily (which isn't free)? If you live in an area where garbage rates depend on the amount of stuff you toss out, recycle. Recycling means less garbage, which means lower trash bills. (Even if you don't pay extra, recycle anyway — it benefits the environment by reducing landfill.)

Transportation

Canada is a car-driven society. In most other countries, cars are a luxury. If more people thought of cars as a luxury, Canadians might have far fewer financial problems (and accidents). Cars not only pollute the air and clog the highways but also cost you a bundle. Purchasing the best car you can and using it wisely can save you big dollars. So can using other transportation alternatives.

Don't try to keep up with the Joneses as they show off their new cars every year — for all you know, they're running themselves into financial ruin just trying to impress you. Let your neighbours admire you for your thriftiness and wisdom instead.

Research before you buy a car

When you buy a car, not only do you pay the initial sticker price, but you're also on the hook for gas, insurance, registration fees, maintenance, and repairs. Don't compare simple sticker prices; think about total, long-term costs of ownership.

Speaking of total costs, remember that you're also trusting your life to the car. With around 3,500 Canadians killed in auto accidents annually, safety should be an important consideration as well. Air bags, for example, or ABS, especially with our ice and snow, may save your life.

The *Consumer Reports Buying Guide* summarizes all the latest information on cars and includes a list of the most reliable used cars in various price categories. For a detailed assessment of defects, repair costs, and safety ratings, check out the *Lemon-Aid Used Cars 1999* by Phil Edmonston (published by Stoddart). The book also details average resale prices by model and year. For you data jocks, *The Complete Car Cost Guide* (published by Intellichoice) is packed with information about all categories of ownership costs, warranties, and dealer costs. The guide rates new cars based on total ownership costs. But can you *really* afford a new car?

Buy your car with cash

The main reason people end up spending more than they can really afford on a car is that they finance it. As we discuss in Chapter 2 and elsewhere, you should avoid borrowing money for consumption purchases, especially for items that depreciate in value like cars. A car is most definitely *not* an investment.

In most situations, leasing is even more expensive than borrowing money to buy a car. Leasing is like a long-term car rental. We all know how well rental cars get treated — well, leased cars are treated just as well, which is one of the reasons leasing is so costly.

Replace high-cost cars

Maybe you've realized by now that your car is too expensive to operate because of insurance, gas, and maintenance costs. Or maybe you bought too much car — people who lease or borrow money to buy a car frequently buy a far more expensive car than they can realistically afford. Nothing says that you're stuck with it until the bitter end.

Dump your expensive car and get something more financially manageable. The sooner you switch, the more money you'll save.

Keep cars to a minimum

We've seen households that have one car per person. Four people, four cars! In most cases, this is unnecessary and very costly. In developing countries like China, cars are a luxury. Bikes are used to carry groceries, the kids, and even large pieces of furniture, thereby reducing transportation costs . . . and the need to diet!

Maintaining two or more cars for most middle-income households is an expensive extravagance. Try to find ways to make do with fewer cars.

But I can't buy a new car with cash!

"Come on, guys," you may be thinking, "how can I and most wage-earners today afford to buy a new car with cash — who has that kind of dough sitting around?!"

Some people feel that it's unreasonable of us to expect them to buy a new car using cash. After all, many publications, which not uncoincidentally derive great advertising revenue from auto dealers and lenders, effectively endorse and encourage borrowing to buy a car.

If you knew us, you'd know that we're very reasonable people. Believe us, we're trying to look out for your best long-term financial interests. Please consider the following:

✔ If you lack sufficient cash to buy a new car, we say, "Don't buy a new car!" Ninety percent of the world's population can't even afford a car, let alone a new one! Buy a car that you can afford, which may not be a new one.

✔ Don't fall for the new car buying rationalization that says that buying a used car means lots of maintenance, repair expenses, and problems. If you do your homework and buy a good used car, you can have the best of both worlds. A good used car costs less to buy and should cost you less to operate thanks to lower insurance costs.

✔ A fancy car isn't needed to impress people for business purposes. Some people we know say that they absolutely must drive a brand-spanking nice new car to set the right impression for business purposes. We're not going to tell you how to manage your career, but we will ask you to consider that if clients and others see you driving an expensive new car, they may think that you spend money wastefully or that you're getting rich off of them!

One way to move beyond the confines of a car is to ride buses or trains or carpool to work. Some employers give incentives for taking public transit to work, and some cities offer assistance in setting up van pools or car pools along popular routes. By leaving the driving to someone else, you can catch up on reading or just relax on the way to and from work. And you're doing your share to cut down on pollution.

When you're considering where to live and the cost of living in different areas, don't forget to consider commuting costs. One advantage of living close to work, or at least close to public transit systems, is that you may be able to make do with fewer cars in your household or with no car at all.

Buy commuter passes

In many areas, you can purchase train, bus, or subway passes to reduce the cost of commuting. Many toll bridges also have booklets of tickets that you can buy at a discount. Some booths don't advertise that they offer these plans — maybe as a strategy to keep revenues up.

Buy regular unleaded gas

A number of studies have shown that "superduperultrapremium" gasoline isn't worth the extra expense. Rather than making a separate trip, fill up your tank when you're on a shopping trip to the warehouse wholesalers (discussed earlier in this chapter). Also don't use credit cards to buy your gas if you have to pay a higher price to do so.

Service your car regularly, before problems develop

Sure, servicing your car (for example, changing the oil every 8,000 kilometres) costs money, but it saves you dough in the long run by extending the operating life of the car. Servicing your car also reduces the chances that your car will crap out in the middle of nowhere, which requires a humongous towing charge to a service station. Even worse is stalling on the highway during peak rush hour and having thousands of angry commuters stuck behind you.

Clothing and accessories

Given the amount of money that some people spend on clothing and related accessories, we've come to believe that people in nudist colonies must be great savers! But you probably live among the clothed mainstream of Canadian society, so here's a short list of economizing ideas:

✔ **Avoid dry cleanables.** When you buy clothing, try to stick with cottons and machine-washable synthetics rather than wools or silks that require dry cleaning. Check labels before you buy stuff.

✔ **Don't chase the latest fashions.** Fashion designers and retailers are constantly working to tempt you to buy more. Don't do it. Recycle the publications that pronounce this season's look.

Fashion, as defined by what people wear, changes quite slowly. In fact, the classics don't ever go out of style. Buy basic, buy classic — don't let fashion gurus be your guide, or you'll be the best dresser in the poorhouse.

✔ **Minimize accessories.** Shoes, jewelry, handbags, and the like can gobble large amounts of money. How many of these accessory items do you really need? The answer is probably very few, and each one should last many years.

Go to your closet or jewelry box and tally up the loot. What else could you have done with all that cash? See the things you regret buying or forgot you even had? Don't make the same mistake again. Have a garage sale if you have a lot of stuff that you don't want. And then save the proceeds.

Debt repayment

In Chapter 5, we discuss strategies to reduce the cost of carrying consumer debt. The *best* way to reduce the costs of debt is to avoid it in the first place when you're making consumption purchases. You can avoid debt by eliminating your access to credit or by limiting your purchases to consumer items that you can pay off each month.

If you pay your balance in full each month, you don't need to keep a credit card that charges you an annual fee. Many no-fee credit cards exist, and some even offer you a benefit for using them:

✔ Bank of Montreal MasterCard (800-263-2263) earns Air Miles, or up to 5 percent of your purchases — to a maximum of $500 a year for five years — toward the purchase of a first home.

✔ CIBC Classic (800-465-4653). The "dividend" card gives you a credit of 0.25 percent on the first $1,500, 0.5 percent on the next $1,500, and 1.0 percent on any amount over $3,000 you charge annually. The Club Z card lets you earn points that can be used for discounts at Zellers.

✔ Royal Bank Classic VISA (800-668-9700) earns you points that can be used to purchase merchandise.

✔ Scotiabank Classic VISA (800-387-6556) is simply a no-fee card.

✔ TD GM Green VISA (800-268-9460) credits 5 percent of charges toward the purchase of a GM-manufactured vehicle. You're limited to $500 of credits a year, and an overall total of $3,500.

If you have a credit card that charges an annual fee, try calling the company and saying that you want to cancel the card because you can get a competitor's card without an annual fee. Many banks will agree to waive the fee on the spot. Some require you to call back yearly to cancel the fee — a hassle that can be avoided by getting a true no-fee card.

If you pay in full each month and charge $10,000 or more annually, consider a card that gives you credits toward a purchase, such as a car or airline ticket. *Note:* Be careful, however, because some people are tempted to charge more on a card that rewards them for more purchases. If you spend more than you would otherwise, it defeats the purpose of getting the credits. The following financial institutions' cards may rebate enough to justify a fee:

✔ CIBC (800-465-4653). The Vacation Gold VISA card (annual fee: $39) earns you points that buy travel packages through CIBC's agency. The Aerogold card (annual fee: $120) earns you air miles with Air Canada.

✔ Royal Bank's (800-668-9700) Canadian Plus VISA Gold credits you one air mile with Canadian Airlines for every dollar charged. Annual fee: $120.

✔ Scotiabank's (800-387-6556) Gold VISA credits you with points for purchasing travel packages. Annual fee: $95.

✔ TD's Gold Travel Card (800-268-9460) credits points that can be used to purchase airline tickets and travel packages. Annual fee: $99.

Stuff to make you and others happy

Having fun, taking time out for R & R, and lavishing gifts on those you love can be money well spent. But in these areas, financial overindulgence can wreck an otherwise good budget.

Gifts

Think about how you approach buying gifts throughout the year — and especially during the holidays. We know people who spend so much money on credit cards at this time of year that it takes them until late spring or summer to pay off their debts!

Although we don't want to deny your loved ones gifts from the heart — or you the pleasure of giving them — spend wisely. Homemade gifts are less costly to the giver and may be more dear to recipients.

Don't make the mistake of equating the value of a gift with its dollar cost. How many expensive gifts have you received that were useless or meaningless to you?

In fact, we've got a good suggestion for getting rid of those old, unwanted gifts. For an entertaining and memorable holiday party, try a "white elephant" gift exchange: everyone brings a wrapped, unwanted gift of the past and exchanges it with someone else. Once the gifts are opened, trading is allowed.

Entertainment

Entertainment doesn't have to cost a great deal of money if you adjust your expectations. Especially in metropolitan areas, many movies, theaters, and museums offer discount prices on certain days and times. Same goes for some restaurants. Cultivate some interests and hobbies that are free or low cost. Seeing friends, reading, hiking, and playing sports can be good for your finances as well as your health.

Vacations

For many people, vacations are a luxury. For others, vacations are essential parts of their routine. Regardless of how you recharge your batteries, remember that vacations aren't investments, so you shouldn't borrow through credit cards to finance your travels. After all, how relaxed will you feel when you have to pay all those bills?

Try vacations that are shorter and closer to home. Have you been to a provincial or national park recently? Take a vacation at home and see the sights in your local area.

If you do travel far and are heading for a popular destination, travel during the off-season for the best deals on airfares and hotels. Keep an eye out for discounts and "bought-but-unable-to-use" tickets advertised in your local paper.

Also, be sure to shop around even when working with a travel agent. Travel agents work on commission, so they may not work very hard to find you the absolute best deals. Tour packages, when they meet your interests and needs, can also save you money. If you have flexible travel plans, you may be able to get a reduced fare or even a free ticket by offering to deliver a package for a courier company (but make sure that the company is reputable).

Value your publications

Everyone has a favorite and not-so-favorite publication. Some people don't realize how much they spend on publications partly because they've never tallied up the cost.

As we discuss elsewhere in this book, "free" publications are often driven by advertisers so we're not encouraging you to load up on them.

But take a close look at how much in total you're spending on publications and how much each one costs. Keep the ones that you're getting sufficient value from and cancel the rest. You can always read them at your local library.

Medical care

Health care is a big topic nowadays, and the cost of it is going up fast. If you are covered under your province's health insurance system, it probably pays for most of your health-care needs. But many plans require you to pay for certain expenses out of your own pocket. (Chapter 18 explains how to shop for extra health insurance.)

Medical care and supplies are like any other services and products — price and quality vary. And medicine in Canada is becoming more and more like a business, and a conflict of interest exists whenever the person recommending treatment benefits financially from providing that treatment. Many studies have documented unnecessary surgeries and other medical procedures.

If you don't have health-insurance coverage for a procedure or health care service, you may end up paying a larger amount out of your own pocket. Investigate buying coverage that pays for care not covered by your provincial plan. Just remember: As with any other service or product that you buy, shop around.

Alternative medicine (holistic and chiropractic, for example) is gaining attention because of its focus on preventive care and treatment of the whole body or person. Alternative treatment for many forms of chronic pain or disease may be worth your investigation. Alternative medicine may lead to better *and* lower-cost health care.

If you must take certain drugs on an ongoing basis and pay for them out-of-pocket, ordering through a mail-order company can bring down your costs and be more convenient for refilling prescriptions. Your health plan may be able to provide more information about this. The following mail order companies also offer generic drugs, which are medically equivalent to brand-name drugs but cost a lot less:

✔ MediTrust Pharmacy Inc. (800-263-8999)

✔ Pharmex Containment Service Inc. (800-269-7898)

Insurance

Insurance is a vast mine field. Part IV explains the different coverages, suggests what to buy and avoid, and reveals how to save on policies. The following are the most common ways people waste money on insurance.

✔ **Keeping low deductibles.** The *deductible* is the amount of a loss that must come out of your pocket. On an auto insurance policy, for example, if your collision deductible is $100 and you get into an accident, you pay for the first $100 of damage and your insurance company picks up the rest. Low deductibles, however, translate into much higher premiums for you. In the long run, you should save money with a higher deductible, even factoring in the potential for greater out-of-pocket costs to you when you do have a claim.

If you have a lot of claims, your insurance premiums will escalate, so you still don't come out ahead with lower deductibles. Plus low deductibles mean more claim forms to file for small losses (more hassle). Filing an insurance claim is usually not an enjoyable or quick experience.

However, if your savings are quite low, don't get carried away with a really high deductible, which could cause financial hardship if you do have a claim.

✔ **Covering small potential losses or unnecessary needs.** You shouldn't buy insurance for anything that wouldn't be a financial catastrophe if you had to pay for it out of your own pocket. For example, although the postal service isn't perfect, insuring inexpensive gifts sent in the mail isn't worth the price.

✔ **Failing to shop around.** Rates vary *tremendously* from insurer to insurer. In Part IV, we recommend the best companies to call first for quotes and other cost-saving strategies.

Taxes

Taxes probably represent one of the largest — if not *the* largest — of your expenditures. (So why is it last here? You'll soon see.)

Retirement savings plans are one of the best and simplest ways to reduce your tax burden. We explain more about retirement savings plans in

Chapter 9. Unfortunately, most people can't take full advantage of these plans because they spend everything they make. So not only do they have less savings, they also pay higher income taxes — a double whammy.

Costly addictions

Human beings are creatures of habit. We all have habits that we wish we didn't have, and breaking those habits can be very difficult. Costly habits are the worst. The following tidbits may nudge you toward breaking your own financially draining habits.

✔ **Kick the smoking habit.** Despite the decline over the past few decades in smoking, 30 percent of all Canadians over the age of 14 still smoke. Using smokeless tobacco, which also causes long-term health problems, is on the increase. Canadians spend around $6 billion annually on cigarettes — that's a staggering $900 per year per smoker. The increased medical costs and lost work time costs are even greater, estimated at anywhere from $3 billion to $7 billion every year. (Of course, if you continue to smoke, you may eliminate the need to even save for retirement.)

Check with local hospitals for smoking-cessation programs. The Canadian Cancer Society (check your local phone directory) offers a helpful brochure, *How to Be a Happy Ex-Smoker*, and maintains up-to-date lists of smoking cessation programs in your area. Branches of the Canadian Lung Association, also found in your phone book, often offer group quit-smoking programs.

✔ **Stop abusing alcohol and other drugs.** Thousands of Canadians seek treatment annually for alcoholism or drug abuse. These addictive behaviors, like spending, transcend all educational and socioeconomic lines in our society. Even so, studies have demonstrated that only one in seven alcoholics or drug abusers seeks help. Three of the ten leading causes of death — cirrhosis of the liver, accidents, and suicides — are associated with excessive alcohol consumption.

In Ontario, the Addiction Research Foundation runs a drug and alcohol information line (800-463-6273, 595-6111 in Toronto, Monday to Friday, 9 a.m. to 5 p.m.). In other provinces, call your provincial Department of Health.

✔ **Don't gamble.** The house *always* comes out ahead in the long run. Why do you think so many governments run lotteries and video lottery terminals? Because governments make money on people who gamble, that's why.

Casinos, horse and dog racetracks, and other gambling establishments are sure long-term losers for you. Getting hooked on the dream of winning is easy and tempting. And sure, occasionally you win a little bit (just enough to keep you coming back). Every now and then a few folks win a lot. But it's built into the odds that your hard-earned capital mostly winds up in the pockets of the casino owners.

If you go just for the entertainment, take only what you can afford to lose.

We've attended many presentations where a fast-talking investment guy in an expensive suit lectures about the importance of saving for retirement and explains how to invest your savings. Yet details and tips about finding the money to save (the hard part for most people) are left to the imagination.

In order to take advantage of the tax savings that come through retirement savings plans, you must first spend less than you earn. Only then can you afford to contribute to these plans. That's why the first part of this chapter is all about strategies to reduce your spending.

Another benefit of spending less and saving more is reduced sales taxes. When you buy most consumer products, you pay GST plus a provincial sales tax. Therefore, the less money you spend and the more you save in retirement plans, the more you reduce income *and* sales taxes. (See Chapter 7 for other tax-reduction strategies.)

Chapter 7
Taking the Trauma Out of Taxes

· ·

· ·

"Our tax system has become a crazy quilt of special incentives, special deductions and special write-offs. . . . Special breaks have made the income tax system more and more complicated."

— Former Finance Minister Michael Wilson

The Winchester Mystery House is a bizarre tourist attraction near San Jose, California. It's named for its former owner, Sarah Winchester, widow of the rifle-manufacturing magnate. As the story goes, Sarah believed that she wouldn't die as long as she continued to build on her property.

Proving that the prospect of death is a powerful motivator, Ms. Winchester kept builders working on her house around the clock for 38 years! Without a plan in mind, contractors added one room at a time. One hundred and sixty rooms later, you can imagine the result. Some staircases appropriately lead upstairs, but others dead-end at ceilings. Some doors and windows open only to reveal walls.

The Winchester Mystery House provides tour guides to lead you through the property. If you were on your own, of course, you'd need a detailed map and a lot of patience and persistence to get from one end of the house to the other.

And so it is with our tax system, which has quite a bit in common with the Winchester Mystery House. There is no master plan.

It's Not You — It's the System

The Canadian tax code has been changed incrementally over the years but has never been examined globally or given an overhaul. And rather than being a fun and interesting tourist attraction, for weary Canadian taxpayers who must comply with its sometimes frightening and unnecessary complexity, our tax system is like a nightmare that never seems to end.

Nearly every year, elected officials make revisions to the tax code, changing, amending, occasionally deleting, but more often adding to the written rules and regulations that determine what is taxable, which deductions are legal, which aren't, and so forth. The revisions are the results of political bargaining that usually ignores the fact that you, the taxpayer, must understand it all.

Of course, not everyone suffers at the hands of the confusing, cumbersome tax code. Some accountants and tax preparers are guaranteed employment as long as bewildered taxpayers need help. And the category of bewildered taxpayers includes most of us.

So don't feel dumb when the time comes to fill out tax forms, because it's not you — it's the system. Nevertheless, even if you hire a tax advisor to help you navigate the tax morass and prepare your annual return, understanding how the system treats certain financial moves you make is worth some of your time. The more you know about taxes, the smarter the financial strategies you devise and the less you need to spend hiring tax advisors.

The value of understanding the system

You pay a lot of money in taxes — probably more than you realize. Most people remember only whether they got a refund or owed money on their return. But when you file your tax return, all you do is settle up with tax authorities over the amount of taxes you paid during the year versus the total tax that you owe based on your income and deductions.

Some people feel lucky when they get a refund, but really, all a refund indicates is that you overpaid in taxes during the year. You should have had this money in your own account all along. If you consistently get big refunds, it may mean you should be paying less tax throughout the year.

Instead of caring about whether you get a refund when you complete your annual tax return, you *should* care about the *total* taxes you pay. The only way to know the *total* taxes you pay is to get out your tax return. On line 435 on the recent federal T1 General form, find your total federal and provincial tax payable. Subtract from this sum any credits deducted from your total tax payable, except for your tax that you've already had deducted (line 437) or any tax you paid in instalments (line 476). The end result will probably be one of the single largest expenses of your financial life (unless you have an expensive home or a huge gambling habit).

The goal of this chapter is to legally and permanently help you reduce the total taxes you pay. The key to reducing your tax burden is to understand the tax system — if you don't, you'll surely pay more in taxes than necessary. And your tax ignorance can lead to mistakes, which can quickly become even more costly if Revenue Canada catches errors in their favour. With the proliferation of computerized information and data tracking at Revenue Canada, discovering mistakes has never been easier for them.

The tax system, like much of public policy, is built around incentives to encourage *desirable* behaviour and activity. Saving for retirement, for example, is considered desirable because it encourages people to take more responsibility for their own financial future (not to mention that it reduces Ottawa's responsibility for you!). Retired citizens who have sufficient savings to support themselves in their later years are supposed to result from RRSPs. Therefore, the government offers the benefits of tax-deferred contributions and tax-deferred growth to those who set up RRSPs in order to encourage people to save for their future.

To understand the tax system is to understand what your government thinks you should be doing. Naturally, not all people follow the path the government encourages — after all, it's a free country. You've spent years rebelling against your parents. Why should the government get better treatment?

However, the difference between rebelling against your parents and being a rebellious taxpayer, of course, is that as a taxpayer, the cost of defiance comes out of your pocket. (We haven't heard of many parents who penalize, in *cash,* their kids' unruliness.) The *fewer* desirable activities that you engage in, the *more* you pay in taxes. If you understand the options, you can choose those that meet your needs as you approach different stages of your financial life.

Many people resent the taxes they pay — they feel that they pay too much and get too little in return. Therefore, another potential benefit of understanding the tax system is that you can become a more informed voter and citizen in the democratic process.

Your marginal income tax rate: The single most important tax number

"What's marginal about my taxes?" we hear you asking. "They're huge! They're not marginal in my life at all!" *Marginal* is a term often applied to those things that are small or minimally acceptable. Sort of like getting a C- on a school report card (or an A- if you're from an overachieving family).

Marginal tax rates are a powerful concept. Once you understand them, you can understand the implications of many financial strategies that affect the amount of taxes you pay. And because you pay taxes on your income from employment as well as on your investments held outside of retirement plans, a lot of personal financial decisions are at stake.

First, you must understand that when it comes to taxes, *not all income is treated equally.* This fact is not self-evident. If you work for an employer and have a constant salary during the course of a year, a steady and equal amount in federal and state taxes is deducted from your pay cheque. Thus, it appears as though all that earned income is taxed equally.

In reality, however, you pay less tax on your *first* dollars of earnings and more tax on your *last* dollars of earnings. For example, if your taxable annual income (a term we define in the next section) totalled $40,000 during 1997, you paid tax at the rate of approximately 27 percent on the first $29,590 of taxable income and 41 percent on income from $29,591 up to $40,000. (You actually don't end up paying tax on your first $6,456 of taxable income, due to a basic federal tax credit of $1,098.)

Table 7-1 gives approximate combined federal/provincial tax rates.

Table 7-1	Combined Federal/Provincial Income Tax Brackets and Rates
Taxable Income	*Federal Tax Rate (Bracket)*
Up to $29,590	27%
$29,590 to $59,180	41%
Over $59,180	50%

Your *marginal tax rate* is the rate of tax that you pay on your *last* or so-called *highest* dollars of income. In the example of a single person with taxable income of $40,000, that person's marginal tax rate is 41 percent. In other words, she effectively pays 40 percent tax on her last dollars of income — those dollars in excess of $29,590.

Alternative minimum tax (say what?)

As if the tax system weren't already complicated enough, there's actually a *second* tax system. Called the Alternative Minimum Tax, or AMT. This second system may raise your taxes higher than they would have been. Let us explain.

The AMT was introduced in 1986 in response to reports of wealthy individuals who were purportedly using loopholes and deductions to reduce their tax bills to next to nothing.

The problem with the AMT is that it hits many more people than just those making excessive use of tax shelters and other sophisticated tax-planning strategies. For example, anyone who receives a very large capital gain — such as a farmer selling his land — may also be thrown in with all the supposed robber barons.

If there's a chance that the rule will affect you, you must calculate your tax both the normal way *and* through the AMT calculations — and then pay the higher tax bill of the two! (The reason it's called the "alternative" minimum tax is *not* because you have a choice in the matter!)

If you think you might be a good AMT candidate, call up Revenue Canada and request the one-page AMT Calculations Sheet. The sheet walks you through recalculating your taxable income.

You start with your taxable income, after having taken away all your allowable deductions. Next, you add back a few of these deductions, including: losses from tax shelters; losses from a partnership if you're a limited partner or passive partner; CCA on Canadian firms; resource write-offs; as well as interest charges and other carrying costs related to these transactions. You also have to add back deductions for RPP contributions, along with employee home relocation and employee stock option deductions. Finally, add back 25 percent of all your capital gains.

Next, deduct the gross-up amount on any dividends you received. Then deduct $40,000 — your "basic minimum tax exemption." The number you're left with is your "adjusted taxable income." Take 17 percent of this to arrive at your federal tax. From this tax figure, you can deduct many personal credits, including your basic credit, as well as any old age, disability, CPP contributions, EI premiums, tuition, medical, education, and charitable credits you're eligible for.

If the figure you end up with is higher than your federal tax bill calculated the regular way, you have to use the higher amount as your federal tax. (One consolation is that, if you have to pay AMT, it can be recovered in future years.) Hope that aspirin is starting to kick in.

Your marginal tax rate allows you to quickly calculate additional taxes that you would pay on additional income. Conversely, you can delight in quantifying the amount of taxes that you save by reducing your taxable income, either by decreasing your income or by increasing your deductions.

Taxable income defined

Taxable income is the amount of income on which you actually pay taxes. You don't pay taxes on your total income for the following two reasons:

- ✔ **Not all income is taxable.** For example, any profit you make when you sell the home you live in — your principal residence — generally isn't taxable.

- ✔ **You get to subtract deductions from your income.** Some "deductions" are available just for being a living, breathing human being. Every taxpayer resident in Canada for the full year receives a basic federal tax credit of $1,098. That basically means you get a deduction for the first $6,456 of taxable income. Another example is RRSP contributions, which are subtracted from your taxable income before your tax bill is calculated.

How to Trim Taxes on Employment Income

You're supposed to pay taxes on any income you earn from work. Countless illegal ways are available to reduce your employment income — for example, not reporting it — but you could very well end up with a heap of penalties and extra interest charges on top of the taxes you owe. And you might even get tossed in jail. Because we don't want you to lose even more money by paying unnecessary penalties and serving jail time to boot, this section focuses on the many *legal* ways to reduce your taxes.

RRSP and retirement plan contributions

An RRSP (or your employer's retirement plan) is one of the few relatively painless and completely legal ways to reduce your taxable income. Besides reducing your taxes, you build up a nest egg so that you don't have to work for the rest of your life.

Money that you contribute to your RRSP (up to your allowable maximum contribution amount) is deductible from your taxable income. Therefore, if you contribute $1,000 to your RRSP and your marginal tax rate is 41 percent, you reduce your taxes by $410. Like the sound of that? How about this: Contribute another $1,000, and your taxes drop *another* $410 (as long as you're still in the same marginal tax rate).

If this process sounds easy, that's because it is. In fact, everyone should invest in a tax-sheltered retirement plan such as an RRSP. You benefit both in the short term and the long term. So why don't more people take advantage of this tax break?

Many people miss this opportunity to reduce their taxes because they *spend* all (or too much) of their current employment income and, therefore, have nothing (or little) left to put into an RRSP. If this scenario sounds familiar, you need to reduce your spending first in order to be able to contribute money to a retirement plan. Take an immediate tour through Chapter 6, which explains how to reduce your spending.

Income shifting

Income shifting, which has nothing to do with money laundering, is a more esoteric tax-reduction technique and is an option only to those who can control *when* they receive their income.

For example, suppose that your employer tells you in late December that you're eligible for a bonus. You're offered the option to receive your bonus in either December or January. Looking ahead, if you're pretty certain that you'll be in a higher tax bracket next year, you should choose to receive your bonus in December.

Or suppose that you run your own business and think that you'll be in a lower tax bracket next year. Perhaps you plan to take time off to be with a newborn or take an extended trip. In this case, you may want to push a big contract off until January so the income is taxed in the next tax year.

Investment Income Reducing Techniques

For investments that you hold in *tax-sheltered* retirement plans (an RRSP or your company's Registered Pension Plan, for example), you don't need to worry about taxes. This money isn't taxed until you actually withdraw your funds.

For investments that you hold outside of tax-sheltered retirement plans, the distributions and profits on those investments are exposed to taxation when you receive them. Interest, dividends, and profits (called *capital gains*) from the sale of an investment at a price higher than the purchase price are all taxed.

Taxes on investment income should definitely concern you if you're in a relatively high tax bracket. If you're in the 41 percent or higher federal bracket (see Table 7-1 for tax brackets), you should pay attention to the rest of this section.

If you're in the 27 percent tax bracket, these strategies may or may not help. Pay close attention to the issues that increase or decrease the benefits of following each of the strategies.

Although this section explains some of the best methods to reduce the taxes on investments exposed to taxation, Chapter 14 discusses in detail how and where to invest money held outside of tax-sheltered retirement plans.

Fill up those retirement plans

If you have money invested outside retirement plans, the distributions and profits on those investments are exposed to taxation. Unless you have that money earmarked for some specific non-retirement purpose such as buying a home, and as long as hefty taxes won't result from selling off those investments at a great profit, the money will probably serve you better in a tax-sheltered retirement plan.

 Taking advantage of opportunities to direct money into retirement plans gives you two possible tax bonuses. First, your contributions to the retirement plan may be immediately tax-deductible (see Chapter 9 for complete details). Second, the distributions and growth of the investments in the retirement plans aren't taxed until withdrawal.

Select other tax-friendly investments

Too often, when selecting investments, people mistakenly focus on past rates of return. We all know that the past is no guarantee of the future. But an even worse mistake is choosing an investment with a reportedly high rate of return without considering tax consequences. What you get to keep after taxes is what matters in the long run.

Mutual funds

Mutual funds are a good example. When comparing two similar funds, most people prefer a fund with average returns of 14 percent per year to a fund earning 12 percent. But what if the 14-percent-per-year fund causes you to pay a lot more in taxes? What if, after factoring in taxes, the 14-percent-per-year fund nets just 9 percent, while the 12-percent-per-year fund nets an effective 10 percent return? In such a case, you'd be unwise to choose a fund solely on the basis of the higher (pre-tax) reported rate of return.

We call investments that appreciate in value and don't distribute much in the way of taxable income *tax friendly*. Examples include growth stocks, which pay low taxable dividends, and mutual funds that invest in such stocks. See Chapter 12 for more information.

Dividends

The most tax-friendly way to earn investment returns are dividends paid out on Canadian equities. Dividends are paid out of a company's after-tax profits. In order not to tax the same profits twice, shareholders get a credit for the tax already paid on the earnings that companies distribute as dividends.

The *dividend tax credit* is arrived at through a convoluted formula. The estimated effect of the dividend tax credit means that, after all the numbers have been crunched, dividends are taxed at a lower rate than your salary. See the following table:

Income Level	Salary Tax Rate	Dividend Tax Rate
Up to $29,590	27%	7%
$29,590 up to $59,180	41%	25%
$59,180 and up	50%	33%

Capital gains

A capital gain is simply the profit you make when you sell an investment for more than you paid for it. Capital gains are spared the full wrath of Revenue Canada's bite. Only 75 percent of any capital gain is included in your taxable income.

Given that only three-quarters of your capital gains are taxed, the effective tax rates compared to tax on your employment income are approximately

Income Level	Salary Tax Rate	Capital Gains Effective Tax Rate
Up to $29,590	27%	20%
$29,591 – $59,180	41%	31%
$59,181 and up	50%	37%

Your principal residence

Any profits you make when you sell your principal residence generally aren't taxed. However, married couples (and common-law couples, since 1992), are allowed to have only one principal residence between them. This means, for example, that you can no longer make tax-free gains on both your home and a cottage.

Strategies to Increase Your Deductions

Deductions are just that: You deduct (subtract) them from your income after totalling your income and before you calculate the tax that you owe. To find out what a deduction is worth to you in tax savings, multiply it by your marginal tax rate.

Child care expenses

You can deduct from your income many of the costs of having others take care of your children. Usually, though, they are only claimable by the spouse who earns the lower income. Baby-sitters, day nurseries, day-care day camps, and boarding school expenses all qualify. The expenses must be incurred either to enable you to work or to take an occupational training course, however.

You can deduct $7,000 for each child who is under 7 at the end of the year, and $5,000 for each child over 7 and under 17. Your total deduction can't be greater than two-thirds of your salary or business income (technically your *earned* income). Quebec residents, however, can choose to allow either spouse to claim the deduction, which is capped at 100 percent of the earned income of the spouse with the lower income.

Alimony and maintenance payments

Alimony or maintenance payments you make to an ex-spouse can be deducted, as long as they are regular, periodic payments (lump payments don't qualify). They must also be made following a decree, order, judgement, or written agreement. Support payments for children, though, are no longer deductible.

Annual union and professional fees

Regular annual dues are deductible, but you can't claim initial fees or special assessments. Fees paid to professional organizations are deductible only if they must be paid in order to maintain a professional standing recognizable by law.

Business losses

If you work or run your own business or professional practise, you can use business losses from these other businesses you're involved in to reduce your employment or professional income.

Say that you have a salaried job in a car plant, and you start up a contracting business. If your business expenses are greater than the income it brings in, you can subtract your losses from your other income.

Interest on investment loans

Any interest you pay on money you borrow in order to buy investments or to earn income from a business may be deducted. (**Note:** This rule doesn't apply to money borrowed to make an RRSP contribution.)

Moving expenses

The moving expenses deduction can put a *load* of cash in your pocket. If you move to take a new job or to start a business, you often can deduct almost all the associated costs. Students who move in order to attend university or other post-secondary institution full-time can deduct moving expenses against taxable scholarships, bursaries, research grants, or fellowships. The move must leave you at least 40 kilometres closer to your new job or school than your old residence. However, moving to Canada from another country doesn't qualify.

Expenses that are eligible include the travelling costs to move you and your family (including food and lodging along the way) and your household belongings, as well as any related storage costs.

In addition, you can deduct the cost of selling your old home, including the real estate commissions, and the legal bills on purchasing your new home.

Students can also claim moving expenses if the move is in order to take a job — including a summer job — or to start a business. Any expenses can only be deducted against income that is earned in the new location. If you are unable to deduct all the expenses in the year of the move, the remainder can be deducted in future years. So don't forget to carry that deduction forward.

Organizing to deduct

The hard part for most people is locating the forms, receipts, and all the other scraps of paper you need when you're completing your tax return. Setting up a filing system can be a *very* big time-saver:

  ✔ **One receptacle.** If you have limited patience for setting up neat file folders and you lead an uncomplicated financial life (that is, you haven't saved receipts throughout the year that you need for tax purposes), you can confine your filing to January and February. During those months, you should receive tax summary statements on wages paid by your employer (T4 slips), taxable dividend income from Canadian corporations (T5s), income from profit-sharing plans (T4PSs), and interest income (T5s for bank account and regular-interest CSB "R" bonds, T5008 for T-Bills). If you're older, you may also get a slip for Old Age Security income (T4AOAS) and Canada/Quebec Pension Plan (CPP/QPP) (T4A(P)). Set up a folder that's labelled with something easy to remember ("1998 Taxes" is a brilliant choice) and dump these papers as well as your tax booklet into it. When you're ready to crunch numbers, you should have everything you need to complete the form.

✔ **Many receptacles.** A more thorough approach is to organize the bills you pay into individual folders during the entire year. This method is essential if you own your own business and need to tabulate your expenditures for office supplies each year. No one is going to send you a form totalling your office expenditures for the year — you're on your own.

✔ **Software as receptacle.** Software programs can help organize your tax information during the year and can save you time and accounting fees come tax-preparation time. See Chapter 22 for more information about tax and financial software.

Shifting or bunching expenses

Because you can control when you make some expenditures that earn you a credit, you can *shift* or *bunch* more of them into the select years in order to boost your tax savings. Take medical expenses: You're allowed to claim a deduction for medical bills for any 12-month period, as long as it ends within the tax year. If you anticipate a large medical bill, perhaps for some major dental work, and your 12-month period runs October to September, try to pay for the work in September rather than October. By having the expense included in the earlier 12-month period, you're able to get a credit for the expense a full year earlier.

Charitable donations is another expense category where grouping and timing your claims makes sense. You and your spouse are allowed to pool your contributions on one return. You can also group donations from up to six years together. The credit for your first $200 of donations each year earns you a combined federal/provincial tax credit of about 27 percent. For donations above a $200 total, though, the credit is worth about 50 percent.

If your annual donations are relatively small, pool them and only claim them every few years to maximize your tax savings.

Trading consumer debt for mortgage debt

If you own real estate and haven't borrowed the maximum amount that you can borrow, and if you've run up high-interest consumer debt, you may be able to trade one debt for another. If you can refinance your mortgage and pull out extra cash to pay off your credit card, auto loan, or other costly credit lines, you may be able to save yourself money.

You can usually borrow at a lower interest rate for a mortgage. You don't reduce the amount you owe, but you can drastically cut your interest charges, which should also make it easier to pay the debt off more quickly.

This strategy involves some danger. Borrowing against the equity in your home can be an addictive habit. We've seen cases in which people run up significant consumer debt three or four times and then refinance their home the same number of times over the years to bail themselves out.

An appreciating home creates the illusion that excess spending isn't really costing you. But debt is debt, and all borrowed money has to be repaid. In the long run, you wind up with greater mortgage debt, and paying it off takes a bigger bite out of your monthly income. Refinancing and establishing home equity lines cost you more in terms of loan application fees and other charges (appraisals, legal costs, and so on).

At a minimum, continued expansion of your mortgage debt handicaps your ability to work toward other financial goals. In the worst case, easy access to borrowing encourages bad spending habits that can lead to bankruptcy or foreclosure against your debt-ridden home.

Strategies to Increase Your Credits

Tax credits are *credited* to you, as if you've already paid that amount in taxes. Once your tax bill has been calculated from your taxable income, any tax credits reduce your taxes by the full amount of the credit. A $500 credit is worth the same amount to everybody — it reduces the tax payable by $500. Most credits are *nonrefundable,* which means that they can't be used to make your tax liability less than zero. If you have $1,500 of credits left over after wiping out your federal tax payable, that's as good as it gets. The government won't send you a cheque for $1,500.

Credits are usually deducted from your federal tax bill before your provincial taxes and surtaxes are calculated. In most provinces, provincial taxes are simply a percentage of your federal tax bill. As a result, a $100 federal tax credit is usually worth around $150 to $160.

Credits are usually described as being 17 percent "of something." For example, you multiply eligible tuition fees by 17 percent to arrive at your federal credit. But once the savings on provincial taxes are figured into the equation, that 17 percent education tax credit is worth about 27 percent.

The following sections discuss credits you should take if you're eligible and offer some suggestions on how to maximize them for your family. *Note:* The dollar figures are from the 1998 tax year. Check your tax guide for the specific amounts for the year for which you are filing.

Personal tax credit

Everyone gets a basic federal credit of $1,098. (When you're going through the form, you claim a "basic personal amount" of $6,456, which then gets multiplied by 17 percent to work out to $1,098.)

This is what became of the old "personal exemption" when it used to be a deduction. As a result of the change into a credit, you likely no longer get anywhere near as big a bang from this item as you once did, especially if you're in a higher tax bracket.

Spousal credit

You can claim a credit of $915 if your spouse (including a common-law spouse) earned less than $538 during the year, and a smaller credit if he or she made between $538 and $5,820. If the spouse makes more than the cut-off amount of $5,820, the lower-earning partner may be able to get under the threshold by making an RRSP contribution.

Equivalent-to-married

You can claim this credit if you're single, separated, or divorced, and support a relative who lives with you. The most common example of this is a single mother. However, you can claim this credit if you're a man or a woman and you're financially responsible for supporting a child, a parent, or other relative. The only conditions are that the dependent must be related to you, completely financially dependent on you, living in Canada, and, except in the case of a parent or grandparent, under 18 years old at some point in the tax year. (The age limit doesn't apply if the person is dependent on you because of a mental or physical disability.)

Charitable donations

As long as you get an official tax receipt, you can earn credits from most contributions made to charities. In addition to cash contributions, you can often gain tax credits if you donate items of significant value, such as a used computer. The amount of the receipt must reflect the item's fair market value. However, you can't get a receipt for your time or the expenses you ring up while doing charitable work.

The first $200 you donate earns you a 17 percent federal tax credit (which works out to about 27 percent once your savings on provincial taxes are accounted for). Once you're past the $200 level, though, your donations give you a 29 percent federal tax credit, worth about 50 percent once the savings on provincial taxes are counted. That makes your donations above $200 worth as much as a deduction if you're in the top (50 percent or so) tax bracket.

If you and your spouse both make charitable donations, combine the receipts and claim them on one return (Revenue Canada lets you do this). If both of you claimed $200 donations, together you would only save $107. By combining the donations onto one return, you can boost your savings to $145.

You're also allowed to pool charitable contributions from up to five consecutive years. If you regularly make donations smaller than $200, hold onto your receipts and claim them every few years. Again, this puts more of your donations over the $200 level, earning you a credit at a higher percentage.

Tuition fees

You can receive a credit worth 17 percent of tuition fees (as long as they total more than $100) paid to a Canadian university, college, or other post-secondary institution during the year. Fees paid to an institution certified by Employment and Immigration Canada are also eligible. Tuition paid to universities outside of Canada may also be eligible, but fees paid to private elementary schools or high schools don't earn you a tax credit. If you study *full time,* you also get to claim a federal educational status credit that starting in 1998 is $35.00 per month (up from $25.50 in 1997 and $17 in 1996).

Sometimes the student in the family doesn't need to use all — or any — of the tuition fee tax credit or the education credit to bring her federal tax bill to zero. In this case, the credits don't go to waste. Up to $850 of the unused portion of either — or both — credits generally can be transferred to a parent, grandparent, or spouse.

Medical expenses

You can include a fairly broad range of medical costs in calculating this credit. The problem with this credit is that it's worth something only if your medical expenses exceed certain minimum amounts. But you can get a much bigger tax break by moving and grouping your medical bills.

Add up any payments to doctors, nurses, dentists, and public or licensed private hospitals for medical or dental care. In addition, you can include payments for any prescription drugs and medications, eyeglasses, and therapy for speech or hearing problems. You can also include any premiums for private health insurance plans. (That includes the cost of travel insurance for your vacations out of the country. See Chapter 18 for more information.) You can't claim any expenses that you get reimbursed for from, say, a company dental plan, but any deductibles you pay qualify.

Out of that total, you can claim only the amount of your expenses that exceed 3 percent of your net income. Your credit is 17 percent of that allowable amount. If your net income exceeds $53,800, you can claim 17 percent of any expenses exceeding $1,614.

To maximize the benefit of this credit, one spouse can and should claim the entire family's medical expenses. The claim generally should be made by the spouse with the lowest income, in order to get over the 3 percent floor as quickly as possible. Further, in any tax year you can claim your expenses for any 12 months ending in that particular year. If you have a lot of bills in the fall and spring, for example, make your claim run from August 1 to July 31.

Disability credit

If you have a severe and prolonged mental or physical impairment, you get a federal credit of $720. Your disability must be certified by a medical doctor or, in the case of a vision impairment, by an optometrist.

If you're unable to use the credit because you haven't earned enough, this credit can be used by your spouse or parent if they support you. (If a parent supports a disabled child who is over 18 years old, the parent is allowed an additional federal credit of $400.)

Pension income credit

If you're 65 or older and receive income of at least $1,000, you probably can claim a federal tax credit of up to $170. (In general, income from an RRSP, private pension plan, life annuity, an annuity arising under a DPSP or an RRSP, and income from a RRIF all qualify, but income from Old Age Security or Canada Pension Plan doesn't.)

If your pension income is less than $1,000, you can claim a credit of 17 percent. If you're unable to use the credit, it may be transferred to your spouse.

Age 65 or older

Another credit for those over 65: If this means you, you can claim a federal tax credit of $592. However, this credit is reduced if your net income is over $25,921, and is completely eliminated if your income is over $49,134.

Self-employment expenses

If you're self-employed, you can deduct a multitude of expenses from your income before calculating the tax that you owe. If you buy a computer or office furniture, you can deduct those expenses (usually they need to be gradually deducted or *depreciated* over time). Salaries for your employees, office supplies, rent or mortgage interest for your office space, and phone expenses are also generally deductible.

Although some business owners cheat on their taxes, some self-employed folks don't take all the deductions they should. In some cases, people simply aren't aware of the wonderful world of deductions. Others are worried that large deductions will raise the risk of an audit.

If you fall into one of these categories, you should spend some time learning more about tax deductions; you'll be convinced that taking full advantage of your eligible deductions makes sense and saves you money.

The following sections describe common mistakes made by people who are their own bosses.

Being an island unto yourself

If you're self-employed, going it alone is usually a mistake when it comes to taxes. You must educate yourself to make the tax laws work for you rather than against you. It's worth the money to hire tax help — in the form of a tax advisor and/or some good tax guide books and computer software. (We recommend some later in this chapter.)

Making administrative tax screwups

When you're self-employed, you're responsible for the correct and timely filing of all taxes owed on your income or on that of your employees. You need to make estimated tax payments on a quarterly basis. And if you have employees, you also need to withhold taxes on their income from each pay cheque they receive and make timely payments to Revenue Canada. In addition to taxes, you also need to withhold and send in Canada Pension Plan (or Quebec Pension Plan) contributions and employment insurance premiums.

Overlooking start-up expenses

Many small-business owners use some of their personal assets when starting a business. For example, perhaps you owned a home computer that you put to service for your new business. When you convert the computer to business use, you can claim depreciation on it.

Receipts, receipts, and more receipts

When you pay with cash, following the paper trail for all the money you spent is hard for you (and Revenue Canada in the event you're ever audited). At the end of the year, how will you remember how much you spent for parking or client meals if you keep no records? Try to keep receipts for every business expenditure you make. Write down the name of the expense and the date, and regularly sort the receipts into categories such as travel, parking, entertainment, business supplies, and so on.

Not depreciating what is deductible

You can't simply deduct the cost of major purchases, such as a computer or a car, that you buy to run your business. You can, however, deduct an amount each year for the depreciation on major items. The income tax system calls writing off depreciation *capital cost allowance,* or *CCA.*

Each asset you buy falls into a specific class that determines the specific rate at which you're allowed to depreciate it. (In general, you want to depreciate your assets as quickly as possible in order to get the savings on your taxes earlier.) The only wrinkle is that you're allowed to depreciate an item at only half the normal rate in the year that you bought it. (*The Business and Professional Income Tax Guide* has a list detailing the CCA class for most items.)

Suppose that you buy a new $5,000 computer. Computers are in class ten, with a CCA rate of 30 percent. Because it's a new purchase, in the first year you can only claim a depreciation expense of $750 ($5,000 × 15 percent). The next year, you can claim the full 30 percent depreciation. But according to Revenue Canada's book, your computer is worth $750 less than when you bought it. So you can deduct 30 percent of the "remaining" value of $4,250, or $1,275. Now Revenue Canada says your computer is "worth" $2,975. The next year, you can deduct 30 percent of this "remaining" value, and so on.

Choosing the wrong entity or form of organization

When you set up your own business, you can structure its legal and tax organization in a variety of ways. To incorporate or not to incorporate is the first question you want to answer. Those motivated to incorporate do so not out of a love of paperwork (which can be considerable) but out of the desire to shield themselves from liabilities and lawsuits that might be brought against the business. A corporation may also offer opportunities for tax savings.

A *corporation* is a separate legal entity from you, the individual. For example, if a customer slips on a stray banana peel at your office and decides to sue, if you're incorporated, the customer can sue your company but can't go after your personal assets. Incorporating makes more sense if you have employees, customers who visit the office, or if you do business with many vendors.

Incorporating isn't always the right answer. For professional services, such as self-employed lawyers, physicians, or tax advisors, incorporating may not necessarily be useful as protection against professional negligence suits related to their work. In such cases, the law may treat the business and the professional as one and the same. The answer for these folks is *professional liability insurance*. Check with the professional associations in your field for information on insurers that offer such policies.

Not funding a retirement plan

We are sometimes shocked by accountants who don't encourage their clients to contribute to retirement plans to reduce taxes. You should save money toward retirement anyway, and you can't beat the tax break. Self-employed people can contribute up to 18 percent of their earned income, less a "pension adjustment" if they also belong to a Registered Pension Plan, to a certain maximum. To learn more about RRSPs and other retirement plans, see Chapter 9.

Not using numbers to help manage business

If you are a small-business owner who doesn't track his income, expenses, staff performance, and customer data on a regular basis, your tax return may be the one and only time during the year when you take a financial snapshot of your business. After you go to all the time, trouble, and expense to file your tax return, make sure that you reap the rewards of all your work: Use those numbers to help analyze and manage your business.

Some bookkeepers and tax preparers can provide you with management information reports on your business from the tax data they compile for you. Just ask! Likewise, software packages can help. See recommendations later in this chapter

Not paying family help

If your children, spouse, or other relatives help with some aspect of your business, consider paying them for the work. Besides showing them that you value their work, this practise may reduce your family's tax liability. For example, a child is usually in a lower tax bracket than you are. So by shifting income to the child, you cut your tax bill.

Tax Preparation and Planning Options

All sorts of ways to prepare your tax return exist. Which approach makes sense for you depends on the complexity of your situation and your level of interest and knowledge about taxes.

Regardless of which approach you take, you should make financial moves during the year to reduce your taxes. By the time you actually file your return the following year, it's usually too late to take advantage of many tax-reduction strategies.

Doing it yourself

Odds are, you do many things for yourself, such as cooking, shopping, and repairing your home. You may do these chores because you enjoy them, because you save money by doing them, or because you want to develop particular skills. For the same reasons, you may also choose to do-it-yourself when it comes time to file your tax return.

By preparing your own tax return, you develop a better understanding of the ins and outs of the tax code and of your own financial situation. Done on your own, a tax return gives you a condensed review of your financial history over the past year; it should also plant some ideas on how to better manage your finances in the year to come.

If your financial situation doesn't change much from year to year, neither does your return. You may need to do a little reading to keep up with the small number of changes in the tax system and laws that might affect your situation.

Revenue Canada publications and phone assistance

If you have a simple, straightforward tax return, filing it on your own using only Revenue Canada's instructions is fine. This approach is as cheap as you can get. The only costs are time, patience, photocopying expenses (you should always keep a copy for your files), and postage to mail the completed tax return. (You may also need to lay in some remedies for headaches and upset stomachs.)

This approach has a lot in common with an Easter egg hunt. If you've ever hunted for Easter eggs, you know the prizes are well hidden (from a child's perspective, anyway) and require some real searching to ferret out. Unless the Easter Bunny in your life was a New Age, cooperative problem-solver, you probably don't recall any large, flashing neon signs reading *DON'T MISS*

THIS ONE! with a blinking arrow pointing to the hidden eggs. Likewise, Revenue Canada publications generally don't have *Tip* or *Warning* icons as this book does. For example, here's something you don't usually see in a Revenue Canada publication:

Stop! One of the most commonly overlooked deductions is making a tax-deductible contribution to a Registered Retirement Savings Plan (RRSP). You still have time to start one and knock off hundreds, maybe thousands of dollars from your tax bill! Hurry!

A danger of relying on Revenue Canada is that it has been known to give wrong information on a more-than-infrequent basis. If you call Revenue Canada with a question, be sure to take notes about your conversation to protect yourself should you be audited. Date your notes and include the name of the tax employee you talked to, what you asked, and the employee's responses. File your notes in a folder with a copy of your completed return. If a large deduction is involved, it may pay to get a tax professional's help on the issue, just to be sure.

In addition to the standard instructions that come with your tax return, Revenue Canada offers a number of free and helpful tax guides that you can pick up at your nearest Revenue Canada centre, or you can call Revenue Canada to request them. These guides serve as useful references and provide more detail and insight than the basic Revenue Canada publications. For the self-employed, many booklets are available depending on your occupation, including *Business and Professional Income, Farming Income, Fishing Income,* and *Rental Income.* Other guides deal with specific circumstances, including *Alimony or Maintenance, Are You Moving?, Canadian Residents Going Down South,* and *Home Buyers' Plan.* For retirement planning, you can read *RRSPs and Other Registered Plans for Retirement, How to Calculate Your RRSP Contribution Limit,* and *When You Retire.*

All of these guides are available free — kind of. Actually, you pay for Revenue Canada guides through your taxes.

Free filing advice

If your return is straightforward, you usually have a way to get some basic advice at no charge on how to prepare your return. And — surprise of surprises — it's all made possible by those helpful folks at Revenue Canada.

Under its long-running Community Volunteer Income Tax program, each year Revenue Canada trains volunteers to know how to prepare simple returns (those without rental income, business expenses, capital gains, and so on). The volunteers come from all walks of life but are often members of charitable organizations and community groups. Advice is usually given in group sessions at local libraries, seniors' homes, and community centres.

Although the program focuses on people who might have special difficulty dealing with their returns — such as new immigrants, the elderly, and the handicapped — the program can benefit anybody. And many Canadians do take advantage of the program. To find out whether a volunteer is giving a tax information session in your area, call your local district office of Revenue Canada, your library, or local volunteer association.

Other preparation and advice guides

Books about tax preparation that are written in clear, simple English and that highlight common problem areas are invaluable. They supplement the official instructions not only by helping you to complete your return correctly but also by saving you as much money as possible. The best ones also offer simple explanations of basic tax-planning techniques that can save you money.

Quite a few preparation guides are on the market. Our favourites are

- ✔ *Canadian Personal Tax Guide* (published by KPMG)
- ✔ *Preparing Your Income Tax Returns* (prepared by Arthur Andersen and published by CCH Inc.)
- ✔ *How to Reduce the Tax You Pay* (published by Deloitte & Touche)
- ✔ *Jacks on Tax* (written by Evelyn Jacks and published by Business McGraw-Hill Ryerson)

Software

If you have access to a computer, tax-preparation software can be helpful. Think of it as having a squadron of accountants in your computer. Plus you don't have to go to the library to get all the forms for your particular return, only to discover that the library is out of them and then call Revenue Canada and wait for your forms to arrive in the mail — the forms are in the software!

Software also has the virtue of automatically recalculating all the appropriate numbers on your return when one number changes — no more whiting out math errors because your dog was sleeping on some of the receipts.

Among the better tax-preparation software packages on the market are

- ✔ Quicktax (for Windows and Macintosh)
- ✔ CanTax (Windows, DOS)
- ✔ GriffTax (Macintosh)

Filing the electronic way

Although the electronic highway is being paved faster than you can say *nanosecond,* it doesn't yet run between your house or office and Revenue Canada.

Right now, only accountants and other tax specialists who have made special arrangements with the tax department, including having a dedicated transmission line installed, can file returns electronically through EFILE. However, if you prepare your own taxes using a computer program, you usually can find someone who will transmit it to Revenue Canada for a fee. Tax preparers such as H&R Block and tax accountants will charge you anywhere from $15 to $100 for the transmission and for going over your return before sending it in (which Revenue Canada requires them to do).

We don't recommend filing this way for most people — you pay a high effective interest rate to get your money sooner, and it can be a hassle to find someone to do it for you.

Hiring help

Some people hire a contractor to help with a home-remodelling project because they lack the time, interest, energy, or skill to do it themselves. For the same reasons, some choose to hire a tax advisor.

Competent tax specialists can save you money — sometimes more than enough to pay their fees — by identifying tax-reduction strategies you may overlook. They can also reduce the likelihood of an audit, which can be triggered by blunders you might make. Mediocre and lousy tax preparers, on the other hand, may make mistakes and not be aware of sound ways to reduce your tax bite.

Tax practitioners come with varying backgrounds, training, and credentials. One credential is not necessarily better than another. The four main types are preparers, certified general accountants (CGAs), chartered accountants (CAs), and tax lawyers (surprised you — no acronym!). The more training and specialization a tax practitioner has (and the more affluent his clients), the higher his hourly fee usually is. Fees and competence at all levels of the profession vary significantly. If you do hire a tax advisor and you're not sure of the quality of work performed and the soundness of the advice, try getting a second opinion.

Preparers

Among all tax practitioners, preparers generally have the least amount of training, and a greater proportion of them work part time. As with financial planners, no national regulations apply to preparers, and no licensing is required.

H&R Block is the largest and most well-known tax-preparation firm in the country with about 1,000 offices nationwide. In addition to Block, there are also lots of mom-and-pop shops. The appeal of preparers is that they're relatively inexpensive — they can do most basic returns for around $100 or so. The drawback, of course, is that you may hire a preparer who doesn't know much more than you do.

Preparers make the most sense for folks who have relatively simple financial lives, who are budget-minded, and who hate doing their own taxes. If you're not good about hanging onto receipts or don't want to keep your own files with background details about your taxes, you should definitely shop around for a tax preparer who's going to be around for a few years. You may need all that stuff someday for an audit, and many tax preparers keep and organize their clients' documentation rather than return everything each year. (Can you blame them for keeping it after they went to the trouble of sorting it all out of the shopping bags you brought them?) Also, going with a firm that's open year-round may be safer (some small shops are open only during tax season) in case tax questions or problems arise.

Certified general accountants

CGAs are often a sound, economical choice for tax advice. Many certified general accountants have large personal tax practices. CGAs are best for people with moderately complex returns who don't necessarily need complicated tax-planning advice throughout the year.

Many CGAs also have expertise in preparing returns for small businesses. A professional who is familiar with the peculiarities of your industry may be able to give you more complete advice on the opportunities for saving and how to organize your business to minimize your tax bill. What's more, he'll likely be able to do your return more quickly, meaning a lower bill. CGAs don't close down when the tax season ends. That means you can go to them for advice and help on *your* schedule, and you'll be able to get help if you have problems after filing your return. Fees for a straightforward return should cost about $100, while more complex situations (a part-time business, investment income, for example) might mean a bill of several hundred dollars.

Chartered accountants (CAs)

CAs are the folks who audit public companies. They tend to have specialities in specific industries or types of businesses. Many CAs work for large firms such as KPMG, Ernst & Young, Price Waterhouse, and Deloitte & Touche that have international operations in both accounting and consulting, so they have the expertise to prepare complicated returns involving investments and earnings in different countries.

CAs are of greatest value to people completing some of the more unusual and less user-friendly schedules, or who have to file in several countries. A typical CA user might be a Canadian who, because she works a portion of the year in the U.S., has to file in both countries and who has numerous tax shelters and real estate investments.

CA fees vary tremendously. Most charge around $100 per hour, but CAs at large companies and in high-cost-of-living areas tend to charge somewhat more. The cost of having a CA prepare your return can range anywhere from $150 to several thousand dollars.

If your return is uncomplicated and your financial situation is stable, hiring a high-priced CA year after year to fill in the blanks is a waste of money. Sometimes you'll be granted an initial interview with a partner, who then has a less-qualified — and lower-paid — associate carry out the work. However, the bill you receive for the associate's advice often will reflect the CA's rate.

Paying for the additional cost of a CGA or CA on an ongoing basis makes sense if you can afford it and if your situation is reasonably complex or dynamic. If you're self-employed and/or file lots of other schedules, it may be worth hiring a CGA or CA. But you needn't do so year after year. If your situation grows complex one year and then stabilizes, consider getting help for the perplexing year and then using preparation guides, software, or a lower-cost preparer in the future.

Tax lawyers

Tax lawyers are hired guns who can tackle major tax problems and issues. Unless you're a super-high-income earner with a complex financial life, it's prohibitively expensive to hire a tax lawyer to prepare your annual return. In fact, many tax lawyers don't prepare returns as a normal practice. Often, their role is to interpret tax regulations and rules and advise accountants and clients on what's an acceptable and what's a risky strategy.

Because of their level of specialization and training, tax lawyers tend to have the highest hourly billing rates — $200, $300, or even $400 per hour isn't unusual. The total bill to have a tax lawyer prepare a return that includes complex off-shore investments will be in the thousands, if not the *tens* of thousands of dollars.

The more training and specialization a tax practitioner has (and the more affluent her clients), the higher her hourly fee is. Select the one that best meets your needs. Fees and competence at all levels of the profession vary significantly. If you're not sure of the quality of work performed and the soundness of the advice, try getting a second opinion.

Help, I Got an Audit Notice!

On a list of real-life nightmares, most people would rank tax audits right up there with rectal exams and needing to appear in court to contest a speeding ticket.

The primary trauma of an audit is that many people feel like they're on trial and are being accused of a crime. Take a deep breath and don't panic.

First of all, you may be one of the tens of thousands of taxpayers whose returns are audited at random. No, Revenue Canada isn't headed by sadists (all appearances and popular rumours aside). Random audits help Revenue Canada identify common areas on tax forms where taxpayers make mistakes or try to cheat.

A second thing to consider: You might be audited simply because a business that reports tax information on you, or someone at Revenue Canada, made an error regarding the data on your return.

Third, you may just have the misfortune of working in an industry or running a type of business that Revenue Canada has targeted this year. In order to close loopholes, not to mention to keep taxpayers on the straight and narrow, Revenue Canada regularly hones in on certain types of employees and professions.

Or, fourth, maybe your return simply stuck out because you claimed abnormally large deductions or credits.

And the final possible explanation for an audit: Certain types of returns are much more likely than the average Joe's to set off the red light for a review. Those returns come from people who participate in real estate, limited partnerships, and research-and-development tax shelters. Certain professions, such as self-employed salespeople, are also much more likely to set the audit bells a-ringing.

Unfortunately, you'll most likely be one of the majority of audit survivors who end up owing more tax money. The amount of additional tax that you owe in interest and penalties hinges on how your audit goes.

Audit preparation

Preparing for an audit is sort of like preparing for a test in school. Revenue Canada informs you of which sections of your tax return the agency wants to examine.

The first decision you face when you get an audit notice is whether to handle it yourself or turn to a tax advisor to represent you. Hiring representation costs money out of pocket but may save you time, stress, and money.

If you normally prepare your own return and are comfortable with your understanding of the areas being audited, then do it yourself. If the amount of tax money in question is small in comparison to the fee you'd pay the tax advisor to represent you, self-representation is probably the answer. However, if you're likely to turn into a babbling, intimidated fool and are unsure how to present your situation, hire a tax advisor to represent you (see the "Hiring help" section earlier in this chapter for information about whom to hire).

If you decide to handle the audit yourself, get your act together sooner rather than later. Don't wait until the night before to start gathering receipts and other documentation. You may find, for example, that you can't find certain documents and need to contact others to get copies.

You need to document and be ready to speak with the auditor only about the areas the audit notice says are being investigated. Organize the various documents and receipts into folders. You want to make it as easy as possible for the auditor to review your materials. *Don't* show up, dump shopping bags full of receipts and paperwork on the auditor's desk, and say, "Here it is — *you* figure it out."

Whatever you do, *don't ignore your audit request letter.* Revenue Canada is the ultimate bill-collection agency. And if you end up owing more money (the unhappy result of most audits), the sooner you pay, the less interest and penalties you'll owe.

The day of reckoning

Two people with identical situations can walk into an audit and come out with very different results. The loser can end up owing much more in taxes and have the audit expanded to include other parts of the return. The winner can end up owing less tax money than he or she really should pay under the tax laws.

Here's how to be a winner:

✔ **Treat the auditor as a human being.** Obvious advice, yes, but very often not practiced by taxpayers. You may be resentful or angry about being audited. You may be tempted to gnash your teeth and tell the auditor how unfair it is that an honest taxpayer like you had to spend scores of hours getting ready for this. You might feel like ranting and raving about how the government wastes too much of your tax money or that the party in power is out to get you. Bite your tongue.

Believe it or not, most auditors are decent people just trying to do their job. They're well aware that taxpayers don't like seeing them. Don't suck up, either — just relax and be yourself. Behave as you would around a boss whom you like — with respect and congeniality.

✔ **Stick to the knitting.** Your audit is to discuss *only* the sections of your tax return that are in question. The more you talk about other areas, the more likely the auditor will probe into other items. Don't bring documentation for parts of your return not being audited. Besides creating more work for yourself, you may open a can of worms that needn't be opened.

✔ **Don't argue when you disagree.** State your case. If the auditor wants to disallow a deduction or otherwise increase the taxes you owe and you don't agree, state once why you don't. If the auditor won't budge, don't get into a knock-down, drag-out confrontation. He or she may not want to lose face and is inclined to find additional tax money — that's the auditor's job. *Remember:* If necessary, you can plead your case with several layers of people above your auditor. If that fails and you still feel wronged, you can take your case to tax court.

✔ **Don't be intimidated.** Most auditors aren't tax geniuses. The work is stressful — being in a job in which people dislike seeing you isn't easy. They may know less about tax and financial matters than you do. So you may not be at such a disadvantage in your tax knowledge after all, especially if you work with a tax advisor.

Chapter 8
Saving for Specific Goals

· ·

In This Chapter

▶ Prioritizing your financial goals

▶ Making RRSP funding a priority

▶ Nonretirement goals and how to fund them

▶ What you need to get through retirement

▶ Ways to make up for lost time

▶ Overcoming objections to saving in RRSPs and other retirement plans

· ·

*M*ost people whom we know have dreams. Here's a list of some of the most common dreams, in no particular order:

✔ **Become part of the landed gentry.** Renting and dealing with landlords can be a financial and emotional drag, so most folks want to own some real estate — most commonly their own home.

✔ **Retire.** No, retiring doesn't imply sitting in a rocking chair watching the world go by while hoping that some long lost friend, your son's or daughter's family, or the neighbourhood dog comes by to visit. *Retiring* is a catch-all term for discontinuing full-time work or perhaps not even working for pay at all.

✔ **Educate the kids.** No, all those diaper changes, late-night feedings, and trips to the zoo aren't enough to get junior out of your house and into the real world as a productive, self-sufficient adult. You may want to help your children get university educations, and, unfortunately, they can cost a truckload of dough.

✔ **Own your own business.** Many employees want to become employers so that they can face the challenges and rewards that come with being the boss. The primary reason that many people continue to dream without actually plunging into their own small business is that they lack the money to do so. Although many businesses don't require gobs of start-up cash, almost all require that you withstand a substantial reduction in your income in the early years.

Each of us may have other goals unique to our personal situations. No matter — accomplishing such goals almost always requires saving money. As one of our favourite Chinese proverbs says, "Do not wait until you are thirsty to dig a well."

The first chapters in this book help you to assess your current financial situation and to begin to develop good savings habits. In this chapter, you move on to more advanced topics, such as determining how much you need to save in order to achieve your important financial goals.

Prioritizing Your Savings Goals

Unless you earn really big bucks or have a large family inheritance to fall back on, your personal and financial desires will probably outstrip your resources. Thus, you must prioritize your goals if you want to accomplish them.

One of the biggest mistakes that we see people make is to rush into financial decisions without considering what's really important to them. Because many of us get caught up in the responsibilities of our daily lives, time for reflection often never happens.

From the experience we've had teaching and talking to people about better personal financial management, we can tell you that the people who accomplish their goals aren't necessarily smarter or higher income earners than those who don't.

People who accomplish their goals first identify their goals and work toward them.

Taking advantage of RRSPs and other tax-deferral plans

Where possible, you should try to save and invest in plans that offer you a tax advantage. That's precisely what RRSPs (Registered Retirement Saving Plans) and other retirement plans do for you — offer tax breaks to people of all economic means (see Chapter 9):

> ✔ **Contributions are usually tax-deductible.** We feel that RRSPs and other retirement plans are misnamed. They should really be called *tax-reduction plans*. If they were, people might be more excited about contributing to them. For many, avoiding higher taxes is the motivating force behind opening the plan and starting the contributions.

Retirement plan contributions, up to certain limits, are excluded from your income when it comes time to calculate how much tax you should pay for the year. If you pay 40 percent tax (refer to Chapter 7 for your tax bracket), a $5,000 contribution to an RRSP lowers your taxes by $2,000.

✔ **Returns on your investment compound over time without taxation.** After money is in a retirement plan, any interest, dividends, and appreciation add to your account without being taxed.

Of course, there's no such thing as a free lunch — these accounts don't allow for *permanent* tax avoidance. Yet, you can get a really great lunch at a discount — you get to defer taxes on all the accumulating gains and profits until you withdraw the money down the road. Thus, more money is working for you over a longer period of time.

Dealing with competing goals

Unless one enjoys paying higher taxes, why would anyone save money outside of an RRSP or other retirement plan? The reason is that accomplishing some financial goals isn't possible through saving in these retirement plans.

If you're accumulating down payment money for a home purchase or to start or buy a business, for example, you need to save that money outside of an RRSP. Why? Because if you withdraw funds from an RRSP, you not only have to pay tax on your withdrawal, but you will have used up a portion of the total amount you're allowed to put into your RRSP without enjoying the benefits of long-term tax-deferred growth.

Because each of us is constrained by our financial resources, we must prioritize our goals. Before funding your retirement plans and racking up those tax breaks, read the rest of this chapter to consider the importance of accomplishing other common goals.

Building Emergency Reserves

If your only source of emergency funds right now is a high-interest credit card, it's in your financial interest to save at least three to six months' worth of living expenses in an accessible account before funding a retirement plan or saving for other goals.

No one can predict the future. There is simply no reliable way to tell what may happen with your job, health, or family. Because you don't know what the future holds, preparing for the unexpected is financially wise. Even if you're the lucky sort who sometimes finds $5 bills on street corners, you can't control the sometimes chaotic world in which we live.

Conventional wisdom says that you should have approximately six months of living expenses put away for an emergency. This particular amount may or may not be right for you because it depends, of course, on how expensive the emergency is. Why six months, anyway? And where should you put it? Unfortunately, no hard-and-fast rules exist. How much of an emergency stash you need depends on your situation.

We recommend saving the following emergency amounts under differing circumstances (in Chapter 14, we recommend good places to invest this money):

- **Three months' living expenses** if you have other sources of funds such as family members and close friends that you could tap for a short-term loan. This minimalist approach makes sense when you're trying to maximize investments elsewhere (for example, in retirement plans) or have very stable sources of income (employment or otherwise).

- **Six months' living expenses** if you don't have other places to turn for a loan and/or have some instability in your employment situation or source of income.

- **Up to one year's living expenses** if you don't have other places to turn for a loan and if your income fluctuates wildly from year to year. If your profession involves a high risk of job loss, and if it could take you a long time to find another job, you also have a greater need for a significant cash reserve.

Establishing an emergency reserve should take priority over saving for other purposes, unless you have access to money through other resources such as family or are willing to borrow from a retirement plan.

Saving to Buy a Home or Business

When you're starting out financially, deciding whether to save money to buy a home or to put money into a retirement plan presents a real dilemma. In the long run, owning your own home is often a wise financial move. On the other hand, starting early to save for retirement makes achieving your goal easier.

The bottom line is: You should be doing both — saving for a home and for retirement. If you're eager to own a home, then you can throw all your savings toward achieving that goal and temporarily put retirement savings on hold. If you're not in a rush, you can save for both purposes simultaneously.

Avoiding early withdrawal penalties

There are times and ways to avoid the early withdrawal penalties that the tax gods normally apply to retirement plans.

Suppose that you read this book at a young age, develop sound financial habits early, and contribute regularly to an RRSP. Later on, you have a few years where your income is low or nonexistent. This may not be by choice if, for example, the company you work for closes. But it may also be due to a lifestyle change you've chosen to make. Maybe you decide to take a couple of years off to sail the seven seas, start a family, or get a small business off the ground. Whatever the cause, the lower your income, the less you're dinged on money you take out of your plan. RRSP withdrawals are simply treated as part of your income to determine the rate at which they're taxed. The lower your overall income, the lower your tax rate, and the more of your withdrawal you can keep.

Although this may mean you will pay little or even no tax on an RRSP withdrawal, don't rush to take money out that you don't need. You'll still be giving up the benefit of your money being able to grow without the income, dividends, or appreciation being taxed.

If you do need to get at some of your RRSP funds, the taxes due will be calculated when you complete your next tax return. However, your financial institution is required to hold onto some of your money when you make your withdrawal as kind of a tax down payment. The rates (unless you live in Quebec) are 10 percent on the first $5,000, 20 percent on the next $10,000, and 30 percent on any amount beyond $15,000. In Quebec, the rates are 25 percent on the first $5,000, 33 percent on the next $10,000, and 38 percent on any amount over $15,000.

These rates are calculated on each individual withdrawal. If you need to withdraw a large amount, only take out $5,000 at a time to minimize the amount of withholding tax.

You may be able to have your cake and eat it too by saving money in an RRSP and then borrowing against it for the down payment. This is allowed under the government's Home Buyers' Plan. Be careful, though. The plan requires that you pay back the loan over the next 16 years. You also lose the tax-deferred compounding on that money when it's outside your plan, and you may find that making your repayments doesn't leave any money to make a new contribution and earn a tax refund.

In saving money for starting or buying a business, you face the same dilemma as when deciding to save to buy a house: If you fund your retirement plan to the exclusion of building money for your small business dreams, your dreams may never become a reality. Generally, we advocate hedging your bets by saving some money in your tax-sheltered retirement plans as well as some toward your business venture. Although an investment in your own small business can produce great rewards, this type of investment is usually a good deal riskier than investing in real estate in the form of your own home.

Saving for Children's Educational Expenses

Wanting to provide for your children's future is perfectly natural. But doing so before you've saved adequately toward your own goals can be a major financial mistake.

It may sound selfish, but you need to take care of *your* future first. If you're not taking advantage of saving through tax-sheltered retirement plans, you should do so before you set aside money in special savings accounts for your kids. This practice isn't selfish — do you really want to have to leech off your kids when you're old and frail because you didn't save any money for yourself?

RRSPs and other retirement savings plans are smart investments for the future of the entire family, and they give you immediate tax breaks. In some cases, that tax break may even provide the extra cash you need to start putting some money away for your kids' education. See Chapter 15 for a complete explanation for how to save for educational expenses.

Saving for Big Purchases

If you want to buy a car or a canoe or plane ticket to France, do not, we repeat, *do not* buy such things with credit or a consumer loan. As we explain in Chapter 5, cars, boats, vacations and the like are consumer items, not investments that build wealth, such as real estate or a small business. A car begins to depreciate the moment you drive it off the sales lot. A plane ticket to France is worthless the moment you land in Paris. (We know your memories will be priceless, but they don't pay the bills.)

Don't deny yourself gratification; just learn how to delay it. Get into the habit of saving for your big consumer purchases and paying for them with cash.

Interest on consumer debt is exorbitantly expensive, up to 18 percent for most credit cards. When contemplating the purchase of a consumer item on credit, add up the total interest you end up paying on your debt and call it the price of instant gratification.

Paying for high-interest consumer debt can cripple your ability not only to save for long-term goals like retirement or a home but also to make major purchases in the future.

If you're saving up for a consumer purchase like a car, a money market account (see Chapter 14) is a good place to store your short-term savings.

Preparing for Retirement

We've never cared much for the term *retire*. It seems to imply idleness or the end of usefulness to society. But if retirement means not having to work at a job (especially one you don't enjoy) and having financial flexibility and independence, then we're all for it.

Part of the typical dream of most Canadians is to be able to retire sooner rather than later. But this idea has some obvious problems. First, you set yourself up for disappointment. If you want to retire by your mid-60s, you'll need enough money to live for an additional 20 years, maybe longer. Two decades is a long time to live off your savings. You're going to need a good-sized chunk — more than most people realize. The earlier you hope to retire, the more money you need to set aside and the earlier you have to start saving. Either that or plan to work part time in retirement to earn more income!

Most people we speak with say that they do want to retire, and most say the sooner the better. Yet only around a quarter of Canadians typically make the maximum allowable contributions to their RRSPs. If you're in this group, and even if you're not, you should determine where you stand financially regarding retirement. If you're like most working people, you need to increase your savings rate for retirement.

What you need for retirement

If you hope to someday cease working or reduce the time you spend working for an income, you'll need sufficient savings to support yourself. Most people — particularly young people and those who don't work well with numbers — underestimate the amount of money needed to retire.

Many people don't even think about saving for retirement until middle age rolls around. As you may already know or will soon see, this mistake can be costly. To figure out how much you should save per month given your retirement goals, you can't avoid crunching a few numbers (but don't worry — this number-crunching is easier than doing your taxes).

Luckily for you, you don't have to start cold. Studies have shown how people typically spend money before and during retirement. Most people need about 70 to 80 percent of their preretirement income throughout retirement to maintain their standard of living.

For example, if your household earns $40,000 per year before retirement, you'll likely need $28,000–$32,000 (70–80 percent of $40,000) per year during retirement to live the way that you're accustomed to living. The 70–80 percent is an average. Some people may need more money simply because they have more time on their hands to spend their money. Others adjust their standard of living and need less.

Can you save too much or spend too little?

Anne Scheiber, on a modest income, started saving at a young age and allowed her money to compound in wealth-building investments such as stocks over many years. The result was that she was able to amass $20 million by the time she passed away at the age of 101.

Scheiber lived in a cramped studio apartment and never used her investments. She didn't even use their interest or dividends — she lived solely on her government benefits and the small pension from her employer. Scheiber was extreme in her frugality and obsessed with her savings. As reported by James Glassman in the *Washington Post,* "She had few friends . . . she was an unhappy person, totally consumed by her securities accounts and her money."

Most people, us included, wouldn't choose to live and save the way that Scheiber did. She saved for the sake of saving: no goal, no plan, no reward for herself. Saving should be a means to an end, not something that makes you mean to the end.

Even those who save for an ultimate goal can often become consumed by their saving habits. We see people pursuing higher-paying jobs and pinching more and more pennies in order to retire early. But sometimes they make too many personal sacrifices today while chasing after some vision of their lives tomorrow.

The problem is that tomorrow might not come. Even if all goes according to plan, will you know how to be happy when you're not working if you spend your entire life making money? More importantly, who will be around to share your leisure time? One of the costs of an intense career is time spent away from friends and family. You may indeed realize your goal of retiring early, but you may put off too much living today in expectation of living tomorrow.

As Charles D'Orleans said in 1465, "It's very well to be thrifty, but don't amass a hoard of regrets."

At the other extreme are spendthrifts who live only for today. As a friend once said, "I'm not into delayed gratification." Shop 'til you drop seems to be the motto of this personality type. "Why bother saving when we might not be here tomorrow?" reasons this type of person.

The danger of this approach is that tomorrow may come after all, and most people don't want to spend all their tomorrows working for a living. The earlier neglect of saving, however, handicaps the possibility of not working when you're older. And if for some reason you can't work and have little money to live on, the situation can be tragic.

Although neither extreme is good, you may be surprised to hear us say that if you must pick an extreme — and we'd rather that you didn't — picking the spendthrift approach is better. At least you're making use of your money and, hopefully, deriving value from it. Just don't live too close to the edge. Remember that the only difference between a person without savings or access to credit and some homeless people is a few months of unemployment. If you're a spendthrift, be sure that you have an emergency reserve and you don't mind continuing to work, assuming your health allows.

Saving money is like eating food: If you don't eat enough, you may suffer. If you eat too much, the extra may go to waste or make you overweight. The right amount, perhaps with some extra to spare, affords you a healthy, balanced, peaceful existence.

You, of course, are a shining example of the diversity that makes our country great. You're unique! You're not average in any way! So how do you estimate what *you* will need?

The simplest and easiest method to estimate what you need is for us to tell you what percentage you need. (We know we've only known each other a short time, but let us have a chance to offer some friendly counselling.) The following three profiles provide a rough estimate of the percentage of your preretirement income that you need during retirement. Pick the one that most accurately describes your situation. If you fall between two descriptions, pick a percentage in between.

To maintain your standard of living in retirement:

✔ You need **65 percent of your preretirement income** if you

- save a large amount (15 percent or more) of your annual earnings

- are a high-income earner

- will own your home free of debt by retirement, and

- don't anticipate leading a lifestyle in retirement that reflects your current high income.

If you're an especially high-income earner who lives well beneath his or her means, you may be able to do with even less than 65 percent. Try picking an annual dollar amount or percentage of your current income that you believe would allow the kind of retirement lifestyle you need.

✔ You need **75 percent of your preretirement income** if you

- save a reasonable amount (5 to 14 percent) of your annual earnings

- will still have some mortgage debt or a small rent to pay by the time you retire, and

- anticipate having a standard of living in retirement that is comparable to what you have today.

✔ You need **85 percent of your preretirement income** if you

- save little or none of your annual earnings (less than 5 percent)

- will have a significant mortgage payment or growing rent to pay in retirement, and

- anticipate wanting or needing to maintain your current lifestyle throughout retirement.

Of course, you can use a more precise approach to figure out how much you need per year in retirement. Those who are more data-oriented may feel comfortable tackling this method: You need to figure out where you're spending your money today (worksheets are located in Chapter 4) and then work up some projections for your expected spending needs in retirement (the information in Chapter 21 may help as well). Be sure to include some of your "dream spending" in your equations. This more personalized method is far more time-consuming, and because you make projections into an uncertain future, it may not be any more accurate than the first method.

If you've been working steadily, you may already have a foundation for your retirement reserves, even if you haven't been actively saving toward retirement. In the pages ahead, we walk you through the probable components of your future retirement income and how to figure how much you should save to reach a particular retirement goal.

Government benefits

A few decades ago, the future looked very bright indeed, and the government laid the plans for what was an ambitious cradle-to-grave system of social support.

A key component of social assistance was the many programs that would ensure that, in their retirement, Canadians could rest assured that they would have a basic level of income. In addition to Old Age Security (OAS), most people are eligible for the Canada Pension Plan (CPP) or the Quebec Pension Plan (QPP).

The bad news is that the Canada Pension Plan is in trouble because it's fast approaching the point where more people will be taking money out of the system than there are workers contributing fresh funds. The good news is that Canadians are quickly learning the importance of not depending solely on the government for their retirement income. A recent poll found that almost two-thirds of Canadians believe that government programs won't provide them with a secure retirement income.

However, there still should be some government programs for you when you retire, no matter how old you are today. Just imagine what would happen to the group of politicians that voted to stop paying benefits. Just recently, for instance, the government moved to increase contributions to the Canada Pension Plan in order to start building up more reserves in the system.

If you think you can never retire because you have no money saved, we're happy to inform you that you're probably wrong. You very likely will be able to receive benefits from at least one or two government programs.

Old age pensions are intended only to provide you with a subsistence level of income in retirement so that you can afford basic necessities, such as food, shelter, and clothing. They aren't intended to be your sole source of income. Few people could maintain their current lifestyles without supplementing government benefits with personal savings and company retirement plans.

How much will I get from the CPP/QPP?

All Canadians who have worked, either for a company or for themselves, are eligible for CPP/QPP. As an employee, both you and your employer contribute equally to the CPP (or Quebec Pension Plan for Quebec residents) in your name. If you're self-employed, you pay both parts of the contribution yourself.

The amount of your monthly benefits in retirement is based on the contributions made on your behalf during your working years. If you're 65, the maximum monthly amount you could receive from the CPP/QPP in 1998 was $744.79, for a maximum yearly pension of $8,937. The payments are set for life and are fully indexed for inflation. The adjustment for inflation is done once a year in January.

If you qualify for CPP/QPP and are disabled and no longer able to work, you are eligible for a disability pension. The maximum amount is slightly higher than the normal CPP/QPP benefits; in 1998, it was capped at $895.36 a month, or $10,744 a year.

If you're a member of the CPP, you'll receive a statement of your contributions every three years. To find out exactly how much you can expect to get, contact Health and Welfare Canada. (Quebec residents should contact the Quebec Pension Plan.) It's also a good idea to check your statement to make sure that your contributions are being reported correctly.

When you die, your family will continue to benefit from the CPP/QPP. Upon your death, the CPP/QPP will pay a lump-sum death benefit to your estate. In 1998, the maximum amounted to $2,500. If your surviving spouse is under 65 and doesn't have a disability or children to support, he or she will receive 37.5 percent of what your pension was, plus a flat rate of $131.40, up to a monthly maximum of $410.70. If your surviving spouse is 65 or over, his or her payments will be 60 percent of your pension, with a 1998 maximum of $446.87 a month.

In order to get a more precise handle on your CPP benefits, call the Income Securities Program information service at 800-277-9914. Checking your earnings record is a good thing to do every few years, because occasional errors do arise and — surprise — they aren't usually in your favour.

When should I start collecting CPP/QPP?

You *can* start collecting as early as age 60 or as late as 70. But the benefits are permanently reduced by 0.5 percent for every month before age 65 that you start drawing your pension — which works out to 6 percent a year. The reduction is permanent. It continues for the rest of your life. (If you choose to delay receiving your CPP/QPP, your benefits will be increased by the same 0.5 percent a month for each month beyond your 65th birthday.)

If you're single and don't foresee living into your 80s or 90s, start drawing your pension earlier. This allows you to get as much out of the system as possible.

If your family has a history of living well into old age and you yourself are in good health (and you trust the government to continue making the payments), consider delaying your pension benefits.

Further, waiting is usually advisable if you are in a high tax bracket. CPP/QPP benefits are taxable, and by delaying, you may move yourself into a lower tax bracket when you do draw the benefit.

Another consideration is the amount of employment income you're still earning. As of 1998, if you earn more than around $8,900 (the yearly maximum benefits from the plan), you can't collect early.

If you're working and want to start drawing your pension, you can retire, start your pension, and then go back to work. Whether you work or not, no one has to make CPP contributions past the age of 65, so make sure your employer isn't taking them out of your pay cheque if you are working and over 65.

Because you're allowed to choose when to start receiving your benefits, don't expect them to magically appear in your mailbox on your 65th birthday. You must notify Health and Welfare Canada or, for Quebec taxpayers, the Quebec Pension Plan, to let them know when you want your payments to begin. Do this well in advance because it takes a while for the paperwork to work through the system. Two months is the minimum, but six months should ensure that your payments start arriving when you want them to. Completely retroactive payments aren't allowed, so if you apply late or simply forget, you'll just have to lump it.

How much will I get from Old Age Security?

OAS is paid out automatically to you once you reach 65. As long as you have lived in Canada for at least 10 years since the age of 18, you will get something out of Old Age Security. As of July 1998, the maximum monthly payment was $408.78. This amount is adjusted four times a year for inflation. To receive the full amount, you must have lived in Canada for at least ten years leading up to the time you apply. If you were born after July 1, 1952, you have to rack up 40 years of Canadian living after turning 18 to qualify for the full amount.

With a maximum $4,905 a year, you obviously shouldn't take the "Security" part of Old Age Security too seriously. What's more, you may not get to keep all the money that comes to you, thanks to the clawback. You have to start paying back some of the OAS when you file your annual income tax return when your net income passes a certain point. In the 1997 tax year, that point was $54,000. By the time your net income is around $84,000, you won't hold on to a single penny of your OAS benefits. Ouch!

What's the problem with the Canada Pension Plan?

Government pension programs have three built-in problems. First, they were designed in anticipation of ever-rosier economic times. Second, they vastly underestimated how long people would be living by the end of the century. Finally, they were created without accounting for the baby boom and Canada's growing retirement population.

And each individual program is also hobbled further. Old Age Security benefits, for example, are paid out of general government revenues. That puts them immediately on the critical list because the debt our politicians have so wisely bestowed on us is finally forcing them to look for ways to cut public spending. In fact, the thin edge of that particular wedge was introduced back in 1989, when those with higher incomes were required to start paying back some or all of their Old Age Security benefits.

The problem with the CPP and QPP is that, when the systems were created, their designers had no idea how long people would live in retirement. Thanks to medical advances, improved living conditions, and better diets, we're living much longer than people were just a few decades ago. As a result, many of today's retirees get back far more in benefits than they paid into the system.

Another problem is that your contributions aren't held in a special account in your name to be repaid specifically to you when you retire. The government uses the contributions you make today to make pension payments to your neighbours who are already retired. In turn, your CPP/QPP benefits are supposed to come out of the pockets of those who will be working when you're retired, and so on. (This is known as a "pay-as-you-go" plan, though the logic of this name escapes us! Perhaps it should be called "you-pay-as-they-go.")

Baby boomers have thrown a very large wrench into this logic. As the large bulge of the population who make up this infamous group reaches retirement age, the number of people drawing from the plan will swell, while the number of contributors (largely, the baby boomers' children) will have shrunk. Various number crunchers, including Statistics Canada, have already warned that the current system will run out of money in 20 years.

Contribution levels will have to be cranked up, the level of payments will have to be cut back, or the retirement age will have to be increased — or perhaps all three — in the near future, if the pension system is to survive, because the CPP/QPP system will be fed by a relatively small number of workers while supporting large numbers of retirees.

So how should you go about planning your retirement if you can't depend on government-sponsored pensions? Don't cut your calculations close and depend on the government's contributions to your retirement years kicking in at the same age and level they do today.

On the other hand, if your retirement income is extremely low, you may be entitled to a top-up by the Guaranteed Income Supplement, or GIS. The maximum benefit in 1998, if you were single or married to a nonpensioner, was $485.80 a month, or $5,829 a year. The maximum drops to $316 a month for those who are married to pensioners. If you were married to a spouse who was also receiving GIS, your monthly maximum in 1997 was $316.

GIS payments aren't taxed. In addition, depending on where you live, your province may provide an additional low-income supplement.

Note: If you qualify for the maximum from the CPP/QPP and OAS, you will receive $13,842 year. There are two lessons in this. First, yes, you're absolutely right: That isn't a whole heck of a lot to live on! The second point is this: To even earn that much, you would need to have a nest egg of somewhere just shy of $200,000 to supply you with that much income (assuming 3 percent inflation and an 8 percent return). This makes you realize just how much of a pile o' cash you need to save for your retirement.

Personal savings/investments

Money that you save toward retirement can include money under the mattress as well as money in a retirement plan such as an RRSP (see Chapter 9). You may also earmark investments in a nonretirement plan toward your retirement.

Equity in rental real estate can be counted as well. Deciding whether to include the equity in your primary residence (your home) is trickier. If you don't want to count on using this money in retirement (for example, you don't want to sell the house and move away), then don't include it when you tally your stash.

In reality, many people do sell their homes when they retire to move to a cheaper region of the country, to move closer to family, or to downsize to a more manageable household. And increasing numbers of older retirees are tapping their home's equity through reverse mortgages. So you may want to count a portion of your home equity in your total assets for retirement.

Pensions

Pension plans are a benefit offered by some employers — mostly larger organizations and government agencies. Even if your current employer doesn't offer a pension, you may have earned pension benefits through a previous job (if you have become fully eligible for retirement benefits, the accumulated amount is still yours when you leave the company).

Don't neglect nonfinancial preparations for retirement

Investing your money is just one, and not even the most important, aspect of preparing for your retirement. In order to enjoy the lifestyle that your retirement savings will provide you, you need to invest energy into other areas of your life as well.

✔ Few things are more important than your health. Without your health, enjoying the good things in life is hard. Unfortunately, many people aren't motivated to care about their health until after they discover problems. By then, it may be too late.

Although regular exercise, a balanced and nutritional diet, and avoiding substance abuse can't guarantee you a healthful future, they go a long way toward preventing many of the most common causes of death and debilitating disease. Regular medical exams also are important in detecting problems early.

✔ In addition to your physical health, invest in your psychic health. It is well documented that people live longer and are happier and healthier when they have a circle of family and friends around them for support. Unfortunately, as they grow older, many people become more isolated as they lose regular contact with business associates, friends, and family members.

Retirees who are happy seem to be busy and involved in volunteer organizations and in new social circles. They may travel to see old friends or to visit younger relatives who may be too busy to visit them.

Treat retirement life like a bubbly, inviting hot tub. You want to ease yourself in, nice and slow; taking a hasty plunge can take most of the pleasantness out of the experience. Abruptly leaving your job without some sort of plan for spending all that free time is an invitation to boredom and depression. Everyone needs a sense of purpose, a sense of routine. Establishing hobbies, volunteer work, or a sideline business while gradually cutting back your regular work schedule can be a terrific way to ease the transition into retirement.

Lower yourself into the tub slowly. Take some time to get used to the temperature change. Ahhh . . . nice isn't it?

The plans we're referring to are known as *defined-benefit plans*. You qualify for a monthly benefit amount to be paid to you in retirement based on your years of service.

Although each company's plan differs, all plans calculate and pay benefits based on a formula. A typical one might credit you with 1.5 percent of your salary for each year of service (full-time employment). For example, if you work ten years, you earn a monthly benefit worth 15 percent of your monthly salary.

This type of benefit is quite valuable. In the better plans, an employer puts away 5–10 percent of your salary to pay your future pension. What the employer is effectively doing is putting money away in an account for your retirement. This money isn't quoted as part of your salary — it's in addition to your salary. You never see it in your pay cheque and it isn't taxed.

To qualify for pension benefits, you don't have to stay with an employer long enough to receive the 20-year gold watch. Employees of the federal public services and private-sector workers in Ontario, Nova Scotia, PEI, Quebec, and Saskatchewan are now fully *vested* (entitled to receive full benefits based on years of service upon attaining retirement age) after two years of full-time service. In Alberta, British Columbia, Manitoba, and New Brunswick, you must wait five years, and, in Newfoundland, ten.

Defined-benefit pension plans are becoming rarer for two reasons:

- First, they're very costly for employers to maintain. Many employees don't understand how these plans work and why they're so valuable, so companies don't get mileage out of their expenditures here — employees don't see the money, so they don't appreciate how generous the company is.

- Second, most of the new jobs being generated in the Canadian economy are with small companies that typically don't offer these types of plans.

More and more employers are offering plans in which the amount of pension you'll receive is determined by how much you and your employer contribute to the plan. Known as *defined-contribution plans,* these plans allow you to save toward your retirement at your own expense, typically adding your own money to money contributed on your behalf by your employer. Thus, more of the burden and responsibility for saving for retirement falls on your shoulders. You need to be educated about how these plans work.

Employers offering defined-contribution plans should educate employees about how to save by using these plans. Defined-contribution plans transfer much of the burden of planning for retirement from the employer to the employee. Most people are ill-equipped to know how much to save and how to invest the money. The retirement planning worksheet in the next section should help.

Group RRSPs

A group RRSP works much like a money purchase pension plan. Instead of contributions going into a pension plan, however, the money goes into individual RRSPs administered by your employer.

Group RRSPs have a number of benefits. You can choose how much you want to contribute, although you're still limited to the maximums for individual RRSP contributions. (See Chapter 9 for details.) Your employer sets up automatic payroll deductions from your pay cheque. Not only is this a relatively painless way to make regular contributions, but the amount of tax deducted from your pay is reduced to give you an immediate benefit from your tax-sheltered contributions. (Normally, you have to wait until late spring of the following year to receive your tax benefits from RRSP contributions.) Some employers will also make contributions to your plan on your behalf.

Another important benefit of group RRSPs is that they give you a good deal of control over how your savings are invested. Most employers offer a choice of mutual funds, usually from a specific mutual fund company, as well as fixed-interest options such as GICs. Others allow you a wider range of options.

Deferred profit-sharing plans

As their name suggests, deferred profit-sharing plans, or *DPSPs,* are savings accounts built up from your employer's profits. DPSPs are particularly popular with small companies because they save money in years in which the company has not fared well by decreasing or eliminating contributions in that year.

Only your employer can contribute to a DPSP — you aren't allowed to make any contributions. Your employer gets a tax write-off for its contributions, and the money is allowed to grow tax free as long as it's in the plan. The amount of money put away in your name depends on the company's profits and your salary level, position, and the length of time you've been with the company.

DPSPs offer you more freedom than a registered pension plan because you're allowed to withdraw the money before you hit a specified retirement age. You have to pay income tax on any withdrawals, however, unless you transfer the money directly into an RRSP or a company pension plan.

Retirement planning worksheet

After you tour through the components of your future retirement income, we'd like you to take a shot at tallying where you stand in terms of retirement preparations. Don't be afraid to do this exercise — it isn't difficult, and you may be surprised that you're not in such bad shape. If you find that you're behind in saving for retirement, we provide specific ideas for how to play catch-up.

Note: The following worksheet (Table 8-1 and the Growth Multiplier Minitable) assumes that you'll retire at age 66 and that your investments will produce an annual rate of return that's 4 percent per year higher than the rate of inflation (for example, if inflation averages 3 percent, this table assumes you'll earn 7 percent per year on your investments).

Table 8-1	Retirement Planning Worksheet
1. Annual retirement income needed in today's dollar (see earlier in this chapter)	$ _____ / year
2. Annual CPP/QPP, OAS, and GIS	– $ _____ / year
3. Annual pension benefits (ask your benefits department). Multiply by .60 if your pension won't increase with inflation during retirement.	– $ _____ / year
4. Annual retirement income needed from personal savings (subtract lines 2 and 3 from line 1)	= $ _____ / year
5. Savings needed to retire at age 66 (multiply line 4 by 15)	$ _____
6. Value of current retirement savings	$ _____
7. Value of current retirement savings at retirement (multiply line 6 by Growth Multiplier in following minitable)	$ _____
8. Amount you still need to save (line 5 minus line 7)	$ _____
9. Amount you need to save per month (multiply line 8 by Savings Factor in following minitable)	$ _____ / month

To get a more precise handle on where you stand in terms of retirement planning, especially if you'd like to retire earlier than your mid-60s, many financial institutions distribute retirement planning booklets. We also recommend retirement planning software in Chapter 22 that can save you a great deal of number crunching.

Growth Multiplier Minitable		
Your Current Age	*Growth Multiplier*	*Savings Factor*
26	4.8	.001
28	4.4	.001
30	4.1	.001
32	3.8	.001

Your Current Age	Growth Multiplier	Savings Factor
34	3.5	.001
36	3.2	.001
38	3.0	.002
40	2.8	.002
42	2.6	.002
44	2.4	.002
46	2.2	.003
48	2.0	.003
50	1.9	.004
52	1.7	.005
54	1.6	.006
56	1.5	.007
58	1.4	.009
60	1.3	.013
62	1.2	.020
64	1.1	.041

How to make up for lost time

If the amount that you need to save per month to reach your goal seems frightening, don't despair. All is not lost. In fact, there are some tried-and-true ways to make up for lost time. Saving money doesn't have as much sex appeal as spending it does, so don't expect much help or praise from your friends and neighbours. But your mother will think she brought you up well, and you'll have the satisfaction of knowing that you're doing the right thing, unless you want to work for the rest of your life.

- ✔ **Question your spending.** There are only two ways to boost your savings: Earn more money or cut your spending (or do both). Most people don't spend their money nearly as thoughtfully as they earn it. Refer to Chapter 6 for spending reduction suggestions and strategies.

- ✔ **Be more realistic about your retirement age.** If you extend the age at which you plan to retire, you get a double financial benefit. You're earning and saving money for more years and spending your nest egg over fewer years. Of course, if your job is making you crazy, this option may not be too appealing. Try to find work that makes you happy and that provides income now and consider working, at least part time, during the years typically considered the retirement years.

✔ **Use home equity.** Psychologically, the prospect of tapping the cash in your home can be troubling. After getting together the down payment, you probably worked for many years to pay off that sucker. You're delighted not to have to mail a mortgage payment to the bank anymore. You've been released from that particular prison. But what's the use of owning a house free of mortgage debt when you have no cash? All that money tied up in the house can help to increase your standard of living in retirement.

You can tap your home's equity in a number of ways. You can sell your home and either move to a lower-cost property or rent. Any capital gains aren't taxed as long as you're selling your primary residence. Another option is a *reverse mortgage* — where you get a monthly income cheque as you build a loan balance against the value of your home. The loan is paid when your home is finally sold (see Chapter 16 for more information about reverse mortgages).

✔ **Get focused on your investment returns.** The faster the rate at which your money grows and compounds, the less you need to save each year to reach your goals. Earning just a few extra percentage points per year on your investments can dramatically slash the amount you need to save. The younger you are, the more powerful the effect.

For example, if you're in your mid-30s and your investments appreciate 6 percent per year faster than the rate of inflation rather than 4 percent, the amount you need to save each month to reach your retirement goals drops by about 40 percent!

✔ **Turn a hobby into supplemental retirement income.** Even if you've earned a living in the same career over many decades, you have skills that are portable and can be put to profitable use. Pick something you enjoy and are good at. Go to the library and do some research on how to market your services and wares. Remember, as people get busier, more specialized services are being created to support their hectic lives. A demand for quality, homemade goods of all varieties also exists. Be creative! You never know — you may wind up on the cover of some business magazine.

✔ **Invest in a tax-wise way.** A free way to boost the effective rate of return on your investments without taking on additional risk is to insulate more of your money from taxation. Many people who are able to save money don't do so in a way that minimizes their taxes.

We don't want to sound like a broken record, but direct your savings into a tax-favoured RRSP or other retirement plan. You get an immediate tax deduction for your contribution. For a typical person, a quarter or more of your contribution represents money you would have had to pay in federal and provincial taxes. This money gets to work for you, rather than for the government, in the years ahead. Plus, the money compounds over the years without taxation.

As for money outside of tax-sheltered retirement plans, if you're in a relatively high tax bracket, you may earn more by investing in tax-favoured investments and other vehicles that don't make a great deal of taxable distributions. (Chapter 14 discusses these investments in detail.)

✓ **Take a look at jobs that offer retirement plans.** When you're evaluating employers, cash is usually king. But having access to a retirement savings plan is a valuable benefit. Even more beneficial is a pension plan that pays you a monthly retirement benefit based on your years of service (a completely pain-free way to plan for retirement). If you're lucky enough to have choices, check out these plans when considering a job offer.

✓ **Think about inheritances.** While we don't endorse knocking off rich relatives whom you don't care for, people do die every day, and their estates (large or small) typically go to their children or grandchildren. Although you should never count on an inheritance to support your retirement, in reality, you may inherit money someday. If you want to see what impact an inheritance has on your retirement calculations, simply add the amount (use a conservative estimate) that you expect to inherit to your current total savings in Table 8-1.

Common objections to saving in RRSPs and other retirement plans

Despite all the great tax benefits of saving in RRSPs and other retirement plans, many people aren't jumping at the opportunity to take advantage of them. The following sections describe the objections to contributing to tax-favoured plans that we hear most frequently. Some of these objections can be overcome; others are legitimate excuses.

Retirement's a long way away

When you're in your 20s or 30s, age 65 seems like the distant future. For many people, it's not until middle age that some warning bells start to stimulate thoughts about one's golden years.

Delaying the age at which you start to sock money away is usually a financial mistake. The sooner you start to save, the less painful it is to save each year because your contributions have more years to compound. Each decade you delay approximately doubles the percentage of your earnings you should save to meet your goals. For example, if saving 5 percent per year in your early 20s would get you to your retirement goal, waiting until your 30s may mean socking away 10 percent; 40s, 20 percent; and so on.

When should you start saving toward retirement? Ideally, you should start saving a small portion of your employment earnings with your very first pay cheque. Start your kids' saving habits when they're young!

Only losers who don't know how to have fun save for retirement

Some people really believe this statement. But we also know losers who don't save for retirement and still don't know how to have a good time. This attitude is just a rationalization. The reality is that if you manage your finances efficiently and start working toward your goals sooner, you can spend more and have more fun in the long run. Besides, who says spending all your money is the only way to have fun?

There are greener investment pastures elsewhere

Real estate is a good example. Some people find retirement plans boring and believe that they can get a better return in the real estate market. Rental real estate can appreciate in value and produce increasing rental income over the years. Investing in real estate is a legitimate reason for not maximizing retirement plan contributions.

However, although real estate provides some tax breaks, consider its drawbacks:

- First, while you accumulate the down payment, you may pay higher income taxes if you're sacrificing contributions to retirement plans that are tax-deductible.

- Second, rental real estate produces income that is taxable and is added to all your other income during the year; it may even push you into a higher tax bracket.

In an RRSP or other retirement plan, the earnings continue to compound without taxation, and you decide when you want to start drawing on the money.

There may be a way for you to have your cake and eat it, too. Many types of investments — stocks, bonds, mutual funds, precious metals, and even real estate — can be held in retirement plans. (See Chapter 13 for more details.)

I have no money left over to save

People who don't save enough and who don't take advantage of the great tax savings that come with retirement plans most often use this excuse. In a very real sense, the extra taxes that you pay because you can't afford RRSPs or other retirement plan contributions are an additional cost of overspending today. So if you can reduce your expenditures (refer to Chapter 6), you can more easily meet your retirement goals. You'll have more money to contribute to retirement plans, and you'll save on your taxes to boot!

In some cases, people have a pile of money not earmarked for specific future needs that's invested outside of tax-sheltered retirement plans. They may use all their monthly employment income to meet their ongoing living expenses. As a result, they believe they can't afford to save in a retirement plan.

If you think this way, you're compartmentalizing your finances. Look at the big picture. For example, what if you contribute $300 per month to your tax-deductible retirement plan? Suppose that doing so reduces your taxes by $100 and thus really costs you only $200 a month. You then can take $100 from your savings outside the retirement plan and put it toward living expenses.

What you're effectively doing is transferring your savings from an outside retirement plan to inside an RRSP or other retirement plan. You're not really saving new money, but you're getting terrific tax savings by playing this perfectly legal investing shell game. Just be careful not to drain your emergency savings reserve down too far.

I love my job and will work forever

Are you one of those people who loves his or her work? You don't plan to retire and therefore don't need to amass a pile of money to live on for 20-plus years? If so, you can get away with saving a lot less than your eager-to-retire friends. You may not, however, be *able* to work at your current job forever. What if you lose your job? What if something happens to your health? You can't assume that you will always be able to work — plan ahead for these what-ifs.

I've saved enough already

Congratulations! This is the single best excuse for not saving more for retirement. If you have a lot of money outside of tax-sheltered retirement plans, you may want to contribute to retirement plans anyway for the tax deductions.

Chapter 9

Registered Retirement Savings Plans (RRSPs)

In This Chapter

▶ The benefits of RRSPs

▶ Tax benefits explained

▶ How your RRSP can make you a millionaire

▶ Strategies to boost your contributions

▶ Ways to collapse (close out) your plan

RRSPs — Registered Retirement Savings Plans — are the single most talked-about financial product for Canadians. Especially during the RRSP contribution season — January and February — you can't escape the pleadings, entreaties, and near-threats to put money into an RRSP that come from banks, fund companies, financial "experts," and the media.

Although they often have their own self-interests at heart, the advice is some of the best you'll come across. Putting money into an RRSP is simply the best, easiest, and most effective way to save for your retirement — and reduce your tax bill.

What Is an RRSP?

The most important (if somewhat bland) word in the RRSP mouthful is *Registered.* That word means you cut a deal with the government. And believe it or not, you come out ahead.

By "registering" your retirement savings plan with the government, you agree to put money away for your retirement and not touch it until that time. In return, the government gives you two valuable benefits:

✔ **An immediate tax deduction.** Money that you contribute to your RRSP is deductible from your taxable income. In other words, any income that you contribute to your savings plan is not taxed.

✔ **Tax-deferred growth.** The government lets the savings in your RRSP grow tax free. Any profits your RRSP investments earn are not taxable (until you collapse your plan and withdraw the funds).

The combined benefits of tax-deductible contributions and tax-deferred growth combine to supercharge your retirement savings. Here's a look at the powerful impact they can have on your ability to save for the future.

Government-subsidized contributions

By agreeing not to tax any income that you put into your retirement savings plan, the government in essence subsidizes your contributions. Suppose that you're in a 50 percent tax bracket, which means that the government takes 50 cents of the last dollar you earn. If you contribute $5,000 to your RRSP, you save yourself $2,500 in tax. So the *real* out-of-pocket cost of a $5,000 contribution is only $2,500. Looked at another way, you can choose to invest $2,500 outside your RRSP, or you can contribute $5,000 to your plan. As you can see in Table 9-1, the tax savings from contributing to an RRSP are substantial, regardless of your tax bracket.

Table 9-1	Short-Term Benefits of Tax-Deductible RRSP Contributions			
Where	*Investment*	*Tax Rate*	*Tax Reduction*	*Net Cost*
Outside RRSP	$5,000	All	$0	$5,000
Inside RRSP	$5,000	27%	$1,350	$3,650
Inside RRSP	$5,000	41%	$2,050	$2,950
Inside RRSP	$5,000	50%	$2,500	$2,500

The benefits of tax-deductible contributions increase over time. Suppose that you're 35 and invest $5,000 of your salary this year outside an RRSP. Assuming that you're in a 40 percent tax bracket, Revenue Canada would first take $2,000 in tax, leaving you with $3,000. You invest that $3,000 in a mutual fund that earns a 10 percent compound return. After 30 years, you would have amassed a tidy $52,000. (This doesn't take into account the taxes you would likely have to pay each year on the distribution of capital gains, dividends, and interest, which would further reduce your average compound return outside an RRSP.)

But what if you had first contributed that money to your RRSP? Because Revenue Canada doesn't take any tax off your contributions, you can invest the full $5,000. Right away, that puts you $2,000 ahead. (In the real world, of course, you would have had the tax already taken off your income as it was earned. But you would receive a $2,000 tax rebate for your $5,000 contribution, so, at the end of the day, the real cost is only $3,000.)

If you invest that $5,000 in the same mutual fund inside an RRSP earning an average 10 percent compound return for 30 years, you're left with $87,000, or almost $35,000 more than you would have if you had put the money in a mutual fund. Table 9-2 shows just how valuable a tax-sheltered RRSP contribution can be to the long-term growth of your savings.

Table 9-2 Long-Term Payoff of Tax-Favoured RRSP Contributions			
Where	*Savings*	*Available for Investment*	*Value in 30 Years (with 10 percent growth)*
Inside RRSP	$5,000	$5,000	$87,000
Outside RRSP	$5,000	$3,000	$52,000

As Table 9-2 demonstrates, the message is simple: The more money you invest to begin with, the more money you end up with for any given investment. And the best way to increase the amount of funds working for you is to use the tax break the government gives you for investing inside your RRSP.

Tax-free compound growth

The second booster rocket that can put your RRSP into orbit is *tax-free compound growth*. If you put your money into an RRSP, any profits you earn with that money aren't taxed until you take the money out of your plan. Over time, the tax-free compounding leads to faster and faster growth of your retirement savings plan.

Tax-free compound growth occurs when interest and earnings on investments aren't taxed, so the full value is added to the original amount. This new, larger amount then earns further gains, which again are added to, or compounded with, your investments. Over time, this compounding leads to exponential growth. Just how well does compound growth work? A good rule to remember is that an investment that earns 10 percent compound growth annually will double about every seven years.

How to Maximize Your RRSP Savings

You need only to keep two basic rules in mind, and your RRSP will turn out to be a real moneymaker!

> ✔ **Begin contributing as early as you can in life.**
>
> ✔ **Maximize the return of your RRSP.**

There. That's it. If you follow these two basic rules, you pretty much take care of your RRSP. Then you can sit back and, except for an occasional tweak here and a shift there, watch as your RRSP all but *prints* money for you.

Start an RRSP when you're young

The earlier you start investing in an RRSP, the greater its final value will be. That's simple enough. But the real value in starting as early in life as possible is not simply the total amount of the extra contributions you manage to put in. The longer you have money in an RRSP, the more time your savings have to compound.

Take someone who starts an RRSP when she is 28, making annual $2,000 contributions each year until she's 65. If she puts her money into a family of mutual funds that earns an average return of 10 percent, the total accumulation would be about $660,000.

But that same amount could essentially have been accumulated if she had begun putting $2,000 a year into an RRSP when she was 21 — and only contributed for seven years total (see Table 9-3). The younger you are, the less money it takes to ring up some big profits in your plan. Even if you're just 25 and have only $1,000 to spare, put it in an RRSP! If you earn an average 10 percent a year, you'll have an extra $45,000 in your plan when you retire at 65. Just like the Concorde, your RRSP needs a good, long runway to really build up some steam. But when it takes off, the sky is the limit.

Table 9-3	The Money-Earning Potential of Starting an RRSP When You're Young		
Age $2,000 Contributions Begun	**Age Ended**	**Total Years**	**Final Value at Age 65**
21	27	7	$664,000
28	65	37	$660,000

Note: Table 9-3 assumes a 10 percent annual rate of return.

Examples like the previous one are commonly used to sell the benefits of putting money into an RRSP from an early age. The problem is that if you aren't young, these examples can be unsettling. If you didn't find out about the benefits of RRSPs when you were young or didn't have money to contribute, you likely find it dispiriting to realize the tax savings and compound growth you missed out on. Whatever you do, don't let that stop you from taking action today.

To rework that old cliché, today is the first day of the rest of your financial life. Even if you have only a few years of contributing money to an RRSP remaining, you can still enjoy the benefits of tax-free contributions and tax-deferred growth and enhance the retirement savings you end up with.

Maximizing your returns

Every February, many people dash around trying get their RRSP contribution invested before the deadline. Rushed contributions, however, are usually made without considering investment options. Often, the only thing on your mind is what you're going to do when your tax rebate arrives in the mail. In this case, you're probably better off putting your money into a money market mutual fund or other cashlike investment, and then moving your money into better-performing investments when you have the time and energy to consider your options. By carefully assessing your RRSP investments, you can greatly boost the value of your plan, which translates directly into thousands of dollars more income to live on during retirement.

When a bargain isn't a bargain

Looking at the benefits of an RRSP contribution is often an excellent way to stem your appetite for a large expense that you may desperately want, but not necessarily need. Say, for example, that you were able to put $6,000 every year into your RRSP and earned an average return of 9 percent. After 30 years, you would have accumulated an impressive $817,845.

But what if you only put in $4,500 annually, using the extra $1,500 to give yourself a week in the sun? Your total would still be a respectable $613,384. But look at it another way. Indulging yourself a little today will cost you over $200,000 on your retirement. Are your "sunfests" really worth having $200,000 less when you retire?

Do you find it tough to come up with anywhere near your maximum allowable contribution when the RRSP deadline comes around? Try an automatic deduction plan. You can tell your financial institution or RRSP holder to take a certain amount out of your bank account every few weeks — for example, when your pay cheque comes in. You likely won't miss the money, and you'll be surprised at how much more you can put away.

Choosing appropriate investments is critical in maximizing the growth of your RRSP. And the more years you have before you have to collapse your plan, the larger the impact of boosting your returns by even just 1 or 2 percent.

Say you contribute $5,000 a year to your plan for 30 years, and you earn an average return of 8 percent. The final value of your plan would be just over $566,000.

But consider the results if you had taken a little more time in choosing your RRSP investments, and you had managed to earn 9 percent a year — just 1 percent more? In 30 years' time, your plan would be worth more than $681,000.

By improving your fund's performance by only 1 percent, you would end up with an extra $115,000! (See Table 9-4.)

Table 9-4	The Pay-Off from Investing Wisely: How a $5,000 Annual Contribution Will Grow	
	Value at growth rate of . . .	
Years	8%	9%
5	$29,333	$29,924
10	$72,433	$75,965
30	$566,416	$681,538

Types of RRSPs

You can get an RRSP from just about any bank, trust company, brokerage house, insurance company, credit union, or mutual fund company. An RRSP contribution is almost the same as making a regular investment with any of these companies. When you specify that your money is to go into an RRSP, however, you get a tax receipt that gives you a tax break on your contributions. In turn, you agree to follow the RRSP rules.

There are two general types of RRSPs. The first are *guaranteed plans,* in which you invest your money in investments where your principal is protected, such as Guaranteed Investment Certificates (GICs) and money market funds. When you do so, you lend your money to a bank or other financial institution in return for regular interest payments. Guaranteed plans pay fixed returns, and your money, if invested in GICs, is usually protected by the CDIC's deposit protection.

The second basic type of RRSP is an investment in mutual funds. There are two benefits to mutual fund RRSPs. First, you can invest in stocks and bonds, which over the long haul will handily beat the returns from guaranteed investments. Second, if you set up an RRSP with a mutual fund company, you can diversify your savings by putting them into several different types of funds with the same company. Mutual fund companies usually charge an annual trustee fee ranging from $25 to $50 a year for RRSP accounts.

Can I have more than one plan?

You aren't limited to a specific number of RRSPs. You could, for example, open up a handful of RRSPs, each investing in different types of fixed-income securities or mutual funds, with different companies. There are drawbacks to having several plans, however. The paperwork can be burdensome, and it can become a real chore to follow your investments. If you invest with a number of different mutual fund companies, the trustee fees can start to add up. Finally, if you have some of your investments in foreign securities, it can be difficult to ensure that you haven't exceeded the maximum allowable foreign holdings (see the sidebar "International investing and your RRSP" later in this chapter).

Self-directed RRSPs

Self-directed plans allow you to invest in a wider range of securities. In addition to GICs and mutual funds, you can invest in individual stocks and bonds, and a wide range of other securities.

Because you have such a choice of investment options, a self-directed plan has the greatest potential for returns. By the same token, though, there is considerable risk attached to a self-directed RRSP. Unlike a mutual fund RRSP, for example, nobody else watches over your money. Unless you have the time and inclination to regularly monitor your savings, you're better off leaving self-directed plans to more sophisticated investors.

You can set up a self-directed plan with most investment dealers and discount brokerages. These companies generally charge an annual fee of around $100. Some institutions are willing to reduce or eliminate their fees for self-directed plans. The discount brokerages run by the big banks and trust companies often waive the first year fee for new plans. If you do have to pay a fee, make sure that you pay it out of your regular savings, not out of the funds in your plan.

Figuring Out Your Contribution

As long as you're age 69 years or younger and have received income from a job or from running a business or even net rental income — that is, as long as you've received *earned income* — you usually can contribute to an RRSP. There is no minimum age requirement. Even a child can have an RRSP, as long as he or she has earned income.

Contribution limits

The most you can contribute to your RRSP in any year is 18 percent of your earned income from the previous year, up to certain maximum amounts. In addition, if you're a member of a company pension plan or a deferred profit sharing plan, that membership further reduces the amount you can shelter in your plan.

In the spring or summer of each year, Revenue Canada sends all taxpayers a Notice of Assessment for the previous year. Your contribution limit for the current year is included on the statement. For example, if you've filed your 1998 tax return, you'll find your allowable contribution for 1999 on your assessment statement, which you should have received in the first half of 1999.

It's important to review your allowable maximum contribution to ensure that the government has come up with the right figure. If Revenue Canada is too high and you overcontribute, you may risk having to pay a penalty. If its figure is too low, your plan will suffer because you won't have maximized your contribution.

International investing and your RRSP

The government wants to keep you investing in Canada, so it limits how much of your RRSP funds can be invested in non-Canadian securities. The maximum you can have invested in non-Canadian assets is 20 percent, based on their cost, or *book value*. If you have a self-directed plan, you're responsible for ensuring that you don't exceed the limit. If you do go over the maximum, a 1 percent per month tax is levied against any amount over the allowable limit.

One way to diversify your RRSP investments internationally without worrying about exceeding the limit is to invest in funds that maintain at least 80 percent of their investments in Canada and still put money into international securities. These funds qualify as 100 percent Canadian content and aren't taken into account when assessing how much "foreign" content you have in your RRSP. All companies will tell you which of their funds are RRSP eligible.

The contribution deadline

For any given tax year, you can make a contribution anytime up to — and including — the 60th day in the next year. The last day you're allowed to contribute for the 1999 tax year, for example, is March 1, 2000. You could have contributed as early as January 1, 1999, of course.

The only positive thing that can be said about leaving your contribution to the last minute is that it's probably good for an adrenaline rush. But consider this: If you plan ahead and make your contributions well in advance, you'll likely earn enough in extra interest over the years to pay for hours of heart-stopping bungee jumping and skydiving when you retire.

One other note: In the year you turn age 69, you must contribute to your plan before December 31.

In the next section, a simple guide (as simple as we could make it) helps you determine your allowable contribution. If you want, you can skip over this part and pick up again at the "RRSP withdrawals" section. You can then come back to review the following information when you get down to the nitty-gritty of working out your RRSP contribution.

Calculating your allowable contribution

To begin with, realize that the government puts absolute maximums on how much people, regardless of their situations, can contribute each year (see Table 9-5).

Table 9-5	Maximum RRSP Contributions		
Tax Year	*RRSP Limit*	*Min. Earned Income Req'd*	*From Year*
1998-2003	$13,500	$75,000	Previous year
2004	$14,500	$80,556	2003
2005	$15,500	$86,111	2004
After 2005	Indexed from 2005 limits		

If your company has a pension plan, your maximum RRSP contribution limit is less than those listed here (see upcoming sections).

A second cap on your contributions is that, for any year, you can contribute only up to 18 percent of your earned income from the *preceding* year.

Now, you probably quite naturally believe that when it comes to your income, you've earned *all* of it. But wouldn't you know it? The government has other ideas. When it taxes your income, Revenue Canada generally wants a piece of the action — all the action. But in determining what qualifies as your "earned income," certain types of earnings are excluded.

Earned income includes only income sources such as these:

- Salary
- Bonuses and commissions
- Net business income
- Any retiring allowances
- Alimony and maintenance payments
- Unemployment benefits
- Net rental income
- Royalties
- Disability pension received under the Canada and Quebec Pension Plans
- Some types of taxable employment incomes, including disability and sick benefits

Revenue Canada's logic (who says contradictions in terms aren't fun?) is that these are the sorts of income that usually stop coming in when you retire. So Ottawa gives you a tax break only on income saved for retirement from these sources.

So what *is* excluded from earned income?

- Pension benefits
- Most investment income
- Family allowance and child tax credit payments
- Unemployment insurance payments
- Adult training allowances
- Money from an income-averaging annuity

If you only have income from these sources, you can't make an RRSP contribution.

If you don't have a company pension plan, the most you can contribute in any given year, then, is the lowest of

 ✔ The annual maximum amount for that year, or

 ✔ 18 percent of your earned income in the previous year

(If no one in your family has a company pension plan, you can skip this section. Those with plans, please stay with the program.)

But if you *are* a member of a pension plan or deferred profit-sharing plan (DPSP), the government further scales back the amount it lets you contribute. The thinking is that because you have alternative sources of retirement income, you shouldn't get the full tax break allotted to people without pensions. The government reduces your otherwise maximum allowable contribution by the value attributed for the contributions that both you and your employer make to your pension or deferred profit-sharing plan. This figure is called your *pension adjustment*, or PA Factor. Just how that figure is arrived at depends on the type of plan you belong to.

Your pension adjustment is then subtracted from 18 percent of your earned income to arrive at your RRSP limit. Your pension adjustment is listed in Box 52 of your T4 slip, which you should receive from your employer before the end of every February. In general, the higher your pension, the larger your pension adjustment and the lower your maximum allowable contribution.

If you belong to a defined benefit pension plan

Under a defined benefit pension plan, the amount you receive when you retire is based upon your years of service and your income level. If you belong to this kind of plan, your pension adjustment (PA Factor) is based on a calculation of the future value attributed to your pension of your previous year of employment. Your maximum contribution for 1998, for example, was 18 percent of your 1997 earned income to a maximum of $13,500, less your 1997 PA Factor.

If you belong to a money-purchase pension plan

Your pension adjustment under this kind of pension plan is the total combined amount put into your pension by both you and your employer for the previous year. Your maximum contribution for 1998, for example, was 18 percent of your 1997 earned income to a maximum of $13,500, less all the 1997 pension contributions (PA Factor).

If you belong to a deferred profit sharing plan

If your employer contributes money to a deferred profit sharing plan on your behalf, your pension adjustment equals the total of the contributions made (up to the maximum allowable DPSP contribution) for the previous year. For example, your 1998 maximum was 18 percent of your 1997 earned income to a maximum of $13,500, minus your 1997 PA Factor.

Calendars and calculators

Figuring out just what you're permitted to contribute to an RRSP can get confusing, especially if you're a member of a company pension plan. On top of the calculations, you can also get lost by the way your numbers work back and forth between years. Here's an example to help you get through the maze.

Say you're trying to work out your allowable contribution for 1999. Your 1998 earned income was $47,000. Eighteen percent of that is $8,460, well below the maximum allowed of $13,500.

Next, to find your pension adjustment, you look at your 1998 T4 slip (or the Notice of Assessment you got in the mail in the late spring or summer of 1999, after you filed your 1998 tax return). Your 1998 T4 slip tells you that your 1998 PA Factor is $3,900; you then subtract that figure from $8,460. The result, $4,560, is your maximum contribution for 1999, which you can contribute up to March 1, 2000, for a deduction on your 1999 tax return.

Note: Retroactive improvement of your pension benefits may further reduce your RRSP limit. In such cases, the amount you can contribute is decreased by a *past service pension adjustment,* which is called (surprise, surprise) a PSPA.

RRSP withdrawals

You can take money out of your RRSP whenever you like, but the government will want to collect the taxes it had earlier foregone on your contributions.

When you withdraw money from your RRSP, the plan holder is required to withhold taxes on your withdrawals. The rates in all provinces (except Quebec) are 10 percent on amounts up to $5,000, 20 percent on the next $10,000, and 30 percent on withdrawals of over $15,000. In Quebec, the withholding rates are 25 percent of amounts up to $5,000, 33 percent on withdrawals up to $10,000, and 38 percent on withdrawals of $15,000 and higher.

(When you do your income tax return, you have to declare your withdrawals as income in the year you took the money out of your plan. For most people, that will mean an additional tax bill because the withholding rates in most cases are lower than the marginal tax rate.)

The withholding tax rates are calculated on each individual withdrawal. If you do need to get at your RRSP funds, take out separate withdrawals of no more than $5,000 each time to minimize the amount of withholding tax.

Collapsing (Closing) Your Plan

You must close out or *mature* your plan by the end of the year in which you turn 69. You can make a final contribution to your RRSP in your last year.

However, instead of having 60 days into the next year to get your money in, the deadline for your final contribution is December 31.

Deciding just when to fold your plan and what to do with your funds are two of the most important financial decisions you'll ever make. Time your moves correctly and make some astute choices, and you'll find you have a much larger financial comfort zone than you expected. However, if you make your decisions at the last minute without doing your homework, you may find that your lack of attention costs you plenty in terms of a lower standard of living.

You're allowed to close out your RRSP earlier than the year in which you celebrate your 69th birthday, but your best strategy usually is to leave your RRSP alone for as long as you're allowed. This is almost always the case if you decide to choose a *Registered Retirement Income Fund* (RRIF). If you choose to go the *annuity* route, collapsing your plan a year or two early can make sense. If interest rates are relatively high, you can lock in a higher-than-average return.

Your Three RRSP Maturity Options

When you close your plan, you have three basic choices. You can simply cash out — take all the money right out of your RRSP and do what you will with it. If you do, Revenue Canada will treat the sum total of your plan as taxable income in that year. The resulting tax bill will lop off anywhere from one-third to half of your retirement savings, right then and there.

Far more practical is using the funds to buy an annuity by handing over your money to a financial institution (usually an insurance company), which then pays out regular sums to you for a period of time that you choose. This can be as short as ten years or as long as the rest of your life.

The third, and often best, choice is to convert your RRSP into another sort of registered plan that continues to enjoy tax-deferred compounding. The only condition of these accounts, called Registered Retirement Income Funds (or RRIFs), is that you take out a certain minimum amount every year.

You aren't limited to choosing one of these three options. You can choose to split your RRSP funds and use two or even all three of these different strategies.

In order to make the right decision for your individual circumstances, you have to consider a lot more than simply how much cash flow each option will bring in. Each strategy has its own specific tax burden and a different schedule on when those tax bills will come due to consider. Further, you need to decide how much control you want to have over how your funds are invested, and whether you want to have access to your funds. Finally, each option offers different levels of estate or survivorship protections.

Registered Retirement Income Funds (RRIFs)

An RRIF allows your money to grow tax deferred, and you can invest your funds in most of the eligible RRSP investments, from money market funds to individual stocks. You can redirect or shift your investments when you want. And, as with an RRSP, you can have one, two, or a handful of different RRIFs. The only difference between an RRIF and an RRSP is that you aren't allowed to put any money into your RRIF. Instead, you're required to take out a certain minimum amount each year.

These payments must start the year after you set up your RRIF. You can choose monthly, quarterly, semi-annual, or annual payments. What's more, you don't have to take your payments in cash. You can move any investment out of your RRIF without selling it. However, you must pay tax on the fair market value at the time of the withdrawal, just as if it had been taken out as income.

The main benefit of an RRIF is that you continue to have control over how and where your money is invested. This control gives you the best chance of earning healthier returns on your money. In particular, it allows you to invest in equities and bonds.

RRIFs also let you have a say about how much income you have. As long as you withdraw the required minimums, you can take out as little or as much as you wish in any given year. If you suddenly come into some money, you can leave your RRIF essentially untouched and keep ringing up tax-free growth. If you have a medical emergency, you can quickly get your hands on as much as you need at the time.

RRIFs are usually a good choice if you

- ✔ Enjoy managing your money
- ✔ Have an indexed company pension plan that guarantees you a basic level of income
- ✔ Don't immediately need to start drawing on your funds

Another advantage of RRIFs is that you can convert them to an annuity at any time, whereas an annuity is for life: Once you sign up for an annuity, there's no changing your mind. Further, with an RRIF you have a lot more control over what happens to your money at your death.

Minimum RRIF withdrawals

Before 1993, you were required to have withdrawn all your money from your RRIF by the time you were 90. The rules changed in 1992 to allow you to maintain your RRIF as long as you live. If you opened an RRIF before 1993, your minimum withdrawals are determined by the pre-1993 rules until you hit 78 or, if you have a younger spouse, when he or she turns 78.

Your minimum withdrawals are a percentage of the market value of your RRIF at the end of the previous year. The requirement for each year is determined by your age on January 1 of that year.

Age	RRIF opened before 1993	RRIF opened 1993 and later
69	4.76%	4.76%
70	5.00%	5.00%
71	5.26%	7.38%
72	5.56%	7.48%
73	5.88%	7.59%
74	6.25%	7.71%
75	6.67%	7.85%
76	7.14%	7.99%
77	7.69%	8.15%
78	8.33%	8.33%
79	8.53%	8.53%
80	8.75%	8.75%
81	8.99%	8.99%
82	9.27%	9.27%
83	9.58%	9.58%
84	9.93%	9.93%
85	10.33%	10.33%
86	10.79%	10.79%
87	11.33%	11.33%
88	11.96%	11.96%
89	12.71%	12.71%
90	13.62%	13.62%
91	14.73%	14.73%
92	16.12%	16.12%
93	17.92%	17.92%
94 and up	20.00%	20.00%

Annuities

When you use your RRSP funds to buy an annuity, you transfer your RRSP funds to over to a financial institution (usually an insurance company), which then pays them back to you a little bit at a time. You don't pay tax on any RRSP funds at the time you turn into an annuity. The regular payments from the annuity, though, are taxable and treated by Revenue Canada as "pension" income. If you have no other pension income, up to $1,000 of the annuity payments will qualify for the Pension Income Tax Credit.

The biggest decision when buying an annuity is the length of time you want your payments to run for. One option is to pick a specific number of years, such as 5, 10, or 20. At the end of the specific time, your payments end and your annuity is fully depleted. Another choice is a *life annuity,* which provides you with payments for the rest of your life, while a *joint-life annuity* continues payments as long as you or your spouse is still alive.

If you select a life annuity, the size of your payments depends on your age and sex. Men tend to die at an earlier age than women do, so life annuity payments for males are generally higher because the funds have to last for fewer years. And obviously, the younger you are, the smaller your payments will be because (hopefully) your payments will have to stretch far into the future.

You can also add a couple of wrinkles to your annuity. If you choose a life annuity, even if you die the very next week, the insurance company gets to keep all the money. But if you choose a *guaranteed annuity,* you ensure that if you die before a certain number of years have passed, the payments will continue and will go to your beneficiaries. You can also choose to have your payments increase gradually from year to year. Such *indexed annuities* help your income keep up with inflation.

Just how much your funds will pay you, how long you want them to continue, and the options you want are all put through complex calculations by the technical climbers of the accounting world, actuaries. Once you decide on your options, your payments can be calculated by using the statistics of how long you're likely to live and the likelihood of your dying at various ages. (Don't ask to see these numbers because you probably don't want to know.) After you select your options, they can never be changed; they will remain in place until the annuity contract ends with your death and, if you chose the spousal survivor option, your spouse dies.

That means that such options as indexing and guarantees all come at a price. Because these features mean that the insurance company will in all likelihood have to pay out more money, your regular payments will be lower than if you choose to go with a basic, stripped-down *defined-term annuity.*

Annuities are usually best if you

- ✔ Have small retirement savings that absolutely need to last a number of years, especially if you're young and your family has a history of living a long time

- ✔ Must have the peace of mind that comes with knowing just how much you have to live on

- ✔ Don't want to have to make ongoing decisions about how to invest your money

On the flip side of these advantages are several drawbacks, including these:

- ✔ You lose all control of your savings.

- ✔ Your rate of return is fixed when you buy your plan and will likely be lower than what you could earn investing in good mutual funds. If the investment world suddenly becomes littered with far more profitable options, you'll just have to lump it.

- ✔ If you don't accept lower payments in return for an indexed annuity, you may be faced with having less buying power over the years if inflation takes off.

- ✔ If you don't take out a guarantee, or you die after the guarantee period expires, your family or other beneficiaries won't get anything on your death.

The largest drawback to annuities is that you lose all input in how your money is invested and in how much it earns for you. You also have to accept lower initial payments if you want your annuity to increase with the cost of living.

Part III
Investing What You Save

The 5th Wave   By Rich Tennant

"WE TOOK A GAMBLE AND INVESTED ALL OUR
MONEY IN A RACE HORSE. THEN IT RAN AWAY."

In this part . . .

You find out what you already know deep down, that earning and saving are hard work and that you should be careful where you invest the fruits of your labor. We lay out the basics of investing and show you how to pick your investments wisely. This part is where you find out the real story on such things as stocks, bonds, mutual funds, the differences between investing in retirement and non-retirement plans, how to invest for university or college, and how to buy a home.

Chapter 10

Important Investment Concepts

*M*aking wise investments need not be complicated. In fact, the investment world is really quite simple. If you have money to invest, you have only two choices! You can either be a lender or an owner.

However, many investors get bogged down trying to analyze and compare the thousands of investments out there. This chapter helps you grasp the important, "bigger picture" issues that will ensure that your investment plan fits with your needs and the realities of the investment marketplace.

First, Set Goals

Jumping right into picking a particular investment is fun and easy. You may have an idea from some reading you've done or from some entertaining, investment-type person touting investments on television or online. Or maybe Uncle Louie is whispering in your ear that he's gonna get you in on the ground floor of a great new opportunity — a real sure thing.

Stop! Wait! Hit the brakes!

Before you immerse yourself in a specific investment, you must first determine your investment needs and goals. Why are you saving this pile of money? What are you going to use it for?

You can't and don't need to earmark *every* dollar, but you should set some major objectives. Doing so is important because the expected use of the money determines how much time is going to be invested. And that, in turn, helps determine which investment you choose to go with.

Suppose the money you plan on using for Uncle Louie's sure-win deal is all the liquid cash you have available. What if Louie's deal is a bust? What are you going to tap in the event of an emergency? Bad things don't just happen to "other" people. You need a safety net in case you lose your job or are hit with unexpected expenses.

If you've been accumulating money toward a down payment on a home that you'd like to buy in a few years, you can't afford much investment risk with that money. You're going to need that money sooner rather than later. Putting that money in the stock market, then, probably isn't a wise move. As you see later in this chapter, the stock market can drop a lot in a year or over several consecutive years. So stocks are probably too risky a place to invest down payment money you plan to use soon.

Perhaps you're saving toward a longer-term goal, such as retirement, that's 20 or 30 years away. In this case, you're in a position to take more risk because you have more time to bounce back from temporary losses or setbacks. A retirement plan that you leave alone for 20 years may be where you should consider investing in growth investments like stocks. You can tolerate year-to-year volatility in the market — you've got time on your side.

For some people, the thought of putting retirement money in the stock market is horrifying. You want to make sure that your retirement nest egg is intact, and perhaps you know what a roller coaster the stock market can be. These concerns are valid.

The risk level of your investments has to meet your time frame *and your comfort level.* There's no sense investing in high-risk vehicles if you're going to spend all your profits on ulcer-induced medical bills. Learn how to weigh your fears against the potential benefits. What's the investment rate of return that you *need* in order to reach your goals? Let that direct how much risk to take.

Lending Investments

You're a *lender* when you invest your money in a bank certificate of deposit, a Treasury bill, or a bond issued by a company like General Motors, for example. In each case, you lend your money to an organization — a bank, the federal government, or GM. You're paid an agreed-upon rate of interest for lending your money. You're also promised to have your original invest-ment (the *principal*) returned to you on a specific date.

The best that can happen with a lending investment is that you're paid all of the interest in addition to your original investment — the *principal* — as promised. Given that the investment landscape is littered with carcasses of failed investments, this is not a result to take for granted.

The worst that can happen is that you don't get everything you were promised. Promises can be broken under extenuating circumstances. When a company goes bankrupt, for example, you can lose all or part of your original investment.

Another risk is that you get what you were promised, but because of the ravages of inflation, your money is worth less — it has less purchasing power than you thought it would. Back in the 1960s, for example, high-quality companies issued long-term bonds that paid approximately 6 percent interest. At the time, buying a long-term bond seemed like a good deal because the cost of living was increasing only 2 percent per year.

When inflation rocketed to 6, 8, and 10 percent and higher, those 6 percent bonds didn't seem so attractive any longer. The interest and principal didn't buy nearly the amount it did years earlier when inflation was lower. Table 10-1 shows the reduction in the purchasing power of your money at varying rates of inflation after just ten years.

Table 10-1	Reduction in Purchasing Power
Inflation Rate	*Reduction in Purchasing Power After 10 Years*
6 percent	– 44 percent
8 percent	– 54 percent
10 percent	– 61 percent

A final drawback to lending investments is that you don't share in the success of the organization to which you lend your money. If the organization doubles or triples in size and profits, neither your principal nor your interest rate doubles or triples in size along with it; they stay the same. On the other hand, such success probably ensures that you'll get your promised interest and principal back.

Ownership Investments

You're an *owner* when you invest your money in an asset, such as a company or real estate, that has the capability to generate earnings or profits. In the first case, suppose that you own 100 shares of Hudson Bay stock. With hundreds of millions of shares of stock outstanding, Hudson Bay is a mighty big company — your 100 shares represent a tiny piece of it.

What do you get for your small slice of Hudson Bay? As a stockholder, you share in the profits of a company in the form of annual dividends as well as an increase (you hope) in the stock price if the company grows and becomes more profitable. That's when things are going well.

The downside is that if Hudson Bay's business declines, your stock can become worth less (or even worthless!). Hudson Bay might be taken over by evil aliens that decide to sell all sorts of "socially irresponsible" products. Everyone may boycott the store, causing your stock to plummet in value.

Real estate is another type of ownership investment. Most folks invest in real estate in order to earn a profit. (The two exceptions are homes you live in yourself, in which case you probably hope that they increase in value, and properties you buy for sentimental or conservation reasons.) Real estate can yield profits by being rented out for income (profits come when rental income exceeds the expense of owning the property) or by being sold at a higher price than what you paid for it.

As with other ownership investments, the value of real estate depends not only on the particulars of the individual property but also on the health and performance of the local economy. If the local economy grows and more jobs are produced at higher wages, real estate should do well. If companies in the community lay people off left and right and excess housing sits vacant because of previous overbuilding, rents and property values will likely fall.

A third way many Canadians have built substantial wealth is through small business. Small business is the engine that drives much of our economic growth. Although firms with fewer than 20 employees account for about 27 percent of all employees, such small firms in the past two decades were responsible for 47 percent of all new jobs created.

You can participate in small business in a variety of ways. You can start your own business, buy and operate an existing business, or simply invest in promising small businesses.

In the chapters ahead, we explain each of these major investment types in detail.

Investing versus Gambling

Although investing is often risky, it isn't gambling.

Gambling is putting your money into schemes that are sure long-term losers. That's not to say that everyone loses or that you lose every time you play. However, the deck is stacked against you. The house wins most of the time.

That's no way to fund government

More and more provinces are getting into the gambling business as a way to bring in more revenue. This business is sad and wrong for many reasons. First, it's been well documented that lotteries and casinos obtain most of their business from those least able to afford them — primarily middle- and low-income earners. They end up creating an additional tax on the less-economically well off and operate on the basis of false hopes.

Second, government endorsement of gambling promotes the get-rich-quick mentality. Why get an education and work hard over the years when you can solve all your financial concerns with the next ticket you buy or slot you pull? Gambling also contributes to our nationally low personal savings rate.

Finally, gambling, like alcohol and tobacco, can be addictive and destructive. In the worst cases, gambling and gambling debts can split up families and lead to divorce or even suicide.

It's bad enough that legalized gambling exists. It's even worse that, in the pursuit of short-term profits and a quick fix, more local governments are piling into this business. Government is fostering an irresponsible attitude toward money.

In some cases, as with horse racing, gambling casinos, and lotteries, the system is set up to pay out 50–60 cents on the dollar. The rest goes to administration of the system and — don't forget that these are businesses — profits. Sure, your chosen horse may win a race or two, but in the long run, you're almost guaranteed to lose about 40 to 50 percent of what you bet. Would you put your money in an "investment" where your expected return was negative 40 percent?!

Gambling in the investment world is *speculation* — these opportunities are found in sales and trading of futures, options, and commodities. Futures, options, and commodities are *derivatives,* financial investments with value derived from the performance of another security such as a stock or bond.

You may have heard the radio ad by the firm of Fleecem, Cheatem, and Leavem, advocating that you buy heating oil futures because the cold weather months lead to the use of more heating oil. You call and are impressed by the smooth-talking vice president who spends so much time with little ol' you. His logic makes sense, and he's spent a lot of time with you, so you send him a check for $10,000.

Doing so isn't much different from blowing $10,000 at the craps tables in Las Vegas. Futures prices depend on short-term, highly volatile price movements. As with gambling, you occasionally win when the market moves the right way at the right time. But in the long run, you're gonna lose. In fact, you can lose it all.

The investing secret of millionaires

Wouldn't it be interesting to see where those who have some discretionary funds to toss around invest their money? They must know some secret. Many millionaires are financially savvy — that's how some of them make their millions. But others are financially illiterate — the difference is that they are (or feel) wealthy enough to hire advisors.

Millionaires invest most of their wealth — nearly three-quarters of it — in ownership investments such as corporate stock, real estate, and businesses. They invest the remaining quarter mainly in lending-type investments.

Options are the same — you bet on short-term movements of a specific security. If you have inside information, as infamous U.S. investor Ivan Boesky did, such that you know in advance when a major corporate development is going to occur, you can get rich. But don't forget one minor detail — insider trading is illegal. You may end up in the slammer like Boesky.

Investment Returns

You know the difference between ownership and lending investments. Hopefully, you can also distinguish gambling and speculation from true investments.

"That's all well and good," you say, "but how do I choose which type of investments to put my money into? How much can I make and what are the risks?"

Good questions. We'll start with the returns you *might* make. We say "might" because we're looking at history, and history is a record of the past. Using history to predict the future, especially the near future, is dangerous. History may repeat itself, but not always in exactly the same fashion and not necessarily when you expect it to.

This century, ownership investments like stocks and real estate have returned around 10 percent per year, handily beating lending investments such as bonds (around 8 to 9 percent) and savings accounts (roughly 3 to 4 percent) in the investment performance race. Inflation has averaged 3 percent per year.

If you already know that the stock market can be risky, perhaps you're wondering why it's worth the anxiety and potential loss of money to invest in stocks. Why bother for a few extra percent per year? Well, over many years, a few extra percent per year can really magnify the growth of your money (see Table 10-2). The more years you have to invest, the greater the difference a few percent makes in your returns.

Table 10-2	The Difference a Few Percent Makes	
At This Rate of Investment Return on $10,000	You'll Have This Much in 25 Years	You'll Have This Much in 40 Years
4% (savings account)	$26,658	$48,010
8% (bond)	$68,484	$217,245
10% (stocks and real estate)	$108,347	$452,592

Investing is not a spectator sport. You can't earn good returns in stocks and real estate if you keep your money in cash and sit on the sidelines. If you do invest in growth investments such as stocks and real estate, don't chase one new investment after another trying to beat the market average returns. *The biggest value is to be in the market, not to beat it.*

Investment Risks

We should put all of our money in stocks and real estate, right? The returns sure look great. So what's the catch?

Investments with a potential for higher returns carry greater risks. Risk and return go hand-in-hand. If you aren't willing to accept more risk, you aren't going to be able to achieve higher rates of return.

The risk with ownership investments is the short-term fluctuations in their values. On average, during this century, stocks have declined by more than 10 percent in a year every five years. Drops in stock prices of more than 20 percent occurred, on average, once every ten years. Real estate prices suffer similar periodic setbacks.

Thus, in order to earn those generous long-term returns, you must be willing to tolerate volatility. That's why you absolutely should not put all your money in the stock or real estate market. At a minimum, you shouldn't invest your emergency money or money you expect to use within the next five years in such volatile investments.

The shorter the time period that you have, the lesser the likelihood that growth-oriented investments like stocks will beat out lending-type investments like bonds. Table 10-3 illustrates the historical relationship between stock and bond returns based on number of years held.

Dollar-cost averaging: Investing lump sums without losing your shirt

Whether through accumulation of funds over the years, an inheritance, or a recent windfall from work that you've done, you have a problem when you have a large chunk of cash to invest. Many people, of course, would like to have your problem. (You aren't complaining, right?) You want to invest your money, but you're a bit skittish, if not outright terrified, at the prospect of investing the lump of money all at once.

If the money is residing in a savings or money market account, you may feel like it's wasting away. You want to put it to work!

Our first words of advice: Don't rush. Nothing is wrong with earning only a few percentage points on your money in a money market account (see Chapter 13 for recommendations of the best money market funds). Remember that a money market fund beats the heck out of rushing into an investment in which you might lose 20 percent or more. We often talk to people in a state of near panic. Typically, these folks have GICs coming due and feel that they must decide exactly where they want to invest the money in the 48 hours before the GIC matures.

Take a deeeep breath. You have absolutely no reason to rush into an important decision. Instruct your friendly banker that when the GIC matures, you'd like the proceeds to be put in their highest-yielding savings or money market account. That way, your money still earns interest while you buy yourself some breathing room.

One approach to investing is called dollar-cost averaging. Dollar-cost averaging is a process in which you invest your money in equal chunks on a regular basis, such as once a month.

For example, if you have $60,000 to invest, you can invest $2,000 per month until it's all invested, which takes a few years. The money that's awaiting future investment isn't lying fallow. You keep it in a money market-account earning a bit of interest while it's waiting its turn.

The attraction of dollar-cost averaging is that it allows you to ease into riskier investments instead of jumping in all at once. The benefit may be that if the price of the investment drops after some of your initial purchases, you can buy some later at a lower price. If you had dumped all your money into the "sure-win" investment at once and then it dropped like a stone, you'd kick yourself for not waiting.

The flip side of dollar-cost averaging is that if your investment of choice appreciates in value, you may wish that you had invested your money faster. Another possible drawback of dollar-cost averaging is that you may get cold feet continuing to pour money into an investment that's dropping in value. Many people who are attracted to dollar-cost averaging out of fear of buying before a price-drop end up bailing out of what feels like a sinking ship.

Dollar-cost averaging can also cause headaches with your taxes when the time comes to sell investments held outside retirement accounts. If you buy an investment at a number of different times and prices, accounting is muddied as you sell blocks of the investment.

Dollar-cost averaging is most valuable when the money you want to invest represents a large portion of your total assets and you can stick to a schedule. Making dollar-cost averaging automatic so that you're less likely to chicken out is best. Most investment firms that we recommend in the next few chapters can provide automatic purchase services.

Table 10-3	Stocks versus Bonds
Number of Years Investment Held	*Likelihood of Stocks Beating Bonds*
1	60%
5	70%
10	80%
20	91%
30	99%

Some types of bonds have higher yields than others, but the risk-reward relationship remains intact. A bond generally pays you a higher rate of interest as compared to other bonds when it is

- ✔ Lower credit — to compensate for the higher risk of default and higher likelihood of losing your investment
- ✔ Longer-term maturity — to compensate for the risk that you'll be unhappy with the bond's interest rate if interest rates move up

Focus on the risks that you can control

Eric always asks his students in his personal finance class to write down what they would like to learn. Here's what one student had to say: "I want to learn what to invest my money in now as the stock market is overvalued and interest rates are about to go up, so bonds are dicey and banks give lousy interest — HELP!"

This student recognizes the risk of price fluctuations in her investments, but she also seems to believe, like too many people, that there's a way to expect or predict what's going to happen. How does *she* know that the stock market is overvalued and why hasn't the rest of the world figured it out? How does *she* know that interest rates are about to go up, and why hasn't the rest of the world figured that out either?

If you're going to invest in stocks and other growth-oriented investments, you must accept the volatility of these investments. Invest the money that you have earmarked for the longer-term in these vehicles. Minimize the risk of these investments through diversification. Don't buy just one or two stocks; buy a number of stocks, which you can easily do through a mutual fund.

Low-risk, high-return investments

Despite what professors teach in the nation's leading business and finance graduate school programs, low-risk investments that almost certainly lead to high returns *are* available.

We can think of at least three such investments:

- **Your health.** Eat healthy, exercise, relax. Low risk, high return!
- **Friends and family.** Improve your relationships with loved ones. Invest the time and effort in making them better. Low risk, high return!
- **Personal and career development.** Learn a new hobby, improve your communication skills, or read widely. Take an adult education course or go back to school for a degree. Your investment will surely pay off in higher pay cheques and greater happiness. Low risk, high return!

Diversification: Managing Risk

Diversification is one of the most powerful investment concepts. All it really means is that you save and place your eggs (or investments) in different baskets.

Diversification requires you to place your money in different investments with returns that aren't completely correlated. This is a fancy way of saying that with your money in different places, when one of your investments is down in value, odds are that others are up.

To decrease the odds of all of your investments getting clobbered at the same time, you must put your money in different types or classes of investments. These include bonds, stocks, real estate, small business, and precious metals. (We cover all these investments and more in Chapter 11.) You can further diversify your investments by investing in domestic as well as international markets.

Within a given class of investments such as stocks, to diversify by investing in different types of stocks that perform well under various economic conditions is important. For this reason, mutual funds, which are diversified portfolios of securities such as stocks or bonds, are a highly useful investment vehicle. You buy into the mutual fund, which in turn pools your money with that of many others to invest in a vast array of stocks or bonds.

You can look at the benefits of diversification in two ways:

✔ Diversification reduces or dampens the volatility in the value of your whole portfolio. In other words, you can achieve the same rate of return that a single investment can provide with reduced fluctuations in value.

✔ Diversification allows you to obtain a higher rate of return for a given level of risk.

Keep in mind that no one, no matter whom he works for or what credentials he has, can guarantee returns on an investment. You can do good research, and you can be lucky, but no one is free from the risk of losing money. Diversification allows you to hedge the risk of your investments.

Asset allocation: Spreading it around

How you spread out your investing dollars over different investment options is known as *asset allocation*. When determining how to allocate your assets, study your financial situation, prioritize your goals, and then weigh the pros and cons of various investment options.

Although stocks and real estate offer investors attractive long-term returns, they can and do suffer significant declines in value from time to time. Thus, these investments are not suitable for money that you think you may want or need to use within, say, the next five years.

Money market and bond investments are good places to keep money that you expect to use sooner. Everyone should have a reserve of money that they can access in an emergency. Keeping about three to six months' worth of living expenses in a money market fund is a good start. Shorter-term bonds or bond mutual funds can serve as a higher-yielding, secondary emergency cushion (refer to Chapter 8 for more on emergency reserves).

Bonds also can be useful for some longer-term investing for diversification purposes. For example, when investing for retirement, placing a portion of your money in bonds helps to buffer stock market declines.

Allocating money for the long-term

In almost any type of retirement account, you have investment options. Most people get big headaches when they try to decide how to spread their money across those choices. (If you have to select the investment options yourself, such as in an RRSP, you have other decisions to make as well. Find out more about this in Chapters 9 and 13.)

Your current age and the number of years until you retire should be the biggest factors in your allocation decision. The younger you are and the more years you have before retirement, the more comfortable you should be with growth-oriented (and more volatile) investments, such as stocks.

One useful guide for dividing or allocating your money between longer-term oriented growth investments such as stocks and bonds is to subtract your age from 100 (or 120 if you want to be aggressive) and invest the resulting percentage in stocks. Invest what's left over in bonds. For example, if you're 30 years old, you could invest from 70 (100 minus 70) to 90 (120 minus 30) percent in stocks. What's left over — 10 to 30 percent — could be invested in bonds.

Table 10-4 lists some guidelines for allocating retirement account money. All you need to figure out is how old you are and the level of risk you're comfortable with.

Table 10-4	Allocating Retirement Account Money	
Your Investment Attitude	*Bond Allocation (%)*	*Stock Allocation (%)*
"Play it safe"	= Age	= 100–age
"Middle of the road"	= Age–10	= 110–age
"Aggressive"	= Age–20	= 120–age

For example, if you're the conservative sort who doesn't like a lot of risk but recognizes the value of striving for some growth and making your money work harder, you're a *middle-of-the-road* type. Using Table 10-4, if you're 40 years old, you might consider putting 30 percent (40–10) in bonds and 70 percent (110–40) in stocks.

In most employer retirement plans, mutual funds are the typical investment vehicle. If your employer's retirement plan includes more than one stock mutual fund as an option, you may want to try discerning which options are best by using the criteria outlined in Chapter 13. If it's safe to assume that all your retirement plan's stock fund options are good, you can simply divide your stock allocation equally among the choices.

Historically, most employees haven't had to make their own investing decisions with retirement money. Pension plans, in which the company directs the investments, were more common in previous years. It's interesting to note that in a typical pension plan, companies choose to allocate the majority of money to stocks (about 60 percent), with a bit less in bonds (about 35 percent) and other investments.

Investment Firms Are Not Created Equal

Thousands of firms sell investments and manage money. Banks, mutual fund companies, securities brokerage firms, and even insurance companies all vie for your hard-earned dough.

Just to make matters more complicated, each industry plays in the others' backyards. You can find banks that offer insurance, insurance firms that are in the mutual fund business, and brokerage firms that offer banking-like accounts and services. You benefit somewhat from all this competition and one-stop shopping convenience. On the other hand, some firms are novices at particular businesses and count on the fact that you shop by brand-name recognition.

Where to focus

The firms with whom you should do business are those that do the following:

✔ **Offer the best value investments in comparison to their competitors.**

Value combines performance and cost. Given the level of risk that you're comfortable with, you want investments that offer the highest possible rates of return, but you don't want to have to pay a small fortune for them. Commissions of all types (front end, back end, or ongoing), management fees, maintenance fees, and other charges can turn a high-performance investment into a mediocre or poor one.

✔ **Employ representatives who don't have an inherent self-interest in steering you into a particular type of investment.**

This criterion has nothing to do with whether an investment firm hires polite, well-educated, or well-dressed people. The most important factor is the way the company compensates its employees. If the investment firm's personnel are paid on commission, we'd consider passing on that firm. You want to work with firms that don't tempt their employees to push one investment over another in order to generate a better commission. As you see in the rest of this part of the book, plenty of such firms with excellent investment products exist.

No-load mutual fund companies

Mutual funds are an ideal investment vehicle for most investors. *No-load mutual fund companies* are firms in which you can invest in mutual funds without paying sales commissions. In other words, every dollar you invest goes to work in the mutual funds you choose. However, almost all no-load funds still pay salespeople ongoing commissions — called *trailer fees* — that make up part of each fund's MER *(management expense ratio)*. See Chapter 12 for the lowdown on investing in mutual funds.

Discount brokers

In one of the most beneficial changes for investors in this century, the Toronto and Montreal stock exchanges deregulated the retail brokerage industry in 1983. For the first time, brokerage firms could charge people whatever their little hearts desired. You may think that this change opened the door to exorbitantly high rates. In fact, it did the opposite. A fair and open free market is good for consumers. Competition inevitably resulted in more and better choices.

Most firms that were in business before that time continued doing business as usual: That is, they continued to pay their brokers based on the amount of trading their customers did and which investments they sold.

Fortunately, many new brokerage firms opened up that didn't do business the old way. They were dubbed *discount brokers* because the fees they charged customers were substantially lower than what brokers charged under the old fixed-fee system.

Even more important than saving the customer money, discount brokers established a vastly improved compensation system that effectively eliminated conflicts of interest. Discount brokers pay their brokers a straight salary. Therefore, they don't have an incentive to encourage the customer to trade, and they also won't steer the customer into one investment over another unless it truly is wiser.

The term *discount broker* actually isn't an enlightening one. It's certainly true that this new breed of brokerage firm saves you lots of money when you invest. You can easily save 50–80 percent through the major discount brokers, such as TD Green Line, Bank of Montreal's InvestorLine, Royal Bank's Action Direct, CT Securities and E*Trade Canada. But these firms' investments are not "on sale" or second rate. Discount brokers are simply brokers without major conflicts of interest. Of course, like any other for-profit enterprise, they want your business and are in business to make money, but they're much less likely to steer you wrong for their own benefit.

Places to consider avoiding

The worst places to invest are those that charge you a lot, have mediocre or poorly performing investments, and have major conflicts of interest.

The prime conflict of interest comes with investment firms that pay their brokers commissions on the basis of how much and what they sell. The result: The investment firms often sell lots of stuff that pays fat commissions, and they may churn your account (because each transaction has a fee, the more you buy and sell, the more money they make).

Folks who call themselves *financial planners* or *financial consultants* work on commission (discussed in Chapter 3) outside the big brokerage firms. Many of them belong to so-called *broker-dealer networks,* which provide back-office support and investment products to sell. If a person claiming to be a financial planner or advisor is part of a broker-dealer network, odds are quite high you're dealing with an investment salesperson. See Chapter 20 for the questions to ask an advisor you're considering hiring.

Commissions and human behaviour

Investment products bring in widely varying commissions. The products that bring in the highest commissions tend to be the ones that money-hungry brokers push the hardest.

Table 10-5 lists the commissions that you pay and that come out of your investment dollars when you work with brokers, financial consultants, and financial planners working on commission.

Table 10-5	Investment Sales Commissions	
Investment Type	*Avg. Commission on $20,000 Investment*	*Avg. Commission on $100,000 Investment*
Annuities	$1,400	$7,000
Initial public offerings (new stock issue)	$1,000	$5,000
Limited partnerships	$1,800	$9,000
Load mutual funds	$1,200	$5,000
Options and futures	$2,000+	$10,000+

Besides the fact that you can never be sure that you're getting an unbiased recommendation from a salesperson working on commission, you're wasting unnecessary money. Many good investments can be bought on a no-load (commission-free) basis. No-load mutual funds are a good example.

If you're unsure about an investment product being pitched to you (and even when you *are* sure), ask for a copy of the prospectus. In the first few pages, check out whether the investment includes a commission (also known as a load).

Investment salespeople's conflicts of interest

Financial consultants (also known as stockbrokers), financial planners, and others who sell investment products can have enormous conflicts of interest in the strategies and specific investment products that they recommend. Commissions and other financial incentives can't help but skew the advice of even the most earnest and otherwise well-intentioned salespeople.

Numerous conflicts of interest can damage your investment portfolio. The following are the most common conflicts to watch out for:

- **Pushing higher-commission products.** As we discuss earlier in this chapter, commissions on investment products vary tremendously. At the worst end of the spectrum for you (and the best for a salesperson) are products like limited partnerships, commodities, options, and futures. At the best end of the spectrum for you (therefore, the worst for a salesperson) are investments such as no-load mutual funds and GICs, both of which are 100 percent commission-free.

  Commission-based investment salespeople should have to provide prospectuses in advance of a sale, and they should be required to disclose any commissions up front and in writing. We suppose if that happened, more people would choose to buy investments elsewhere and politicians might start telling the truth!

- **Recommending active trading.** Investment salespeople sometimes advise you to trade frequently *(churn)* into and out of different securities. They usually base their advice on current news events or an analyst's comments on the security. Sometimes, these moves are valid; more often, they aren't. In extreme cases, brokers trade on a monthly basis. By the end of the year, they've churned through your entire portfolio; needless to say, all these transactions cost you big money in trading fees.

  Diversified mutual funds (discussed in detail in Chapter 12) make more sense for most people. You can invest in mutuals free of sales commissions. Beside saving money on commissions, you earn better long-term returns by having an expert money manager work for you.

- **Failing to recommend investing through employer's retirement plans.** If you aren't taking full advantage of your employer's retirement savings plans (see Chapters 9 and 13), you may be missing out on valuable tax benefits. An investment salesperson isn't likely to recommend that you contribute to your employer's retirement plan because such contributions cut into the total stash of money you have available to invest with your friendly salesperson. If you're self-employed, salespeople are somewhat more likely to recommend that you fund a retirement plan because they can set up such plans for you. You're better off doing so yourself through a no-load mutual fund company (see Chapters 11 and 12).

- **Pushing high-fee products.** Many brokerage firms that used to sell investment products only on commission are moving into fee-based investment management. This change is an improvement for investors because it reduces some of the conflicts of interest caused by commissions.

  On the other hand, these brokers charge extraordinarily high fees (which are usually quoted as a percentage of assets under management) on their managed investment (wrap) accounts.

Wrap or managed accounts

Wrap, or managed, accounts are all the rage among commission-based brokerage firms. These accounts go under a variety of names but are similar in that they charge a fixed percentage of the assets under management to invest your money through money managers.

Two major problems exist with wrap accounts. First, their management expenses are extraordinarily high — often up to 3 percent per year (some even higher) of assets under management. Remember that in the long haul, stocks can return about 10 percent per year before taxes. So, if you're paying 3 percent per year to have the money managed in stocks, 30 percent of your return (before taxes) is siphoned off. And although wrap fees are tax-deductible, you'll pay tax on any returns beyond that 3 percent, so your net after-tax return may only be 4 to 5 percent.

No-load (commission-free) mutual funds offer investors access to the nation's best investment managers for a fraction of the cost of wrap accounts. You can invest in dozens of top-performing funds for an annual expense of 1 percent per year or less.

So how do brokerage firms trick investors into paying 3 times as much for access to investment managers? Marketing. Slick, seductive, deceptive, misleading pitches that include some outright lies.

You may be told that you're getting access to investment managers who don't normally take money from small-fry investors like you. Not a single study shows that the performance of money managers has anything to do with the minimum account they handle. Besides, no-load mutual funds hire many of the same managers who work at other money management firms.

You also may be told that you earn a higher rate of return, so the extra cost is worth it. You could have earned 18–25 percent per year, they say, had you invested with the "Star of Yesterday" investment management company. The key word here is "had." History is history. Many of yesterday's winners become tomorrow's losers or mediocre performers.

You also must remember that, unlike mutual funds, whose performance records are audited, wrap account performance records may include marketing hype. The most common ploy is showing only the performance of selected accounts — those that performed the best!

How valuable is brokerage research?

One of the arguments frequently advanced by brokerage firms and the brokers who work for them is that their research is better. With their insights and recommendations, they say, you'll do better and "beat the market averages."

Don't believe them. A number of studies clearly demonstrate that their research is barely worth the cost of your morning paper (sometimes not even that)!

Analysts are chronically overly optimistic when it comes to predicting corporate profits. (Hey, it's better than being a sad sack all the time!) If analysts were simply inaccurate or bad estimators, you would expect that they would sometimes underestimate and other times overestimate companies' earnings. Doesn't happen. They almost always overestimate. The discrepancy identifies yet another conflict of interest among many of the brokerage firms.

Brokerage firm analysts are loathe to write a negative report about a company because the firms these analysts work for also solicit companies to issue new stock to the public. What better way to show your potential for selling shares at a high price to the public than by showing how much you believe in certain companies and writing glowing reports about their future prospects?

Brokerage analysts can't be completely objective. Investment banking (the business of helping companies sell new securities) can't be done objectively by companies supposedly evaluating and rating the same securities for the investing public.

If you want research on individual securities, check out the *Value Line Investment Survey,* which we mention in detail in Chapter 11.

Experts Who Predict the Future

A common mistake that many investors make is believing that they can increase their investment returns if they follow the prognostications of certain gurus. The sage predictions in an investment newsletter or by an "expert" who is repeatedly quoted in financial publications make you feel protected. It's sort of like Linus and his security blanket in the comic strip *Peanuts.*

We have some bad news for you investment newsletter subscribers and guru followers. Go buy yourself a warm blanket. It has a lot more value and costs a whole lot less. No one can predict the future. If they could, they would be so busy investing their own money and getting rich that they wouldn't have the time and desire to share their secrets with you.

Investment newsletters

Many investment newsletters purport to time the markets, telling you exactly the right time to get into and out of certain stocks or mutual funds (or the financial markets in general). Such a time approach is doomed to failure in the long run. By failure, we mean that this approach won't beat the tried-and-true strategy of buy and hold.

We see many people paying hundreds of dollars annually to subscribe to all sorts of market-timing and stock-picking newsletters. Ken, an attorney and a client of Eric's, had subscribed to several newsletters. When asked why, Ken said that their marketing materials claimed that if you followed their advice, you would make 20 percent per year return on your money. But in the four years that he had followed their advice, Ken had actually *lost* money, despite appreciating financial markets overall.

Before you ever consider subscribing to any investment newsletter, you should examine its historic track record. The newsletter's marketing materials typically hype the supposed returns that a letter's recommendations have produced. Sadly, newsletters seem to be able to make lots of bogus claims without suffering the timely wrath of securities regulators.

Mark Hulbert tracks the performance of the recommendations made by newsletter writers. Hulbert's organization looks at the cold, hard facts of actual returns and shows how your portfolio would have done if you had followed the recommendations of given newsletters.

If you had been so omniscient as to know in advance which five newsletters would give the best advice during the past 15 years (see Table 10-6), after adjusting for the level of risk that each had taken, you would have done worse in all five cases than the overall rate of return of the Wilshire 5000 index, the broadest measure of the overall performance of small, medium, and large companies' U.S. stocks.

Table 10-6	The "Best" Newsletters
Newsletter	*Risk-Adjusted Performance Ranking*
Value Line Investment Survey	97.5
The Chartist	93.2
Growth Stock Outlook	82.6
No-Load Fund X	73.3
The Prudent Speculator	72.0
Wilshire 5000 Index	100.0

Source: Hulbert's Financial Digest

Hulbert uses *risk-adjusted returns,* which are corrected for the differences in the amount of risk different newsletters took in their recommendations. For comparative purposes, the risk-adjusted return of the Wilshire 5000 index is set at 100. The best newsletter listed in Table 10-6, which has a rating of 97.5, has produced a –2.5 percent lower return than expected given the level of risk it takes. The fact that all of the newsletters in Table 10-6 have a rating less than 100 implies that their recommendations, given the risk entailed, performed worse than the Wilshire 5000 index.

What to do if you're fleeced by a broker

You can't sue a broker just because you lose money on that person's investment recommendations. That's life in the big city. However, if you've been the victim of one of the following cardinal financial sins, you may have some legal recourse:

- ✔ **Misrepresentation and omission.** If you were told, for example, that a particular investment guaranteed returns of 15 percent per year and the investment ends up plunging in value by 50 percent, you were misled. Misrepresentation can also be charged if you're sold an investment with a hefty commission but were originally told that it was commission free.

- ✔ **Unsuitable investments.** Retirees who need access to their capital are often advised to invest in limited partnerships (discussed in Chapter 11) for safe, high yields. The yields on most LPs end up being anything but safe. LP investors have also discovered how illiquid their investments are — some can't be liquidated for up to ten years or more.

- ✔ **Churning.** If your broker or financial planner is constantly trading your investments, odds are that his or her weekly commission cheque benefits at your expense.

- ✔ **Rogue elephant salespeople.** If your planner or broker buys or sells without your approval or ignores your request to make a change, you may be able to collect for losses caused by these actions.

Two major types of practitioners — lawyers and arbitration consultants — stand ready to help you recover your lost money. You can find lawyers by looking under "Lawyers " in the Yellow Pages or by calling your local bar association for referrals. Arbitration consultants can be found under "Arbitration Service." If you come up dry, try contacting a broker or financial advisor, or someone else who works in the securities industry. These sources may be able to give you names and numbers of folks they know.

Most lawyers and consultants usually ask for an up-front fee ranging from several hundred to several thousand dollars to help them cover their expenses and time.

You generally don't end up in a courtroom *L.A. Law* style. You'll probably go to arbitration — an agreement you made (probably not realizing it) when you set up an account to work with the broker or planner.

The good news is that arbitration is usually much quicker, cheaper, and easier for you. You can even choose to represent yourself. Both sides present their case to a panel of arbitrators who make a decision that both sides can't squabble over or appeal.

If, by bad luck, you had been suckered into following the advice of some of the worst newsletters, your investment results would have been disastrous, especially in comparison to what you could have earned in Treasury bills or the Wilshire 5000 stock index. Check out Table 10-7.

Table 10-7	The Worst Newsletters Compared to the Market
Newsletter Portfolio	*Past Five-Year Return*
Granville Market Letter	- 99 %
Overpriced Stock Price	- 95 %
Futures Hotline	- 88 %
Option Advisor	- 78 %
PQ Wall Street	- 73 %
The Dines Letter	- 52 %
Investment Reporter	- 48 %
Wilshire 5000 Index	+ 78 %

Source: Hulbert's Financial Digest

Never use a newsletter for predictive advice. If people were that smart about the future of financial markets, they would be money managers making lots more money. The only types of investment newsletters and periodicals that you should consider subscribing to are those that offer research and information rather than predictions. We discuss those that fit the bill in the subsequent investment chapters.

Investment gurus

Every year, new gurus emerge. All it seems to take to leap to guru status these days is one right call or one good stock pick. Recently, for example, prognosticators who recommended one of the high-flying technology stocks were nearly vaulted to instant guru status as the stocks continued climbing.

Pundits who pitched investing in Presstek and Iomega attracted fairly large followings as these stocks seemed to defy gravity and rationale valuations as their stocks rocketed ever skyward. These stocks and their promoters were brought back to reality during 1996 when their stocks plummeted by more than 65 percent.

And like other high-flying stocks and the pundits made famous by them, many investors weren't attracted to invest in Presstek and Iomega until nearly everybody was talking about them. By then, those stocks were peaking and those who bought got clobbered.

Herb Greenberg, a business writer for the *San Francisco Chronicle,* had a stock market contest in which a group of 13-year-olds won. The reason: They put most of their money into Iomega while it was still heading up. Does this make these 13-year-olds investing geniuses to whom we should look to for guidance on the next hot stock? Of course not. Treat other pundits who happened to guess right the same way.

Commentators and experts interviewed in the media can't predict the future. Don't make investing decisions based on any prognostications. The very few people who have a slight leg up on everyone else aren't going to share their investment secrets — they're too busy investing their own money!

Avoid These Common Investment Mistakes

This section is one of the most important of the book. Before you jump into selecting your investments, we'd like to give you a quick education in the investing school of hard knocks. Whether you're just starting to save money to invest or have millions to play with, mistakes can cost you dearly. Everyone makes at least one.

We don't define a mistake as an investment that doesn't turn a profit. No one can predict which investments will produce great profits. Aside from doing your homework before making an informed investment decision, there's an occasional element of luck in picking a high-yielding investment.

What we mean by an *investment mistake* is a bad decision that you could or should have avoided — either because better options were available or because the odds were heavily stacked against your making money. A mistake is the result of not doing your homework, surrendering to a sales pitch against your better judgement, or being greedy and believing that you can get something for nothing.

The following are the most common blunders, costly errors, and painful regrets. If you can avoid major investment errors, you're more than halfway down the road to investment success. So sit back, relax, swallow your pride, and learn from the mistakes of others.

✔ **Neglecting to pay off high-interest consumer debt:** Although "saving money and watching it grow" may be the most psychologically gratifying approach to investing, you may ultimately lose money if you neglect paying off a credit card bill or an auto loan.

If you're paying 10, 14, or 18 percent interest on an outstanding balance, pay that bill off first — it's your best investment. To get a comparable return through other investment vehicles (after the government takes its share of your profits), you would have to start a new career as a loan shark. If you're in a 41 percent tax bracket, and you're paying 12 percent interest on a consumer loan, you'd need to annually earn a whopping 20 percent on your interest-earning investments pre-tax to justify not paying off the debt. Good luck!

If your only source of funds to pay off debt is a small emergency reserve equal in size to a few months living expenses, paying off debt may involve some risk. Only tap into your emergency reserves if you have a backup source — for example, the ability to borrow from a willing family member.

✔ **Investing based on sales solicitations:** Companies that advertise aggressively or sell investments by telemarketing offer some of the worst financial products with the highest commissions. Companies with great products don't have to reach their prospects this way.

✔ **Purchasing investments you don't understand:** The mistake of not understanding the investments you purchase usually follows from the preceding no-no — buying into a sales pitch. If you don't understand an investment, odds are good that it won't be right for you. Before you put your money into an investment, be sure you know its track record, its true costs, and how liquid it is.

✔ **Not understanding risks:** Many of us have a simplistic understanding of what risk means and how to apply it to our investment decisions. For example, when compared to the yo-yo motions of the stock market, a bank savings account may seem like a less risky place to put your money. Over the long term, however, the stock market usually beats out the rate of inflation; money in a savings account does not. Thus, if you're saving your money for a long-term goal like retirement, a savings account can be a "riskier" place to put your money.

Before you invest, determine your goal, your timeline, and the historical volatility of the investment and whether it suits your comfort level and timeline. Only then can you match your savings goals to their most risk-appropriate investment vehicles. In Chapter 8, we help you consider your savings goals and timeline. We deal with investment risk and returns later in this chapter.

✔ **Paying commissions and high management fees:** Avoid investments that carry high sales commissions and management fees (usually disclosed in a *prospectus*). Virtually all investments today can be purchased without a salesperson. And management fees create a real drag on investment returns, while often supporting lavish offices, glossy brochures, and skyscraper salaries, or propping up small, inefficient operations.

↙ **Putting all your eggs in one basket:** *Diversification* means putting your money in different investments that perform well under differing market conditions. A common mistake is investing too much retirement money in your employer's stock. If your employer falls on hard times, you may lose your job and the value of your investments.

Another common mistake with diversification is that some conservative-minded investors think that they diversify their long-term investment money by buying several bonds, some GICs, and a few T-bills. The problem, however, is that all these investments pay a relatively fixed-rate of return. There's no real upside or growth potential.

↙ **Buying after major price increases:** By the time an investment gets front-page coverage and everyone is talking about its stunning rise, it's time to take a reality check. The higher the value of an investment rises, the greater the danger that it's overpriced. Its next move may be downward.

↙ **Selling after major price declines:** When the Montreal Canadiens won hockey's prized Stanley Cup in 1969, they looked like they were on a roll. But the very next year, they played terribly, and were one of the few teams that didn't even make it to the first round of the play-offs. Suddenly, their future looked very dim. But the very next season, the Canadiens came back like gangbusters and won the Cup again in 1971. When things look bleak, giving up hope is easy — who wants to be associated with a loser? If you could have invested in the Canadiens, though, 1970 would have been a great time to do so. Things couldn't have gotten much worse for the team, and the price of stock would have been cheap. But you gotta have faith.

Likewise, the stock market is full of fair-weather fans. Investors who panicked and sold *after* the October 1987 stock market crash missed out on a tremendous buying opportunity. People like buying everything from clothing to cars to ketchup on sale — yet whenever the stock market has a clearance sale, most investors stampede for the exits instead of snatching up great buys. Demonstrate your courage; don't follow the herd.

↙ **Ignoring tax consequences:** Even if you never become an investment expert, you're smart enough to know that the less money you pay in taxes, the more you have to invest and play with. Channeling investment money into an RRSP or other retirement plans allows your money to grow without taxation, and therefore faster, over time (see Chapter 13). For investments outside retirement plans, you need to match the types of investments to your tax situation (see Chapter 14).

↙ **Believing self-proclaimed gurus and soothsayers:** Ignore the predictions and speculations of self-proclaimed gurus. No one has a crystal ball — and even if someone did, she wouldn't waste her time publishing a mass-market newsletter to tell you what she saw.

Chapter 11

Investment Vehicles

- -

- -

*I*n the investment world, you can place your money in many different types of investment vehicles. Decent investment vehicles work their way methodically around the racetrack, rarely deterred but also never at a fast rate. The best ones make their way through the course at a faster clip, only occasionally slowed by a bump or detour. The worst ones sputter in fits and starts and sometimes crash and burn in a flaming heap.

Which vehicle you choose for your trip depends on where you're going, how fast you want to get there, and what risks you're willing to take along the way.

If you haven't yet read Chapter 10, please do so now. In it, we cover a number of investment concepts, such as the difference between lending and ownership investments, that will enhance your ability to choose among the common investment vehicles we discuss in this chapter.

Lending Vehicles for Slow-Trip Money

Everyone should have some money riding in stable, safe investment vehicles. For example, as we discuss in Chapter 8, money that you earmark for your short-term bills, both expected and unexpected, should have a seat belt on in the back seat of a Volvo. Likewise if you're saving money for a home purchase within the next few years, you certainly don't want to risk that money on the roller coaster of the stock market.

The vehicles that follow are appropriate for money that you don't want to put at great risk. In the chapters that follow, you should be happy to know, we recommend the best specific investments to satisfy varying financial needs and goals.

Transaction/chequing accounts

These accounts are best used for depositing your monthly income and paying for your expenditures. If you want to have unlimited cheque-writing privileges and access to your money with an ABM card, chequing accounts at local banks are your best bet. Make sure that you shop around for accounts that don't ding you $1 here for each use of an ABM machine and $10 there for a low balance.

With interest rates as low as they are now, focus on avoiding monthly service charges rather than chasing after a chequing account with a slightly higher interest rate. Some banks, for example, don't require you to maintain a minimum balance to avoid a monthly service charge when you direct-deposit your pay cheques.

If you don't need access to ABM machines on every other street corner — an option usually available through larger banks — you can generally get a better chequing account deal at a credit union or a smaller bank.

In any event, you should only keep enough money in the account to service your monthly bill payment needs. If you consistently keep more than a few thousand dollars in a chequing account, get the excess out. You can earn more in a savings or money market account, which we describe next.

Savings and money market accounts

Savings accounts can be found at banks; money market funds are available through mutual fund companies and most major banks. Savings accounts and money market funds are nearly identical except that money market funds generally pay a better rate of interest. The interest rate paid to you, also known as the *yield,* fluctuates over time, depending on the level of interest rates in the overall economy.

Savings account are protected (up to the $60,000 limit) by the Canada Deposit Insurance Corp. (CDIC). Money market funds are not. Should you prefer a bank account because your investment (the *principal*) is insured? No. In fact, you should prefer money market funds because the better ones are higher yielding than the better bank savings accounts, and money market securities generally are extremely safe. Dozens of money market funds invest billions of Canadian individuals' and institutions' money. We aren't aware of an individual losing even a penny of principal in these funds.

Money market funds can only invest in the most credit-worthy securities and must have an average maturity of 180 days or less. Money market funds usually maintain a constant value per share of either $1 or $10. In the unlikely event that an investment in a money market's fund portfolio goes sour, a large money market fund would almost certainly cover the loss.

General-purpose money market funds invest in Government of Canada Treasury bills, provincial Treasury bills, and corporate short-term commercial paper (short-term debt), which is issued by the largest and most credit-worthy companies.

If the lack of insurance on money market funds still spooks you, here's a way to get the best of both worlds: Select a money market fund that invests exclusively in government securities that are virtually risk-free because they're backed by the full strength and credit of the federal and provincial governments.

Bonds

Bonds are the most common lending investments traded on securities markets. When you invest in a bond, you really lend your money to an organisation. When a bond is issued, it includes a specified maturity date at which time the principal is repaid. Bonds are also issued at a particular interest rate or what's known as a *coupon*. That rate is fixed on most bonds. So, for example, if you buy a five-year, 7 percent bond issued by IBM, you lend your money to IBM for five years at an interest rate of 7 percent per year.

The value of a bond is based on changes in interest rates. For example, if you hold a bond issued at 8 percent and rates increase to 10 percent on comparable, newly issued bonds, your bond decreases in value. (Why would anyone want to buy your bond at the price you paid if it yields just 8 percent and she can get bonds with 10 percent yields elsewhere?)

More and more bonds issued today are tied to variable interest rates. For example, you can buy bonds that are indexed to the rate of inflation.

Bonds differ from each other in the following ways:

- ✔ The type of institution to which you lend your money — provincial government, federal government, mortgage holder, or a corporation.

- ✔ The credit quality of the borrower to whom you lend your money (in other words, the probability that the borrower will pay you the interest and return your principal as agreed).

- ✔ The length of maturity of the bond. Short-term bonds mature within a few years, intermediate bonds within 7 to 10 years, and long-term bonds within 30 years. Longer-term bonds generally pay higher yields but fluctuate more with changes in interest rates.

Bonds are rated by major credit-rating agencies for their safety, usually on a scale on which AAA is the highest-possible rating. For example, high-grade corporate bonds (AAA or AA) are considered the safest (that is, most likely to pay you back). Next in safety are general bonds (A or BBB), which are still safe but just a little less so. Junk bonds (rated BB or lower), made popular by Michael Milken and Drexel Burnham, actually aren't all that junky; they're just lower in quality and have a slight (1 or 2 percent) probability of default.

Some bonds are *callable,* which means that the lender can decide to pay you back earlier than the previously agreed-upon date. This event usually occurs when interest rates fall and the lender wants to issue new, lower-interest rate bonds to replace the higher-rate bonds outstanding. To compensate you for early repayment, the lender typically gives you a small premium or bonus over what the bond is really worth.

Ownership Vehicles to Build Wealth

The three best, legal ways to build wealth are to invest in stocks, real estate, and small business.

Stocks

Stocks are the most common ownership investment vehicle and represent shares of ownership in a company. When companies go "public," they issue shares of stock that people can purchase on the major stock exchanges, such as the Toronto Stock Exchange, Montreal Stock Exchange, Vancouver Stock Exchange, New York Stock Exchange, American Stock Exchange, and NASDAQ (National Association of Securities Dealers Automated Quotation system) or the over-the-counter market.

As the economy grows and companies grow with it and earn greater profits, stock prices generally follow suit. Stock prices don't move in lockstep with earnings, but over the years, the relationship has been pretty close. In fact, the *price-earnings ratio* — which measures the level of stock prices relative to (or divided by) company earnings — of U.S. stocks has averaged approximately 14 during this century. While the ratio has varied and has been as high as 27 and as low as 6, it tends to fluctuate around 14. A price-earnings ratio of 14 simply means that stock prices per share on average are selling at about 14 times those companies' earnings per share.

Companies that issue stock (called *publicly held* companies) include automobile manufacturers, computer software producers, fast food restaurants, hotels, magazine and newspaper publishers, supermarkets, wineries, zipper manufacturers, and everything in between! By contrast, some companies, known as privately held companies, elect to have their stock held by senior management and a small number of affluent outside investors. Privately held companies' stocks don't trade on a stock exchange. That means that folks like you can't buy stock in such firms.

Companies differ in size and in what industry or line of business they're in. In the financial press, you often hear companies referred to by their *market capitalization,* which is the value of their outstanding stock. When describing the size of companies, Bay Street has done away with such practical adjectives as "big" and "small" and replaced them with babbling expressions like "large cap" and "small cap" (cap standing for capitalization). Such is the language of financial geekiness.

As with raising children or going mountain climbing, investing in the stock market involves occasional setbacks and difficult moments, but the overall journey should be worth the effort. Over the past two centuries, North American stock markets have produced an annual average rate of return of about 10 percent. However, the market does fall — often dramatically. For instance, the Dow Jones Industrial Average has fallen more than 20 percent during 16 different periods in this century. On average, these periods of decline lasted less than two years. So if you can withstand a temporary setback over a few years, the stock market is a terrific place to invest for long-term growth.

You can invest in stocks by making your own selection of individual stocks or by letting a mutual fund manager (discussed in Chapter 12) do it for you.

GICs are overused

Another type of bond is a Guaranteed Investment Certificate (GIC), which is issued by a bank. With a GIC, as with a real bond, you agree to lend your money to a bank for a predetermined number of months or years. Generally, the longer you agree to lock up your money, the higher the interest rate you receive.

Unlike bonds, GICs are not liquid; that is, you can't get your money back whenever you want

it. If you want your money back before the end of the GIC's term, you generally get whacked with the loss of a number of months' worth of interest. Some GICs don't let you cash out early, period. GICs also don't tend to pay very competitive interest rates. You can usually beat the interest rate on shorter-term GICs (those that mature within a year or so) with the best money market mutual funds, which offer complete liquidity without any penalty.

International stocks

Not only can you invest in company stocks that trade on the Canadian stock exchanges, but you can also invest in stocks in the U.S. and overseas. Aside from folks with business connections abroad, why would the average citizen want to do so?

Several reasons. First, the majority of investment opportunities lie outside of Canada. If you look at the total value of all stocks outstanding worldwide, the value of Canadian stocks is very definitely in the minority (about 3 percent).

Another reason for investing in international stocks is that when you confine your investing to Canadian securities, you miss a world of opportunities, not only because of business growth available in other countries but also because you get the opportunity to diversify your portfolio further. International securities markets don't move in tandem with Canadian markets. During the 1987 stock market crash, for example, most international stock markets dropped less. Some actually rose in value. Also, you protect part of your portfolio from a prolonged drop in the Canadian dollar.

Some people hesitate to invest in overseas securities for silly reasons. In some cases, people read idiotic columns like one we recently ran across in a fairly big city paper. It was entitled "Plenty of Pitfalls in Foreign Investing: Timing is all in earning a decent return." The piece went on to say, "But as with sex, commuting, and baseball, timing is everything in the stock market." Smart stock market investors know better than to try to time their investments. The piece also ominously warned, "Foreign stock markets have been known to evaporate overnight." We wish we could say the same for the jobs of boneheaded financial journalists.

Others are concerned that international investing hurts the Canadian economy and contributes to a loss of jobs. We have some counterarguments. First, if you don't profit from the growth of economies overseas, someone else will. If there's money to be made, Canadians may as well be there to participate. Profits from a foreign company are distributed to all stockholders, no matter where they live. Dividends and stock price appreciation know no national boundaries.

Also, you must recognize that you already live in a global economy — making a distinction between Canadian and non-Canadian companies is no longer appropriate. Many companies headquartered in Canada also have overseas operations. Some Canadian firms derive a large portion of their revenue from their international divisions. Conversely, many firms based overseas also have operations here. Increasing numbers of companies are worldwide operations.

The danger of individual stocks

Investing in individual stocks generally should be avoided. Success is difficult to attain; the drawbacks and pitfalls are many:

✔ **Significant research time and cost required.** You should know a lot about the situation of the company you're investing in when you consider the purchase of an individual security. Relevant questions to understand are: What products does it sell? What are its prospects for future growth and profitability? How much debt does the company have? You need to do your homework not only before you make your initial investment but also on an ongoing basis as long as you hold the investment.

Don't fool yourself or let others fool you into believing that picking and following individual companies and their stocks is simple, requires little time, and is far more profitable than investing in mutual funds.

✔ **High transaction costs.** Even when you use a discount broker (described in Chapter 10), the commissions you pay to buy or sell securities are substantial. It may cost you about $30 to buy 100 shares of a $20 security through a discounter, which amounts to around 35 cents per share or almost 2 percent of the amount invested. A large institution, such as a mutual fund company, that buys securities in blocks of 10,000 shares or more pays a penny or two per share when trading. So you're effectively paying 20 to 40 times more in commissions than mutual fund companies do.

✔ **Less likely to diversify.** Unless you have tens of thousands of dollars to invest in different stocks, you probably can't cost-effectively afford to develop a diversified portfolio. For example, when you're investing in stocks, you should hold companies in different industries, different companies within an industry, and so on. Not diversifying adds to the risk of losing your shirt.

✔ **Accounting and bookkeeping.** When you invest in individual securities outside retirement accounts, when you sell a specific security at a profit, you must report that transaction on your tax return. Even if you pay someone else to complete your tax return, you still have the hassle of keeping track of statements and receipts.

✔ **Generally forced to do so in taxable accounts.** If you work for an employer, it's highly unlikely that his or her retirement plan allows you to invest in individual stocks. Thus, you may be relegated to investing in individual stocks in a nonretirement plan, which thus exposes your stock investments to taxation. You're taxed whenever dividends are paid as well as whenever you sell a stock at a profit.

If you use your nonretirement savings to play the stock market game and don't fully fund your RRSP, you sacrifice substantial tax benefits. That isn't wise investing.

Researching individual stocks can be more than a full-time job, and if you choose to take this path, remember that you'll be competing against the professionals who do so on a full-time basis.

Isn't the stock market just legalized gambling?

A student in Eric's personal finance class brought in a copy of a *The New York Times* article entitled "Gaming on Wall Street." In the piece, the writer said, "Increasingly, the stock market itself has become just another commodity — as its recent volatility has shown."

After having read this, the student put her comment/question to Eric in writing: "Unless you're a superstar in your field, have stock options in a high tech company, or inherited wealth, it's increasingly difficult for a working person to provide for the future merely with hard work and savings. One is forced to invest in a stock market that is acting more like a commodity and has little to do with economic rules or real value. It is more and more like gambling. I resent turning over my hard-earned money to something that resembles a casino, but there's really no other game in town. Your thoughts?"

First, Eric suggested to the student that she might choose better reading material. The writer of this piece hadn't bothered to do his homework. If he had, he would know that, in the years before this piece was published in early 1996, by historic standards, the U.S. stock market was actually less volatile than normal. He also implied that the increasing stock prices were inflated and unjustified by the economy. In fact, corporate profits have been booming in recent years, and that inevitably drives stock prices higher.

Second, Eric told his student that although the stock market can sometimes be temperamental, in the long run, the market is driven by the performance of our economy. That's not gambling — that's investing.

Third, as we discuss later in this chapter, the stock market is hardly the only game in town. To build wealth, in addition to the stock market, you can invest real estate, small business, or your own career.

A capitalistic economy isn't always fair. But it rarely rewards pessimists, spectators, and those unwilling to take some risks.

The relative advantages of mutual funds

Efficiently managed mutual funds offer investors of both modest and substantial means low-cost access to high-quality money managers. Mutual funds span the spectrum of risk and potential returns from nonfluctuating money market funds (which are similar to savings accounts) to bond funds (which generally pay higher yields than money market funds but fluctuate with changes in interest rates) to stock funds (which offer the greatest potential for appreciation but also the greatest short-term volatility).

Mutual funds make better sense than individual securities for investors regardless of the amount of money they have to invest. Investing in individual securities should be done only by those who really enjoy doing it. Mutual funds, if properly selected, are a low-cost way to hire professional money managers.

In the long haul, you're not going to beat full-time professional managers who invest in securities of the same type and risk level that you do. Even if you think that you can do as well as the best, remember that most "superstar" money managers only beat the market averages by a few percent per year.

If you derive sheer ecstasy from picking and following your own stocks or want an independent opinion of some stocks you happen to own now, probably the best research reports available are from the *Value Line Investment Survey*. This superb publication provides concise, user-friendly, single-page summaries of about 1,700 stocks, including about 70 Canadian companies. Libraries with good business sections sometimes carry this publication. You can subscribe for $680 U.S. per year, or on a ten-week trial basis for $77 U.S. by calling Value Line at 800-833-0046.

Real estate

Investing in real estate is another time-tested method for building wealth. Over the generations, real estate owners and investors have enjoyed rates of return comparable to the stock market.

Real estate is not a gravy train or a simple way to get wealthy. Like stocks, real estate goes through good and bad performance periods. Most people who make money investing in real estate do so because they invest over many years.

The best place to start investing in real estate is to buy your own home. The *equity* (difference between the market value of the home and loan owed on it) in your home that builds over the years can become a significant part of your net worth. Among other things, this equity can be tapped to help finance other important financial goals such as retirement, university, and starting or buying a business.

Over your adult life, owning a home should generally be less expensive than renting a comparable home. The reason: As a renter, your housing costs are fully exposed to inflation (unless you're the beneficiary of rent-controls). As a homeowner, the bulk of your housing costs — your monthly mortgage — isn't exposed to inflation over the term of your mortgage. And when you sell your home, the capital gains are tax free.

See Chapter 16 to learn the best ways to buy and finance your home purchase.

Real estate: Not your ordinary investment

Besides providing solid rates of return, real estate is quite different from most other investments. Here's what makes real estate unique as an investment.

✔ **Usability.** You can't live in a stock, bond, or mutual fund (although we suppose you could build yourself a pretty substantial fortress with all the paper these companies fill your mailbox with each year). Real estate is the only investment that you can use (live in or rent out) to produce income.

✔ **Land is in limited supply.** Last time we checked, the percentage of the earth occupied by land wasn't increasing. And because humans like to reproduce, the demand for land and housing continues to grow. Consider the areas that have the most expensive real estate prices in the world — Hong Kong, Tokyo, Hawaii, San Francisco, and Manhattan. In these densely populated areas, there is virtually no new land upon which to build.

✔ **Zoning shapes potential value.** Local government regulates the zoning of property, and zoning determines what a property can be used for. In many communities these days, local zoning boards are against big growth. This bodes well for future real estate values. Also know that, in some cases, a particular property may not have been developed to its full potential. If you can see how to develop the property, you can reap large profits.

✔ **Leverage.** Real estate is also different from other investments because to buy it, you can borrow a lot of money — up to 80–90 percent or more of the value of the property. This is known as exercising *leverage:* With only a small investment of 10–20 percent down, you're able to purchase, own, and control a much larger investment. If the value of your real estate goes up, you make money on your investment and on all the money that you borrowed.

For example, suppose that you plunk down $20,000 to purchase a property for $100,000. If the property appreciates to $120,000, on paper you've made a profit of $20,000 on an investment of just $20,000. In other words, you've made a 100 percent return on your investment. But leverage cuts both ways. If your $100,000 property decreases in value to $80,000, even though it's only dropped 20 percent in value, you've actually lost (on paper) 100 percent of your original $20,000 investment.

✔ **Hidden values.** In an *efficient market,* the price of an investment accurately reflects its true worth. Some investment markets are more efficient than others because of the large number of transactions and easily accessible information. Real estate markets can be *in*efficient at times. Information is not always easy to come by, and you may find an ultramotivated or uninformed seller. If you're willing to do some homework, you may be able to purchase a property below — perhaps by as much as 10–20 percent — its fair market value.

Good real estate investment options

If you want to invest directly in real estate, residential housing — such as single-family homes or small multiunit buildings — is a straightforward and attractive investment for most people. Before you venture into real estate investing, be sure that you have sufficient time to devote to it. Also be careful not to sacrifice tax-deductible contributions to RRSPs or other retirement plans in order to own investment real estate. In the early years of rental property ownership, many investors find that their property's expenses exceed its income. This negative cash flow can siphon off money that you could otherwise direct into your RRSP to earn tax benefits.

Although it is in some ways unique, real estate is like other types of investments in that prices are driven by supply and demand. You can invest in homes or small apartment buildings and rent them out. In the long run, investment-property buyers hope that their rents and the value of their properties will increase faster than their expenses.

Real estate versus stocks

Real estate and stocks have historically produced comparable returns. Deciding between the two depends less on the performance of the markets than it does on you and your situation. Consider the following major issues in deciding which investment may be better for you.

The first and most important question to ask yourself is whether you're cut out to handle the responsibilities that come with being a landlord. Real estate is a time-intensive investment. Investing in stocks can be time-intensive as well, but it doesn't have to be if you use professionally managed mutual funds.

An often-overlooked drawback to investing in real estate is that you earn no tax benefits while you're accumulating your down payment. RRSPs give you an immediate tax deduction as you contribute money to them. If you haven't exhausted your contributions to your RRSP or other retirement plan, consider doing so before chasing after investment real estate.

Also ask yourself which investments you know more about. Some folks feel uncomfortable with stocks and mutual funds because they don't understand them. If you have a better handle on what makes real estate tick, you have a good reason to consider investing in it.

Finally, what will make you happy? Some people enjoy the challenge that comes with managing and improving rental property. It's a bit like running a small business. If you're good at it and have some good luck, you can make money and derive endless hours of enjoyment.

Although few will admit it, some real estate investors get an ego rush from a tangible display of their wealth. Sufferers of this "edifice complex" can't obtain similar pleasure from a stock portfolio that's detailed on a piece of paper (although others have been known to boast of their stock market prowess and wealth).

When selecting real estate for investment purposes, remember that local economic growth is the fuel for housing demand. In addition to a vibrant and diverse job base, a limited supply of both existing housing and land on which to build is a thing to look for. When you identify potential properties in which you might invest, run the numbers to understand the cash demands of owning the property and the likely profitability. See Chapter 16 for background on how to think about the costs of real estate ownership.

If you don't want to be a landlord — one of the biggest drawbacks of investment real estate — consider investing in real estate through real estate investment trusts (REITs). *REITs* are diversified real estate investment companies that purchase and manage rental real estate for investors. A typical REIT invests in different types of property, such as shopping centres, apartments, and other rental buildings.

You can invest in REITs either through purchasing them directly on the major stock exchanges or through a real estate mutual fund that invests in numerous REITs. (See Chapter 12 for more information on buying mutual funds.)

Not-so-good real estate investments

Not all real estate investments are good; some aren't even real investments. These bad ones are characterized by burdensome costs and problematic economic fundamentals:

- ✓ **Limited partnerships.** Limited partnerships (LPs) sold through brokers and financial consultants should be avoided at all costs. LPs are inferior investment vehicles. They're so burdened with high sales commissions and ongoing management fees that deplete your investment that you can do better elsewhere. The investment salesperson who sells you such an investment stands to earn a commission of up to 10 percent or more — so only 90 cents of your dollar gets invested. Each year, LPs typically siphon off another several percent for management and other expenses. Most partnerships have little or no incentive to control costs. In fact, they have a conflict of interest to charge more to enrich the managing partners.

  Unlike a mutual fund, you can't vote with your dollars. If the partnership is poorly run and expensive, you're stuck. LPs are *illiquid.* You can't get your money out until the partnership is liquidated, typically seven to ten years after you buy in.

  Brokers who sell LPs often tell you that, while your investment is growing at 20 percent or more per year, you get handsome dividends of 8 percent or so per year. Many of the yields on LPs have turned out to be bogus. In some cases, partnerships propped up their yields by paying back investors' principals (without telling them, of course). As for returns — well — most LP investors of a decade ago are lucky to have half their original investment left.

The only thing limited about a limited partnership is its ability to make you money.

✔ **Time shares.** Time shares are another nearly certain money loser. With a time share, what you buy is a week or two per year of ownership, or usage, of a particular unit, usually a condominium in a resort location. If you pay $8,000 for a week (in addition to ongoing maintenance fees), you're paying the equivalent of more than $400,000 for the whole unit, but a comparable unit nearby may sell for only $150,000. All the extra markup pays the salespeople's commissions, administrative expenses, and profits for the time share development company.

People usually get lured into buying a time share when they're enjoying a vacation someplace. They're easy prey for salespeople who want to sell them a souvenir of the trip. The cheese in the mousetrap is an offer of something free (for example, a free night's stay in a unit) for going through the sales presentation.

If you can't live without a time share, consider buying a used one. Many previous buyers, who almost always have lost a good hunk of money, are trying to dump their shares (which should tell you something). You may be able to buy a time share at a fair price. But why commit yourself to taking a vacation in the same location and building at the same time each year? Many time shares let you trade your weeks for other times and other places; however, doing so is a hassle, you're charged an extra fee, and your choices are usually limited to time slots that other people don't want — that's why they're trading them!

✔ **Second homes.** A sometimes romantic notion and extended part of the so-called Canadian dream is the weekend getaway — a place you can escape to a couple of times a month. When it's not in use, you may be able to rent it out and earn some income to help defray the expense of keeping it up.

If you can realistically afford the additional costs of a second — or vacation — home, we're not going to tell you how to spend your extra cash. But please don't make the all-too-common mistake of viewing a cottage or cabin as an investment. The way most people use them, they're not. Most second-home owners rent out their property very little — 10 percent or less of the time. As a result, cottages and cabins are usually money drains.

Part of the allure of a second home is the supposed tax benefits. Even when you qualify for some or all of them, tax benefits only partially reduce the cost of owning a property. And because the rental potential is so small for most family cottages (due to a potentially high "personal use" component), Revenue Canada often doesn't allow cottage owners to claim "rental expenses" in vacation properties. We've seen more than a few cases in which the second home is such a cash drain that it prevents its owners from contributing to and taking advantage of tax-deductible retirement savings plans.

If you don't rent out a second home property most of the time, ask yourself whether you can afford such a luxury. Can you accomplish your other financial goals — saving for retirement, paying for the home in which you live, and so on — with this added expense? Keeping a cottage or cabin is more of a consumption than an investment decision. Few people can afford more than one home.

Investing in small business

With what type of investment have more people built great wealth? If you said the stock market or real estate, you're wrong. The answer is small business. You can invest in small business by starting one yourself (and thus finding yourself the best boss you've ever had), buying an existing business, or investing in someone else's small business.

Launching your own enterprise

If you have self-discipline and a product or service you can sell, starting your own business can be both profitable and fulfilling. Consider first what skills and expertise you possess that you can use in your business. You don't need a "eureka"-type idea or an invention like Velcro to justify going into small business. Millions of people operate successful businesses such as dry cleaners, restaurants, tax preparation firms, and so on that are hardly unique. *Small Business For Dummies* by Eric Tyson and Jim Schell, published by IDG Books Worldwide, Inc., tells you what you need to know.

Start exploring your idea first by developing a written business plan. Such a plan should detail what your product or service will be, how you will market it, who your customers and competitors are, and what the economics of the business are, including the start-up costs.

Of all your small business options, starting your own business involves the greatest amount of work. Although you can do this work on a part-time basis in the beginning, most people end up in their business full time — it's your new job, career, or whatever you want to call it.

We've run our own businesses for most of our working years and wouldn't give it up. That's not to say that running your own business doesn't have its drawbacks and down moments. But in our experience with small-business owners, we've seen many people of varied backgrounds, interests, and skills succeed and be happy with running their own business.

In the eyes of most people, starting their own business is the riskiest of all small-business investment options. But if you go into a business that utilizes your skills and expertise, the risk is not nearly as great as you may think.

Many businesses can be started with little cash by leveraging your existing skills and expertise. You can build a valuable company and job if you have the time to devote to building "sweat equity." As long as you check out the competition and offer a valued service at a reasonable cost, the principal risk with your business is that you won't do a good job marketing what you have to offer. If you can market your skills, you're home free.

As long as you're thinking about the risks of starting a business, consider the risks of staying in a job you don't enjoy or that isn't challenging or fulfilling you. If you never take the plunge, you may regret that you didn't pursue your dreams.

Buying someone else's business

If you don't have a specific product or service you want to sell but are skilled at managing and improving the operations of a company, buying a small business might be for you. Finding and buying a good small business takes much time and patience, so be willing to devote at least several months to the search. You will probably also need to enlist the help of financial and legal advisors to help inspect the company, look over its financial statements, and put a deal together.

Although you don't have to go through the riskier start-up period if you take this route, you will likely need more capital to buy a going enterprise. You also need to be able to deal with stickier personnel and management issues. The history of the organization and the way things work will predate your ownership of the business. If you don't like making hard decisions, firing people who don't fit with your plans, and coercing people into changing the way they did things before you arrived on the scene, buying an existing business likely isn't for you.

Some people perceive buying an existing business as safer than starting one. Buying someone else's business can actually be riskier. You're likely to shell out far more money, in the form of a down payment, up front to buy a business. If you don't have the ability to run the business and it does poorly, you have a lot more to lose financially. Another risk is that the business is for sale for a reason — it's not very profitable, it's in decline, or it's generally a pain in the neck to operate.

Good businesses for sale don't come cheaply. If the business is a success, the current owner has removed the start-up risk from the business, so the price of the business should be at a premium to reflect this lack of risk. If you have the capital to buy an established business and you have the skills to run it, consider going this route.

Sticking your money in someone else's business

If you like the idea of profiting from successful small businesses but don't want the day-to-day headaches of being responsible for managing the enterprise, investing in someone else's small business may be for you.

Although this route may seem easier, fewer people are actually cut out to be investors in other people's businesses. The reason: Finding and analyzing opportunities isn't easy.

Are you astute at evaluating corporate financial statements and business strategies? Investing in a small, privately held company has much in common with investing in a publicly traded firm. One difference is that private firms aren't required to produce comprehensive, audited financial statements that adhere to certain accounting principles the way that public companies are. Thus, you have a greater risk of not having sufficient or accurate information when evaluating a small private firm.

Another difference is that it's harder to unearth private small business investing opportunities. The best private companies seeking investors don't generally advertise but instead find prospective investors through networking with people such as business advisors. Increase your chances of finding private companies to invest in by speaking with tax, legal, and financial advisors who work with small businesses. You can also find interesting investing opportunities through your own contacts or experience within a given industry.

Consider investing in someone else's business only if you can afford to lose what you're investing. Unlike investing in a diversified stock mutual fund (see Chapter 12), you can lose all your investment when investing in a small, privately held company. Also, make sure you have sufficient assets so that what you invest in small, privately held companies is only a small portion (20 percent or less) of your total financial assets.

Investment Odds and Ends

In Chapter 10, we tell you that the investment world offers you only two flavours: lending investments and ownership investments. Well, we sort of oversimplified.

The investments that we discuss in this section sometimes belong on their own planet. Following are the basics on these other common, but odd, investments.

Precious metals

Gold and silver have been used by many civilizations as currency or as a medium of exchange. One advantage of precious metals as a currency is that they can't be debased by the government. With a paper-based currency, such as Canadian dollars, the government can print more to pay off debts.

This process can lead to the devaluation of a currency and inflation. It takes a whole lot more work to make more gold. Just ask Rumplestiltskin.

Holdings of gold and silver can provide a so-called *hedge* against inflation. In Canada in the late 1970s and early 1980s, inflation rose dramatically. This largely unexpected rise in inflation depressed stocks and bonds. Gold and silver, however, rose tremendously in value — in fact, more than 500 percent (even after adjusting for inflation) from 1972 to 1980.

Periods like 1972 to 1980 are unusual. Over many decades, precious metals tend to be lousy investments. Their rate of return will keep up with the rate of inflation, but it won't come out ahead.

If you want to invest in precious metals as an inflation hedge, your best option is to do so through mutual funds. For more information about determining how mutual funds fit with the rest of your investments and how to buy them, be sure to read Chapter 12.

Don't purchase precious metals futures. They aren't investments; they're short-term gambles on which way gold or silver prices might head over a short period of time. You should also stay away from firms and shops that sell coins and *bullion* (not the soup but bars of gold or silver). Even if you can find a legitimate firm (not an easy task), the cost of storing and insuring gold and silver is quite high. You don't get good value for your money. We hate to tell you, but the Gold Rush is over.

Collectibles

Collectibles are a catchall category for antiques, art, autographs, baseball cards, clocks, coins, comic books, diamonds, dolls, gems, photographs, rare books, rugs, stamps, vintage wine, and writing utensils — in other words, any material object that through some kind of human manipulation has become more valuable to certain humans.

However, as an investment vehicle, collectibles are far from valuable; in fact, they're lousy. Dealer markups are enormous, maintenance and protection costs are draining, research is time-consuming, and people's tastes are quite fickle — all this for returns that, after you factor in the huge markups, rarely keep up with inflation.

If you buy collectibles, do it for your love of the object, not for financial gain. Treat it as a hobby, not as an investment.

When buying a collectible, try to avoid the big markups by cutting out the middlemen. Buy directly from the artist or producer if you can.

Life insurance with a cash value

Life insurance should not be used as an investment, especially if you haven't exhausted your contributions to retirement plans. Agents love to sell it for the high commissions. Life insurance that combines life insurance protection with an account that has a cash value is usually known as *universal, whole,* or *variable life.*

The only reason to consider buying accumulating cash-value life insurance is so that you can use the accumulation to secure a tax-free bank loan in the future and, on your death, the proceeds will retire the bank borrowings free of tax. (See Chapter 18 for more on life insurance and why term life insurance is best for the vast majority of people.)

Chapter 12

Mutual Funds: Investments for All of Us

. . . .

In This Chapter

▶ Why funds?

▶ The different types of funds

▶ Choosing the best mutual funds

▶ Good and bad information sources

▶ Making sense of fund performance numbers

. . . .

Mutual funds are managed by investment companies that pool your money with that of thousands of other like-minded individuals and invest it in stocks, bonds, and other securities. It's kind of like a big investment club without the meetings. When you invest through a typical mutual fund, several million to a billion dollars or more are invested along with your money.

Mutual Fund Benefits

Mutual funds rank right up there with microwave ovens, videocassette recorders, sticky notes, and plastic wrap as the best inventions of modern times. To understand their success is to grasp how and why funds can work for you. Read on to discover their benefits:

> ✔ **Professional management.** Mutual funds are managed by a portfolio manager and research team whose full-time jobs are to screen the universe of investments for those that best meet the stated objectives of the fund. The portfolio management team calls and visits companies, analyzes companies' financial statements, and speaks with companies' suppliers and customers. In short, the team does more due diligence and research than you can ever hope to do in all of your free time.

BANK STOCKS ARE

MUTUAL FUNDS IN ITSELF

DIVERSIFIED CUSTOMERS / BALANCED .

Fund managers are typically graduates of the top business and finance schools in the country, where they learn the principles of portfolio management and securities valuation and selection. (Despite their time in the groves of academe, most of them do a good job of investing money.) The best fund managers typically have five or more years of experience in analyzing and selecting investments.

✔ **Low cost.** The most efficiently managed stock mutual funds cost less than 2 percent per year in fees (bonds and money market funds cost much less). Because mutual funds typically buy or sell thousands of shares of a security at a time, their transaction fees are generally 80 to 90 percent less per share than what you pay to buy or sell a few hundred shares on your own. Recent innovations in the technology of information management further reduce the cost of monitoring and managing millions of dollars of investor money.

In addition, when you buy a *no-load fund,* you avoid paying brokerage commissions on your transactions. We write more about these types of funds later in this chapter.

✔ **Diversification.** Mutual fund investing enables you to achieve a level of diversification that is difficult without several hundred thousand dollars and a lot of time to invest. To go it alone, you need to invest money in at least 8 to 12 different securities in different industries to ensure that your portfolio can withstand a downturn in one or more of the investments. Proper diversification allows a mutual fund to receive the highest possible return at the lowest possible risk given its objectives.

We're not suggesting that mutual funds are able to escape share price declines during major market downturns. For example, mutual funds that invested in Canadian and U.S. stocks certainly declined during the October 1987 stock market crash. However, the most unlucky investors that month were individuals who had all of their money riding on only a few stocks. Some shares plunged in price by as much as 80 to 90 percent that month. (Of course, if you held on to your stocks during the plunge, you would have enjoyed the past decade's generous returns.)

✔ **You don't need big bucks.** Most mutual funds have low minimum-investment requirements, especially for RRSP investors. And when you invest in a mutual fund, you get the same attention given to the rich and famous: full-time, professional money management.

Even if you have a lot of money to invest, you should also consider mutual funds. Join the increasing number of companies and institutions (which have the biggest bucks of all) that are turning to the low-cost, high-quality money-management services that you can get in a mutual fund.

✔ **Audited performance records and expenses.** In the prospectuses, all mutual funds are required to disclose historical data on returns, operating expenses, and other fees. The securities regulators in each province oversee these disclosures for accuracy.

✔ **Flexibility in risk level.** Among the enormous variety of different mutual funds, you can choose a level of risk that you're comfortable with and that meets your personal and financial goals. If you want your money to grow over a long period of time, you may want to select funds that invest more heavily in stocks. If you need current income and don't want investments that fluctuate in value as widely as stocks, you may choose more conservative bond funds. If you want to be sure that your invested principal doesn't drop in value because you may need your money in the short term, you can select a money market fund.

✔ **Freedom from salespeople.** Stockbrokers (also known as financial consultants) and commission-based financial planners make more money by encouraging trading activity and by selling you investments that provide them with high commissions — limited partnerships and mutual funds with high load fees, for example. No-load (commission-free) mutual fund companies don't push products. Their toll-free telephone lines are staffed with knowledgeable people who earn salaries, not commissions. Their recommendations don't carry inherent conflicts of interest.

Fund Types

One of the major misconceptions about mutual funds is that they're all invested in stocks. They're not. Figure 12-1 shows how the money Canadians have currently invested in mutual funds breaks down:

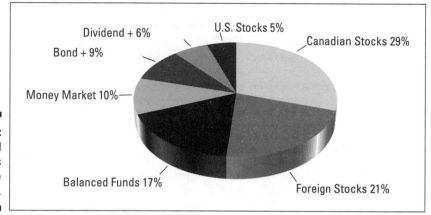

Figure 12-1: How mutual fund assets are invested.

So, as you can see, the majority of mutual fund money is *not* invested in stocks.

BANK FUND
BEST OF TWO WORLDS
+ NO RISK
+ GROWTH

BANK SAVINGS ACCOUNT PLUS GROWTH

When you hear folks talk about the "riskiness" of mutual funds, even in the media, you'll know that they're overlooking this fact: All mutual funds are not created equal. Some funds, such as money market funds, carry virtually *no* risk that your investment will decline in value.

Throughout this discussion, remember that when mutual fund companies package and market their funds, the names they give their funds aren't always completely accurate or comprehensive. For example, a stock fund may not be *totally* invested in stocks. Some of it may be invested in bonds or short term government Treasury bills. Don't assume that a fund invests exclusively in Canadian companies, either — it may invest in international firms as well.

Note: If you haven't yet read Chapters 10 and 11, which provide an overview of investment concepts and options, doing so will enhance your understanding of the rest of this chapter.

Money market funds

ZERO RISK / GOT BANKS

Money market funds are the safest type of mutual funds if you're worried about losing your principal. Money market funds are like bank savings accounts in that the value of your original investment doesn't fluctuate. As with money you'd put into bank savings accounts, money market funds are suitable for money that you can't afford to let fluctuate in value.

Bond funds

Bonds are IOUs. When you buy a bond, you lend your money, typically to a corporation or government agency. A bond mutual fund is nothing more than a large group (pack, herd, gaggle, whatever) of bonds.

Bond funds typically invest in bonds of similar *maturity* (the number of years to elapse before the borrower must pay back the money you lend). The names of some bond funds include a word or two to provide clues about the average length of maturity of their bonds. For example, a short-term bond fund concentrates its investments in bonds maturing in the next two to three years. An intermediate-term fund generally holds bonds that come due within seven to ten years. The bonds in a long-term fund usually mature in 20 years or so.

In contrast to an individual bond that you buy and hold until it matures, a bond fund is always replacing bonds in its portfolio to maintain its average maturity objective.

There's safety in numbers

Mutual funds have a virtually zero risk of bankruptcy. Unlike banks and insurance companies, which have failed and will continue to fail, mutual funds have never failed and probably won't in the future. The situation in which the demand for money back *(liabilities)* exceeds the value of a fund's investments *(assets)* can't occur with a mutual fund.

Of course, the value of a fund fluctuates with the value of the securities in which it is invested. But this variation doesn't lead to the failure or bankruptcy of a mutual fund company.

In contrast, hundreds of banks and dozens of insurance companies have failed in North America in the past decade alone. Banks and insurers can fail because their liabilities *can* exceed their assets. When a bank makes too many loans that go sour at the same time depositors want their money back, the bank fails. Likewise, if an insurance company makes several poor investments or underestimates the number of claims that will be made by insurance policyholders, it too can fail.

And as for security, you don't have to worry about mutual fund companies stealing your money. The specific securities in which a mutual fund is invested are held at a custodian — a separate organization independent of the mutual fund company. The employment of a custodian ensures that the fund-management company can't embezzle your funds and use assets from a better-performing fund to subsidize a poor performer.

Bond funds are useful when you want to live off income or when you don't want to put all your money in riskier investments such as stocks and real estate (perhaps because you plan to use the money soon). Shorter-term bond funds are typically less volatile than longer-term bond funds.

Hybrid funds

Hybrid funds invest in a mixture of different types of securities. Most commonly, they invest in bonds and stocks. These funds are usually less risky and volatile than funds investing exclusively in stocks. In an economic downturn, bonds usually hold up in value better than stocks do. However, during good economic times when the stock market is booming, the bond portions of these funds tend to drag down their performance a bit.

Hybrid mutual funds are typically known as balanced or asset allocation funds. *Balanced funds* generally try to maintain a fairly constant percentage of investment in stocks and bonds. *Asset allocation funds* tend to adjust the mix of different investments according to the portfolio manager's expectations of the market. Of course there are exceptions — some balanced funds make major shifts in their allocations whereas some asset allocation funds maintain a relatively fixed mix. You should note that most funds that shift money around instead of staying put in good investments have done a dismal job in beating the market averages.

Hybrid funds are a way to make fund investing simple. They give you instant diversification across a variety of investing options. They also make it easier for stock-skittish investors to invest in stocks while avoiding the high volatility of pure stock funds.

Stock funds

Stock mutual funds, as their name implies, invest in stocks. These funds are often referred to as *equity* funds. (Equity — not to be confused with equity in real estate — is another word for stocks.) Stock mutual funds are usually categorized by the type of stocks they invest in.

Stock types are first defined by size of company (small, medium, and large). The total market value (capitalization) of a company's outstanding stock determines its size. Small- and midcompany stocks, for example, are usually defined as companies with total market capitalization of less than $500 million.

Stocks are further categorized as growth or value. *Growth stocks* are companies that are experiencing rapidly expanding revenues and profits. These companies tend to reinvest most of their earnings back into their infrastructure to fuel future expansion. Thus, growth stocks pay low dividends.

At the other end of the spectrum are *value stocks*. Value stock investors look for good buys. They want to invest in stocks that are cheaply priced in relation to the assets and profits of the company.

These categories are combined in various ways to describe how a mutual fund invests its money. One fund may focus on large-company growth stocks; another fund limits itself to small-company value stocks. Funds are further qualified by the geographical locations of their investments: Canadian, U.S., international, worldwide, and so on.

For more background on stocks, see Chapter 11.

Canadian, U.S., international, and global funds

Canadian funds focus their investments in Canada unless they have words like *international, global, worldwide,* or *world* in their names. But even funds without one of these terms attached often invest money internationally.

The only way to know for sure where a fund is currently invested (or where the fund may invest in the future) is to ask. You can start by calling the 800 number of the mutual fund company that you're interested in.

The term *U.S. fund* means a fund that concentrates on investing almost exclusively in U.S. companies. *International* typically means that a fund can invest anywhere in the world except Canada. The term *worldwide* or *global* generally implies that a fund can invest anywhere in the world, including Canada. But just because they can pick from investments all over the world doesn't make these funds instant winners. First, thoroughly following the financial markets and companies in so many parts of the world is difficult for a fund manager. Following financial markets and companies is hard enough to do solely in Canada or the U.S. or in a specific international market. Second, some of these funds charge high operating expenses — often well in excess of 2 percent per year — which puts a drag on returns.

Exceptions to this rule are a number of strong funds, including Saxon World Growth Fund, Templeton Growth Fund, Trimark Fund, and Cundill Value Fund.

Index funds

Index funds are funds that can be (and are, for the most part) managed by a computer. An index fund's assets are invested to replicate an existing market index such as the TSE 300, an index of 300 large Canadian company stocks.

Over long periods (ten years or more), U.S. index funds outperform about three-quarters of their peers! How is that possible? How can a computer making mindless, predictable decisions beat out an intelligent, creative, MBA-endowed portfolio manager with a crack team of research analysts scouring the market for the best securities? The answer is cost. The computer does not demand a high salary, nor does the computer need a big corner office. And index funds don't need a team of research analysts.

OUR BANK FUND

Most active fund managers can't overcome the handicap of high operating expenses that pull down their funds' rates of return. As we discuss later in this chapter, operating expenses include all the fees and profit that a mutual fund extracts from a fund's returns before the returns are paid out to you. For example, the average U.S. stock fund has an operating expense ratio of 1.2 percent per year. So a U.S. stock index fund with an expense ratio of just 0.2 percent per year has an advantage of 1 percent per year.

But index funds have performed less well in Canada, and the reason lies in our higher expense ratios. The management (or operating) expense ratios on Canadian index funds range from 0.87 percent up to the whopping 2.52 percent charged by Great-West Life, which stunningly is almost the same expense ratio charged for its actively managed Canadian equity funds. Those higher expenses undermine the returns of Canadian index funds and have contributed to their relative unpopularity.

Another not-so-inconsequential advantage of index funds is that you can't underperform the market by much more than the expense ratio. Other types of funds, though, can do far worse due to the burden of high fees and poor management. If you were unfortunate enough to have been involved in the following loser mutual funds in the past ten years, you fared about 5 to 15 percent worse per year in your rate of return than if you had invested in a boring old index fund (Bank of Montreal's First Canadian Equity index fund over the same time period provided an average annual rate of return of 10.1 percent). See Table 12-1.

Table 12-1	Mutual Funds That Will Fetch a Stick (Bow Wow!)
Fund	**Average Annual Rate of Return (10 years) up to July 31, 1998**
Cambridge Special Equity	−3.7%
Friedberg Double Gold Plus	−2.4%
Industrial Equity	−0.1%
Royal Japanese Stock	−2.7 %

For money invested outside retirement plans, index funds have an added advantage: Fewer taxable distributions (discussed later in this chapter) are made to shareholders because less trading of securities is conducted and a more stable portfolio is maintained.

Yes, index funds may seem downright boring. When you invest in them, you give up the opportunity to brag to others about your shrewd investments that beat the market averages. On the other hand, you have no chance of doing much worse than the market, which more than a few mutual fund managers do.

Index funds make sense for a portion of your investments because it's very difficult for portfolio managers to beat the market.

Specialty (sector) funds

Specialty funds don't fit neatly into the previously discussed categories. These funds are often known as *sector* funds because they tend to invest in securities in specific industries.

OUR
FUND
BANKS

[handwritten: BANK FUND IS DIVERSIFICATION / 6 BANKS EVERY CAN INDUSTRY]

In most cases, you should avoid investing in specialty or sector funds. Investing in stocks of a single industry defeats a major purpose of investing in mutual funds — diversification. Another good reason to avoid sector funds is that they tend to carry much higher expenses than other mutual funds.

Specialty funds that may make sense for a small portion (10 percent or less) of your investment portfolio are funds that invest in real estate or precious metals (refer to Chapter 11). These types of funds can help diversify your portfolio because they can do better during times of higher inflation.

Selecting the Best Mutual Funds

Selecting the best funds for you requires an understanding of your invest-ment goals and risk tolerance. A good fund for your next-door neighbour is not necessarily a good fund for you. You have a unique financial profile. If you've determined your needs and goals already, terrific! If you haven't, refer to Chapter 8.

Understanding yourself is a good part of the battle. But don't shortchange yourself by not being educated about the investment you're considering. Although most mutual fund investors are rewarded for their efforts, there are no guarantees. You can, however, follow some simple, common-sense guidelines that will keep you on the trail and increase your chances of investment success and happiness. The following issues in this section are the main ones you should consider.

Cost

[handwritten: LOW FIXED COSTS]

The charges you pay to buy or sell a fund, as well as the ongoing fund operating expenses, can have a big impact on the rate of return you earn on your investments. Many novice investors pay too much attention to a mutual fund's prior performance (in the case of stock funds) or to the fund's current yield (in the case of bond funds). Doing so is dangerous because a fund can inflate its return or yield in many (risky) ways. And what worked yesterday may flop tomorrow.

A recent study conducted by the Investment Company Institute in the U.S. confirms what we've long observed among fund buyers. Only 43 percent of recent fund buyers surveyed bothered to examine the fees and expenses of the fund they ended up buying. The majority of fund buyers — 57 percent to be exact — don't know what their funds charge them to manage their money!

Fund costs are an important factor in the return that you earn from a mutual fund. Fees are deducted from your investment. All other things being equal, high fees and other charges depress your returns.

Loads

Loads are up-front commissions paid to brokers and other financial advisors who sell mutual funds. Loads typically range from 2 percent to as high as 6 or 7 percent of your investment. Sales loads have two problems:

ONE TIME COST!

✔ **First, sales loads are a needless cost that drags down the returns of your investment money.**

Because commissions are paid to the salesperson and not to the fund manager, the manager of a load fund doesn't work any harder and isn't any more qualified than a manager of a no-load fund. Common sense suggests and studies confirm that load funds perform *worse,* on average, than no-loads when the load is factored in.

And don't think that spotting a load fund is easy. Just as some jewellers flog fake diamonds on late-night TV commercials, increasing numbers of brokers and financial planners sell bogus funds that they *call* no-loads, but these funds are *not* no-loads — they just hide the sales commissions. *NO FREE ROLL!!*

"Stay in this fund for five to seven years," the broker tells you, "and you don't have to pay the back-end sales charge that would normally apply upon sale of the investment." Although this claim may be true, it's also true that the fund probably charges you very high ongoing operating expenses (often 1 percent more per year than true no-load funds) that the fund uses to pay the salesperson a hefty commission. So one way or another, the broker gets his pound of flesh (that is, his commission) from your investment dollars.

✔ **The second problem with sales loads is the power of self-interest.**

Although this issue is rarely discussed, it is even more problematic than the issue of extra sales costs. Brokers who work for a commission are interested in selling you commission-based investment products; therefore, their best interests often conflict with your best interests.

Although you may be mired in high-interest debt or underfunding your RRSP, salespeople may not advise you to pay off your credit cards or put more money into your mortgage. To get you to buy, they may exaggerate the potential benefits and obscure the risks and drawbacks of what they sell. They don't take the time to educate investors. We've seen too many people purchase investment products through brokers without understanding what they're buying, how much risk they're taking, and how these investments will affect their overall financial lives.

The only way to be sure that a fund is truly no-load is to look at the prospectus for the fund. Only there, in black and white and without marketing hype, must the truth be told about sales charges and other fund fees. (An astonishing 73 percent of fund buyers surveyed by the Investment Company

Institute didn't review whether the fund they bought charged a sales load!) If you need advice about investing, hire a financial advisor on a fee-for-service basis (see Chapter 20). Doing so ends up costing you less and eliminates potential conflicts of interest in product sales and recommendations.

If you want to buy a load fund — and there are plenty of good choices available — remember that the load is the maximum, not the required sales commission allowed. If you have enough business to offer them, some planners and brokers will even sell you load funds at minimal cost, or even with no sales charge at all, because they receive ongoing commissions called trailer fees as long as you keep your money in a fund.

Operating expenses

All mutual funds charge ongoing fees. The fees pay for the operational costs of running a fund — employees' salaries, marketing, servicing the toll-free phone lines, printing and mailing published materials, computers for tracking investments and account balances, accounting fees, and so on.

A fund's operating expenses are quoted as an annual percentage of your investment. A mutual fund's operating expenses are essentially invisible to you. That's because they're deducted before you're paid any return. The expenses are charged on a daily basis, so you have no need to worry about trying to get out of a fund before these fees are deducted.

Socially responsible funds

Increasing numbers of mutual funds label themselves *socially responsible*. This term means different things to different people. In most cases, though, it implies that the fund avoids investing in companies, such as tobacco manufacturers, that harm people or the world at large. Because cigarettes and other tobacco products kill hundreds of thousands of people and add billions of dollars to health-care costs, most socially responsible funds shun tobacco companies.

Socially responsible investing presents a couple of problems. For example, your definition of social responsibility may not match the definition of the investment manager who runs a fund. Another problem is that even if you can agree on what's socially irresponsible (such as selling tobacco products), funds aren't always as clean as you would think or hope. Although a fund may avoid tobacco manufacturers, it may well invest in retailers that sell tobacco products.

If you want to consider a socially responsible fund, call the investment company and ask it to send you a recent report that lists the specific investments that the fund owns.

You can find a fund's operating expenses in the fund's prospectus. Look in the expenses section and find a line that says something like "Total Fund Operating Expenses." You can also call the fund's 800 number and ask a representative.

TIP

Within a given sector of mutual funds (for example, money market, short-term bonds, or international stock), funds with low annual operating fees can more easily produce higher total returns for you.

Although expenses matter on all funds, some types of funds are more sensitive to high expenses than others. Expenses are critical on money market mutual funds and very important on bond funds. Fund managers already have a hard time beating the averages in these markets; with higher expenses added on, it's nearly impossible.

With stock funds, expenses are a less important (but still important) factor in picking a fund. Don't forget that over time, stocks have averaged returns of about 10 percent per year. So if one stock fund charges 1 percent in operating expenses more than another, you're already giving up an extra 10 percent of your expected returns.

Some people argue that stock funds that charge high expenses may be justified in doing so if they generate higher rates of return. Evidence doesn't show that they do generate higher returns. In fact, funds with higher operating expenses tend to produce *lower* rates of return. This trend makes sense because operating expenses are deducted from the returns that a fund generates.

REMEMBER

Stick with funds that maintain low total operating expenses and that don't charge sales loads (commissions). Both types of fees come out of your pocket and reduce your rate of return.

You have no reason to pay a lot for the best funds, as Table 12-2 shows.

Table 12-2	Mutual Fund Operating Expense Ratios	
Fund Type	**Expense Ratio Range**	**Who's Got Good Ones**
Money market funds	0.50% to 1.00%	Beutel Goodman, Bissett, BPI, C.I., Green Line, PH&N, Scotia
Bonds funds	0.57% to 1.65%	Altamira, C.I., Green Line, Mawer, PH&N, Trimark
Canadian stock funds	1.33% to 1.75%	Bissett, Saxon, Sceptre, Scudder, Trimark
International stock	1.52% to 2.69%	Fidelity, Templeton, Trimark
Index	0.80% to 1.21%	Bank of Montreal, Green Line

Historic performance

A fund's *performance,* or historic rate of return, is another important factor to weigh when selecting a mutual fund. As all mutual funds are required to tell you, past performance is no guarantee of future results. Analysis of historic mutual fund performance proves that some of yesterday's stars turn into tomorrow's skid-row bums.

Many former high-return funds achieved their results by taking on high risk. Funds that assume higher risk should produce higher rates of return. But high-risk funds usually decline in price faster during major market declines. Thus, in order for a fund to be considered a *best* fund, it must consistently deliver a favourable rate of return given the degree of risk it has taken.

When assessing an individual fund, compare its performance and volatility over an extended period of time (five or ten years will do) to a *relevant* market index. For example, compare funds that focus on investing in large Canadian companies to the TSE 300 index. Funds that invest in U.S. stocks of all sizes can be compared to the Wilshire 5000 index. Indexes also exist for bonds, foreign stock markets, and almost any other type of security you can imagine.

Fund manager and fund family reputation

Much is made of who manages a specific mutual fund. As Peter Lynch, retired and famous former manager of the Fidelity Magellan fund, said, "The financial press made us Wall Street types into celebrities, a notoriety that was largely undeserved. Stock stars were treated as rock stars. . . ."

Although the individual fund manager is important, no fund manager is an island. The resources and capabilities of the parent company are equally important. Different companies have different capabilities and levels of expertise in relation to different types of funds. For example, Templeton has a pool of talented stock fund managers upon which to draw when a manager leaves the firm or moves to another fund, while Phillips, Hager, & North is terrific at money market, bond, and conservative stock funds, thanks to its low operating expenses and investing approach.

When you consider a particular fund — for example, the Barnum & Barney High-Flying Foreign Stock fund — examine the performance history and fees not only of that fund but also of similar foreign stock funds at the Barnum & Barney company. If Barnum's other foreign stock funds have done poorly or Barnum & Barney offers no other such funds because it's focused on its circus business, those are strikes against its High-Flying fund.

Tax-friendliness

Investors often overlook tax implications when selecting mutual funds for nonretirement accounts. Numerous mutual funds effectively reduce their shareholders' returns because of their tendency to produce more taxable distributions — that is, capital gains and dividends, which we discuss later in this chapter.

"Ranking Mutual Funds on an After-Tax Basis," a pioneering study conducted by John B. Shoven and Joel M. Dickson at Stanford University, demonstrated that mutual fund capital gains distributions have a significant impact on an investor's after-tax rate of return. The Shoven and Dickson study found large differences between the before-tax and after-tax rates of return generated by stock mutual funds.

The following example highlights the dangers of picking a stock mutual fund for a nonretirement account simply on the basis of its reported rate of return.

Over a recent three-year period, Altamira Equity fund averaged a 10.9 percent annual rate of return, outpacing the Green Line Canadian Equity fund, which averaged 9.5 percent per year. On the surface, it would seem that Altamira, beating its rival by 1.4 percent per year, is the better of the two funds.

But that's only part of the story. All mutual fund managers buy and sell stocks during the course of a year. Whenever a mutual fund manager sells securities, any gain or loss from those securities must be distributed to fund shareholders. Securities sold at a loss can offset those sold at a profit.

If a fund manager has a tendency to cash in more winners than losers, investors in the fund receive a high amount of taxable gains. Over the past three years, Altamira Equity fund has made capital gains and interest distributions. Green Line Canadian Equity fund, on the other hand, had essentially no capital gains and interest distributions. That meant someone in the top tax bracket would only be able to pocket 68 cents for every dollar received. In other words, the after-tax rate of return was closer to 7.5 percent, not counting dividends. So, even though the Altamira fund says it produces higher total returns, *after* factoring in taxes, it doesn't.

Choosing mutual funds that minimize capital gains distributions helps you defer taxes on your profits. By allowing your capital to continue compounding as it would in an RRSP or other retirement plan, you as a fund shareholder receive a higher total return.

If you're a long-term investor, you benefit most from choosing mutual funds that minimize capital gains distributions. The more years that appreciation can compound without being taxed, the greater the value to you as the investor.

Investors who purchase mutual funds outside tax-sheltered retirement plans should also consider the time of year they purchase shares in funds. December is the most common month in which mutual funds make capital gains distributions. When making purchases late in the year, ask if and when the fund may make a significant capital gains distribution. Consider delaying purchases in such funds until January.

Best Places for Fund Investing

The mutual fund field has attracted a lot of new competitors tempted by the riches that early winners have accumulated. Unfortunately, many companies sell funds with high fees, subpar performance, or both.

Here's a short list of the leading firms to consider when investing in funds. Please note that fund companies not on this short list have some excellent funds, and not all funds offered by each of the top companies are worthy of your fund dollars.

Phillips, Hager & North

Based in Vancouver, Phillips, Hager & North (800-661-6141) is one of the country's best-performing and best-kept secrets in the mutual fund world. With nearly $5 billion in under management, half of which comes from individual investors, it ranks as one of the largest no-load families.

The company's reputation is steadily growing, despite its purposefully low profile. In fact, it has an advertising budget of exactly zero. The fund is also exceedingly rare in that it doesn't pay trailer fees — ongoing commissions — to people who sell its funds.

Part of what limits its general appeal is its steep minimum investment — $25,000 — for its funds. However, if you invest for an RRSP, the minimum initial investment is only $5,000 per fund. Given that the company doesn't even charge RRSP holders an annual trustee fee, this is more than generous.

Phillips, Hager & North funds consistently lead in their groups. Its U.S. Equity, Balanced, and Bond funds are especially good choices, but its Canadian equity funds also turn in solid performances.

What we really like about this company is its attitude. It's all summed up by the fact that it calls its investors *clients*, not customers. Another great feature is its commitment to keeping MERs (*management expense ratios,* also called operating expenses) low. Its Canadian Bond fund, for example, is a consistently strong performer, and its MER is just 0.57 percent, well below the median 1.65 percent on other Canadian Bond funds.

Sceptre Investment Counsel

One of the largest pension fund managers in the country, Sceptre Investment Counsel also has about three quarters of a billion invested in its family of six no-load mutual funds. The funds are strong performers, partly due to their low management expenses.

The company has stated that its goal is to have fees that are lower than at least 75 percent of funds in the same category.

Part of what helps keep expenses down is that, like Phillips, Hager & North, Sceptre does not pay trailer fees, nor does it advertise, another feature that recommends the company to value-conscious investors.

Investors in Ontario and B.C. can buy directly from the company at no charge, while those outside the province must go through a broker or discount brokerage firm, paying a commission of up to 2 percent.

Fidelity Investments

Headquartered in Boston, Massachusetts, Fidelity Investments is the largest mutual funds company in the U.S., with over $400 billion under management. Fidelity set up shop in Canada in 1987, and now has over $10 billion under management here, making it one of Canada's largest fund companies as well.

Fidelity offers more than two dozen funds, and has strong performers in almost every category. Fidelity is an especially good bet if you follow our advice and maximize the amount of foreign investments in your RRSP, or have non-registered funds and are investing globally. Drawing on the expertise of its small army of researchers, Fidelity has good funds that invest in the U.S., Europe, the Far East, and internationally. If there is a fault to be found here, it's Fidelity's operating expenses, which on many of its funds are above average.

Banks and Trust Companies

Canadian financial institutions have jumped into the mutual fund fray with both feet, and the results have largely been good news for consumers. Each institution has come up with a separate name for its family of funds, but they can all be bought from any of the institutions' many branches. In addition to being a no-load, most bank and trust company funds have below-average management or operating expense ratios (MERs).

Here's an overview of the offerings of the big banks and trust companies, with some recommendation of funds worth looking at.

- **Bank of Montreal (First Canadian funds).** A wider range of funds is now offered, with the standouts including First Canadian Growth, First Canadian Special, First Canadian Dividend Income, and specialized funds such as First Canadian Far East Growth.

- **Canada Trust (Everest funds).** Boasts a lot of middle-of-the-road performers. Best bets are Canada Trust Amerigrowth Fund, Canada Trust Money Market, and Canada Trust Dividend Income.

- **CIBC** The Bank of Commerce has been adding funds, hiring new managers, and dropping some fees in order to address its funds' overall performance, which has been mediocre at best. Decent results have been turned in by CIBC Balanced, Canadian Bond, and Mortgage funds. While their track records are still too short to know whether they can maintain above-average numbers, the results have been impressive so far on CIBC Canadian Index, CIBC Canadian Energy, CIBC Global Technology, and CIBC U.S. Index RRSP.

- **Royal Bank (Royal Funds and Royal Trust Funds).** Royal has more money under its management than any other no-load fund company. Top funds here include Royal Canadian Equity, Royal U.S. Equity, Royal Balanced, Royal Dividend, and Royal Trust International Bond.

- **Scotiabank (Excelsior funds).** This fund family includes Montreal Trust's old line of funds, which was merged with Scotia Funds in 1995. This family offers solid performance from its Scotia Excelsior Canadian Growth, Dividend, and American Equity funds. Its top performers, though, are Scotia CanAm Money Market Fund, Scotia Excelsior Latin American, Scotia Excelsior Mortgage Fund, and Scotia Excelsior Pacific Rim.

- **TD (Green Line funds).** TD offers a great variety of funds to choose from, with several real winners in the bunch. Funds that deserve special attention include Green Line Balanced Growth, Green Line Canadian Equity, Green Line Canadian Bond, Green Line Money Market, Green Line Science & Technology, and Green Line Value.

The banks and trust companies spend a good deal of time and money on training, but you shouldn't expect their sales representatives to be mutual fund experts. They simply have far too many products to know about and different job functions to carry out to be able to keep up with the latest in the mutual fund field. However, you can easily get your basic questions answered, and many of these institutions put out newsletters that cover everything from explaining basic concepts to suggesting model portfolios.

Tracking Fund Rankings and Performance

Whether you're a novice or an experienced mutual fund investor, trying to get a handle on which funds are the best in various categories (such as international stocks or mortgage bonds) through mutual fund information and rating services can be overwhelming.

Many publications track and recommend mutual funds. However, because they're usually listed alphabetically, going over the lists and trying to compare hundreds of different funds is often a fruitless task.

A good list should rate funds over a reasonably long period of time. Anything shorter than five years won't give you a good read on the fund's long-term performance (except for index funds, where you know what you're getting). Also, make sure that the grouping isn't comparing apples and oranges, either by type of fund or by the period over which the funds are evaluated.

Finally, the best sources of information give you some sense of the fund's riskiness, or *volatility*. If a fund comes out at the top of its class but continually answers a stellar year with a year in which it plummets in value, you might be better off considering a fund that has a slightly lower overall return, but that rings up nice, steady gains each year. A breakout of a fund's performance year by year, such as the one you'll find in the *Globe and Mail's* Mutual Fund Report from time to time, is a terrific and easy way to gauge the volatility and safety of a particular fund.

Chapter 13 recommends the best mutual funds by using criteria discussed earlier in the chapter.

Beware the worst sources

With the popularity of mutual funds, more and more business, personal finance, and news magazines publish mutual fund articles and rankings. For a variety of reasons, much of this information isn't useful to folks trying to make informed decisions. In fact, making decisions based on some of these so-called mutual fund studies is downright dangerous.

A large business magazine committed a number of major errors in its recent "Top Funds" analysis. First of all, the article awarded higher rankings to funds with high returns, without paying any attention to risk or volatility. Funds that took more risk and were able to generate higher rates of return were awarded higher rankings.

The most egregious error was the ranking of funds solely on the basis of rate of return over a three-year period. Three years is a very short time to look at fund performance. This particular three-year period witnessed a nearly uninterrupted upward march in stock and bond prices. Imagine betting on an athlete to win the Olympic decathlon after the shot-put competition. Sure, a stocky, muscular type can shot-put farther than his competitors, but he may be huffing and puffing his way around the track in the mile run.

Be careful of reports that rate funds using letters or grades just like your junior high school teacher did. The reason is your teacher's system was probably more sound. Some reports grade funds within broad categories based solely on total return, completely ignoring risk. The performance rankings that wind up in some newspapers can be for periods as short as *one year.*

Another mistake that some publications commit in published mutual fund rankings is dumping a truckload of data on you. They then order the mutual funds alphabetically so that you sift through page after page of rows and columns of numbers. You have better things to do with your time.

Sadly, one of the reasons some publications confuse more than they convey is *advertising.* Eric once got a call from a financial reporter. Mr. Reporter had an outline for an article he wanted to write about mutual fund investing in which he would profile mutual fund investors that had specific fund companies' investments. The list included a number of load funds, all of which were heavy advertisers in the magazine.

Reading prospectuses and annual reports

Mutual fund companies produce information that can help you make decisions about mutual fund investments. Every fund is required to issue a *prospectus.* This legal document is reviewed and audited by securities regulators. Most of what's written isn't worth the time it takes to slog through it.

The most valuable information — the fund's investment objectives, costs, and performance history — is summarized in the first few pages of the prospectus. This part you should read. Skip the rest, comprised mostly of tedious legal details.

Funds also produce annual reports that discuss how the fund has been doing and provide details on the specific investments that a fund holds. If, for example, you want to know which countries an international fund invests in, you can find this information in the fund's annual report.

As best as Eric could tell, the reporter, who came from a political background, had little — if any — experience with the financial services industry. A few minutes into the conversation, he asked Eric to explain a couple of terms he had used. He didn't know the difference between a stock fund and a bond fund! We hope you enjoy the fact that, having read this chapter, you know a lot more about mutual funds than this reporter did.

Understanding your fund's performance

When you look at a statement for your mutual fund holdings, odds are that you won't understand it. It isn't you — it's the statement.

The hardest part is getting a handle on how you're doing. Most people want to know, and have a hard time figuring out, how much they've made or lost on their investment.

You can't deduce your return by comparing the share price of the fund today versus the share price that you originally paid for the fund. Why not? Because mutual funds make distributions, both of dividends and capital gains, which lead to your getting more shares of the fund (see the section on taxes and funds earlier in this chapter).

Distributions create an accounting problem because they reduce the share price of a fund. (Otherwise, you could buy into a fund just before it made a distribution and make a profit from the distribution.) Therefore, over time, following just the share price of your fund doesn't tell you how much money you've made or lost.

Imagine that the share price of your mutual fund is like a balloon with a small rock tied to the end of a string attached to it. The balloon (representing fund share price) struggles to rise, but the rock (representing fund distributions) keeps pulling down on the balloon.

The only way to figure out exactly how much you've made or lost on your investment is to compare the total value of your holdings in a fund today versus the total dollar amount you originally invested. If you've invested chunks of money at various points in time, this exercise becomes much more complicated, if you want to factor in the timing of your various investments. (Check out recommended investment software in Chapter 22 if you want your computer to help you crunch your own numbers.)

The *total return* of a fund is the percentage change of your investment over a specified period. For example, a fund may tell you that in 1996, its total return was 15 percent. Therefore, if you had invested $10,000 in the fund on the last day of 1995, your investment would be worth $11,500 at the end of 1996. To get a fund's total return, you can call the fund company's 800 number or read the fund's annual report.

The following three components make up your total return on a fund:

- Dividends and/or interest
- Capital gains
- Unit price changes

Dividends and interest

Dividends are income paid by investments, typically preferred and common shares (stocks). Bonds generally pay interest, although they can also provide you with capital gains. When a dividend or interest distribution is made, you can receive it as cash (which is good if you need money to live on) or as more shares in the fund. In either case, the share price of the fund drops by an amount to offset the payout. So if you hope to strike it rich by buying into a bunch of funds just before their dividends are paid, don't bother. You'll just end paying more in income taxes.

If you hold your mutual fund outside an RRSP or other retirement savings plan, the dividend, interest, and capital gains distributions are taxable whether or not you reinvest them as additional shares in the fund.

Capital gains

When a mutual fund manager sells a security in the fund, net gains realised from that sale (the difference from the purchase price) must be distributed to you as a *capital gain*. Typically, funds make one annual capital gains distribution in December.

As with a dividend or interest distribution, you can receive your capital gains distribution as cash or as more shares in the fund. In either case, the share price of the fund drops by an amount to offset the distribution.

For funds held outside RRSPs, RRIFs, and so on, your capital gains distribution is taxable. As with dividends and interest distributions, capital gains are taxable whether or not you reinvest them in additional shares in the fund.

As we discuss in more detail in the next chapter, you may want to check with a fund to determine when capital gains are distributed if you want to avoid making an investment in a fund that's about to make a capital gains distribution. This increases your current-year tax liability for investments made outside of retirement plans.

Unit price changes

You also make money with a mutual fund when the unit price increases. This occurrence is just like investing in a stock or piece of real estate. If it's worth more today than when you bought it, you've made a profit (on paper, at least). In order to realize this profit, you need to sell your units in the fund.

There you have it — the components of a mutual fund's total return are the following:

Dividends/Interest + Capital Gains + Unit Price Changes = Total Return

Following and selling your funds

How closely you follow your funds is up to you, depending on what makes you happy and comfortable. We don't recommend tracking the share prices of your funds (or other investments for that matter) on a daily basis. It's time-consuming, nerve-racking, and will make you lose sight of the long term. You're more likely to panic when times get tough. And for investments held outside of retirement plans, every time you sell an investment at a profit, you get hit with taxes.

A weekly, monthly, or quarterly check-in is more than frequent enough to follow your funds. Many newspapers now carry total return numbers over varying periods, so you can determine the exact rate of return that you've been earning.

Trying to time and trade the markets to buy at lows and sell at highs rarely works. Yet an entire industry of investment newsletters, hotlines, online services, and the like have sprung up purporting to be able to tell you when to buy and sell. Don't waste your time and money on such nonsense (refer to Chapter 10 for more about gurus and newsletters).

You should consider selling a fund when it no longer meets the criteria mentioned in the section "Selecting the Best Mutual Funds," earlier in this chapter. If a fund has underperformed its peers for at least a two-year period, or if a fund jacks up its management fees, it may be a good time to sell. But if you do your homework and buy good funds from good fund companies, you should need to do little trading.

Chapter 13

Investing Money Inside Retirement Plans

. . . .

In This Chapter

▶ Investments to avoid in retirement plans

▶ How to allocate money in employer-sponsored plans

▶ How to allocate money in plans that you design

▶ How to transfer retirement plans

. . . .

*T*his chapter explains how to make decisions about investing money you currently hold inside RRSPs or other retirement plans, or money you plan to contribute to a retirement plan.

Compared to the often overwhelming world of investing outside retirement accounts, investing inside tax-sheltered retirement plans is far less complicated. There are two reasons for this:

✔ **The range of possible retirement plan investments is more limited.** Direct investments, such as real estate and investments in small, privately owned companies, are not generally available or accessible in most retirement plans.

✔ **When investing in a retirement plan, your returns aren't taxed as you earn them.** Money inside retirement plans compounds and grows without taxation. You only pay taxes on these funds when you withdraw money from the plan (direct transfers to a retirement plan at another investment firm aren't withdrawals, so they aren't taxed). So when you choose an investment for your retirement plan, don't rack your brain over dividends and capital gains; save all that worry for your money in nonretirement accounts.

Inappropriate Retirement Plan Investments

Some investments for retirement plans are simply inappropriate. The basic problem stems from otherwise intelligent folks forgetting, ignoring, or simply not knowing that retirement plans are sheltered from taxation so you therefore want to maximize that benefit by selecting investment vehicles that would otherwise be taxed. This section discusses investments that you should *not* make in retirement plans.

Annuities

Annuities have no place inside retirement plans. Annuities allow your investment dollars to compound without taxation. In comparison to other investments that don't allow such tax deferral, annuities carry much higher annual operating expenses, which depress your returns.

Purchasing an annuity inside an RRSP or other registered retirement plan is like wearing a belt and suspenders together. Either you have a peculiar sense of style, or you spend too much time worrying about your pants falling down. In our experience, many people who mistakenly invest in annuities inside retirement plans have been misled into it by investment salespeople.

Annuities pay hefty commissions, sometimes as high as 10 percent or more of the amount invested. In some cases, we think, the salespeople aren't being conniving and unethical — they just don't know any better. The insurance companies behind these products, in their enthusiasm to pump up salespeople to peddle them, conveniently skip over the details about when investing in annuities is appropriate and when it isn't.

Limited partnerships

Limited partnerships, which are sold through investment salespeople, are treacherous, high-commission, high-cost, and hence low-return investments. Part of their supposed allure, however, is the tax benefits that they generate. But when you buy and hold a limited partnership in a retirement plan, you lose the ability to take advantage of many of the tax deductions. The illiquidity of LPs may also mean that you can't make required retirement plan withdrawals when needed. These are just some of the many reasons to avoid investing in limited partnerships. For more reasons, see Chapter 11.

Allocating Your Money in Retirement Plans

With good reason, people are concerned about placing their retirement plan money in investments that can decline in value. You may feel that you're gambling with dollars intended for the security of your golden years.

But in order to attain that security, most working folks need to make their money work hard in order for it to grow fast enough. That involves taking some risk; you have no way around it. Luckily, if you have 15 to 20 years or more before you need to draw on the bulk of your retirement account assets, time is on your side. If some of your investments drop a bit over a year or two, what's the big deal as long as the value of your investments has time to recover? The more years until you retire, the greater your ability to take risk.

If you haven't yet done so, read the section in Chapter 10 on asset allocation. That section helps you decide how to divide your money among different investment options based upon your time frame and risk tolerance.

Prioritizing retirement contributions

If you have access to more than one type of retirement account, prioritize which accounts to use first by what they give you in return. Your first contributions should be to employer-based plans that match your contributions. After that, contribute to any other employer plan or your RRSP, as long as your contributions are tax-deductible.

Setting up an RRSP

No-load (commission-free) mutual fund and discount brokerage firms are your best bet for setting up an RRSP. (Find specific recommendations for investments to use inside your plan later in this chapter.)

Investments and account types are different issues. People sometimes get confused when discussing the investments they make in retirement plans, especially people who have RRSPs at banks. They don't realize that you can have your RRSP at a variety of financial institutions (for example, a mutual fund company or brokerage firm). At each financial institution, you can choose among the firm's investment options for putting your RRSP money to work.

Allocating money when your employer selects the investment options

In some company-sponsored pension plans, you're limited to the predetermined investment options your employer offers. Plans differ in the specific options they offer, but they usually offer similar basic choices. In what follows, we discuss a pension plan's typical investment options, in order of increasing risk and, hence, likely return.

Money market/savings accounts

For regular contributions coming out of your pay cheque, the money market or savings account option makes little sense. Some people who are skittish about the stock and bond markets are attracted to money market and savings accounts because those accounts can't drop in value. However, the returns are low . . . so low that you run the risk — we would venture to say high probability — that your investment won't stay ahead of, or even keep up with, inflation and taxes (which are due upon withdrawal of your money from the retirement plan).

For those of you who may be tempted to use a money market fund as a parking place until the time that you think stocks and bonds are cheap, don't. In the long run, you won't do yourself any favours if you do so. As we discuss in Chapter 10, timing your investments to attempt to catch the lows and avoid investing at the peaks is impossible. If you can figure out how to do that, you're wasting your time in whatever occupation you're now employed. You could make a fortune as a money manager.

You may need to temporarily keep money in the money market investment option if you plan to cash in the account in the near future in order to facilitate a transfer to another retirement plan.

Bond mutual funds

Bond mutual funds (which we describe in Chapter 12) invest in a mixture of typically high-quality bonds. Bond funds pay a higher rate of interest or distributions than money funds. Depending on whether your plan's option is a short-term, intermediate-term, or long-term fund, the bond fund's current yield is probably a couple percent or so higher than the money market fund's yield.

Bond funds carry higher yields than money market funds, but they also carry greater risk because their value can fall if interest rates increase. However, bonds tend to be more stable in value than stocks.

Aggressive, younger investors should keep a minimum amount of money in bond funds. Older folks who want to invest more conservatively may want to invest more money this way.

Guaranteed Investment Certificates (GICs)

GICs are backed by a bank, trust company, or insurance company, and offer you a fixed rate of return projected anywhere from a few months to five years forward. The return is always positive and certain — thus you don't have the uncertainty that you would normally face with bond or stock investments.

The attraction of these investments is that your account value doesn't fluctuate (at least, not that you can see). The financial institution normally invests your money mostly in bonds and maybe a bit in stocks. The difference between what these investments generate and what you get paid in interest is profit to the GIC seller. The yield is usually comparable to that of a bond fund.

For people who would hit the eject button the moment that a bond fund slides a bit in value, GICs are soothing to the nerves. And they're certainly higher yielding than a money market or savings account.

Like bonds, however, GICs don't give you the opportunity for long-term growth of your money. Over the long haul, you should earn a better return in a mixture of bond and stock investments. In GICs, you pay for the peace of mind of a guaranteed return in the form of lower long-term returns.

Balanced mutual funds

Balanced mutual funds invest in a mixture primarily of stocks and bonds. This one-stop shopping concept makes investing easier and smoothes out fluctuations in the value of your investments — funds investing exclusively in stocks or in bonds make for a rougher ride. These funds are solid options and, in fact, can be used for a significant portion of your retirement plan contributions. Refer to Chapter 12 to learn more about balanced funds.

Stock mutual funds

Stock mutual funds invest in stocks, which usually provide greater long-term growth potential but also wider fluctuations in value from year to year. Some companies offer a number of different stock funds, including funds that invest overseas. Unless you plan to borrow against your funds for a home purchase (if your plan allows), you should have a healthy helping of stock funds.

Stock in the company you work for

Some companies offer employees the option of investing in the company's stock. We generally advocate avoiding this option for the simple reason that your future income and other employee benefits are already riding on the success of the company. If the company hits the skids, you may lose your job and your benefits. You certainly don't want the value of your retirement plan to be dependent on the same factors.

If your employer does not offer you other retirement plan investing options, complain. Start with your benefits department. If your employer's stock is the one and only option, that doesn't pass muster.

If you think that your company has its act together and the stock is a good buy, investing a portion of your retirement plan is fine — but no more than 25 percent. Now, if your company is on the verge of hitting it big and the stock is soon to soar, you'll of course be kicking yourself for not putting more of your money into the company's stock. But if you place a big bet on your company's stock, be prepared to suffer the consequences if the stock tanks. Don't forget that lots of smart investors track companies' prospects, so odds are that the current value of your company's stock is fair.

Some employers offer employees the ability to buy company stock at a discount, sometimes as much as 15 percent, compared to its current market value. If you can do this, so much the better. If you sell the stock when your employer's plan allows, usually after a certain length holding period, you should be able to lock in a decent profit.

Some examples

Using the methodology that we outline in Chapter 10 for allocating money, Table 13-1 shows a few of examples of how people in typical employer plans may choose to allocate their pension plan investments among the plan's investment options.

Table 13-1	Allocating Registered Savings Plan Investments		
Risk	25-Year-Old, Aggressive	45-Year-Old, Moderate Risk	60-Year-Old, Moderate Risk
Bond Fund	0%	35%	50%
Balanced Fund (50% stock/ 50% bond)	10%	0%	0%
Blue Chip/ Larger Company Stock Fund(s)	45%	25%	25%
Aggressive/ Smaller Company Stock Fund(s)	25%	20%	10%
International Stock Fund(s)	20%	20%	15%

Please note that making allocation decisions is not a science. Use the formulas in Chapter 10 as a guideline.

Allocating money in plans that you design

With RRSPs, particularly self-directed plans, you get to select the investment options as well as the allocation of money among them.

In the sections that follow, we give some specific recipes that you may find useful for investing. To set up your RRSP at one of these firms, simply pick up your telephone and dial the company's toll-free number and ask them to mail you an account application. At the time you call, you can also have them mail you background on specific mutual funds that you may be interested in.

The following sections discuss some sample portfolios to consider, one designed for someone keeping her RRSP with Phillips, Hager & North, the other for an investor with TD Bank's Green Line. There are many other strong fund groups out there to work with, but we've chosen these two to give you an idea of how to spread your investments over a company's different fund offerings.

Don't forget, though, that self-directed RRSPs cost $100 to $150 a year in administration fees. A self-directed plan lets you choose from a wide range of funds offered by many different companies. (If you're considering a mutual fund RRSP, we advise setting up a no-load plan.)

Note: In the sections that follow, we recommend a conservative and an aggressive portfolio. These terms are used in a relative sense. Because some of the recommended funds don't maintain fixed percentages of their different types of investments, the actual percentage of stocks and bonds that you end up with may vary slightly from the targeted percentages. Don't sweat it.

Where you have more than one fund choice, you can pick one or split the suggested percentage between them. If you don't have enough money today to divide it up as we suggest, you can achieve the desired split over time as you add more money to your retirement accounts.

Don't forget that you can greatly expand your universe of good mutual fund choices by dealing with a brokerage that charges you a modest commission or no commission at all on load funds.

Green Line

The following two Green Line (800-268-8166) recommendations are for a conservative mix and an aggressive mix, respectively.

A conservative portfolio with 50 percent stocks, 50 percent bonds

Green Line Value — $^1/_3$

Green Line Canadian Bond — $^1/_3$

Green Line Balanced Income — $^1/_3$

An aggressive portfolio with 80 percent stocks, 20 percent bonds

Green Line Canadian Equity — 30 percent

Green Line Value — 30 percent

Green Line Global Select — 20 percent

Green Line Canadian Bond — 20 percent

Phillips, Hager & North

The following two Phillips, Hager & North (800-661-6141) recommendations are for a conservative mix and an aggressive mix, respectively.

A conservative portfolio with 50 percent stocks, 50 percent bonds

Phillips, Hager & North Canadian Equity Plus — $^1/_3$

Phillips, Hager & North Bond — $^1/_3$

Phillips, Hager & North Balanced — $^1/_3$

An aggressive portfolio with 80 percent stocks, 20 percent bonds

Phillips, Hager & North Canadian Equity — 30 percent

Phillips, Hager & North Canadian Equity Plus — 30 percent

Phillips, Hager & North U.S. Equity — 20 percent

Phillips, Hager & North Bond — 20 percent

Self-directed or discount brokerage choices

The following recommendations are for a conservative mix and an aggressive mix, respectively.

A conservative portfolio with 50 percent stocks, 50 percent bonds

AGF Bond, Green Line Global RRSP Bond/ C.I. Canadian Bond/Dynamic Global Bond — 30 percent (Canadian Bond)

Green Line Global RRSP Bond/ C.I. Global Bond RSP/ Dynamic Global — 10 percent (International Bond funds that qualify as Canadian content)

Should I use one investment firm or more than one?

The firms listed in this chapter offer a large enough variety of investment options, managed by different fund managers, that you can feel comfortable concentrating your money at one firm. The advantages of a focused approach are needing to learn the nuances and choices of just one firm rather than several, and having fewer administrative hassles.

If you like the idea of spreading your money around, you may want to invest through a number of different firms. If you open a discount brokerage account (refer to Chapter 10), you can have your cake and eat it, too. You can diversify across different mutual fund companies through one brokerage firm. However, you'll generally pay small transaction fees on some of your purchases and sales of funds (refer to Chapter 11 for more details).

Bissett Retirement/ Sceptre Balanced/ Phillips, Hager & North Balanced/ Global Strategy Income Plus/ Ivy Growth and Income/ Trimark Income Growth — 20 percent (Balanced)

AIC Advantage/ Bissett Canadian Equity/ Ethical Growth Or Clean Environment Equity/ Ivy Canadian/ Spectrum Unit Canadian Equity/ Trimark Canadian — 20 percent (Canadian Equity)

AGF International Value/ Cundill Value/ Dynamic International/ Fidelity International Portfolio/ Templeton Growth/ Trimark — 20 percent (International Equity)

An aggressive portfolio with 80 percent stocks, 20 percent bonds

AGF Bond, Green Line Global RRSP Bond/ C.I. Canadian Bond/Dynamic Global Bond — 20 percent (Canadian Bond)

AIC Advantage/ Bissett Canadian Equity/ Ethical Growth Or Clean Environment Equity/ Ivy Canadian/ Spectrum United Canadian Equity/ Trimark Canadian — 40 percent (Large-Cap Canadian Equity)

BPI Canadian Small Companies/ Bissett Small Cap/ Sceptre Equity Growth — 20 percent (Canadian Small-Cap Equity)

AGF international Value/ Cundill Value/ Dynamic International/ Fidelity International Portfolio/ Templeton Growth/ Trimark — 20 percent (International)

Transferring RRSPs and Other Retirement Plans

You can move your money held in an RRSP to almost any major investment firm you please. Moving the money is pretty simple. If you can dial an 800 number, fill out a couple of short forms, and send them back in a postage-paid envelope, you can transfer a plan. The investment firm to which you transfer your account does the rest.

Here's a step-by-step list of what you need to do to transfer an RRSP or other registered plan such as a RRIF to another investment firm. Even if you work with a financial advisor, you should be aware of this process to ensure that no hanky-panky takes place on the advisor's part:

1. **Decide where you want to move the account.**

   We profile many of the best investment companies in Chapter 12, and we recommend some investment options within those firms in the previous section of this chapter.

2. **Obtain an account application and asset transfer form.** Call the 800 number of the firm you're transferring the money to and ask for an *account application and asset transfer form* for the type of account you're transferring — for example, RRSP, RRIF, or RESP.

   Never, ever sign over assets such as cheques and security certificates to a financial advisor, no matter how trustworthy and honest he or she may seem. The advisor could abscond with them quicker than you can say Bonnie and Clyde. Transfers should not be completed this way. Besides, you'll find it easier to handle the transfer the way we describe in this section.

3. **Complete and mail the account application and asset transfer form.** Completing these for your new investment firm opens your new account and authorizes the transfer.

   You shouldn't take possession of the money in your retirement plan yourself to get it over to the new firm. The tax authorities impose huge penalties if you do a transfer incorrectly. Let the company to which you're transferring the money do the transfer for you.

   If you have questions or problems, the firms to which you're transferring your account have armies of capable employees waiting to help you. Remember, these firms know that you're transferring your money to them, so they should roll out the red carpet.

4. **Figure out which securities you want to transfer and which need to be liquidated.** Transferring existing investments in your plan to a new investment firm can sometimes be a little sticky. If you're transferring cash (money market funds) or securities that trade on any of the major stock exchanges, transferring such assets isn't a problem.

If you own publicly traded securities, transferring them *as is* to your new investment firm is better, especially if the firm offers discount brokerage services. You can then sell your securities through that firm more cheaply.

If you own mutual funds unique to the institution you're leaving, check with your new firm to see if it can accept them. If not, you need to contact the firm that currently holds them to sell them.

GICs are tricky to transfer. Ideally, you should send in the transfer forms several weeks or so before the GICs mature — few people do this. If the GIC matures soon, call the bank and instruct it that, when the GIC matures, you would like the funds to be invested in a savings or money market account that you can access without penalty when your transfer request lands in its mailbox.

5. **(Optional) Let the firm from which you're transferring the money know that you're doing so.** If the place you're transferring from doesn't assign a specific person to your account, definitely skip this step. If you're moving your investments from a brokerage firm where you've dealt with a particular broker, the decision is more difficult.

   Most people feel obligated to let their representative know that they're moving their money. In our experience, calling the person with the bad news is usually a mistake. Brokers or others who have a direct financial stake in your decision to move your money will try to sell you on staying. Some may try to make you feel guilty for leaving, and some may even try to bully you.

   Writing a letter may seem the coward's way out, but writing usually makes leaving your broker easier for both of you. You can polish what you have to say, and you don't put the broker on the defensive. Or (although we don't mean to encourage lying) not telling the *whole* truth may be better. Excuses, such as you have a family member in the investment business who will manage your money for free, may help you to avoid an uncomfortable confrontation.

   Then again, telling an investment firm that its charges are too high or that it misrepresented and sold you a bunch of lousy investments may help the firm to improve in the future. Don't fret too much — do what's best for you and what you're comfortable with. Brokers aren't your friends. Even though the broker may know your kids' names, your favourite hobbies, and your birthday, you have a *business* relationship.

Transferring your existing assets typically takes a month or longer to complete. If the transfer is not completed within six weeks, get in touch with your new investment firm to determine what the problem is. If your old company isn't cooperating, call a manager to help get the ball rolling.

The unfortunate reality is that an investment firm will cheerfully set up a new account to *accept* your money on a moment's notice, but it will drag its feet — sometimes for months — when the time comes to relinquish your money. To light a fire under the behinds of the folks at the investment firm, tell a manager at the old firm that you're sending letters to your province's securities regulator if it doesn't complete your transfer within the next week.

Moving Money from Your Employer's Retirement Account

If you leave a job and you've earned the right to some of your pension benefits (called vesting), you have the option of transferring them into a locked-in retirement account (LIRA). In some provinces, these are called Locked-in RRSPs. Check with your employer's benefits department or a tax advisor for details.

If you want to transfer your pension funds, simply inform your employer where you want your money to be sent. Prior to doing so, you should establish an appropriate account with the investment firm you intend to use. Then tell your employer's benefits department what investment firm you would like your retirement money transferred to. You can give your employer the Revenue Canada forms and lock-in agreements (if required) that have been signed by the investment firm's retirement account trustee. These forms will detail the investment firm's mailing address and your account number.

When you leave a job, particularly if you're retiring or being laid off after many years of service, money-hungry brokers and financial planners probably will be on you like a pack of bears on a tree leaking sweet honey. Tread carefully and slowly if you seek financial help — be sure to read Chapters 3 and 20 to avoid the pitfalls in hiring (or paying commissions for) such assistance.

Chapter 14

Investing Money Outside Retirement Plans

. . . .

In This Chapter

▶ Taking advantage of frequently overlooked investment options

▶ Factoring taxes into your investment decisions

▶ Where to invest your emergency reserve

▶ Recommended short-, intermediate-, and long-term investments

. . . .

*1*n this chapter, we discuss investment options for money held *outside* RRSPs or other retirement plans and include specific mutual fund recommendations. Chapter 13 reviews investments for money inside RRSPs and other retirement plans. This distinction may seem somewhat odd — this distinction isn't made in most financial books and articles — but we have our reasons.

Thinking of the two pots of money differently is useful.

✔ Investments held outside an RRSP (or your company pension plan) are subject to taxation. You have a whole range of different investment options to consider when taxes come into play.

✔ Money held outside RRSPs or other registered plans is also more likely to be used sooner than funds held inside tax-deferred plans. Why? Because you generally have to pay far more in income taxes to access money inside rather than outside retirement plans.

✔ Funds inside retirement RRSPs and registered savings plans have their own nuances. For example, when you invest through your employer's retirement plan, your investment options are usually limited to a handful of choices. And special rules govern transfer of your retirement plan balances.

Getting Started

Suppose you've got some money sitting around in a bank savings account or money market mutual fund. Your money is earning several percent in interest, but you want to invest it more profitably. Never forget two things about investing this type of money:

- ✔ **Earning a few percent is better than losing 20 to 50 percent or more.** Just talk to most people who bought limited partnerships in the past decade (refer to Chapter 11). So be patient. Educate yourself *before* you invest.

- ✔ **To earn a higher rate of return, you must be willing to take more risk.** Earning a better rate of return means considering investments that can fluctuate in value — and, of course, the value can drop as much as it can rise.

You approach the vast sea of investment options and start stringing up your rod to go fishing. You hear stories of people catching big ones — cashing in big on stocks or real estate that they bought years ago. Even if you don't have delusions of grandeur, you'd at least like your money to grow faster than the cost of living.

But before you cast your investment line, consider the following frequently overlooked ways to put your money to work and earn higher returns without as much risk.

- ✔ **Pay off high-interest debt:** Many folks have credit card or other consumer debt that costs more — often *far* more — than 10 percent per year in interest. Paying off this debt with savings is like putting your money in an investment with a guaranteed, after-tax return equal to the rate you pay on the debt. Refer to Chapter 5 for more details if you still aren't convinced.

- ✔ **Pay off some or all of your mortgage:** This financial move isn't quite as clear because the interest rate is lower than on consumer debt. (See Chapter 16 for more details on this decision.)

- ✔ **Contribute to an RRSP:** If you have a chunk of money, make sure that you take advantage of the *terrific* tax benefits offered by RRSPs. (Retirement plan options are discussed in Chapter 13.)

These options may not be as exciting as hunting the big fish out there, but they're financially astute and should improve your financial health.

Taxes and Your Investments

When you invest money outside of an RRSP, *investment distributions* — such as interest, dividends, and capital gains — are all exposed to taxation. Too many folks (and too many of their financial advisors) ignore the tax impact of their investment strategies. You need to pay attention to the tax implications of your investment decisions *before* you invest your money.

Many people make the mistake of not considering the potential tax implications of their investments *before* they invest. For example, consider a moderate-income person in the combined 41 percent tax bracket (federal plus provincial taxes) who keeps extra cash in a taxable bank savings or money market account paying 4 percent interest. She pays 41 percent of her interest earnings in taxes and ends up keeping only about 2.4 percent. If she wasn't using that money as an emergency fund, she might consider putting it into a dividend-producing investment, such as a dividend mutual fund. The effective tax rate on dividend income for someone in the 41 percent tax bracket is only 25 percent — 16 percent less than the rate at which straight interest is taxed.

In the sections that follow, we give specific advice about investing your money while keeping an eye on taxes.

Investing Your Savings/ Emergency Reserve

In Chapter 8, we explain the importance of keeping sufficient money in an emergency reserve account. From such an account, you need two things:

- ✔ **Accessibility.** When you need to get your hands on the money for an emergency, you want to be able to do so quickly and without penalty.

- ✔ **Highest possible return.** You want to get the highest rate of return possible without risking your principal. This doesn't mean that you should simply pick the money market or savings option with the highest yield, because taxes are a consideration. What good is earning a slightly higher yield if you pay a lot more in taxes?

Bank, trust company, and credit union accounts

If you have a few thousand dollars or less, your best and easiest path is to keep the money in a local bank, trust company, or credit union. Look first to the institution where you keep your chequing account.

Keeping this stash of money in your chequing account, rather than in a separate savings account, makes financial sense if the extra money helps you avoid monthly service charges because your balance occasionally dips below the minimum. Compare the service charges on your chequing account with the interest earnings from a savings account.

For example, suppose that you have $2,000 that you're keeping in a savings account to earn 4 percent interest versus earning no interest on your chequing account money. So over the course of a year, you earn $80 interest on that savings account. At the same time, though, you're incurring a $9 per month service charge on your chequing account — $108 a year — because your balance is too low to have your service fees eliminated. In this case, keeping your extra $2,000 in a chequing account may be better if that keeps you above a minimum balance and erases that monthly service charge. (However, if you're more likely to spend the extra money if it's in your chequing account, keeping it in a separate savings account where you won't be tempted to spend it might be better.)

Money market mutual funds

Money market funds, a type of mutual fund, are just like bank savings accounts — but better, in most cases (refer to Chapter 12). The best money market funds pay higher yields than bank savings accounts and offer you cheque-writing privileges.

The yield on a money market is an important consideration. The operating expenses deducted before payment of distributions is the single biggest determinant of yield. All other things being equal (which they usually are with different money market funds), lower operating expenses translate into higher yields for you.

Another factor that may be important in your choice of a money market fund is what other types of fund investing you can do at the fund company where you establish a money market fund. Doing most or all of your fund shopping, money market and otherwise, at one good fund company can reduce the clutter in your investing life; chasing after a slightly higher yield offered by another company sometimes isn't worth the extra paperwork and administrative hassle. On the other hand, there's no reason why you can't invest in funds at multiple firms (as long as you don't mind the extra paperwork), using each for its relative strengths.

Most mutual fund companies don't have many local branch offices, so you'll probably open and maintain your money market mutual fund through the fund's toll-free phone line and the mail. Distance has its advantages. Because you can conduct business by mail and phone, you don't need to schlep into a local branch office to make deposits and withdrawals. Major banks and trust companies offer a large choice of mutual funds, including money market funds.

Despite the distance, your money often is still accessible via cheque writing, and you can also have money wired to your local bank on any business day. If you're worried about a deposit to the fund being lost in the mail, don't. It rarely happens, and no one can legally cash a cheque made payable to you anyway. Just be sure to endorse the cheque with the notation "For Deposit Only" under your signature. (For that matter, driving or walking to your local bank isn't 100 percent safe, either. Imagine all the things that could happen to you or your money en route to the bank!)

If you buy money market funds from your trust company or bank, moving money in and out of the fund is as simple as making a deposit or withdrawal from your chequing account. However, if you sell units in a money market fund, you typically will have to wait until the next business day before the money is available to you.

Never, ever pay a commission to buy or sell a money market fund. Be sure to ask if there are any "loads," as some are actually sold with a deferred sales charge (DSC), meaning you'll get hit with a commission when you move your money out of the fund.

In Table 14-1, we recommend good money market mutual funds.

Table 14-1	Recommended Money Market Funds	
Fund	**Operating Expense (MER)**	**Minimum to Open Account***
Beutel Goodman Money Market	0.58%	$2,500
C.I. Money Market	0.75%	$1,000
Green Line Canadian	0.84%	$2,000 ($100 inside RRSP)
Maxxum Value Advantage	0.84%	$500
McLean Budden Money	0.75%	$5,000
Sceptre Money Market	0.75%	$5,000
Talvest Money Market	0.77%	$500
Trimark Interest	0.75%	$500

*If you agree to invest regularly with a fund company by signing up for a pre-authorized chequing plan, most fund companies will allow you to invest with them for as little as $25 to $50 a month.

Canadian Treasury bill (T-bill) money market funds are appropriate if you prefer a money fund that invests solely in government-issued debt, which has the safety of government backing. Note that some of these funds are permitted to invest in other money market securities. Call the specific fund to ensure it is 100 percent in T-bills before you invest, if the additional security if important for you.

Table 14-2 lists a few that we recommend.

Table 14-2	Recommended T-Bill Money Market Funds	
Fund	*Operating Expense (MER)*	*Minimum to Open Account**
Altamira T-Bill Money Market	0.24%	No minimum
B.P.I. T-Bill Money Market	0.65%	No minimum
Green Line Canadian T-Bill Money Market	0.86%	$2,000 ($100 inside RRSP)

*If you agree to invest regularly with a fund company by signing up for a pre-authorized chequing plan, most fund companies will allow you to invest with them for as little as $25 to $50 a month.

For parking your cash, a strong alternative to money market funds is ING Direct (800-464-3473). The company offers a very competitive rate on its savings accounts, which often beats the returns of many money market funds. Once set up, you can move money between your other accounts and your ING account over the phone.

Investing Money for the Longer Term

Important Note: This section assumes that you have a sufficient emergency reserve and are already taking advantage of tax-deductible RRSP contributions as discussed in Chapter 8.

Which investments you should consider depends on your comfort level with risk. But your choice of investments should also be suited to how much *time* you have until you plan to use the money. We're not talking about investments that you won't be able to sell on short notice if need be (most of them you can). Investing money in a more volatile investment is riskier if you need to liquidate it in the short term.

For example, suppose that you're saving money for a down payment on a house and are about one year away from having enough to make your foray into the real estate market. If you had put this money into the stock market in the beginning of 1987 (or 1972 or 1968 for that matter), a year later, you'd have been a mighty unhappy camper. You could have seen 30 to 40 percent of your money *vanish* in short order and your home dreams put on hold.

Most of the following recommended investments are different types of *no-load* (commission-free) mutual funds. Mutual funds are very *liquid* — they can be sold on any business day with a simple phone call. Funds come with all different levels of risk, so you can choose funds that match your time frame and desire to take risk. (Chapter 12 discusses all the basics of mutual funds.)

The different investment options in the remainder of this chapter are organized by time frame. All the recommended investment funds that follow assume that you have *at least* a several-year time frame. The recommended investments are also organized by your tax situation. (If you don't know your current tax bracket, visit Chapter 7.) Following are summaries of the different time frames:

✔ **Short-term investments.** These investments are suitable for a period of a few years — perhaps you're saving money toward a home or some other major purchase in the near future.

When investing for the short-term, look for liquidity and stability — features that rule out real estate and stocks. Recommended investments include shorter-term bond funds, which are higher-yielding alternatives to money market funds. If interest rates increase, these funds drop slightly in value — a couple of percent or so (unless rates rise tremendously). We also discuss T-bills and Guaranteed Investment Certificates later in this chapter.

✔ **Intermediate-term investments.** These investments are appropriate for more than a few but less than ten years. Investments that fit the bill are intermediate-term bonds and very low-risk, well-diversified hybrid funds that include some stocks.

✔ **Long-term investments.** If you have a decade or more, you can consider potentially higher-return (and therefore riskier) investments. Stocks, real estate, and other growth-oriented investments can earn the most money if you're comfortable with the risk involved.

Bond funds

Bond funds pay taxable distributions (mostly interest) that generally are taxed at your full marginal tax rate. Just like interest earned from a savings account, you have to pay tax on any interest generated by bond funds each year, whether the interest is distributed to you or reinvested in your fund. As a result, you're far better off holding bond funds inside your RRSP where the interest isn't taxed and the full amount of your earnings can be reinvested.

Table 14-3 lists some bond funds we recommend.

Table 14-3	Bond Funds		
Fund	*Investments*	*Operating Expense (MER)*	*Minimum to Open Account**
Short- to Midterm			
Green Line Short-Term Income	Government, Corporate	1.10%	$2,000 ($100 inside RRSP)

(continued)

Table 14-3 *(continued)*

Fund	Investments	Operating Expense (MER)	Minimum to Open Account*
Short- to Midterm			
InvestNat Short-Term/ Government Bond	Mostly Government	1.32%	No minimum
Scotia Excelsior Defensive Income	Mostly Government	1.37%	$500
Talvest Income	Government, Corporate	1.69%	$500
Longer Term			
AGF Canadian Bond	Mostly Government	1.93%	$1,000
Altamira Income	Mostly Government	1.0%	No minimum
Beutel Goodman Income	Government, Corporate	0.66%	$2,500
Green Line Canadian Bond	Government, Corporate	0.94%	$2,000 ($100 in RRSP)
McLean Budden Fixed Income	Government, Corporate	1.00%	$5,000
Phillips, Hager & North Bond	Government, Corporate	0.58%	$10,000
Royal Bond	Mostly Government	1.95%	$500
Sceptre Bond	Mostly Government	0.95%	$5,000

If you agree to invest regularly with a fund company by signing up for a pre-authorized chequing plan, most fund companies will allow you to invest with them for as little as $25 to $50 a month.

Inflation-indexed bonds

Many countries, including Canada, now issue *inflation-indexed* bonds. Because a portion of their return is pegged to the rate of inflation, these bonds offer investors a safer type of bond investment option.

To understand the relative advantages of an inflation-indexed bond, take a brief look at the relationship between inflation and a normal bond.

When an investor purchases a normal bond, he commits himself to a fixed yield over a set period of time — for example, a bond that matures in ten years and pays 7 percent interest. However, changes in the cost of living (inflation) aren't fixed and are difficult to predict.

Asset allocation

Asset allocation is the process of figuring out how much of your vast wealth you should invest in different types of investments. You frequently (and most appropriately) practise asset allocation with your RRSP. Ideally, more of your saving and investing should be conducted through tax-sheltered retirement plans. That's generally the best way to lower your long-term tax burden (refer to Chapter 13 for more details).

If you have sufficient assets that you plan to invest outside your RRSP and other retirement plans, specific recommendations follow this section. For that portion of your investments that you intend to hold for the long term (ten or more years), you can allocate according to the "Suggested asset allocations" section in Chapter 10.

Suppose an investor had put $10,000 into a regular bond in the 1970s. During the life of his bond, he would have unhappily watched escalating inflation. During the time he held the bond and by the time his bond matured, he would have witnessed the erosion of the purchasing power of his $700 of annual interest and $10,000 of returned principal.

Enter the inflation-indexed bond. Say you have $10,000 to invest and you buy a ten-year, inflation-indexed bond that pays you a *real rate of return* (this is the return above and beyond the rate of inflation) of 3.5 percent. This portion of your return is paid out in interest. The other portion of your return is from the inflation adjustment to the principal you invested. The inflation portion of the return gets put back into principal. So if inflation were running at about 3 percent, as it has in recent years, your $10,000 of principal would be indexed upward after one year to $10,300. In the second year of holding this bond, the 3.5 percent real return of interest would be paid on the increased ($10,300) principal base.

If inflation skyrocketed and was running at 10 percent rather than 3 percent per year, your principal balance would grow 10 percent per year, and you'd still get your 3.5 percent real rate of return on top of that. Thus, an inflation-indexed bond investor wouldn't see the purchasing power of his invested principal or annual interest earnings eroded by unexpected inflation.

As long as inflation doesn't unexpectedly take off, you can expect inflation-indexed bonds to yield slightly lower returns — perhaps 0.5 to 0.75 percent less — than normal bonds: Such is the cost of insurance against inflation.

The inflation-indexed bonds can be a good investment for conservative, inflation-worried bond investors, as well as taxpayers who want to hold the government accountable for increases in inflation.

Don't buy GICs for the CDIC insurance

Much is made, particularly by bankers, of the CDIC insurance that comes with bank and trust company GICs. The lack of this insurance on high-quality dividend income mutual funds shouldn't be a big concern for you, though. Dividend income funds invest almost exclusively in safe preferred shares and blue-chip common stocks. The companies behind these shares only infrequently suspend dividends; even if a fund held a stock that did stop paying a dividend, that stock would probably be only a small fraction of the value of the fund, so it would have little impact.

Besides, the CDIC itself is no Rock of Gibraltar. Banks have failed and will continue to fail. Yes, you are insured if you have $60,000 or less in a bank or trust company, but if the institution crashes, you may have to wait a long time and settle for less interest than you thought you were getting. You are not immune from harm, CDIC or no CDIC.

If the insurance promised by CDIC backing allows you to sleep better, you can invest in Treasury bills, which are government-backed bonds.

Guaranteed Investment Certificates (GICs)

For many decades, Guaranteed Investment Certificates (GICs) have been the investment of choice for folks with some extra cash that they don't need in the near term. The attraction is that you get a higher rate of return on a GIC than on a bank savings account or money market fund. GICs are also widely available at banks, trust companies, and life insurance companies. GICs include a number of drawbacks in comparison to bonds.

- ✔ First, in a GIC, your money is not usually accessible unless you cough up a fairly big penalty — typically six months' interest. With a no-load (commission-free) bond fund, if you need some or all of your money next week, month, or year, you can access it without penalty.

- ✔ Another and less-often-noted drawback of GICs is that a good deal of your earnings on them usually end up in Revenue Canada's hands. The interest earned on a GIC is taxed at your full marginal tax rate, the same rate as your salary (unless you hold it in your RRSP).

In the long run, you earn more and have better access to your money in bond funds than in GICs. If you're in the lowest tax bracket (27 percent), and you have a bad day whenever your bond fund takes a dip in value, then consider GICs. Just make sure that you shop around to get the best interest rate.

Dividend funds

If you want regular income from an investment outside your RRSP, consider dividend funds, which come with terrific tax savings built in. These funds invest primarily in the preferred shares of Canadian companies, as well as common shares that usually pay regular dividends. The income you receive from the fund will benefit from the dividend tax credit, which means that you pay a lower tax rate on dividend income than on regular interest income.

The only drawback to dividend income funds is that they have a slightly higher risk than other fixed-income funds that invest in bonds or mortgages. Also, some funds broaden their investments to include common stocks that have lower yields in the hope of using capital gains to boost their performance. The main purpose of an income fund, though, is strong after-tax returns, so be sure to find a fund that almost exclusively invests in preferred shares or common stocks with regular, strong dividends.

Table 14-4 lists recommended dividend funds.

Table 14-4		Recommended Dividend Funds			
Company	*Fund*	*1 year*	*3 year*	*5 year*	*Operating Expense (MER)*
AGF	Dividend	5.9%	21.0%	17.4%	1.87%
Bissett	Dividend/Income	9.2%	21.6%	16.8%	1.50%
Maxxum	Dividend	7.6%	19.8%	16.5%	1.73%
Royal	Dividend	16.3%	26.1%	18.4%	1.77%

Performance numbers are as of July 31, 1998

Stock funds

Listed in Table 14-5 are stock funds, which are appropriate if you don't want current income and have many years — preferably at least ten — to invest.

Note that *all* the funds in Table 14-5 are intended as long-term investments.

Table 14-5		Recommended Stock Funds			
Company	*Fund*	*1 year*	*3 year*	*5 year*	*Operating Expense (MER)*
Small- to Medium-Cap Canadian Funds					
Bissett	Small Cap	−7.7%	20.0%	15.1%	2.27%
Colonia	Special Growth	−6.1%	22.8%	19.4%	1.90%
Mawer	New Canada	−3.3%	14.5%	13.1%	1.46%

(continued)

Table 14-5 *(continued)*

Company	Fund	1 year	3 year	5 year	Operating Expense (MER)
Small- to Medium-Cap Canadian Funds					
Saxon	Small Cap	14.3%	21.5%	15.0%	1.75%
Sceptre	Equity Growth	−12.0%	15.6%	20.5%	1.42%
Large-Cap Canadian Funds					
AIC	Diversified	21.8%	40.6%		2.39%
Bissett	Canadian Equity	8.1%	24.6%	18.3%	1.33%
Ethical	Growth	0.9%	18.1%	14.3%	2.10%
Green Line	Value	−4.4%	18.2%		2.09%
GBC	Canadian Growth	2.9%	20.4%	14.7%	1.90%
Mackenzie	Ivy Canadian	10.9%	17.9%	14.9%	2.38%
Spectrum	United Canadian Equity	−0.3%	15.1%	12.8%	2.35%
Trimark	Canadian	−6.4%	10.0%	11.3%	1.52%
International Funds					
AGF	International Value	18.6%	20.1%		2.77%
Fidelity	International Portfolio	19.2 %	21.1%	18.3%	2.69%
Saxon	World Growth	−0.5%	10.1%	15.2%	1.75%
Sceptre	International	−4.8%	9.5%	12.2%	2.07%
Templeton	Growth	4.5%	13.5%	15.4%	2.00%
Trimark	Fund	3.7%	13.5%	17.6%	1.52%

Performance numbers are as of July 31, 1998

Real estate

Real estate can be a financially and psychologically rewarding investment. It can also be a money pit and a real headache. We discuss real estate as an investment in Chapter 11 and the basics of real estate in Chapter 16.

Small-business investments

Investing in your own business or someone else's established small business can be a high-risk but potentially high-return investment. The best options are those you understand well. See Chapter 11 for more information.

Chapter 15

Investing for Educational Expenses

*I*f you're like most parents or potential future parents, just turning to this chapter makes you break out in a cold sweat. Your anxiety is understandable. Much of what you read about educational expenses, particularly university expenses, says that if costs keep rising at the current rate, you'll have to spend tens of thousands of dollars to give your youngster a quality education.

Quality education for your child need not, and probably won't, cost you as much as those gargantuan projections suggest.

Whether you've already started saving or are about to begin a regular post-secondary education investment plan, odds are quite high that your emotions are leading you astray. The hype about educational costs may scare you into taking a path that's less financially beneficial than others that are available.

The Big Mistake: Neglecting RRSPs

If you're a parent, it's a given that you want what's best for your children. Not only do you want to be able to provide good learning opportunities for them when they are young, but you also want to give them choices. When little Homer and Gwendolyn fill out their university applications, you don't want to have to say that you can't afford to send them to their dream school.

Being considerate and thoughtful parents, you may start investing money in a separate account for them, perhaps in their name or through some other financial product, such as a life insurance policy or an *RESP* (Registered Education Savings Plan). Doing so may actually be a financial mistake in both the short and long term.

We know that you're going to think that our advice sounds selfish. But you have to provide for your own financial security *before* saving for your child. Let us explain.

If you're a frequent flier, think back to your most recent trip by airplane. Remember what the flight attendants instructed you to do in an emergency? In the event of a loss of air pressure that necessitates the use of oxygen masks, put your oxygen mask on *first.* Only then should you help your children with their oxygen masks.

Consider for a moment why airlines recommend this approach. Although your instinct may be to ensure that your children are safe before taking care of yourself, by taking care of yourself first, you're stronger and better able to help your children.

Similarly, in regard to your personal finances, you need to take care of yourself first. You should save and invest through an RRSP or other retirement savings plans that give you significant tax benefits.

Take care of your long-term financial needs (for example, by saving through an RRSP) first. By doing so, you strengthen your financial health, which better enables you in the long run to help your kids with their educational expenses. (See Chapter 8 to learn how to save for retirement and reduce your taxes.)

How Will You Pay Educational Expenses?

If you concentrate today on contributing to your RRSP or company retirement savings plan and paying down your mortgage, you'll have a number of options when your kids graduate from high school. If you've paid down some — or all — of your mortgage, you can borrow against the paid-up value of your home (your *home equity*), usually at or near the lowest interest rate available (the *prime rate*).

Second, if you've been building up your retirement savings, you already have some strong momentum and compounding going on. You've also established a savings habit. When your kids get close to university age, you can divert your RRSP or other retirement plan contributions to help pay their education costs. When they graduate, you can easily resume your RRSP contributions. If you have any extra cash, you can even take advantage of the allowable RRSP contributions you missed out on because you're allowed to carry forward unused contributions indefinitely. (Revenue Canada tracks this for you. You'll find a summary on the income tax return assessment notice you receive every year.) This will leave you in much better financial shape than if you had foregone contributions to your RRSP or company retirement savings plan when you were younger in order to start an educational savings program.

Further, when your kids are ready to go to university, you'll likely be in your peak earning years, so some extra funds will hopefully be available.

However, in most cases, even if you have some liquid cash that can be directed to pay the university bills as they come in, you will, in all likelihood, have to borrow *some* money.

Government student loan programs

The Canada Student Loan program provides loans to university and college students through the banking system. Run by the federal government, the loans are administered by the provinces through their own separate student aid offices. Each province also has its own loan scheme that's rolled in with the Canada Student Loan program.

Students make only one combined application to receive loans from both programs, although interest and conditions on the federal loan and the provincial loan differ slightly. To qualify, students must be citizens or permanent residents of Canada, attend an institution recognized by the program, and be full-time students, which means taking at least three full courses out of the full course load of five.

Regardless of where they're going to go to school, your kids must apply to the province in which they live. Applications can be obtained from any university or college or by calling your provincial student loans program. Find the number in the blue pages of your telephone book.

Part of the assessment of your application involves examining your entire family's income and its ability to pay for the costs of going to university. The assessment is based entirely on income. Assets don't come into the picture at all, so it doesn't pay to neglect contributing to your RRSP or company retirement savings plan, or paying down your mortgage.

The loan programs demand that parents assist in paying the education costs of any dependent children. Even if parents absolutely refuse to assist their children, their ability to pay will still be taken into account when the application is assessed. In order not to be classified as a dependent, a child must have graduated from high school at least four years earlier or have been in the work force at least 24 months.

If the loan is approved, your children should go to the financial aid office when they enrol at their university or college. They'll be given some loan documents, which they can then take to the bank of their choice. (The loans are administered through the big banks, but they're guaranteed by the provincial and federal governments.) A number of credit unions and *caisse populaires* are also approved student loan providers. The maximum amount available varies depending on which province the student lives in.

While your child is in school, the federal and provincial governments pay the interest on the debt every three months until the student either graduates or withdraws. At that point, the federal government stops paying its share of the interest, and the student is responsible for the debt. Some of the provinces, however, will continue to pay the debt costs on their part of the loan for an additional six months.

The interest rate on the two components is calculated differently. The rate on the federal part of the loan is fixed once a year at a percent or so above the best rates offered by financial institutions (the prime rate). The provinces tend to use a floating rate. For example, a province might charge prime plus 1 percent on its loans, with the rate rising and falling along the going prime rate.

Even though the federal government stops paying the interest on its portion of the combined loan at graduation, students aren't required to start repaying the federal or provincial component of their loan until six months after graduation. Generally, this due date falls on November 1. At that time, students must negotiate a schedule with their bank. While students are largely free to choose whatever repayment time-frame they like, both the federal and provincial loans must be completely paid off within 114 months (ten years minus six months). After the student signs agreements for the two separate loans, most institutions will consolidate the debts and work out a single payment schedule.

Once upon a time, many students saw these loans as giveaways because the government didn't seem all that interested in collecting from people who walked away from their obligations. Those days are long gone. Both Ottawa and the provinces have become aggressive in tracking down delinquents and getting their money back. The federal government can even take what it's owed out of tax refunds of those who are behind on their payments. Worse yet, many past-due student loans are now routinely handed over to collection agencies, and the students end up with a nick on their credit rating.

Some tips: Loans, grants, and scholarships

A number of grant programs are available through schools and the government as well as through independent sources. Specific universities, colleges, and private organisations (including employers, banks, credit unions, and community groups) also offer grants and scholarships.

Many scholarships and grants don't require any extra work on your part — simply apply for financial aid through universities and colleges. Other programs need seeking out — check directories and databases at your local library, your child's school counselling department, and college financial aid offices. Also try local organizations, churches, employers, and so on. You have a better chance of getting scholarship money through these avenues.

Postsecondary scholarship search services are generally a waste of money; in some cases, they're scams. Some of these services charge up to $100 just to tell you about scholarships that either you're already being considered for or that you aren't even eligible for.

Your child can work and save money during high school and university. In fact, if your child qualifies for financial aid, he or she may be expected to contribute a certain amount to education costs from savings and from employment during the school year or summer breaks. Besides giving your child a stake in his or her own future, this training encourages sound personal financial management down the road.

Students who support a spouse or child or who have a disability can also often obtain nonrepayable grants. Disabled students can get up to $3,000 a year in grants from the Canada Student Loan program and anywhere from $1,000 to more than $2,000 from their province, depending on where they live.

The borrowing versus saving debate

More than a few investment firms and financial planners argue that, in the long run, saving for your children's university expenses is far cheaper than borrowing for them. This claim isn't always true. If you have finite funds and contribute to an RRSP instead of saving for your child's education, and then separately borrow the money needed for college costs later, you can come out ahead.

These organizations and planners have a conflict of interest in that they can't sell you investments if you channel your savings into your employer's retirement plan. They have every reason to scare you into action (and into their hands).

What will university or college cost?

University or college can cost a lot. The total costs vary substantially from school to school and from program to program. The average annual cost (including tuition, fees, books, supplies, room, board, and transportation) is around $9,000 per year. Higher-level professional degrees, such as an M.B.A, will cost even more because of their higher tuition fees.

Is all this expense worth it? Although many critics of higher education claim that tuition shouldn't be rising faster than inflation and that costs can (and therefore should) be contained, it is hard to deny the value of a post-secondary school education. Whether it's a local community college, your friendly local university, or some hallowed college at Oxford or Cambridge, investing in education is worth the effort and the risk.

The definition of an *investment* is an outlay of money for an expected profit. Unlike a car that depreciates in value each year that you drive it, an investment in education yields monetary, social, and intellectual profit. A car is more tangible in the short term, but an investment in education (even if it means borrowing money) gives you more bang for the buck in the long run.

Universities and colleges are now finding themselves subject to the same types of competition that for-profit companies confront on a daily basis. As a result, schools are clamping down on rising costs. As with any other product or service purchase, it pays to shop around. You *can* find good values — schools that don't cost an arm and a leg *and* provide a quality education.

Setting realistic savings goals

If you have money left over *after* taking advantage of retirement plans, by all means try to save for your children.

Be realistic about what you can afford for university expenses given your other financial goals, especially saving for retirement (refer to Chapter 8). Being able to pay the full cost of a postsecondary education or anything approaching the full cost is a luxury of the affluent. If you aren't a high income earner, consider trying to save enough to pay a third or at most half of the cost. You can easily make up the balance through loans, your child's employment before and during university, and the like.

Fill out Table 15-1 to help get a handle on how much you should be saving.

Note: Don't worry about correcting for inflation. This worksheet takes care of that through the assumptions made on the returns of your investments as well as the amount that you save over time. This way of doing the calculations works because you assume that the money you're saving will grow at the rate of college inflation.

If your child has expensive taste in schools, you may want to tack on 20 to 30 percent to the following average figures:

✔ Average cost of a four-year university education today: $40,000.

✔ Average cost of a four-year private U.S. college education today: $90,000 U.S.

Table 15-1	How Much to Save for University	
Figure Out This	*Write It Here*	
1. Cost of school you think your child will attend.	$ _____	
2. Percent of costs you'd like to pay (for example, 20% or 40%).	x _____	%
3. Line 1 times line 2 is amount you'll pay (in today's dollars).	= $ _____	
4. Number of months until your child reaches university age.	_____	months
5. *Amount to save per month (today's dollars). Line 3 answer divided by line 4 answer.	= $ _____	/ month

* The amount you need to save (calculated in line 5) needs to be increased once per year by the increase in university inflation — 5 or 6 percent should do.

Good and Bad Investments for Educational Funds

Many financial companies pour millions of dollars into advertising for investment and insurance products that they claim are the best ways to make your money grow for your little gremlins — we mean, children.

What makes for good and bad investments in general applies to investments for educational expenses, too. Stick with basic, proven, lower cost investments. Chapter 10 gives a thorough overview of what to look for and what to beware of. This section focuses on considerations specific to university funding.

Good investments: No-load mutual funds

As we discuss in Chapter 12, the professional management and efficiency of no-load mutual funds makes them a tough investment to beat. Chapters 13 and 14 provide recommendations for investing money in funds both inside as well as outside tax-sheltered retirement plans. The important issue is to gear the investments to the time frame involved until your children need to use the money. The closer your child gets to attending university and using the money saved, the more conservatively the money should be invested.

Bad investments

Life insurance policies that have cash values are some of the most oversold investments to fund university costs. The usual pitch is: Because you need life insurance to protect your family, why not buy a policy that you can borrow against to pay for college? Makes sense, doesn't it?

The reason you shouldn't is that you're better off contributing to an RRSP. An RRSP gives you an immediate tax deduction that saving through life insurance doesn't. Because life insurance that comes with a cash value is more expensive, parents are more likely to make a second mistake — not buying enough coverage. If you need and want life insurance, you're better off buying lower-cost term life insurance (see Chapter 18).

Another poor investment for university and college expenses is one that fails to keep you ahead of inflation, such as savings or money market accounts. You need your money to grow to afford educational costs down the road.

Prepaid tuition plans should generally be avoided. A few schools have developed plans to allow you to pay university or college costs at a specific school (calculated for the age of your child). The allure of these plans is that by paying today, you eliminate the worry of not being able to afford rising costs in the future.

This logic doesn't work for several reasons. First, odds are quite high that you don't have the money today to pay in advance. If you have that kind of extra dough around, you're better off using it for other purposes (and you're unlikely to worry about rising costs anyway). You can invest your own money — that's what the school will do with it anyway.

Besides, how do you know which university or college your child will want to attend and how long it might take Junior to get through? Coercing your child into the school you've already paid for is a sure ticket to long-term problems in your relationship with your teenager.

How to Save for Educational Expenses

If you have sufficient funds to take care of your other needs like contributing to an RRSP and want to start saving for your children's postsecondary education, just as important as the investments you choose is the way in which you organize your savings efforts.

You can set up an effective savings plan for postsecondary education expenses two basic ways. When she reaches the age of majority, she then assumes control of the funds. The first option is a Registered Education

Savings Plan (RESP). RESPs have recently become much more attractive, thanks to increased contribution limits and a government plan to subsidize your contributions. The second is to use an *in-trust account*. Under this arrangement, you put money into a special account and invest it on your child's behalf. Which approach is best suited to you depends on your financial situation as well as your assessment of just how likely it is that your children will attend university or college.

RESPs

Until recently, Registered Education Savings Plans were, at best, a reasonable way to save for your child's education. However, if your child didn't end up going to university or college, you had to forfeit every penny of earnings on the money you had put away. But recent changes to the RESP rules have turned them into an attractive and profitable way to build up an education fund.

You can put up to $4,000 for each child into an RESP each year, up to a total lifetime maximum of $42,000 per child. You're allowed to contribute money for up to 21 years, but the plan must be closed down within 25 years of being set up. Money that you contribute to an RESP isn't tax deductible, but any gains inside the plan aren't taxed. When your child is ready to go to school, money from the plan can be taken out tax-free and used for a variety of education-related expenses.

Before the regulations were updated, the biggest drawback to RESPs was that if your child didn't go to a postsecondary institution, you forfeited the earnings. They either had to go to another child, to an educational institution, or in the case of pooled or "scholarship" RESPs, to other children in the program.

New rules, though, mean that, starting in 1999, you transfer up to $50,000 of earnings from an RESP to your RRSP or a spousal RRSP, as long as you have the contribution room available. Any earnings that can't be transferred in this way can still be moved out of the RESP, but they're taxed at your marginal tax rate, plus an additional 20 percent penalty. You can take out your original contributions — your principal — without any penalties or restrictions.

The big kicker that has made RESPs truly worthwhile, though, is the new RESP grant. The government will contribute to your RESP an additional 20 percent of any contribution you make for a child, up to a maximum grant of $400 per year. The grant is available in every year the child is 17 or under on December 31. If you don't contribute enough in any year to get the full $400 grant, you can earn the unused portion in later years. The total lifetime maximum you can receive under this program (CESG, or Canada Education Savings Grant) is $7,200.

How Scholarship RESPs work — and often don't pay!

Scholarship RESPs are offered by a number of organizations, including the Canadian Scholarship Trust, University Scholarship Trust, and Children's Education Trust of Canada.

The traditional offerings were *pooled funds*. Your contributions were pooled with those of other considerate parents and grandparents and invested in safe but low-earning investments, such as T-bills, Canada Savings Bonds, and mortgages. These type of RESPs have three major strikes against them.

First, because they invest in guaranteed investments, their rate of return is much lower than your money could earn in a broadly based conservative international equity mutual fund. To ride out the ups and downs of the equity markets, you should generally be able to leave your money invested for seven to ten years. If you start an RESP savings program when your child is born, you have more than enough time — two to three times in fact — to be able to benefit from the long-term higher returns offered by stocks (unless of course, you have a little genius on your hands who will toddle off to university before he's old enough to baby-sit).

The second drawback is highlighted by the word *scholarship,* which these plans usually feature in big, bright letters in their marketing materials. Don't let this fool you. A true scholarship is something your child earns on his or her own by earning high grades, by excelling at a particular subject, or by developing an interest or expertise in a particular area. The only justification for calling the payout from these plans a scholarship is that some children in the plans receive more than the combined value of their families' contributions and the earnings on that money. The reason is that with traditional "pooled" plans, if your child doesn't go to a qualifying educational institution, you forfeit all the earnings on your money. You only get back your original contributions. The interest is distributed between the other children in the plan who do go on to university or college.

Finally, these pooled plans typically have lots of costs and fees that can really add up. Those can include a sales charge, often disguised by the cute name "enrolment fee," as well as deposit charges, trustee and administration fees, and so on.

Now that the RESP rules have changed to allow you to get back the earnings on your contributions (either by transferring them to your RRSP or by paying a hefty tax), the scholarship-type fund providers have come up with a new offering. In addition to their traditional "pooled" funds, most offer individual accounts, where your contributions earn interest for your child alone. If your child doesn't use the money to go to school, then you can claim the earnings. Although this makes them somewhat more attractive, you still have to deal with the many administrative charges, and your contributions are still typically invested in guaranteed investments, limiting the growth of your savings.

If you have more than one child, open a multibeneficiary plan. If one child doesn't go to a postsecondary institution, the funds in the plan can be used by other children named in the plan.

There are two basic types of RESPs. The first are so-called "Scholarship" plans. Because these plans are limited to investing in mostly guaranteed investments, the rate of return on your plan is mediocre. Read the sidebar "How Scholarship RESPs work — and often don't pay!" to see how you can actually end up losing all the gains earned on your contributions.

A much better choice are self-directed or mutual fund RESPs. You can open these with most brokerage and mutual fund firms, often at no charge. A self-directed or mutual fund RESP allows you to choose from a wide range of investments. If you start an RESP when your children are still in diapers, these plans are a much better choice because they allow you to benefit from the larger earnings potential of equities and equity mutual funds.

In-trust accounts

Also known as informal trusts, *in-trust accounts* allow you to save money for your child's future and have a portion of your earnings compound tax free. These accounts also go by the name ITF, which stands for "in-trust for" account. The account is "in-trust" because minors can't enter into financial contracts. There are no restrictions on contributions to an in-trust account. You can put in as much or as little you wish at any time.

Once money is inside an informal trust, it belongs to the child. All profits on investments inside the trust are taxed. The person who contributes the money pays taxes on the dividends and income, but the child is responsible for paying taxes on any capital gains. Because most children have insufficient income to actually have to pay any tax, that portion of the account can compound tax-free. Because of this, the best investments for an in-trust account, especially if there are many years left before the child will need the money, are equity mutual funds where most of the profits are in the form of capital gains.

If you set up an in-trust account and only contribute Child Tax Benefit payments, the above tax rules don't apply. All the gains, whether they're in the form of capital gains, interest, or dividends, are taxed to the child.

The big drawback to informal trusts is that when the child turns 18, the money and all the profits legally become hers to spend as she wishes. There are no rules about what the money must be spent on, so your child could use it for purposes other than an education, such as starting his or her own small business. Although you can hope that little Johnny or Jenny will spend the money wisely, there's nothing you can do if on the day of his 18th birthday, Johnny empties his account and buys a convertible.

Certain steps are involved in setting up an in-trust account. You must clearly lay out when you open the account the role of everybody involved. The person who puts money into the account is known as the "settlor" or contributor. The law requires that a different person have the responsibility of overseeing how the money is invested (the trustee) on behalf of the child (the beneficiary). When you set up an account, ensure that you use the proper phrasing: your name (if you are the trustee) followed by "in trust for" and then your child's name.

Overlooked investments: Time and attention

Too often, we see parents knocking themselves out to make more money so that they can afford to send their kids to more expensive (and therefore supposedly better) private high schools and universities. Sometimes families want to send younger children to costly elementary schools, too. Families stretch themselves with outrageous mortgages or complicated living arrangements to get into neighbourhoods with top-rated public schools or to send their kids to expensive private elementary schools that they can barely afford.

The best school in the world for your child is you and your home. The reason many people we know, including us and our siblings, were able to attend some of the top educational institutions is that concerned parents worked hard, not just at their jobs, but at spending time with the kids while they were growing up. Rather than working to make more money (with the best of intentions to buy educational games or trips or to send the kids to better schools), in our humble opinion, some parents could do more for their kids by focusing more time on the child.

We see parents scratching their heads about their children's lack of interest in academic achievement — they blame the school or TV or society at large. These factors may contribute, but education begins in the home. Schools can't do it alone.

This is another reason not to continually raise your spending and living standards to use your income fully. Living within your means not only allows you to save more of your income, but it also can free more of your time to raise and educate your children.

Chapter 16

Real Estate 101

- -

- -

*B*uying a home or investing in real estate can be a financially and psychologically rewarding experience. On the other hand, owning real estate can be a real pain in the butt. Purchasing and maintaining property can be one of the most time-consuming, emotionally draining, and financially painful experiences in managing your personal finances.

Perhaps you want to escape your rented apartment and buy your first home. Or maybe you're interested in cornering the local real estate market and making millions in investment property. In either case, you can learn many lessons from real estate buyers who have travelled before you.

Note: Although this chapter focuses primarily on real estate in which you would live — otherwise known by those in the trade as *owner-occupied property* — much of what is in the chapter is relevant to real estate investors. For additional information on buying investment real estate — property that you rent out to others — see Chapter 10.

To Buy or Continue Renting?

You may be tired of moving from rental to rental. Perhaps your landlord doesn't keep up the place as well as you'd like, or you have to ask permission to hang a picture on the wall. You may want the financial security and rewards that seem to come with home ownership. Or maybe you just want a place to call your own.

Any one of these reasons is a good enough reason to *want* to buy a home. But you still need to take stock of your life and your financial health *before* you know if you can or should buy a home and how much you can really afford to spend. It's time to ask yourself some bigger questions.

What's my timeline?

From a financial standpoint, you really shouldn't buy a place unless you can anticipate being there for at least three years and preferably five or more. Buying and selling a property entails a lot of expenses, including the costs of getting a mortgage and an inspection, moving, and paying real estate agents' commissions. To cover these transaction costs plus the additional costs of ownership, a property needs to appreciate about 10 percent.

If you need or want to move in a couple of years, counting on that kind of appreciation is risky. If you're lucky and happen to buy before a sharp upturn in housing prices, you may get it. If you're not, you'll probably lose money on the deal.

Some people are willing to invest in real estate even when they don't expect to live in it for long and would consider turning their home into a rental. Doing so can work well financially in the long haul, but don't underestimate the responsibilities that come with being a landlord. Also, most people need to sell their first home in order to tap all the cash that they have in it to buy the next one.

Can I afford it?

Although buying and owning your own home can be a wise financial move in the long run, it's a major purchase that can and probably will send shock waves through the rest of your personal finances. You'll probably take out a mortgage that will take you 25 years to repay (the *amortization*) to finance your purchase. The home you buy will need all sorts of maintenance over the years. Owning a home is a bit like running a marathon: Just as you have to be in good physical shape to run a marathon, you have to be in good financial health when you buy a house. For as long as you own the home, you'll be paying for something or other all the time. *Before* you make a commitment to buy, you must take stock of your overall financial health.

Lenders look primarily at annual income when determining how much a potential home buyer can borrow; they pay little attention to a borrower's global financial picture. Whether you have no money already tucked away into retirement savings or have several children to clothe, feed, and help pay for university, you qualify for the same size loan as other people with the same income (assuming equal outstanding debts).

So don't trust the lender when she tells you what you can afford according to some formulas that the bank uses to determine what kind of a credit risk you are. Only you can figure out how much you can afford, because only you know what your other financial goals are and how important they are to you.

Here are some important financial questions no lender will ask you or care about but that you should ask yourself before buying a home:

- ✔ Are you saving enough monthly to reach your retirement goals?

- ✔ How much do you spend (and want to continue spending) on fun things such as travel and entertainment?

- ✔ How willing are you to budget your expenses in order to meet your monthly mortgage payments and other housing expenses?

- ✔ How much of your children's expected university educational expenses do you want to be able to pay for?

The other chapters in this book can help you answer these important questions. Chapter 8 in particular helps you save for important financial goals.

Many new homeowners run into financial trouble because they don't know their spending needs and priorities and don't know how to budget for them. Some of these owners have trouble curtailing their spending despite the large amount of debt they just incurred; in fact, some spend even more because all sorts of furniture and remodelling expenditures can be made for their home. Many people prop up their spending habits with credit. For this reason, a surprisingly large percentage — some studies say about half — who borrow additional money against their home equity use the funds to pay consumer debts.

Don't let your home control your financial future. We have seen too many people fall in love with a home and make a rash decision without taking a hard look at the financial ramifications. Take stock of your overall financial health, especially where you stand in terms of retirement planning, *before* you buy property or agree to a particular mortgage.

How much will lenders allow you to borrow?

All mortgage lenders want to know your ability and the likelihood of your repaying the money you borrow. So you have to pass a few tests that calculate the maximum amount the lender is willing to lend you. For a home in which you will reside, lenders total up your monthly housing expense. They define your housing costs as

Mortgage Payment + Property Taxes + Insurance

Lenders will typically lend you up to about 30 to 32 percent of your monthly gross (before taxes) income to buy a home. This is know as the *gross debt-service ratio*. If you're self-employed, it's not quite as simple. Lenders will often want to see your financial statements and your income tax returns from the last several years, and many decide on a case-by-case basis.

Lenders also consider your other debts when deciding how much to lend you. A lot of other debt diminishes the funds available to pay your housing expenses. To your monthly housing expense, lenders add the amount you need to pay down your other consumer debt (auto loans, credit cards). The monthly total costs of these debt payments plus your housing costs typically can't exceed 40 percent. This is known as your *total debt-service ratio*.

An old rule says that you can borrow up to three times (or $2^1/_2$ times) your annual income when buying a home. But this is a really rough estimate. The maximum that a mortgage lender lends you depends on interest rates. If rates fall (as they have during much of the past decade), the monthly payment on a mortgage of a given size also drops.

Table 16-1 gives you a ballpark idea of the maximum that you're probably eligible to borrow. Multiply your gross annual income by the number in the second column to determine the maximum-size mortgage you can get. For example, if you get a mortgage with a rate around 7 percent and your annual income is $50,000, multiply 3.5 × $50,000 to get $175,000, the approximate maximum mortgage allowed. Lower interest rates make buying real estate much more affordable.

Table 16-1   What's the Approximate Maximum You Can Borrow?

When Mortgage Rates Are	Multiply Your Gross Annual Income* by This Figure to Determine the Maximum You May Be Able to Borrow
4%	4.6
5%	4.2
6%	3.8
7%	3.5
8%	3.2
9%	2.9
10%	2.7
11%	2.5

If you're self-employed, this is your net income (after expenses but before taxes).

What's more expensive: Owning or renting?

An important financial consideration for many renters is the cost of owning a home. Some people assume that owning costs more. In fact, owning a place doesn't have to cost a truckload of money. It may even cost less than renting.

On the surface, buying a place seems a lot more expensive than renting. You're probably comparing your monthly rent (a couple hundred dollars to more than $1,000, depending on where you live) to the purchase price of a property, which is usually a number with a whole lot more digits — $100,000, $200,000, or more. When you consider a home purchase, you're forced to think about your housing expenses in one huge chunk rather than in small monthly instalments like a rent cheque.

Tallying up the costs of owning a place can be a useful and not-too-complicated exercise. To make fair the comparison between ownership and rental costs, you need to figure what it would cost on a *monthly basis* to buy a place you want versus what it would cost to rent a *comparable* place. The worksheet in Table 16-2 enables you to do such a comparison. *Note:* In the interest of reducing the number of variables, all this figuring assumes a fixed-rate mortgage. (We discuss mortgages later in this chapter.)

Table 16-2	Monthly Expenses: Renting versus Owning
Figure Out This	*Write It Here ($ per month)*
1. Monthly mortgage payment (see the section on "Mortgage")	$
2. Plus monthly property taxes (see the section on "Property taxes")	+ $
3. Equals total monthly mortgage plus property taxes	= $
4. Plus insurance ($30 to $150/mo., depending on property value)	+ $
5. Plus maintenance (1% of property cost divided by 12 months)	+ $
6. Equals total costs of owning (add lines 3, 4, and 5)	= $

Now, compare Line 6 in Table 16-2 with the monthly rent on a comparable place to see which comes out (roughly) ahead, owning or renting.

Mortgage

To determine the monthly payment on your mortgage, simply multiply the relevant number from Table 16-3 by the size of your mortgage expressed in (divided by) thousands of dollars. For example, if you will be taking out a $100,000 mortgage amortized over 25 years at 9 percent, then multiply 100 by 8.27 for a $827 monthly payment.

Table 16-3	Your Monthly Mortgage Payment	
Interest Rate (%)	15-Year Amortization (%)	25-Year Amortization (%)
5.0	7.88	5.82
5.5	8.14	6.10
6.0	8.40	6.40
6.5	8.66	6.70
7.0	8.93	7.00
7.5	9.21	7.32
8.0	9.49	7.63
8.5	9.77	7.96
9.0	10.05	8.27
9.5	10.34	8.61
10	10.62	8.94
10.5	10.92	9.29
11	11.21	9.62
11.5	11.51	9.97
12	11.81	10.32

Property taxes

Ask a real estate person, mortgage lender, or your local assessor's office what your annual property tax bill would be for a house of similar value to the one you're considering buying. Divide this amount by 12 to arrive at your monthly property tax bill.

Consider the long-term cost of renting

When you crunch the numbers to see what owning rather than renting a comparable place may cost you on a monthly basis, you may discover that owning isn't quite as expensive as you thought. Or you may find that owning costs somewhat more than renting. This discovery may tempt you to think that, financially speaking, renting is cheaper than owning.

Be careful not to jump to conclusions. Remember that you're looking at the cost of owning versus renting *today*. What about 5, 10, or 25 years from now? As an owner, your biggest monthly expense — the mortgage payment — doesn't increase steadily over the years; it only fluctuates as interest rates change. Your property taxes, homeowner's insurance, and maintenance expenses — which are generally far less than your mortgage payment — are the items that increase with the cost of living.

As a renter, however, your entire monthly rent is subject to the vagaries of inflation. The exception to this rule is if your dwelling is covered by rent controls, where the annual increase allowed in your rent is capped. Rent control doesn't eliminate price hikes; it just limits them.

Suppose that you're comparing the costs of owning a home that costs $200,000 to renting an equivalent home for $1,200 a month. Table 16-4 compares the monthly cost of owning the home to your monthly rental costs over 25 years. (This assumes that you take out a mortgage loan equal to 75 percent of the cost of the property at a fixed rate of 10 percent for average payments of $1,342 a month. It also assumes that the rate of inflation of your homeowner's insurance, property taxes, maintenance, and rent is 4 percent per year.) What happens to the value of the property is ignored in these calculations.

Table 16-4	Cost of Owning versus Renting over 30 Years	
Year Ownership	**Cost per Month**	**Rental Cost per Month**
1	$1,600	$1,200
5	$1,642	$1,404
10	$1,706	$1,708
15	$1,783	$2,078
25	$1,991	$3,076

As you can see in Table 16-4, it costs a little bit more in the first few years to own the home than to rent it. In the long run, however, owning becomes less expensive. This is because more of your rental expenses increase with inflation. And don't forget that you're building equity in your property as a homeowner, and that equity will be quite substantial by the time you have your mortgage paid off.

If you've been paying attention, you may be thinking that if inflation doesn't rise 4 percent per year, renting could end up being cheaper. This isn't necessarily so. Suppose that no inflation exists at all. Your rent shouldn't escalate, but home ownership expenses (property taxes, maintenance, and insurance) shouldn't, either. And with no inflation, you should be able to get a very low rate on your mortgage. If you do the math, you find that owning should still cost less in the long run with lower inflation, but the advantage compared to renting is less than during periods of higher inflation.

Mortgages: Side Effect of the Home-Ownership Dream

After you look at your financial health, figure out your timeline, and compare renting to owning costs, you can give yourself the green light to pursue the dream of owning your own home. Well, now you need to face the reality that part of the dream is acquiring a large amount of debt — in this case, it's called a mortgage. The *mortgage* is the loan from a bank or other source that makes up the difference between the cash you already have and the agreed-upon selling price of a piece of real estate. Without a mortgage, most people can't buy the homes their hearts desire.

The monthly mortgage payments, which consist of interest and principal to repay your loan balance, are huge expenses. Did you know that you may end up paying more for the *interest* on your mortgage than you will for your humble abode itself?

Assume that your new pad costs $160,000. To buy it, you borrow $120,000 and contribute $40,000 from your savings for the down payment. Let's say that your loan is *amortized* (a fancy word that means spread) over the standard 25 years, and your initial interest rate is 9.5 percent. (It won't, of course, stay at that rate, but we say more about that later.) Over the life of the loan, you'll end up paying almost $190,000 *in interest.* (Although you'll pay back some of these interest dollars many years from now when the dollar will likely, thanks to inflation, be worth less than it is today, you're still going to spend a truckload of dollars in interest.)

So taking the time to educate yourself about how to get the best possible deal on a mortgage and related fees is a very wise financial move. More importantly, you won't be able to buy your dream home unless you can finance its purchase.

For many households, mortgage payments are the single largest monthly expenditure (besides taxes). Like many other financial products, zillions of different mortgages are available to choose from. The differences can be important or trivial, expensive or cost free.

First, the big differences. There are three major ways in which mortgages differ: the length of the *term,* whether the loan is *open* or *closed,* and whether the interest rate is *fixed* or *variable.* You also have to select your *amortization* period — the number of years you want to spread your mortgage over.

Short-term and long-term mortgages

Just how long your home loan runs for is the *term*. The *term* is the length of your specific agreement with your lender. There was a time when the term was for the length of the amortization, but no more. Terms now run from six months or a year to five years. Some lenders also offer seven- and ten-year terms. Generally, the longer the term you choose, the higher your interest rate.

Selecting a *long term* (four or five years) guarantees your payments for that entire period, often an important consideration for those who are on tightly controlled budgets. But you do pay a premium for this insurance.

A *short term,* such as a six-month or one-year agreement, means that you have to renew much more frequently, putting you at the mercy of current interest rates. If rates go up, so do your monthly payments. On the other hand, if rates fall, you profit from the drop.

Choosing between a short-term and a long-term mortgage

This is the single most important nail-biter of a decision you have to make (not to put any pressure on you) when choosing a mortgage.

The worry is backing the wrong horse, because this is largely a gamble. If you choose a short-term, you risk having rates rise between now and your next renewal date. If you go long and rates don't rise, you pay more than you need to.

There's no simple rule as to whether you should go short (six months or a year) or long (four to five years). Both approaches have advantages and disadvantages.

Going long

This approach is usually chosen by people in the early years of home ownership. Once you're locked in, you know exactly how much your mortgage will cost for years to come. You don't have to make any decisions for a long time. And your heart won't jump every time interest rates do. But this peace of mind comes at a price.

Lenders demand higher rates of interest for long-term mortgages. Five-year rates, for example, almost always range from 1 percent to more than 3 percent higher than six-month rates. You pay a kind of insurance premium to protect yourself against the possibility of higher rates in the future. Ask yourself if the cost is worth it. Often, you'll find that both the financial and security risks of going short is not as great as you think.

Longer terms are worth considering if you're just starting out, or you find your finances stretched to the limit. If an unexpected jump in rates would push your payments beyond what you can comfortably handle, then lock in at a rate you know you can afford for several years.

When shouldn't almost anybody choose a long-term mortgage? When rates are at historical all-time highs. Remember, the reason for going long is to lock in a rate that protects you from renewing at an even higher rate. Otherwise, everyone would select a short term. Sure, it's hard to know if rates have peaked. But by staying short, you can quickly capture the gains when rates fall back down again.

Staying short

Choosing a short term means you have to take your chances at the mortgage rate roulette wheel more often. If you can handle the uncertainty, you'll be rewarded by rates that are consistently lower than long-term rates. Making decisions more often also allows you to fine-tune your strategy and gives you more opportunity to reduce your principal.

Be warned, however, that interest rates fluctuate. If they jump quickly, they can just as easily fall back to where they started or even lower. The moral of the story is *don't base your decisions on short-term movements.*

Make sure that you have enough of a financial cushion to afford the higher payments that you'll have to make if rates have risen by the time your renewal date rolls around.

Assessing your best choice

Your decision depends on your ability to live with risk. Staying short means more uncertainty, but you're almost certain to have lower mortgage costs unless rates keep marching up without coming back down. Choose long, and you may sleep better, but you pay a premium for those worry-free nights.

If you're still unsure about which route to follow, don't worry. It's something that everybody goes through. Next time you're at a party, just start asking people about the choices they've made with their mortgages. The tales about thousands of dollars lost or saved are rivalled only by stories from the stock market.

Open and closed mortgages

When you choose a *closed mortgage,* you're stuck with the terms of the deal until your loan agreement ends, or *matures.* You can refinance only if your lender lets you, and often that can involve paying stiff penalties. The upside of a closed mortgage is that, because the lender knows it can depend on your regular payments, your rates are lower.

Growing competition, however, has forced lenders to build in ways for you to pay off significant portions of your loan even within a closed mortgage. For example, the right to pay off 10 percent of your initial principal amount on each anniversary of your agreement is common.

In contrast to a *closed mortgage,* an *open mortgage* allows you to pay off part or all of the loan at any time without penalty. That can be a valuable option if you expect to come into a substantial sum of money or if you know you'll sell your home shortly. By completely paying off an open mortgage, you effectively terminate your contract with the lender. An open loan gives you flexibility to adapt your loan to changes in your financial picture or the economic situation. You have to pay more for this feature, usually 1 to 2 percent.

If falling rates are too tough to resist, but you want something less risky than a variable rate, consider a *fixed open mortgage.* Your rate is guaranteed, but if rates fall to an even more attractive level, you can lock in at that point without any penalty. If you want to play the interest game, this allows you to keep your options open while still protecting you should rates go up instead of down. It's usually not worth paying the premium that lenders charge for open mortgages, though, and you have other options.

Today's numerous prepayment options allow you to pay down significant sums during the life of your mortgage. In addition, more and more home-owners opt for shorter and shorter terms. Simply rolling over six-month terms, for example, is often a very sound strategy. At the end of each term, you're free to pick whatever term you like, from whatever lender you want, if you meet the lender's basic requirements. You also have the option of paying off any amount of your principal that you choose.

Otherwise, however, if you're trying to take advantage of low or falling rates, there is now a much better alternative available, called a *six-month convertible.* We talk more about convertible mortgages later in this chapter.

Fixed- and variable-rate mortgages

Fixed-rate mortgages were the standard before variable-rate mortgages came into being. *Fixed-rate mortgages* have interest rates that never, ever change. Not all fixed-rate mortgages offered by different banks have the same interest rate, but, with a fixed-rate mortgage, you lock in an interest rate that won't change over the term or your mortgage.

With a fixed-rate mortgage, there's nothing complicated to track, and there's no uncertainty. If you like getting your daily newspaper delivered at the same time every day, you're gonna like fixed-rate mortgages.

In contrast to a fixed-rate mortgage, a *variable-rate mortgage,* (sometimes referred to as an *adjustable* mortgage) carries an interest rate that (no surprise here!) varies. Usually tied to the lender's prime rate, it moves, jumps, rises, falls, and otherwise can't sit still, just like a fidgeting child.

The return for putting up with this volatility is that the rate is usually the lowest available at any point in time. Variable rates generally are set at, or slightly above, the lender's prime rate, and they rise and fall accordingly.

Some lenders offer protection from soaring rates by putting an absolute ceiling on how high your rate can go. You pay a slightly higher rate for a capped variable, usually around 1 percent above that of a regular variable.

If rates are on their way up, you're better off locking into a fixed-rate mortgage before the rates go any higher. And if rates are going down, you should select a variable rate and go along for the ride. So some people ask, "Shouldn't the likelihood of interest rates going up or down determine whether I take a fixed-rate or variable-rate mortgage?"

Good question. The problem is, there really is no accurate way to predict which way rates are going. Even the pros on Bay Street can't make these predictions with any consistent accuracy, as you see in Part III.

But if you feel that rates are likely to fall and prefer the variable option, you should understand the risks involved. A rise in interest rates can mean that at some point your monthly payment won't even cover the interest cost of your loan. If this happens, the outstanding interest is added to your balance. Once that figure hits about 105 to 110 percent of the original loan amount, you can expect to hear from your lender. You'll either have to make a lump-sum payment against your principal or lock into a fixed term.

If you decide that a variable-rate mortgage is the way to go, you also have to pass some extra tests. Due to their volatility, variable-rate mortgages often have lower lending limits. Many lenders won't let you borrow more than 70 percent of your property's appraised value. In some cases, you must also select an amortization period of 20 years or less.

Variables are variable in another way: No other type of mortgage differs so much from lender to lender. Every aspect, from the terms available and how your payments are calculated to whether you can pay the loan off early, varies widely depending on the institution. It's important to ask specific questions about any variable mortgage — and make sure that the answers are there on paper — before signing on the dotted line.

There's a relatively unpromoted player on the mortgage scene that can save you from having to decide whether the potential savings from lower rates is worth all this worry. It's called a *convertible mortgage,* and it's one of the best-kept secrets in the mortgage game. A convertible loan offers many of the benefits of a variable-rate mortgage, with very little downside. For more information, see the sidebar on "Convertible mortgages."

How to boost your down payment

When you buy a home, ideally you should make a down payment of at least 25 percent of the purchase price of the property. Why? Because you'll generally be able to qualify for the most favourable terms on a mortgage with such a down payment, and you'll also be able to avoid the added cost of mortgage insurance. Lenders usually require insurance, which on a typical mortgage costs several hundred dollars per year, to protect against their losing money in the event you default on your loan.

Many people don't have the equivalent of 25 percent or more of the purchase price in savings to buy a home without mortgage insurance. Here are a number of ways to come up with that 25 percent faster or to buy with less money down to lose those down payment blues:

TIP

- **Go on a spending diet.** One sure way to come up with a down payment is to raise your savings rate by slashing your spending. Take a tour through Chapter 6 to learn strategies for doing so.

- **Consider lower-priced properties.** Some buyers want their first home to be a palace. Smaller properties and ones that need some work can help to keep down the purchase price and, therefore, the required down payment.

- **Find partners.** You can usually get more home for your money when you buy a building in partnership with one, two, or a few people. Make sure to write up a legal contract to specify what will happen if a partner wants out.

- **Get assistance from family.** If your parents, grandparents, or other relatives have money dozing away in a savings account or GIC, they may be willing to lend (or even give) you the down payment. You can pay them a higher rate of interest than they've been earning (but still lower than what you would pay to borrow from a bank) and thus be able to buy a home — a win/win situation.

How to buy with less money down

It's important to remember that the conditions for conventional mortgages were put in place to protect the financial industry from massive defaults. That also means that, at least statistically, you're more likely to be able to handle your payments if you have at least a 25 percent down payment.

Convertible mortgages

Although convertible mortgages vary from lender to lender, the basic principle remains the same. You get six months or a year of security, usually at the same rate as a fixed mortgage for the same term — usually the lowest rate going. At any point during that time, you can "convert" your mortgage to a different term; you can also choose between an open or closed loan.

The benefit of convertibles is that they allow borrowers to avoid paying a premium for longer-term fixed rates. At the same time, you're protected against rapidly rising rates because you can lock in at any time, rather than having to wait until your term expires or paying a hefty penalty. If rates should suddenly rise, you can simply lock in a longer term rate. Meanwhile, you also save yourself the extra premium for an open mortgage.

If rates are falling, you can lock in the lower rates at any point. It often pays to simply ride out the term, and if rates are still falling at that point, to just sign up for another six-month convertible.

The important point with a convertible loan is to check the fine print for specific conditions. One institution, for example, allows you to convert only to a five-year term. Even if you let the six months elapse, you're automatically signed up. In essence, this is really a 5$\frac{1}{2}$ year mortgage, with the possibility of lower rates for a maximum of the first six months.

Most lenders allow you to convert at any time to any term you wish. The only across-the-board restriction is that you can't convert during the term to another six-month convertible. The other drawback to convertibles is that if you want to renew partway through the six months, you can't change lenders. That means losing some bargaining power, which can cost you a quarter or $\frac{1}{2}$ of a percentage point.

You can get a mortgage with a lower down payment, but that may not always be a good thing — neither for the financial industry nor for you. Not being able to afford a conventional mortgage can be a red flag warning you that you should put your dreams on hold. Stop and think about why you need to buy that house now and what it really means to your financial life. You may just decide that it's better to wait and buy that wonderful house later on when you're on a little firmer financial footing.

If you don't have the 25 percent down payment needed for a conventional mortgage and feel that you can handle the higher risk of buying a home, you have a few options.

High-ratio mortgages

If you have a down payment of at least 10 percent of the purchase price, you can obtain a *high-ratio mortgage* from most lenders. The rate and features usually are the same as for a regular loan. The big difference is that you're required to buy special mortgage insurance. If your application is approved, your lender will organize this for you. The insurance is provided by the Canada Mortgage and Housing Corporation (CMHC), which is run by the federal government. It's important to realize, though, that the insurance is there to protect not you but your *lender* in case you fail to meet your payments.

Your down payment determines your insurance rate, which can run as high as 2.5 percent. You only pay the premium once — when you take out your mortgage. You're required to insure the entire loan, not just the difference between your down payment and the 25 percent required for a conventional loan. On a $100,000 mortgage, that could mean paying up to $2,500 in insurance. If you don't have the money, you can ask your lender to add the insurance premium to your loan. Of course, that means you'll likely end up paying twice or three times that amount back over the life of the mortgage once all the interest costs are considered.

CMHC's 5 percent down option

First-time home buyers may be able to get away with putting down as little as 5 percent under a special program run by CMHC. The total amount of your loan is restricted to certain levels, depending on where in the country you live. You can select any term you want, just as for a regular mortgage. However, you must meet a debt-service test: Your cash flow has to be sufficient to meet the payments on a three-year term. You also have to buy mortgage insurance, which can be as high as 2.5 percent of your loan.

Taking a second mortgage

Another option is to take out a traditional mortgage for the first 75 percent and then to arrange a second mortgage on the remainder. You'll likely have to arrange this through a mortgage broker for a fee. You'll usually have to pay 2 to 3 percent more than the rate on your first mortgage.

If you select a short term — a six-month or a one-year — the premium you'll pay for the second mortgage will be even bigger — up to 4 or even 5 percent above the conventional rate.

Choosing the best strategy

The critical factor to look at is your cash flow. If things are tight and you don't expect your situation to change over the next few years, choose a high-ratio mortgage. You have to pay an insurance premium of up to 2.5 percent, but over the long haul, a high-ratio mortgage is cheaper than the cost of carrying a second mortgage. One other benefit of high-ratio mortgages is that because they're insured by CMHC, you can eventually get out of them. After three years, you can pay off any CMHC-insured loan by paying a penalty of three months' interest.

On the other hand, if you expect a cash inflow from, say, a maturing GIC within a year or two, a second mortgage is the best choice. Although they're expensive, by paying off a big chunk quickly, you minimize most of those premium-priced interest payments. And you save yourself the insurance costs of a high-ratio loan.

The RRSP Home Buyers' Plan

The federal government's Home Buyers' Plan allows you to borrow up to $20,000 from your RRSP to buy a house. You can remove the money without paying any tax or any interest. The only condition: You must repay the money into your RRSP within 15 years. The minimum you have to repay each year is the equivalent of $1/15$ of the amount borrowed.

For hopeful home buyers, the plan can be useful, but it is by no means perfect. True, you get to take the money out both tax and interest free. However, the plan comes with a number of strict conditions. And some potentially big costs are involved, too.

Unfortunately, you have to wade through a bunch of details to understand the pros and cons of the plan. Bear with us. It's vital that you understand these specifics, despite their positively desert-like aridity. Knowing what you're getting into now can save you a lot of financial worries down the road.

For starters, neither you nor your spouse is allowed to make a contribution to your RRSP in the year that you withdraw funds under the plan. Why? Because the government doesn't want people to put money into their plan, get the tax break, and then draw on the same funds to use as part of a down payment. If you've been making regular contributions to your RRSP, and you've been building the tax refund into your budget, you need to prepare for this loss in cash flow.

Repayment rules

The basic requirement is that you have to repay the borrowed funds in equal instalments over the next 15 years. Those payments aren't considered RRSP contributions, and you don't get any tax write-offs for them. If you miss a payment or part of a payment, the government treats that money as if you had withdrawn it directly from your RRSP. The sum is included as part of your income for that year, and you have to pay tax on it. Ouch!

If you're already finding it difficult to put money into your RRSP, it will be twice as hard if you use your retirement funds for a down payment. Before you can even think of making a fresh contribution, you have to replace the required portion of the borrowed funds for that year. If that leaves you unable to make a direct RRSP contribution for that year, you miss out on a big tax break and a large tax refund. You also forego the tax-free compound growth you could have earned from that new contribution.

Loss of potential growth in your RRSP

By taking money out, you lose all the potential growth from those funds as long as that money isn't in your plan. The younger you are, the higher the cost is to you. Unfortunately, the only way to understand the dangers this option poses for your RRSP is to do battle with a few numbers.

Suppose that you're 30 and that you borrow $18,000 from your plan to buy a home. You have to repay $1,200 a year, or $100 a month, for the next 15 years. The alternative would have been to borrow the money, say, as a second mortgage. If you borrowed the money at 10 percent and spread the loan over 15 years, the monthly payments would be $193.50. So the extra cost of borrowing the money from a bank or trust company instead of your RRSP is $93.50 a month.

But you have to balance that off against the gains possible by leaving that $18,000 in your RRSP. Earning an average of 10 percent a year, in 40 years that money would grow to more than $800,000. By comparison, if it were left in for 35 years, it would be worth just over $500,000.

This is an extreme example, but it amply demonstrates the true cost of borrowing "free" from your RRSP. The actual cost depends on how old you are and how quickly you're able to repay the borrowings. In general, if you're over 40, the price may not be too steep. In addition, if you use the plan to buy a home and it appreciates steadily, the growth on the value of your house will offset some of the foregone growth in your RRSP. You may be able to get the best of both worlds by borrowing from your RRSP and repaying the loan quickly, say in the first three or four years after you have settled into your new home.

 In general, you're probably better off borrowing the money, even if that means taking out a second mortgage or a high-ratio mortgage. Just make sure that you can afford the higher interest rate charges or the mortgage insurance premium.

Should you consider faster mortgage payoff?

The appeal of paying off your mortgage years sooner is enticing. So if you can afford higher payments on your mortgage, you'd be silly not to take them, right? Not so fast. You're really asking whether you should pay off your mortgage slowly or more quickly. And the answer isn't as simple as you think. It depends.

You need to think through this decision despite the fact that entire books have been written extolling the virtues of owning your home without mortgage debt as soon as possible. Those books come complete with endless rows and columns of numbers so that you can look up how much you save through a quicker payback.

The decision about whether to pay off a mortgage faster isn't that simple.

If you have the time and inclination (and a good financial calculator), you can calculate how much interest you can save or avoid through a quicker payback. We have a friendly word of advice about spending hours crunching numbers: *Don't.* You can make this decision by considering some qualitative issues.

First, think about *alternative uses* for the extra money you'd be throwing into the mortgage paydown. What's best for you depends on your overall financial situation and what else you can do with the money. If you would end up blowing the extra money at the racetrack or on an expensive car, pay down the mortgage. That's a no-brainer.

But suppose you instead contribute the extra money to an RRSP or other retirement savings plan. That step may make financial sense. Why? Because contributions to your RRSP are tax deductible. When you add an extra $200 to your mortgage payment to pay off your mortgage faster, you get no tax benefits. Zero, *nada,* zippo! When you dump that $200 into an RRSP, you get to subtract that $200 from the income on which you pay taxes. If you're paying 41 percent in federal and provincial taxes, you shave $82 (that's $200 multiplied by 41 percent) off your tax bill.

In fact, choosing between putting more money into your RRSP or paying down your mortgage involves a lot of serious number-crunching, and the results depend on your mortgage rate, how many years you have left before your mortgage is paid off, as well as the return you'll earn in your RRSP. Because of all these variables — some of which are hard to nail down — a good compromise is to maximize your RRSP contributions and to take the tax refund that the contributions earn you and put it down against your mortgage.

Cut your costs at renewal time

No matter how long your mortgage is amortized for, your actual contract with your lender expires at the end of each term. When you renew, you're really entering into an entirely new agreement. This gives you complete flexibility to change any or all of the terms of your mortgage, from payment levels and the amortization period to the frequency of instalments. You can even change lenders if you wish.

A few months before your renewal date, shop around for guaranteed rate offers from a handful of lenders. Sixty- and sometimes 90-day guarantees are common. Getting your renewal rate guaranteed in advance protects you from sudden increases in rates before your renewal. You can also use the guarantee to negotiate better rates from your current mortgage company. If it won't match the competition, you're free to transfer your mortgage to another financial institution.

Here are some other proven methods to cut your mortgage down in size, fast!

Switch from monthly to biweekly payments

Accelerating your payment schedule is a simple, easy, and automatic way to cut years off your mortgage. It also makes budgeting that much simpler because most people get paid on a biweekly basis. Your salary goes in, and your mortgage payment comes out.

Regardless of what terms you choose, have your lender calculate the regular monthly payment. To find what you should pay every second week, simply divide that figure by two. You'll end up making 26 payments each year. That's the equivalent of an extra month's payment every 12 months.

The appeal of this strategy is that because the increased payment is so spread out, it's reasonably gentle on your pocketbook. The great attraction is that it's automatic.

Shorten the amortization

If you don't say any different, your lender will amortize your mortgage over 25 years as a matter of course. But you can choose almost any shorter amortization period you like.

If you can handle even slightly higher monthly payments, shortening your amortization is a good way to reduce your mortgage. One approach is to figure out what kind of monthly payments you'd feel comfortable with, and then see what the corresponding amortization would be. Let's say you're looking at a $100,000 mortgage at 10 percent. Over 25 years, your monthly payment would be $894.49. After checking your budget, you decide that you can afford to pay $100.00 more per month. Bumping up your payments to $994.49 would mean that your loan would be paid off in just under 18 years. All you would need to do now is ask your lender to reduce your amortization to 18 years.

Maintain your payments when rates fall

Lower rates at renewal time offer another easy, relatively pain-free way to bring down your mortgage costs. If rates have dropped by the end of your current term, tell your lender you want to keep your actual payments at the same level. You've been getting by with what you've been paying for months and possibly years, so your financial situation won't change. If you could use a little extra cash flow, set your payments somewhere between what you've been paying and the new minimum amount.

Make annual lump-sum payments

The right to put down a lump sum annually against your mortgage is now almost a standard feature. The usual amount allowed is 10 percent of your original principal, although some lenders have boosted that to 20 percent.

Any lump-sum payment goes directly to reducing your principal. If you can afford the full 10 percent, this is the fastest way to retire your mortgage. For example, if you manage to find the funds to take full advantage of this option every year, the results will be phenomenal. On a $100,000 mortgage at 10 percent, this approach alone saves you a total of $128,227 and means that you can burn your mortgage certificate in just seven years. Wow!

One relatively pain-free way to gather a lump sum is through your Registered Retirement Savings Plan. Contribute as much as you can afford to your RRSP. Then, when you get your tax refund, immediately put your refund toward your mortgage. This way, you build your retirement savings *and* pay off your home.

Finding the best lender

As with other financial purchases, you can save a lot of money by shopping around. It doesn't matter whether you do so on your own or hire someone to help you. Just do it!

On a 25-year, $120,000 mortgage, for example, getting a mortgage that costs 0.5 percent less per year saves you about $11,500 in interest over the life of the loan (given current interest rate levels). That's enough to buy a nice car! On second thought, save it.

Doing it yourself

You can find many mortgage lenders in most areas. Although having a large number to choose from is good for competition, it also makes shopping a chore.

Large financial institutions whose names you recognize from their ads don't necessarily offer the best rates. Make sure that you check out some of the smaller credit unions and trust companies in your area as well.

Real estate agents also can refer you to lenders with whom they've done business. Those lenders don't necessarily offer the most competitive rates — the agent simply may have done business with them in the past.

Look also in the real estate section of one of the larger newspapers in your area for charts of selected lender interest rates. These tables are by no means comprehensive or reflective of the best rates available. In fact, many of them are sent to newspapers for free by firms that distribute mortgage information to mortgage brokers. Use them as a starting point by calling the lenders that list the best rates.

Hiring a mortgage broker

Insurance agents peddle insurance, real estate agents sell real estate, and mortgage brokers deal in mortgages. They buy mortgages at wholesale prices from lenders and then mark them up to retail to you. The difference, or *spread,* is their income. The terms of the loan obtained through a broker are generally the same as you would obtain from the lender directly.

A mortgage broker gets paid a percentage of the loan amount — typically 0.5 to 1 percent. This commission is negotiable, especially on larger loans that are more lucrative. You have no reason not to ask a mortgage broker what his cut is. Many people don't, so some brokers may act taken aback when you inquire. Remember, it's your money!

The chief advantage of using a mortgage broker is that the broker can shop among various lenders to get you a good deal. If you're too busy or disinterested to shop around for a good deal on a mortgage, a competent mortgage broker can probably save you money. A broker can also help you through the tedious and draining process of filling out all those horrible documents lenders demand before giving you a loan. And if you have credit problems or an unusual property, a broker may be able to match you with a hard-to-find lender willing to offer you a mortgage.

In evaluating a mortgage broker, be on guard for those who are lazy and don't continually shop the market looking for the best mortgage lenders. Some brokers place their business with the same lenders all the time — lenders who don't necessarily offer the best rates. Also watch out for those who are salespeople who earn big commissions pushing certain loan programs that aren't in your best interests. They aren't interested in taking the time to understand your needs and discuss your options. Check a broker's references.

Even if you plan to shop on your own, talking to a mortgage broker may be worthwhile. At the very least, you can compare what you find with what brokers say they can get for you. Just be careful. Some brokers tell you what you want to hear — that is, that they can be your best find — and then aren't able to deliver when the time comes.

If a mortgage broker quotes you a really good deal, make sure to ask who the lender is. (Most brokers refuse to reveal this information until you pay the few hundred dollars to cover the appraisal and credit report.) You can check with the actual lender to verify the interest rate the broker quotes you and make sure that you're eligible for the mortgage.

Increasing your approval chances

A lender can take several weeks to complete your property appraisal and evaluation of your loan package. When you're under contract to buy a property, having your loan denied after waiting several weeks could mean that you lose the property as well as the money you spent on legal fees and having the property inspected. Some property sellers may be willing to give you an extension, but others won't. Spending all that time and emotional energy getting so close to owning a special property and then losing it can be disappointing.

You can do a number of smart things to increase your chances of having your mortgage approved:

✔ **Get your finances in shape before you shop.** You're not going to have a good handle on what you can afford to spend on a home until you whip your personal finances in shape. Do so before you begin to make offers on properties. This chapter and book can help you.

If you have consumer debt, get rid of it, pronto! The more credit card, auto loan, and other consumer debt you rack up, the less mortgage you qualify for. In addition to the high interest rate on consumer debt and the fact that it encourages you to live beyond your means, you now have a third reason to get rid of it. Hang onto the dream of a home and plug away at paying off your debts before you buy a home.

✔ **Clear up credit report problems.** Late payments, missed payments, or debts that you never bothered to pay can come back to haunt you. If you think there are problems on your credit report, get a copy (the major agencies are listed in the Yellow Pages) before you apply for your mortgage.

Mistakes cropping up on credit reports is not unusual. The only way to fix mistakes, unfortunately, is to get on the phone to the credit bureau and start squawking. If specific creditors have reported erroneous information, call them, too. If the customer service representatives you talk with are no help, dash off a nice letter to the president of each company. Let the head honcho know that his or her organization is tarnishing your credit report and that you're going to report them to government consumer agencies.

If bona fide problems are documented on your credit report, start by trying to explain them to your lender. If the lender is unsympathetic, try calling other lenders. Tell them your credit problems up front and see whether you can find one willing to give you a loan. Mortgage brokers (discussed earlier) can also help you shop for lenders in these cases.

✔ **Get preapproved or prequalified.** *Prequalified* means that a you've spoken with a lender about your financial situation and the lender has calculated the maximum it will lend you based upon what you've told it. *Preapproval* is more in-depth and includes a lender's actual review of your financial statements. Although neither is binding upon a lender to actually make you a mortgage loan, preapproval means more, especially in qualifying you financially in the eyes of a seller. Just be sure not to waste your time and money getting preapproved if you're not really ready to get serious about buying.

✔ **Be up-front about problems.** The best defence against loan rejection is to avoid it in the first place. You can sometimes head off potential rejection by disclosing to your lender anything that may cause a problem before you apply for the loan. That way, you have more time to correct problems and find alternate solutions.

✔ **Work around low/unstable income.** If you're self-employed or have been changing jobs, your recent economic history may be as unstable as a communist country trying out capitalism. One way around this problem is to make a larger down payment.

If you're a lending risk because you don't have the income to qualify for the loan you want, you may need to get a co-signer. You can try parents, other relatives, or even rich friends as potential co-signers. As long as they aren't borrowed up to their eyeballs, they can help you qualify for a larger loan than you can get on your own. Be sure that all parties understand the terms of the agreement, including who is responsible for monthly payments!

Should you lie to get a mortgage?

Eric knows more than a few folks who have lied to get a mortgage. It's not that he associates with unethical people. Working as a financial planner, he just tends to hear a lot of juicy tales. Mortgage brokers, who end up working with more of the borrowers who have less-than-perfect situations, can tell you lots of war stories of trickery and deception to close a deal. Some brokers even coach people into lying so they can qualify for a loan.

In most cases, not qualifying for the loan that you want is for your own good. Lenders have criteria to ensure that you'll be able to repay and don't get in over your head.

On the other hand, we're sympathetic to some of the complaints we've heard about bankers and other mortgage lenders who can sometimes be as compassionate and flexible as a totalitarian government agency. They have their rules and regulations and qualifying ratios. You either meet them or you don't. It's black or white. They have their reasons, but sometimes their rules don't fit your situation.

Don't lie. Besides the obvious legal ramifications, you could end up with more mortgage debt than you can really afford and possibly worse. You have alternatives if you're cash-constrained. For example, loans that don't require documentation of income are available when you make a large down payment, generally 30 percent or more. These loans cost a little more than conventional loans, but they also allow you to avoid lying. You could also get a co-signer.

Finding the Right Property and Location

Shopping for a home can be fun. You get to peek inside other people's refrigerators and drawers. But for most people, finding the right house at the right price can take a lot of time. It can also entail a lot of compromise when you're buying with partners or a spouse (or children, if you choose to share the decision making with them).

A good agent (or several in different areas) can help with the legwork. Here are the main things to consider:

Condo, townhouse, co-op, or detached home?

Some people's image of a house is a single-family dwelling — a stand-alone house with a lawn and white picket fence. In some areas, however, particularly in higher-cost neighbourhoods, non-single-family housing is more common. *Condominiums* (you own the unit and a share of everything else), *townhouses* (attached or row houses), and *co-operatives* (you own a share of the entire building) are higher-density housing units.

The allure of non-single family housing is that it's generally less expensive. In some cases, as an owner, you don't have to worry about some of the general maintenance because the owners' association (which you pay for, directly or indirectly) takes care of it.

 If you don't have the time, energy, or desire to keep up a property, these types of shared housing can make sense. They may also provide you with better security than a stand-alone home, and you generally get more living space for your dollar.

As investments, however, single-family homes generally do better in the long run. Shared housing is easier to build and hence easier to overbuild; on the other hand, single-family houses are harder to put up because more land is required. But most people, when they can afford it, still prefer a stand-alone home.

That said, you should remember that a rising tide raises all boats. In a good real estate market, all types of housing appreciate, although single-family homes tend to do better. Shared housing values tend to increase best in densely populated urban areas with little available land for new building.

 If you can afford a smaller single-family home instead of a larger shared-housing unit, buy the single-family home. Be especially wary of buying shared housing in suburban areas with lots of developable land.

Cast a broad net

Before you start your search, you may have an idea about the type of property and location that you're interested in or think you can afford. You may think, for example, that you can afford only a condominium in the neighbourhood you want. But if you take the time to check out other communities, you may be surprised to find one that meets most of your needs and has affordable single-family homes. You'd never know that, though, if you narrowed your search too quickly.

Even if you've lived in an area for a while and think that you know it well, look at different types of properties in a number of different areas before you start to narrow your search. Be open-minded and be sure to know which of your many criteria for a home you *really* care about. You may have to be flexible on some of your preferences.

If you're working with an agent, make sure you don't overlook homes that are *for sale by owner* (that is, not listed with real estate agents). Otherwise, you may miss out on some good properties.

Find out actual sale prices

Don't look at just a few homes listed at a particular price and get depressed because they're all dogs or you can't afford what you really want. Before you decide to renew your lease on your apartment, remember that properties often sell for less than the price at which they're listed. Find out how much some of the places you look at end up selling for. Doing so gives you a better sense of what you can really afford as well as what some places seem to really be worth. If you're working with a real estate agent, he or she can easily obtain such sales price information.

Research the neighbourhood and area

Even (and especially) if you fall in love with a house at first sight, go back to the neighbourhood at different times of day and on different days of the week. Knock on a few doors and meet your potential neighbours. You may discover, for example, a flock of chickens in the backyard next door or that the street and basement flood every other winter.

What are the schools like? Go visit them. Don't rely on statistics about test scores. Talk to parents and teachers — what's really going on at the school? Even if you don't have kids, the quality of the local school has direct bearing on the value of your property. Is crime a problem? Call the local police department. Will future development be allowed? If so, what type? Talk to the planning department. What will your property taxes be? Is the property located in an area susceptible to major risks, such as floods, mud slides, fires, or earthquakes? Consider these issues even if they aren't important to you, because they can affect the resale value of your property.

Once you buy a home, you're stuck with it. Make sure that you know what you're getting yourself into *before* you buy.

Working with Real Estate Agents

Odds are that when you buy (or sell) a home, you'll work with a real estate agent. Real estate agents, like many people who call themselves "financial consultants," earn their living on commission. As such, their incentives are different from yours and can sometimes be at odds with what's best for you.

Unlike commission-based financial consultants, who are really salespeople with a loftier sounding title, real estate agents don't hide the fact that they get a cut of the deal. Property buyers and sellers usually understand the real estate commission system. We credit the real estate profession for calling its practitioners "agents" and not coming up with some silly title such as "housing consultants."

A top-notch real estate agent can be of significant help in your purchase or sale of property. On the other hand, a mediocre, incompetent, or greedy agent can be a real liability. Real estate agents don't have as bad a reputation as used car salespeople, but it's not great, either.

Real estate agents' top conflicts of interest

Because they work on commission, real estate agents face numerous conflicts of interest. Some agents may not even recognize the conflicts in what they're doing. This section discusses the most common tipoffs to conflicts of interest at work.

Buy now, sell now

"You must buy now! Prices and interest rates are low, but they could rise any day."

"The market could worsen before it gets better — you'd better sell now."

Because agents work on commission, it costs them when they spend time with you and you don't buy or sell. They want you to complete a deal, and they want that deal as soon as possible — otherwise, they don't get paid.

Don't expect an agent to give you objective advice about what you should do given your overall financial situation. Examine your overall financial situation *before* you decide to work with an agent.

Spend more

Because real estate agents get a percentage of the sales price of a property, they have a built-in incentive to encourage you to spend more. The more you spend, the higher their commission.

I don't waste my time working with small fries like you

Because agents work on commission and get paid a percentage of the sales price of the property, many aren't interested in working with you if you can't or simply don't want to spend a lot. Some agents may reluctantly take you on as a customer but then give you little attention and time. Before you hire an agent, check references to make sure that they've worked well with buyers like you.

Buy in my area

Real estate agents typically work a specific territory. As a result, they usually can't objectively tell you the pros and cons of the surrounding region. Most won't admit that you may better meet your needs by looking in another town (or some other part of town) where they don't normally work. Before you settle on an agent (or an area), spend time on your own learning the pros and cons of different territories. If you do want to look seriously in more than one area, find an agent in each who specializes in that area.

Buyer's brokers

Increasing numbers of agents market themselves as *buyer's brokers*. Supposedly, they represent your interests as a property buyer exclusively.

Legally speaking, buyer's brokers may sign a contract saying that they represent your — and only your — interests. Before this enlightened era, all agents contractually worked for the property seller.

The title buyer's broker is one of those things that sounds better than it really is. Agents representing you as buyer's brokers still get paid only when you buy. And they still get paid on commission as a percentage of the purchase price. So they still have an incentive to sell you a piece of real estate, and the more expensive it is, the more commission they make.

Get your loan from my favourite lender

If you don't get approved for a mortgage loan, your entire real estate deal will unravel. So it's a good thing that real estate agents want you to get approval for a loan. But it may cause them to refer you to a more expensive lender who has the virtue of high approval rates. Shop around — you can probably get a loan and get it more cheaply.

Also, beware of agents who may refer you to mortgage lenders and mortgage brokers who pay agents referral fees. Such payments clearly bias a real estate agent's "advice."

Use this inspector — he's easy

Home inspectors are supposed to be objective third parties who are hired by prospective buyers to evaluate the condition of a property. The inspector's job is to uncover problems that your novice eye can't see. We've heard of tougher (nit-picky) inspectors referred to as "deal killers" by disgruntled real estate agents. Some inspectors get more referrals from agents because they aren't tough. But you'll be the one who's sorry if your newly acquired home has undiscovered problems due to an inadequate inspection.

I'm helping the seller cover up problems

Some agents, under pressure to sign a seller, agree to be criminal accomplices and not disclose known defects or problems with the property. In most cases, it seems, the seller may not explicitly ask an agent to help cover up a problem, but the agent may look the other way or not tell the whole truth. Never buy a home without having a home inspector look it over from top to bottom.

I'd rather credit back than reduce the purchase price

After an initial agreement on a sales price, negotiations in real estate deals can begin again if circumstances change or new information surfaces. For example, your inspections may uncover problems you weren't previously aware of. Agents involved in your deal are far more likely to suggest and favour a *credit back,* wherein the seller credits money to you at closing instead of reducing the original sales price.

Agents prefer the credit back because it doesn't reduce their commission, which is based on the sales price. But a price reduction may benefit both the buyer, whose property taxes usually are based on the sales price, and the seller, who pays a sales commission as a percentage of the sales price. Some agents are willing to go along with an overall price reduction if their commission is based on the previously agreed upon (higher) price.

They scratch my back, and I scratch theirs

Some agents (as do many in other occupations) refer you to lenders, inspectors, and lawyers who have referred them business. A referral, of course, should first and foremost be based on the competence of the person to whom you're being referred. Too often in referrals, this criterion is minor or, in some cases, non-existent. Some agents also solicit and receive referral fees (or bribes) from mortgage lenders, inspectors, and contractors to whom they refer business.

Qualities to look for in real estate agents

Whether you're hiring an agent to work with you as a buyer or seller, you want someone who is competent and with whom you can get along. Working with an agent costs you a lot of money — make sure that you get your money's worth.

Interview several agents. Check references. Ask agents for the names and phone numbers of at least three clients with whom they've worked in the past six months in the geographical area in which you're looking.

You should look for these traits in any agent you work with:

- **Full-time employment.** Some agents work in real estate as a second or even third job. Information in this field changes constantly — keeping track of it is hard enough on a full-time basis. To be a really good agent, an agent must work full time to stay on top of the market.

- **Experience.** With a real estate deal, you've got a lot at stake financially and emotionally. You want to do the best that you can. Hiring someone with experience doesn't necessarily mean looking for an agent who's been kicking around for decades. Many of the best agents come into the field from other occupations, such as business or teaching. Some sales, marketing, negotiation, and communication skills can certainly be learned in other fields, but experience in this field does count.

- **Honesty and integrity.** You're trusting your agent with a lot. If the agent doesn't level with you about what a neighbourhood or particular property is really like, you suffer the consequences.

- **Interpersonal skills.** An agent must be able to get along not only with you but also with a whole host of other people involved in a typical real estate deal: other agents, property sellers, inspectors, mortgage lenders, and so on. An agent doesn't have to be Mr. or Ms. Congeniality, but he or she should be able to put your interests first without upsetting others.

✔ **Negotiation skills.** Putting a real estate deal together involves negotiation. Will your agent exhaust all avenues to get you the best deal possible? Be sure to ask the agent's references how well the agent negotiated for them.

✔ **High quality standards.** Sloppy work can lead to big legal or logistical problems down the road. If an agent neglects to recommend an inspection, for example, you may be stuck with undiscovered problems after the deal is done.

Buying and selling real estate require somewhat different skills. Few agents can do both equally well. No law or rule says that you must use the same agent when you sell a property as when you buy. Don't feel obliged to sell through the agent who worked with you as a buyer just because he sends you holiday cards every year asking how the garden is growing. Remember, he works on commission.

Agents sometimes market themselves as *top producers,* which means that they sell a relatively larger volume of real estate. This title doesn't count for much for you, the buyer. It may be a red flag for an agent who focuses on completing as many deals as possible. When you're buying a home (as opposed to selling), you need an agent who has the following additional traits:

✔ **Patience (not a hard-sell).** When you're buying a home, the last thing you need or want is an agent who tries to push you into making a deal. You need an agent who is patient and willing to allow you the necessary time to get educated and make the best decision for yourself.

✔ **Local market and community knowledge.** If you're looking for a home in an area in which you're not currently living, an informed agent can have a big impact on your decision.

✔ **Financing knowledge.** As a buyer, especially a first-time buyer or someone with credit problems, you should look for an agent who can refer you to lenders who can handle your type of situation, which can save you a lot of legwork.

Putting Your Deal Together

After you do your homework on your personal finances, understand how to choose a mortgage, and research neighbourhoods and home prices, you'll hopefully soon close in on your goal. Eventually, you'll find a home you'd like to buy. Before you make that first offer, though, you need to understand the importance of negotiations, inspections, and other elements of a real estate deal.

Buying without a real estate agent

A competent and ethical real estate agent can add enough value to your purchase to warrant the commission you pay. However, the claim that it doesn't cost you anything as a buyer to buy through an agent is false. If you aren't working with an agent, a seller may be willing to accept a lower offer because he or she needs to pay just one agent's commission.

You can purchase on your own if you're willing to do some additional legwork. You need to do the things that a good real estate agent does, such as searching for properties, scheduling appointments to see them, and negotiating and coordinating inspections. If you're experienced or savvy about real estate and

have found a property on your own, there's no reason you can't put a deal together yourself.

If you don't work with an agent, you should consider having a lawyer review the contracts, unless you're a legal expert yourself. Besides, in most cases, real estate agents aren't legal experts anyway.

One possible drawback to working without an agent is that you must do the negotiations yourself. If you're a good negotiator, doing so can work to your advantage. But if you get too caught up emotionally in the situation, negotiating for yourself can backfire.

Negotiating 101

When you work with an agent, the agent usually carries the burden of the negotiation process. But you need to have a plan and strategy in mind — otherwise, you might overpay for your home. Here are some recommendations for getting a good deal:

✔ **Never fall in love with a property.** If you've got money to burn and you can't imagine life without the home you've just discovered, then pay what you will. Otherwise, always remind yourself that other good properties are out there. Having an actual backup property in mind never hurts.

✔ **Learn about the property and owner before you make your offer.** How long has the property been on the market? What are its flaws? Why is the owner selling it? For example, if the seller is moving because she got a job in another town where she's about to close on a home purchase, she may be eager to get her money out and may be willing to reduce the price. The more you understand about the property that you want to buy and the seller's motivations, the better you'll be able to draft an offer that meets both parties' needs.

✔ **Get comparable sales data to support your price.** Too often, home buyers and their agents pick a number out of the air when making an offer. But if the offer has no substance behind it, the seller will hardly be persuaded to lower his asking price. Point to recent and comparable home sales to justify your offer price.

✔ **Remember that price is only one of several negotiable items.** Sometimes sellers get fixated on selling their homes for a certain amount. Perhaps they want to get at least what they paid for it themselves several years ago. You may be able to get a seller to pay for certain repairs or improvements or to offer you an attractive loan without all the extra loan fees that a bank would charge. Likewise, the real estate agent's commission is negotiable, too.

The thirst for a commission brings out the worst in agents. They'll tell you numerous fibs to motivate you to buy on the seller's terms. One common one is to say that other offers are coming in on the property you're interested in. Or they'll say that the seller already turned down an offer for *x* dollars because he's holding out for a higher offer.

Another tactic is the car dealer trick — blaming the office manager for not allowing them to reduce their commission. The bottom line is that if it's not in writing, be sceptical. Be sure to spend the time needed to find a good agent and to understand agents' potential conflicts of interest (see the section on agents earlier in this chapter).

Conventional wisdom says that the seller pays the agent's commission, so it doesn't concern or cost you as a buyer. Wrong! If the agents involved in your real estate deal agree to reduce their commissions, the seller may be willing to accept less money for the property.

If the buyer and the property seller aren't that far apart on price, suggest that the agents lower their commissions. To get a deal done, you may be surprised at what agents are willing to do. Read the section later in this chapter about negotiating real estate agents' commissions.

Inspect, inspect, inspect

When you buy a home, you're probably making one of the biggest (if not *the* biggest) financial purchases and commitments of your life. Unless you've built homes and done contracting work yourself, you probably have no idea what you're getting yourself into when it comes to furnaces and termites.

Spend the money and time to hire inspectors and other experts to evaluate the major systems and potential problem areas of the home. Areas that you want to check include

- ✔ Overall condition of the property
- ✔ Electrical, heating, and plumbing systems
- ✔ Foundation
- ✔ Roof
- ✔ Pest control and dry rot
- ✔ Seismic/slide risk

Inspection fees often pay for themselves. If you uncover problems that you weren't aware of, the inspection reports give you the information you need to go back and ask the property seller to fix the problems or reduce the purchase price of the property to compensate you for correcting the deficiencies yourself.

As with other professionals whose services you retain, interview a few inspection companies. Ask which systems they inspect and how detailed a report they'll prepare for you (ask for a sample copy). Ask them for names and phone numbers of three people who used their service within the past six months.

Never accept a seller's inspection report as your only source of information. When a seller hires an inspector, she may hire someone who won't be as diligent and critical of the property. What if the inspector is buddies with the seller or agent selling the property? By all means, review the seller's inspection reports if available, but get your own as well.

And here's one more inspection for you to do. The day before you close on the purchase of your home, do a brief walk-through of the property to make sure that everything is still in the condition it was before and that all the fixtures, appliances, curtains, and other items that were to be left as per the contract are still there. Sometimes, sellers (and their movers) "forget" what's to be left or try to test your powers of observation.

After You Buy

After you buy a home, over the months and years ahead, you'll make a number of important decisions regarding your castle (or shoe box). This section discusses key issues and what you need to know to make the best decision for each.

Refinancing early

Three reasons motivate people to refinance early. One is obvious: to save money because interest rates have dropped. Refinancing can also be a way of raising capital for some other purpose. A final reason is to get out of one type of loan and into another. The following sections should help you decide whether refinancing makes sense for you.

Refinancing options

Lower rates look very appealing when you look at how much more money would stay in your bank account every month by cutting your mortgage payments. That's hard cash you could put toward other purposes or use to pay down your principal.

If you have an open mortgage, of course, you can renew whenever current rates are more attractive. Find a new term you're comfortable with and sit back and count your savings. Better yet, keep your payments at the previous level and use the drop in rates to take years off your mortgage. And remember: When you refinance, you terminate your deal with your current lender. You're free to shop around your mortgage to other lenders. Or you could get a few offers to use as leverage to get your current lender to chop a quarter or even half a percent off its published rates.

Most mortgages, however, are closed. And although your lender may be willing to allow you to refinance early, it will want to be compensated for some — or all — of its losses. After all, if you want to refinance to reduce your rate from 11 percent to 8 percent, the banks aren't exactly going to leap at the chance to profit 3 percent less from your loan, now are they?

The first step is to get your mortgage agreement out and read the fine print. Growing competition means that some lenders have made it easier for you to get out of your current loan. But this is a marketing edge they don't particularly want to tout unless they have to. After all, if you don't read your agreement and simply assume that you're stuck paying higher rates than you may need to, you don't really expect banks and trust companies to bring that to your attention — do you?

The three months' interest penalty

Your mortgage agreement may allow you to refinance your loan by paying the equivalent of three months' interest on your outstanding balance. This refinancing rule applies to all CMHC-insured loans. In addition to high-ratio mortgages, loans financed by mortgage-backed securities must be insured with CMHC; it can be worth your while to check with your lender to see if this rule applies to you. Further, by law, any mortgage with a term longer than five years also becomes open on the fifth anniversary, with the same three-month penalty applying.

Although they don't widely promote the fact, several of the big banks now also allow you to refinance under the same terms at any point after the third anniversary of your present agreement. But remember, it's unlikely that your lenders will alert you to the money you could be saving.

Whether the three-month penalty is worth paying is different in every case. It depends on the difference between your existing rate and what current rates are as well as on how much remains in your principal. Your best bet is to ask your lender to work the numbers out for you. The lender may not be that happy about doing so, but you should get the answers you need.

The interest rate differential (IRD) penalty

The most common penalty is something called the *interest rate differential*. The IRD is the value today of the income the lender gives up by allowing you to refinance.

Say you're paying 10 percent and have two years left in your term. Your lender calculates how much it can make by taking the balance of your loan and lending it out elsewhere. Then it will ask you to make up the difference so that it can break even on the deal. The problem is that paying the IRD leaves *you* breaking even as well. The money you save with lower rates will be wiped out by the compensation you'll have to pay.

Another potential problem is that nobody can say with certainty where interest rates are headed. You lose out if rates fall and are lower at the end of your present term. If that happens, you've gone through an awful lot of tedious paperwork only to be locked in at a higher term than you would be paying if you had simply sat tight.

Mortgage life insurance

Shortly after you buy a home or close on a mortgage, you'll start getting mail from all kinds of organizations that keep track of publicly available information about mortgages. Most of these organizations want to sell you something, and they don't tend to beat around the bush.

"What will your dependents do if you meet with an untimely demise and they are left with a gargantuan mortgage?" they ask.

Fair enough. In fact, this is a good financial-planning question. If your family is dependent upon your income, can they survive financially if you and your income disappear from life as we know it?

Don't waste your money on mortgage life insurance. You may need life insurance to provide for your family and help meet large obligations such as mortgage payments or educational expenses for children. But mortgage life insurance is grossly overpriced. (Read the life insurance section in

Chapter 18 for advice about term life insurance.) You should consider mortgage life insurance only if you have a health problem and the mortgage life insurer doesn't require a physical examination. Be sure to compare it with term life options.

Is getting a reverse mortgage a good idea?

Increasing numbers of homeowners are finding, particularly in their later years of retirement, that they lack cash. Their largest asset is usually the home in which they live. Unlike other investments, such as bank accounts, bonds, or stocks, a home does not provide any income to the owner unless he or she decides to rent out a room or two.

A *reverse mortgage* allows a homeowner who's low on cash to tap into home equity. For an elderly homeowner, this can be a difficult thing to do psychologically. Most people work hard to feed a mortgage month after month, year after year, until finally it's all paid off. What a feat and what a relief after all those years!

Taking out a reverse mortgage reverses this process. Each month, a bank or other financial institution sends you a cheque that you can spend on food, clothing, travel, or whatever suits your fancy. The money you receive each month is really a loan against the value of your home, which makes the monthly cheque free from taxation. Other advantages of a reverse mortgage are that it allows you to stay in your home and use its equity to supplement your monthly income.

The main drawback is that a reverse mortgage can deplete the estate that you may want to pass onto your heirs or use for some other purpose. Also, some loans require repayment within a certain number of years. The fees and the effective interest rate you're charged to borrow the money can also be quite high.

Because some loans require the lender to make monthly payments to you as long as you live in the home, lenders assume that you'll live a very long time so that they don't lose money in making these loans. If you end up keeping the loan for only a few years because you move, for example, the cost of the loan is extremely high.

An excellent book that explores all the mechanics of reverse mortgages and how to shop for them is *Have Your Home and Money Too,* by P.J. Wade, published by Wiley.

You may be able to create a reverse mortgage within your own family network. This technique can work if you have family members who are financially able to provide you with monthly income in exchange for ownership of the home when you pass away.

There are also other alternatives to tapping home equity. One is to simply sell your home and buy a less-expensive property or rent a place. Any profits you make when you sell the home you live in are tax free.

Selling your house

The day will someday come when you will want to sell your house. If you're going to sell, make sure that you can afford to buy the next home you desire. Be especially careful if you're a trade-up buyer — that is, you're buying an even more expensive home. All the affordability issues discussed at the beginning of this chapter apply. Also consider the following issues:

Selling through an agent

Selling and buying a home demand agents with different strengths. When you're selling a property, you want an agent who can get the job done efficiently and for as high a price as possible. As a seller, you should seek agents who have marketing and sales expertise and are willing to put in the time and money necessary to get your home sold. Don't necessarily be impressed by an agent who works for a large company. What matters more is what the agent is going to do to market your property.

When you list your home for sale, the contract that you sign with the listing agent includes specification of the commission to be paid if the agent is successful in selling your home. In most areas of the country, agents usually ask for a 6 percent commission.

Regardless of the commission an agent says is "typical," "standard," or "what my manager requires," *always* remember that commissions are negotiable.

Because the commission is a percentage, you have a much greater ability to negotiate a lower commission on a higher-priced home. If an agent makes 6 percent selling both a $200,000 home and a $100,000 home, the agent makes twice as much on the $200,000 home. Yet selling the higher-priced home does not take twice as much work. (Selling a $400,000 home certainly doesn't take four times the effort of a $100,000 home sale.)

If you live in an area with higher-priced homes (above $200,000), you have no reason to pay more than a 5 percent commission. For expensive properties ($400,000 and up), a 4 percent commission is reasonable. You may find, however, that your ability to negotiate a lower commission is greatest when an offer is on the table.

In terms of the length of the listing sales agreement you make with an agent, three months is reasonable. If you give an agent too long a listing (6 to 12 months), the agent may simply toss your listing into the multiple listing book and not expend much effort to get your property sold. Practically speaking, you can fire your agent whenever you want, regardless of the length of the listing agreement. But a shorter listing may be more motivating for your agent.

Selling without a real estate agent

The temptation to sell without an agent is usually to save the commission that an agent deducts from your home's sale price. If you have the time, energy, and marketing experience, you can sell your home and possibly save some money.

The major problem with attempting to sell your home on your own is that you can't list it in the *multiple listing service* (MLS), which only real estate agents can access. Some people have said, and we concur, that the MLS functions as an effective near-monopoly over the selling of homes. And if you're not listed in the MLS, many potential buyers will never know that your home is for sale. Agents working with buyers don't generally look for or show their clients homes that are for sale by owner.

Discount brokers charge less than traditional real estate agents to help you sell your home. They may help you develop advertisements, prepare contracts, and negotiate with potential buyers. You may be responsible for showing the home to prospective buyers.

Discounters usually charge a fixed fee or a percentage of the sales price. The cost should be much less than a traditional agent would charge. Try contacting Peartree Home Marketing (abotex@sympatico.ca), which has franchise operations across the country. Alternatively, try negotiating a better commission from a regular agent.

Should you keep your home until prices go up?

Many homeowners are tempted to hold onto their properties when they need to move if the property is worth less than when they bought it or if the real estate market is soft. It's probably not worth the hassle of renting out your property or the financial gamble of holding onto it. If you need to move, you're better off in most cases selling your home.

You may reason that in a few years, the real estate storm clouds will clear and you can sell your property at a much higher price. Here are three risks associated with this way of thinking:

✔ First, you can't know what's going to happen to property prices in the next few years. They might rebound, but they could stay the same or drop even further. A property generally needs to appreciate at least a few percent per year just to make up for all the costs of holding and maintaining it.

✔ If you haven't been a landlord, don't underestimate the hassle and headaches associated with this job.

✔ Once you convert your home into a rental property, you need to pay capital gains tax on some of your profit when you sell it if it does appreciate (talk to your friendly neighbourhood tax advisor for more details). This tax wipes out much of the advantage of having held onto the property until prices recovered.

The only good reason we can think of to hold onto a home that has plunged in value is that you would realize little cash from selling *and,* combined with your other savings, you wouldn't have enough money for a down payment on your next property.

Should you keep your home as investment property if you move?

It's worth considering converting your home into rental property if you need to or want to move. Don't consider doing so unless it really is a long-term proposition (ten or more years). As discussed in the preceding section, selling rental property has tax consequences.

One advantage to keeping your current home as an investment property after you move is that you already own it. Locating and buying investment property takes time and money. You also know what you have with your current home. If you go out and purchase a property to rent, you're starting from scratch.

If your property is in good condition, consider what damage renters might do — few renters will take care of your home the way that you do. Also consider if you're cut out to be a landlord.

For more information, read the section in Chapter 11 that discusses real estate as an investment.

Part IV
Protecting What You've Got

The 5th Wave
By Rich Tennant

"You may want to talk to Phil – he's one of our more aggressive financial planners."

In this part . . .

You discover that just because insurance is boring doesn't mean you can ignore it. Therefore, we show you how to obtain the right kind of insurance to shield you from the brunt of unexpected major expenses and protect your future earnings and your assets. We reveal which types of insurance you do and do not need, what you should avoid, what to include and what not to include in your policies, and how much of which things you should insure. Plus, you finally face other creepy but important stuff such as wills, probate, and taxes payable when you die.

Chapter 17

Insurance Basics

· ·

In This Chapter

▶ The three laws of buying insurance

▶ How to save thousands of dollars and get the insurance coverage you need

▶ What to do if you're denied coverage

▶ How to get 'em to cough up your claim money

· ·

*U*nless you work in the industry (by choice), insurance is, for most people, a dreadfully boring topic. Most people associate insurance with disease, death, and disaster and would rather do just about anything other than review or spend money on insurance. But because you don't want to deal with money hassles when you're coping with catastrophes — illness, disability, death, fires, floods, earthquakes — you must take care of insurance well before you need it.

Insurance is probably the least-understood and least-monitored area of personal finance. Most people are overwhelmed by all the jargon in sales and policy statements. As a result, people get insurance from the wrong companies, pay more than is necessary for their policies, or get insured through companies with poor reputations for servicing customers with claims on their policies.

The Three Laws of Buying Insurance

We know that your patience and interest in learning about insurance may be limited, so we boil it down to three fairly simple but powerful concepts that can easily save you thousands of dollars over the rest of your insurance-buying years. And while you're saving money, you can still get the coverage you need to avoid a financial catastrophe.

Law I: Insure for the big stuff, don't sweat the small stuff

Imagine, for a moment, that you're offered a chance to buy insurance that reimburses you for the cost of a magazine subscription in the event the magazine folds and you don't get all the issues you paid for. Because a magazine subscription doesn't cost much, we don't think you would buy that insurance.

What if you could buy insurance that pays for the cost of a restaurant meal if you get food poisoning? Even if you're splurging at a fancy restaurant, you don't have a lot of money at stake, so you'd probably decline that coverage as well.

The point of insurance is to protect against losses that would be financially catastrophic to you, not to smooth out the bumps of everyday life. The examples above are silly, but some people buy equally silly policies without knowing it, as we illustrate in this section.

Avoid small-potato policies

A good insurance policy can seem expensive. A policy that doesn't cost much, on the other hand, can fool you into thinking that you're getting something for next to nothing. Policies that cost little also cover little — they are priced low because they don't cover large potential losses.

As you read through the following list, you may very well find examples of policies that you yourself have bought and that you feel more than paid for themselves. We can hear you saying, "But I collected on that policy you're telling me not to buy!" Sure, getting the satisfaction (the revenge?) of being "reimbursed" for the hassle of something being lost or going wrong is always nice. But consider all such policies that you've bought or could buy over the course of your life. You're not going to come out ahead in the aggregate — if you did, insurance companies would lose money! These policies aren't worth the cost relative to the small potential benefit. On the average, insurance companies pay out just 60 cents in benefits on every dollar collected. Many of the following policies pay you back even less — around 20 cents in benefits (claims) for every dollar you spend in insurance premiums.

The following are examples of common, "small-potato" insurance policies that are generally a waste of your hard-earned dollars.

Extended warranty and repair plans

Isn't it ironic that right after the salesperson persuades you to buy a television, computer, or car — in part by saying how reliable the goods are — he or she tries try to convince you to spend more money to insure against the failure of the item? If the stuff is so good, why do you need insurance?

Product manufacturers' warranties typically cover any problems that occur in the first three months to a year. And should you need to pay for a repair out of your own pocket, it won't be a financial catastrophe. Extended warranty and repair plans are expensive and unnecessary insurance policies.

Home warranty plans

If your real estate agent or the seller of the home wants to pay the cost of a home warranty plan for you, turning down the offer would be ungracious (as Grandma would say, you shouldn't look a gift horse in the mouth). But don't buy this type of plan for yourself. In addition to requiring some sort of fee (around $30 to $50) if you need a contractor to come out and look at a problem, home warranty plans limit how much they pay for major problems.

Your money is much better spent on hiring a competent inspector to uncover problems and fix them *before* you buy the home. Everyone buying a house should expect to spend money on repairs and maintenance — that's just being realistic! To buy insurance for the smaller repairs and maintenance is a waste of money.

Dental insurance

If your employer pays for dental insurance, take advantage of it. But you shouldn't pay for this coverage on your own. Dental insurance generally covers a couple of teeth cleanings each year and limits payments for more expensive work.

Credit life and credit disability policies

Many direct-mail firms try to sell policies that pay a small benefit in case you die with an outstanding loan (a credit life policy) or that pay a small monthly income in the event of a disability (a credit disability policy). These policies are usually sold by credit card companies such as VISA, MasterCard, and American Express. Some companies even sell you insurance to pay off your credit card bill in the event of your death or disability.

The cost of this insurance seems low, but that's because the potential benefits are small. In fact, given how little insurance you're buying, these policies are extraordinarily expensive. If you need life or disability insurance, purchase it. But get enough coverage and buy it in a separate, cost-effective policy (see Chapter 18 for more details).

One exception to the above rule is if you're in poor health and you can buy these insurance policies without a medical evaluation. In that case, these policies may be the only ones you have access to. This is another reason that these policies are expensive. If you're in good health, you pay for the people with poor health who can enroll without a medical examination and who undoubtedly make more claims.

Insuring packages in the mail

You buy a $40 gift for a friend, and when you go to the post office to ship it, the friendly postal clerk asks if you want to insure it. For a couple of bucks, you think, why not? Canada Post may have a bad reputation for many reasons, but it rarely loses or damages things. Go spend your money on another gift instead!

Contact lens insurance

The things that people come up with to waste money on just astound us. Contact lens insurance really does exist! The money goes to replace your contacts if you lose or tear them. Lenses are cheap. Don't waste your money on this kind of insurance.

Little stuff riders

Many policies that are worth buying, such as auto and disability insurance, have all sorts of add-on riders. These are extra bells and whistles that insurance agents and companies like to sell because of the high profit margin (for *them*). On auto insurance policies, for example, you can buy a rider for a few bucks per year that pays you $25 each time your car needs to be towed. Having your vehicle towed isn't going to bankrupt you, so it isn't worth insuring against. (Besides, what are you doing to necessitate repeated towings?)

Likewise, small insurance policies that are sold as add-ons to bigger insurance policies are usually not necessary and are overpriced. For example, you can buy some disability insurance policies with a small amount of life insurance added on. If you need life insurance, purchasing a sufficient amount in a separate policy is less costly.

Take the highest deductible you can afford

Most insurance policies have *deductibles* — the maximum amount you must pay in the event of a loss before your insurance coverage kicks in. On many policies, such as auto and homeowner's/renter's coverage, most folks opt for a $100 to $250 deductible.

Here are two benefits to taking a higher deductible:

✔ **You save premium dollars.** Year in and year out, you can enjoy the lower cost of an insurance policy with a high deductible. You may be able to shave 15 to 20 percent off the cost of your policy. Suppose, for example, that you can reduce the cost of your policy by $150 per year by raising your deductible from $250 to $1,000. That $750 worth of coverage is costing you $150 per year. Thus, you would need to have a claim of $1,000 or more every five years — highly unlikely — to come out ahead. And if you are that accident-prone — guess what? — the insurance company will crank up your premiums.

✔ **You don't have the hassles of filing small claims.** If you have a $300 loss on a policy with a $100 deductible, you need to file a claim to get your $200 (the amount you're covered for after your deductible). Filing an insurance claim can take hours of time and can be an aggravating experience. In some cases, you may even have your claim denied after jumping through all the necessary hoops.

If you have low deductibles, you may file more claims (although this doesn't necessarily mean that you'll get more money). If you file more claims, you may be rewarded with jacked-up premiums — in addition to the headache of preparing those blasted forms! If you file too many claims, you may even have your coverage cancelled!

Buy insurance to cover financial catastrophes

You should insure against what could be a huge financial loss for you. The price of insurance isn't cheap, but it's relatively small in comparison to the potential total loss. Many people make the mistake of not insuring against what could be a financial catastrophe.

The beauty of insurance is that it spreads risks over millions of other people. If your home burns to the ground, paying the rebuilding cost out of your own pocket probably would be a financial catastrophe. If you have insurance, the premiums paid by you and all the other homeowners collectively can easily pay the bills.

Think for a moment about what your most valuable assets are. (No, it's not your dry wit or your charming personality.) Also consider potential large expenses.

✔ If you're still in your working years, your most valuable asset is probably your future earnings. If you were disabled and unable to work, what would you live on? That's why long-term disability insurance exists. If you have a family that's financially dependent on your earnings, how will your family manage financially if you die? Life insurance can fill the financial void left by your death.

✔ If you're a business owner, what would happen if you were sued for $1,000,000 for negligence in some work that you messed up? Liability insurance can bail you out.

✔ In this age of soaring medical costs, you can easily rack up a $100,000 hospital bill in the U.S. in short order. That's why you need out-of-Canada medical health insurance coverage. And, yet, a surprising number of people don't carry any travel insurance, particularly those who make short trips south of the border by car. (See Chapter 18 for more on out-of-the-country medical insurance.)

Psychologically, buying insurance coverage for many of the little things that are more likely to occur is tempting. You don't want to feel like you're wasting your insurance dollars. You want to get some of your money back, darn it! You're more likely to get into a fender bender with your car or have a package lost in the mail than you are to lose your home to fire or suffer a long-term disability. But if the fender bender costs $500 (which you end up paying out of your pocket because you took our advice to take a high deductible), it isn't going to be a financial disaster. You probably won't be happy about having to pay for it, but you can and will.

If, on the other hand, you lose your ability to earn an income because of a disability or are sued for $1,000,000 but aren't insured against such catastrophes, you'll not only be extremely unhappy but will also face financial ruin. "Yes, but what are the odds," we hear people rationalize, "that I'll suffer a long-term disability or that I'll be sued for $1,000,000?" We agree that the odds are quite low. But the odds aren't as low as zero. The risk is there. The problem is that you just don't know what bad luck will befall you or when.

And don't make the mistake of thinking that you can figure the odds better than the insurance companies can. The probability of your making a claim, large or small, is predicted with a great deal of accuracy by the insurance companies. That's why they employ armies of number-crunching actuaries to calculate the odds of bad things happening and the frequency of current policyholders making particular types of claims. The companies price their policies accordingly.

Buying or not buying insurance based on your perception of the likelihood of needing the coverage is just plain dumb.

Law II: Buy broad coverage

Another major mistake people make when buying insurance is purchasing coverage that's too narrow. The policies often seem like cheap ways to put their greatest fears to rest. For example, instead of buying life insurance, some folks buy flight insurance at an airport self-service kiosk. They seem to worry more about their mortality when getting on an airplane than they do when getting into a car. If they die on the flight, their beneficiaries collect. But if they die the next day in an auto accident or if they get some dreaded disease — which is statistically far more likely than going down in a jumbo jet — the beneficiaries don't collect anything from flight insurance.

The medical equivalent of flight insurance is cancer insurance. Older people, fearful of having their life savings depleted by a long battle with this deadly disease, are easy prey for unscrupulous insurance salespeople pitching this narrow insurance. If you get cancer, cancer insurance pays the bills. But what if you get heart disease, diabetes, AIDS, or some other disease? The cancer insurance doesn't pay these costs.

Our misperceptions of risks

How high are your risks of dying prematurely if you're exposed to toxic wastes or pesticides or if you live in a dangerous area that has a high murder rate? These risks are actually quite small when compared to the risks you subject yourself to when you get behind the wheel of a car or light up yet another cigarette.

John Stossel, the crack ABC reporter, was kind enough to share with Eric the results of a study done for him by physicist Bernard Cohen who compared different risks. Cohen's study showed that our riskiest behaviors are smoking and driving. Smoking whacks an average of seven years off a person's life, whereas driving a car results in a bit more than half a year of life lost on average. Toxic waste shaves an average of one week off an American's life span.

Knowing what's risky and what isn't is part of what you need to know. Unfortunately, you can't buy a formal insurance policy to protect yourself against all of life's great dangers and risks. But that doesn't mean that you must face these dangers as a helpless victim. Simple changes in behavior can help you fight the odds.

Personal health habits are a good example. If you're overweight; eat fatty, high cholesterol foods; drink excessively; and don't exercise, you're asking for trouble, especially during post-middle age. Engage in these habits, and you dramatically increase your risk of heart disease and cancer.

So does this mean that we should all eat bean sprouts, stay out of cars, never light up, and cease being concerned about toxic waste? No. But understanding the consequences of your behaviors before you engage in them and prioritizing risks worth worrying about is important.

If you're reading this chapter, you obviously want to find out about insurance. Our point is this: You can buy all the types of real insurance that we recommend in this book and still not be well-protected for the simple reason that you're overlooking uninsurable risks. But just because you can't buy formal insurance to protect against some risks doesn't mean that you can't drastically reduce your exposure to such risks through modifying your behaviour.

Your fears in life are natural and inescapable; they're also often arbitrary and irrational. Although you may not have control over the emotions that your fears invoke, you must often ignore those emotions in order to make rational insurance decisions. In other words, getting shaky in the knees and sweaty in the palms when boarding an airplane is okay, but letting your fear of flying cause you to make poor insurance decisions isn't okay, especially when those decisions affect the lives of your loved ones.

You can't possibly predict what's going to happen to you. You want to get the broadest possible coverage that you can. Buy life insurance, not flight insurance. Buy major medical coverage, not cancer insurance.

Law III: Shop around and consider buying direct

The cost of insurance varies tremendously from insurer to insurer. Whether you're looking at auto, home, life, disability, or other types of coverage, some companies may charge double or triple the rates that other companies charge for the same coverage. The companies charging the higher rates may not be better about paying claims, however. You may even end up with the worst of both possible worlds — high prices *and* lousy service.

Most insurance is sold through agents and brokers who earn commissions based on what they sell. This, of course, tends to bias what they recommend that you buy. We see this bias in action all the time. A study done by Cummins and Weisbart and cited in Andrew Tobias's book *Invisible Bankers* confirms this bias: ". . . 48% of the time, an agent's decision on where to place a customer's business was based on which insurer paid the highest commission."

Not surprisingly, policies that pay agents the biggest commissions also tend to be more costly. In fact, insurance companies compete for the attention of agents by offering bigger commissions than other insurers. If you browse through magazines and other publications targeted to insurance agents (we're sure you're anxious to do this), you see ads in which the very largest text is the commission percentage offered to agents who sell the advertiser's products.

Besides the attraction of policies that pay higher commissions, agents also get hooked, financially speaking, to companies whose policies they sell frequently. Once an agent has sold a certain number of a company's insurance policies, he is rewarded with higher commission percentages on any future sales. Just as airlines bribe frequent fliers with mileage bonuses, insurers bribe agents with fatter commissions for their loyalty.

Shopping around is a challenge not only because most insurance is sold by agents working on commission but also because insurers set their rates in mysterious ways. Every company has a different way of analyzing how much of a risk you are; one company may offer low rates to you but not to your cousin, and vice versa.

Despite the obstacles, several strategies exist for obtaining low-cost, high-quality policies. Chapters 18 and 19 recommend how and where to get the best deals on specific types of policies. The following tips offer smart ways to shop for insurance.

The straight scoop on commissions and how insurance is sold

The commission paid to an insurance agent is never disclosed through any of the documents or materials that you receive in the process of buying insurance. This information ought to be disclosed by insurers and agents, just as sales charges on mutual funds are disclosed through a prospectus.

The only way you can know what the commission is on a policy and how it compares with other policies is to ask the agent. Nothing is wrong or impolite about asking. It's your money, after all, that pays the commission. You need to know whether a particular policy is being pitched harder because of its higher commission.

Commissions are typically paid as a percentage of the first year's premium on the insurance policy. (Many policies pay smaller commissions on subsequent years' premiums.) On life and disability insurance policies, for example, a 50 percent commission on the first year's premium is not unusual. On life insurance policies that have a cash value, commissions of 80 to 100 percent of your first year's premium are possible. Commissions on health insurance are lower, but generally not as low as commissions on auto and homeowner's insurance.

Insurance without sales commissions

A good bet for getting a good insurance value is to buy policies from the increasing number of companies that sell their policies directly to the public, cutting the insurance agent and the agent's accompanying commission out of the picture. Just as you can purchase no-load mutual funds directly from an investment company without paying any sales commission (see Chapter 12), you also can buy no-load insurance. Be sure to read Chapters 18 and 19 for more specifics on how to buy insurance directly from insurance companies.

Employer and other group plans

When you buy insurance as part of a larger group, you generally get a lower price because of the purchasing power or clout of the group. Most health and disability policies that you can access through your employer are less costly than equivalent policies that you can buy on your own.

Likewise, many occupations have professional associations through which you may be able to obtain lower-cost policies. Not all associations offer better deals on insurance, so make sure you compare what they offer with other options available to you.

Insurance agents who want to sell you an individual policy can come up with 101 reasons why buying from them is preferable to buying through your employer or some other group. In most cases, agents' arguments for buying an individual policy from them include a lot of self-serving marketing hype. In some cases, agents tell outright lies (which are hard to detect if you're not insurance-savvy).

One valid issue agents will raise is that, if you leave your job, you'll lose your group coverage. Sometimes that may be true. If you know that you'll be leaving your job to become self-employed, securing an individual disability policy before you leave your job makes sense. However, your employer's health and dental insurer may allow you to convert your health and dental insurance policy into an individual one when you leave. And if you have no immediate plans to leave your job, why throw away money on an over-priced individual policy if you have access to low-cost, high-quality group coverage?

In the chapters that follow, you find out exactly what you need in the policies that you're looking for so that you can determine whether a group plan meets your needs. In almost all cases, group plans, especially through an employer, offer the necessary benefits. As long as the group policy is cheaper than an identical policy you could buy as an individual, you'll save money buying through the group plan.

One exception to the rule that group policies offer better value than individual policies is with life insurance. Group life insurance plans usually aren't cheaper than the best life insurance policies that you can buy individually. If the policies are competitively priced, however, group policies may have the attraction of convenience (ease of enrolment and avoidance of long-winded sales pitches from life insurance salespeople). Group life insurance policies that allow enrolment without a medical evaluation will probably be more expensive because such plans attract more people with health problems who couldn't get coverage on their own. If you're in good health, you should definitely shop around for life insurance (see Chapter 18 for how).

Dealing with Insurance Problems

When you seek out insurance or have insurance policies, sooner or later you're bound to hit a roadblock. Although insurance problems can be among the more frustrating in life, in the sections ahead, we explain how to calmly and successfully deal with the most common obstacles.

Help! I've been denied coverage!

Just as you can be turned down when you apply for a loan, you can also be turned down when applying for insurance. For medical, life, or disability insurance, a company may reject you if you have an existing medical problem (a pre-existing condition) and are therefore more likely to file a claim. When it comes to insuring assets such as a home, you may have difficulty getting coverage if the property is deemed to be in a high-risk area.

The financial health of your insurers

In addition to the price of a policy and the insurer's reputation and track record for paying claims, an insurer's financial health is an important consideration when you choose a company. If you faithfully pay your premium dollars year after year, you'll be more than a little bummed out if the insurer goes bankrupt right before you have a major claim.

Insurance companies can fail just like other companies. A number of organizations evaluate and rate, with some sort of letter grade, the financial viability and stability of insurance companies. The major rating agencies include TRAC Insurance Services, Dominion Bond Rating Service, Canadian Bond Rating Service, A.M. Best, Moody's, and Weiss Research.

The agencies' letter-grade rating system works just the way it does in high school: A is better than B or C. Each company uses a different scale. Some companies have as their highest rating AAA, and then AA, A, BBB, BB, and so on. Others use A, A-, B+, B, B-, and so on. Just as some teachers grade more easily, some firms, such as A. M. Best, have a reputation for giving out a greater number of high grades. Others, such as Weiss Research, are tough graders. Unlike in school, however, you want the tough critics when researching where to put your money and future security

TRAC is a good starting point because it reviews almost every Canadian insurer. It puts each company through eight tests and then ranks them from 1 to 8, depending on how many tests they pass. If a company hasn't passed at least five, you should probably look elsewhere.

Just as it's a good idea to get more than one medical opinion, two or three financial ratings can give you a better sense of the safety of an insurance company. Stick with companies that are in the top two — or, at worst, three — levels on the different rating scales. The insurance companies recommended in the following chapters meet this criterion.

You can obtain current rating information about insurance companies, free of charge, by asking your agent or the company itself for a listing of the current ratings.

Although the financial health of an insurance company is important, it's not as big a deal as some insurers (usually those with the highest ratings) and agents make it out to be.

In most insurance company failures, claims still get paid. The people who usually lose out are those who had money invested in life insurance or annuities with the failed insurer. Even then, you'll typically get back 80 or 90 cents on the dollar, but you may have to wait years to get it.

Here are some strategies to employ if you're denied coverage:

✔ **Ask the insurer why you were denied.** Perhaps the company made a mistake or misinterpreted some information that you provided in your application. If you're denied coverage because of a medical condition, see what information the company has on you and whether the information is accurate.

✔ **Request a copy of your medical information file.** Many people don't know that just as you have a credit report file that details your use (and misuse) of credit, you also have a medical information report. You can request a current copy of your medical information file by writing the Medical Information Bureau at 330 University Avenue, Suite 501, Toronto, Ontario, M5G 1R7. You can also call them at 416-597-0590. If a mistake is on your report, you have the right to request that it be fixed. As with changing your credit report, the burden is on you to prove that the information in your file is incorrect. This can be a major hassle — you may even need to contact physicians who you've seen in the past, because their medical records could be the source of the incorrect information.

✔ **Shop other companies.** Just because one company denies you coverage doesn't mean that all insurance companies will. Some insurers better understand certain medical conditions and are more comfortable approving applicants with those conditions. Most insurers, however, charge a person with a blemished medical history a higher rate than a person with a perfect health record, but some companies penalize you less than others. That's why you must shop around even harder if you have a medical condition. A broker who sells policies from multiple insurers can be helpful because he or she can shop among a number of different companies.

✔ **Learn about provincial high-risk pools.** Check with your provincial insurance regulator (see the government section of your local white pages phone directory) if you're turned down for auto or property insurance. A number of provinces act as the insurer of last resort and provide insurance for those who can't get it from insurance companies. Provincial high-risk pool coverage — sometimes known as the Facility Association — is usually bare bones, but it sure beats going without any coverage at all.

✔ **Check for coverage availability before you buy.** If you're considering buying a home, for example, and you can't get coverage, the insurance companies are trying to tell you something. What they're effectively saying is, "We think that property is so high risk, we're not willing to insure it even if you pay a high premium." (A few insurance companies in America's coastal Florida areas hard hit in recent years by hurricanes are actually paying existing policyholders to leave their companies. How's that for a sign that you live in a high-risk area?)

Help! My insurer is hassling me about paying a claim!

In the event that you suffer a loss and file an insurance claim, you may hold the happy belief that your insurance company will cheerfully and expeditiously pay your claims. Given all the money that you've shelled out for coverage and all the hoops you jumped through to be approved for coverage in the first place, that's a reasonable expectation.

Insurance companies may refuse to pay you what you think you're owed for many reasons, however. In some cases, they may actually be right — your claim may not be covered under the terms of the policy. At a minimum, the insurer wants documentation and proof of your loss. Other people who have come before you have been known to cheat, so insurers aren't about to take your word for anything, no matter how honest and ethical you are.

In other cases, though, you're right, and the insurance company is just jerking you around. Some companies view paying claims as an adversarial situation and take a "negotiate tough" stance. Thinking that all insurance companies are going to pay you a fair and reasonable amount is a mistake.

The tips that we discuss in this section help you to ensure that you get paid everything your policy entitles you to.

Document your assets and case

When you're insuring assets, such as your home and its contents, having a record of what you own helps your case. A videotape is the most efficient record, but a handwritten list detailing your possessions works, too. Just remember to keep this record away from your home — if your home burns to the ground, you'll lose your documentation, too!

If you're robbed or are the victim of an accident, get the names, addresses, and phone numbers of witnesses. Take pictures of property damage and solicit estimates for the cost of repairing or replacing what's lost or damaged. File police reports if appropriate, if for no other reason than to bolster your documentation for the insurance claim.

The best offense is a good defence. If you've kept records of valuables and can document their costs, you should be in good shape.

Prepare your case

Filing a claim should be approached the same way as preparing for a court trial or a Revenue Canada audit. Any information that you provide verbally or in writing can and will be used against you to deny your claim. First, you should understand whether the policy you bought covers your claim (this is why getting the broadest coverage possible helps). Unfortunately, the only way to find this out is by getting out the policy and reading it. Policies are hard to read because they use legal language in confusing ways.

A possible alternative is to call the claims department and, *without* providing your name, ask a representative whether a particular loss (such as the one that you just suffered) is covered under its policy. You have no need to lie to the company, but you have no need to tell the representative who you are and that you're about to file a claim, either. Your call is informational so that you can understand what your policy covers. Some companies aren't willing to provide very specific information, however, unless a specific case is cited.

After you initiate the claims process, keep records of all conversations and all copies of documents that you give to the insurer's claims department. If you have problems down the road, this evidence may bail you out.

For property damage, you should get at least a couple of reputable contractors' estimates. Demonstrate to the insurance company that you're trying to shop for a low price, but don't agree to use a low-cost contractor without knowing that he or she can do quality work.

Remember, your claim is a negotiation

To get what you're owed on an insurance claim, you must approach most claims filings for what they are — a negotiation that often isn't cooperative. And the bigger the claim, the more your insurer will play the part of adversary.

When Eric filed a homeowners' insurance claim after a winter storm significantly damaged his backyard, he was greeted on a weekday by a perky, smiley adjuster. Once the adjuster entered his yard and started to peruse the damage, her demeanor changed dramatically. She had a combative, hard-bargainer type attitude that he last witnessed during his days as a consultant when he worked on some labour-management negotiations.

While standing on his back porch a good distance away from the fences in his yard that had been blown over by wind and crushed by two large trees, the adjuster said that his insurer preferred to repair damaged fences rather than replace them. "With your deductible of $1,000, I doubt this will be worth filing a claim for," she said.

The fence that had blown over, she reasoned, could have new posts set in concrete. As he and his wife had already begun to clean up some of the damage for safety reasons, Eric presented to her some pictures of what the yard looked like right after the storm; she refused to take them. She took some measurements and said she'd have a settlement cheque sent out in a couple of days. The settlement she faxed was for $1,119, nowhere near what it would cost Eric to fix the damage that was done.

Be persistent

If you take an insurance company's first offer and don't fight for what you're due, you could be leaving a lot of money on the table. To make Eric's long fence repair story somewhat shorter, after *five* rounds of haggling with the adjusters, supervisors, and finally managers, he was awarded payment to replace the fences and clean up most of the damage. Although the contractors he had contacted all recommended that the work be done this way, the insurance adjuster discredited their recommendations by saying, "Contractors try to jack up the price and recommend work once they know an insurer is involved."

His final total settlement came to $4,888, more than $3,700 higher than the insurer's first offer. Interestingly, Eric's insurer backed off its preference for repairing the fence when the contractor's estimates for doing that work exceeded the cost of a new fence.

Eric, quite understandably, was disappointed with the behaviour of his insurance company. As he admits, "Boy, was I naive! I know from conversations with others that my homeowners' insurance company is not unusual in its adversarial strategy, especially with larger claims. And to think that my insurer has one of the better track records for paying claims!"

Enlist support

If you do your homework and you're not making progress with the insurer's adjuster, ask to speak with supervisors and managers. That's what Eric had to do to get the additional $3,700 needed to get things back to where they were before the storm.

The agent who sold you the policy may be helpful in preparing and filing the claim. A good agent can help increase your chances of getting paid and getting paid sooner. If you're having difficulty with a claim for a policy obtained through your employer or other group, speak with the benefits department or a person responsible for interacting with the insurer. These folks have a lot of clout because of the potential threat to the agent and/or insurer of losing the entire account.

For policies that you buy on your own, if you're having problems getting a fair settlement from the insurer, try contacting your provincial insurance department or commission. You can find the phone number in the provincial government white pages of your phone book or possibly in your insurance policy.

Another option is to hire a public adjuster who, for a percentage of the settlement payment (typically 5 to10 percent), can negotiate with insurers on your behalf.

If all else fails and you have a major claim at stake, try contacting a lawyer who specializes in insurance matters. You can find these specialists in the

Yellow Pages of your phone directory under *Lawyers.* Expect to pay around $150 per hour or so. Consider looking for a lawyer who's willing to negotiate on your behalf, help draft letters, and so on, on an hourly basis without filing a lawsuit. Your provincial department of insurance, the local bar association, or other legal, accounting, or financial practitioners also may be able to refer you to someone.

Yikes! My Insurance Company Has Gone Bust!

If your insurance company goes down in flames, it usually doesn't mean your policy also has gone up in smoke. It's very likely that a substantial portion of your policy will be covered under an industry-run compensation scheme.

In 1990, Canadian life insurance companies got together and created a plan that would help compensate policyholders if their insurance companies failed. The plan works much like the Canada Deposit Insurance Corporation, which protects your savings and most other bank and trust company investments, up to certain limits.

The compensation is provided by CompCorp, (the Canadian Life and Health Insurance Compensation Corporation), an organization set up by the industry.

If your insurer bites the dust, CompCorp entitles you to set amounts of coverage, depending on your policy:

- ✔ Up to $200,000 per life insured with a company. (Insure with two separate insurers and you double your coverage, if you need more than $200,000.)

- ✔ A one-time payout of up to $60,000 for each policyholder who decides to cash in an RRSP or RRIF.

- ✔ If you have a Registered Retirement Income Fund or a cashable annuity with the company, you have the option of forgoing the $60,000 lump sum. In exchange, you get a life annuity insured for up to $2,000 a month.

- ✔ Up to $2,000 a month for someone who already receives income from a noncashable life annuity or disability income policy.

It still pays, though, to take the time to check on the financial health of an insurance company before buying any of its policies. Should your insurance company fail, even if you're eligible for compensation under CompCorp, you may find that your policy is not 100 percent protected.

Chapter 18

Insurance on You

Multiply your typical annual income by the number of remaining years you plan to work — you come up with a pretty big number, don't you? Didn't realize you were worth that much, did you? That dollar amount equals one of your most valuable assets — your ability to earn an income — and you probably need to protect it. You need to buy insurance on you.

This chapter explains the ins and outs of buying insurance that protects your income: life insurance, in case of death; and disability insurance, in case an accident or illness prevents you from working. We tell you which types of insurance may be right for you, which types you should avoid, and where you should look for the insurance you do need.

In addition to protecting your income, you also need to insure against financially catastrophic expenses. We are not talking about December's credit card bill — you're on your own on that one. We are talking about the type of bills that are racked up from a major surgery and a six-week stay in a U.S. hospital. Medical expenses in a foreign country today can make even the most indulgent shopping mall spending spree look dirt cheap. To protect yourself from potentially astronomical medical bills, you also need to buy some out-of-country health insurance.

Life Insurance

You generally only need life insurance when other people are dependent on your income. That means that a lot of people don't need life insurance to protect their incomes: single people, working couples who could maintain an acceptable lifestyle if one of the incomes were gone, independently wealthy people who don't need to work, and retired people who are living off of their retirement nest egg.

But if people in your life are either fully or partly dependent on your pay cheque (usually a spouse and/or children), you should buy life insurance, especially if you have major financial commitments such as a mortgage or years of child-rearing ahead. Considering life insurance if an extended family member is currently or likely to be dependent on your future income also makes sense.

How much do you need?

If you need life insurance, deciding how much to buy is as much a subjective thing as it is a quantitative decision. We've seen some worksheets that are incredibly long and tedious (some are worse than your tax returns). There's no need to get fancy. If you're like us, your eyes start to glaze over if you have more than 20 lines of calculations to complete. Figuring out how much life insurance you need doesn't have to be that complicated.

The main purpose of life insurance is to provide a lump sum payment that replaces the deceased person's income. The question you need to ask yourself is, "How many years of income do I want to replace?" Table 18-1 provides a simple way to calculate how much life insurance you should consider purchasing. To replace a certain number of years of income, simply multiply the appropriate number in the table by the person's annual after-tax income.

Table 18-1	Life Insurance Need Calculation
Years of Income to Replace	*Multiply Annual After-Tax Income* by*
5	4.5
10	8.5
20	15
30	20

* You can roughly determine your annual after-tax income in one of two ways. You can get out last year's tax return and calculate it by subtracting the federal, provincial, and social security deductions (UIC and CPP/QPP) that you paid from your gross employment income. Or you can estimate your after-tax income by multiplying your gross income by 80 percent if you're a low-income earner, 70 percent if you're a moderate-income earner, or 60 percent if you're a high-income earner. (You need to replace only after-tax, not pre-tax, income because life insurance policy payouts aren't taxed.)

Another way to determine the amount of life insurance to buy is to think about how much you'll need to pay for major debts or expenditures, such as your mortgage, other loans, and university for your children. If, for example, you'd like your spouse to have enough of a life insurance death benefit to be able to pay off half of your mortgage and pay for half of your children's university educations, then simply add half of your mortgage amount to half of their estimated university costs (refer to Chapter 15 for approximate numbers) and buy that amount of life insurance.

Don't waste your money on life insurance for your children

You've surely heard of Gerber baby food. Well, the folks at Gerber knew that their brand name had clout with parents, so they sat around racking their brains about what other products they could pitch to parents.

So Gerber established a life insurance company that now has billions of dollars of life insurance in force. The only problem is that they specialize in selling life insurance policies on individuals who don't need it: children.

Gerber's "Grow-Up" policy provides $5,000 of life insurance for children. The marketing materials say, "Life insurance for the child you love . . . $1 a week at most ages. . . ."

Sounds like such a deal, but it's really a rip-off that contradicts the entire logic of life insurance. Unless your kid was the star of the *Home Alone* movies, you aren't financially dependent on any of your children; your children are dependent on you! As any parent knows, kids *cost* a good deal of money — kids don't *earn* money!

And if a person does need life insurance coverage, of what use is a piddling $5,000

worth of coverage?! And a buck a week is hardly a deal — a young adult could buy about ten times that amount of coverage ($50,000) for that cost!

Insurance agents love to prey on the emotional bond between parents and children. In one written sales pitch an agent made to one of Eric's counselling clients, the agent said, ". . . as long as the policies remain in force, your signature(s) will always be there as a reminder of your very thoughtful financial gift."

Agents also love to sell cash value life insurance on kids because such policies pay the agent a hefty commission. Part of the supposed allure is that the huge premiums that you pump into such policies partly go into a savings account for the child's future. As you see later in this chapter, cash-value life insurance is a costly life insurance and investment choice. If you want to secure your children's financial future, follow the advice in this book and pass this information on to your children. Don't waste money on life insurance on your kids — they don't need it.

If you belong to the CPP/QPP, your estate will receive a lump-sum death benefit. As of 1998, the maximum was $2,500. You may also be eligible for other government benefits known as survivors' benefits. If your spouse is under age 65, he or she receives 37.5 percent of your CPP/QPP benefits, plus $131, up to a combined maximum of $410 for 1998. If your surviving spouse is 65 or older, the survivor benefits are 60 percent of your pension, up to a maximum of $446. To find out the approximate amount your family can expect, contact the Income Security Programs information department at 800-277-9914.

Suppose that this benefit amounts to 10 percent of your current income. Then you need to purchase only approximately 90 percent (100 percent minus 10 percent) of the amount of life insurance that you calculated in Table 18-1.

Term versus cash-value life insurance

In the next ten seconds, we're going to tell you how you can save hours of time and thousands of dollars. Ready? *Buy term life insurance.* (The only exception is if you have a high net worth — a couple million bucks or more — in which case, you may want to consider other options. See Chapter 19.) If you've already figured out how much life insurance to purchase and this is all the advice you need to go ahead and buy it, you can skip the rest of this section (and go to the head of the class!).

The following information is for the rest of you who want all the details behind our recommendation for term insurance. Or maybe you've heard (and have already fallen prey to) the sales pitches from life insurance agents, most of whom love selling cash-value life insurance because of the huge commissions it pays.

Cash-value life insurance is the most oversold insurance and financial product in the history of the financial services industry. As you'll soon discover, cash-value life insurance makes sense for only a very small percentage of people.

Let us start with some background. Despite the variety of names that life insurance marketing departments have cooked up for policies, life insurance basically comes in two flavours:

- **Term insurance** is pure life insurance. You pay an annual premium for which you receive a predetermined amount of life insurance protection. If the insured person passes away, the beneficiaries collect; otherwise, the premium is gone. In this way, term life insurance is similar to auto or homeowner's insurance.

- **Cash-value insurance.** All other life insurance policies (whole, universal, variable, and so on) combine life insurance with a supposed savings feature. Your premiums not only pay for life insurance, but some of your dollars are also credited to an account that grows in value over time, assuming you keep paying your premiums. On the surface, this sounds potentially attractive. People don't like to feel that all their premium dollars are getting tossed away.

    But there's a very big catch. For the same amount of coverage (for example, for $100,000 of life insurance benefits), cash-value policies cost you anywhere from four to about ten times (*that's a stunning 1,000 percent!*) more than comparable term policies.

Agents know the buttons to push to get you interested in buying the wrong kind of life insurance. Here are typical arguments that they make for purchasing cash-value polices, followed by the real truth.

"It's all paid up after x number of years. You don't want to be paying life insurance premiums for the rest of your life, do you?"

Agents pitching cash-value life insurance show you all sorts of projections that imply that after the first 10 or 20 years of paying your premiums, you won't need to pay more premiums to keep the life insurance in force.

The only reason that you may be able to stop paying premiums is that you've poured too much extra money into the policy in the early years of payment. Remember that cash-value life insurance costs four to ten times as much as term. Imagine that you currently pay $500 a year for auto insurance, and an insurance company comes along and offers you a policy for $4,000 per year. The representative tells you that after ten years, you can stop paying and still keep your same coverage. We're sure that you wouldn't fall for this sales tactic, but many people do when they buy cash-value life insurance. You need to recognize that only by overcharging today can the insurer afford to continue your coverage in later years without a premium payment.

You also need to be wary of the projections because they often include unrealistic and lofty assumptions about the investment return that your cash balance can earn. When you stop paying into a cash-value policy, the cost of each year's life insurance is deducted from the remaining cash value. If the rate of return on the cash balance isn't high, the cash balance could begin sliding, and eventually you could receive notices saying that your policy needs more funding to keep the life insurance in place.

"You won't be able to afford term insurance when you're older."

As you get older, the cost of term insurance increases because the probability of your dying rises. But life insurance isn't something you need all your life! It's typically bought in a person's younger years when financial commitments and obligations outweigh financial assets. Twenty or 30 years later, the reverse should be true.

If you retire 20 or 30 years from now, you probably won't need life insurance to protect your employment income because there won't be any to protect! You may have needed life insurance when you were raising a family and/or had a substantial mortgage you were responsible for, but by the time you retire, the kids should be out on their own (you hope!) and the mortgage should be paid down.

In the meantime, term insurance saves you a tremendous amount of money. For most people, it takes 20 to 30 years for the premium they're paying on a term insurance policy to finally catch up to (equal) the premium they've been paying all along on a comparable amount of cash-value life insurance purchased today.

One exception to the preceding comment is the case of a small business-owner who owns a business worth more than, say, $1 or $2 million, and who wouldn't want heirs to be forced to sell the business to pay capital gains taxes in the event of his or her death.

"You can borrow against the cash value at a low rate of interest."

Such a deal! It's your money in the policy, remember? If you deposited money in a savings or money market account, how would you like to pay for the privilege of borrowing your own money back? Borrowing on your cash-value policy is not only expensive but also dangerous: You increase the chances of the policy exploding on you — leaving you with nothing to show for all the premiums you pay.

"Your cash value grows tax-deferred."

At last, a glimmer of truth. The fact that the cash-value portion of your policy grows without taxation until you withdraw it is true. But if you want tax-deferral of your investment balances, you should first take advantage of an RRSP (refer to Chapter 9) that gives you an immediate tax deduction for your current contributions in addition to growth without taxation until withdrawal.

Life insurance tends to be a mediocre investment. The insurance company quotes you an interest rate for the first year only. After that, the company pays you what it wants. If you don't like the future interest rates, you can be penalized for quitting the policy (see "How to get rid of cash-value life insurance," later in this chapter). Would you ever invest your money in a bank account that quoted an interest rate for the first year only and then penalized you for moving your money within the next seven to ten years?

"It's forced savings."

Many agents argue that a cash value plan is better than nothing — at least it forces you to save. This is silly reasoning because so many people drop out of cash value life insurance policies after just a few years of paying into them.

If you like the idea of forced savings, you can accomplish it without using life insurance. An RRSP can be set up for automatic monthly transfers. If your employer offers such a plan, it can deduct your contributions right out of your pay cheque — and it doesn't shave a commission off the top! You can also set up monthly electronic transfers from your bank chequing account to contribute to mutual funds (refer to Chapter 12).

Buying term insurance

Term insurance policies have several features to choose from. So that you can make an informed decision about purchasing term insurance, we briefly go over these features in this section.

How often your premium adjusts

As you get older, the risk of dying increases, so the cost of your insurance goes up. Term insurance can be purchased such that your premium adjusts (goes up) annually or every 5, 10, 15, or 20 years. The less frequently your premium adjusts, the higher the initial premium and its incremental increases will be.

The advantage of a premium that locks in for, say, 15 years is that you have the security of knowing how much you'll pay each year for the next 15 years. You also don't need to go through medical evaluations as frequently to qualify for the lowest rate possible.

The disadvantage of a policy with a long-term rate lock is that you pay more in the earlier years than you would on a policy that adjusts more frequently. In addition, you may want to change the amount of insurance you carry as your circumstances change, so you throw money away if you dump a policy with a long-term premium guarantee before its rate is set to change.

Policies that adjust the premium every five to ten years offer a happy medium between price and predictability.

Guaranteed renewability

This feature guarantees that the policy can't be cancelled because of poor health; guaranteed renewability is standard practice on better policies. Don't buy a life insurance policy without this feature unless you're sure that your life insurance needs will disappear when the policy is up for renewal.

Guaranteed renewal rates

The short-term cost is usually the biggest concern when you buy a policy. But as you get older, the costs at renewal time rise significantly. Ensure that future rates are guaranteed and laid out term-by-term in your policy.

Where to buy term insurance

A number of sound ways are available to obtain high-quality, low-cost term insurance. If you choose to buy through a local agent — because you know her or because you'd prefer to buy from someone close to home — you should invest a few minutes of your time to get quotes from one or two sources to get a sense of what's available in the insurance market. If nothing else, your familiarity with the market can prevent an agent from selling you an overpriced, high-commission policy.

The number of insurers who sell term insurance directly to the public is slowly but steadily growing. Many of the banks have insurance-selling divisions, including CIBC and Canada Trust. Good plans to start your search include Belair Direct, CIBC, Canada Trust, and TD Bank. Here's how to contact these companies that sell life insurance directly to individuals:

- ✔ **Belair Direct** (800-268-8551)
- ✔ **Canada Trust Financial Insurance** (888-883-3888)
- ✔ **CIBC Insurance** (888-275-2422)
- ✔ **Green Line Insurance Access** (888-982-0080)
- ✔ **Royal Bank Insurance.** Sold through Lifeco (800-991-0707)

How to get rid of cash-value life insurance

If you were snookered into buying a cash-value life insurance policy and want to get rid of it, go for it. *But don't cancel the coverage until you first secure new term coverage.* If you need life insurance, you don't want to leave open a period when you're not covered (Murphy's Law says *that's* when disaster strikes).

Cashing in a cash-value life insurance policy has tax consequences. For most of these policies, you must pay tax on the amount you receive that's in excess of the premiums you paid over the life of the policy. If you want to withdraw the cash balance in your life insurance policy, consider checking with the insurer or a tax advisor to clarify what the tax consequences may be.

Disability Insurance

As with life insurance, the purpose of disability insurance is to protect your income. The only difference is that you're protecting the income for yourself (and perhaps also your dependents). If you're completely disabled, you still have living expenses, but you probably can't earn an income.

For most people, dismissing the need for disability coverage is easy. The odds of suffering a long-term disability seem so remote — and they are. But if you meet with bad luck, disability coverage can relieve you (and possibly your family) of a major financial burden.

We're talking here about long-term disabilities. If you throw out your back while reliving your athletic glory days with your aging adult body and wind up in bed for a couple of weeks, that won't be as much of a disaster to your finances as it is to your ego! What would be a financial disaster, however, is if you're disabled in such a way that you can't earn an income for several years.

Most large employers offer disability insurance to their employees. Many smaller company employees and all self-employed people are left to fend for themselves. As a result, many people don't have disability coverage. Being without disability insurance is a risky proposition, especially if, like most working people, you need your employment income to live on.

Don't assume that you're adequately covered just because you see the words "disability benefits" in your company's benefits brochure. Many corporate plans offer only minimal levels of coverage, and some policies have very tight conditions you must meet in order to receive any benefits. Get out your policy or talk to your benefits department. If you don't have enough coverage and can't boost it by paying a premium at work, buy extra on an individual basis.

If you're married and your spouse earns a large-enough income that you can make do without yours, then you may consider skipping disability coverage. The same is true if you've already got enough money accumulated for your future years (you're financially independent). Keep in mind, though, that your expenses may go up if you are disabled and require special care or medical attention.

Most disabilities are caused by medical problems, such as arthritis, heart conditions, hypertension, and back/spine or hip/leg impairments. Some of these ailments are caused by advancing age, but more than a third of disabilities are suffered by people under age 45. The vast majority of these medical problems can't be predicted in advance, particularly those caused by accidents, which happen at random.

If you think that you have good disability coverage through the following government programs, think again:

- **Government benefits.** Canada Pension Plan or Quebec Pension Plan pays long-term benefits only if you're unable to perform any substantial, gainful activity and your disability is severe and prolonged and/or likely to lead to your death. Furthermore, disability payments are quite low because they're intended to provide only for basic, subsistence-level living expenses. The maximum in 1998 was $895 a month.

- **Worker's compensation.** Worker's compensation, if you have such coverage through your employer, pays you if you're injured on the job but doesn't pay any benefits if you get disabled away from your job. You need coverage that kicks in regardless of where and how you are disabled.

How much disability insurance do you need?

You need enough disability coverage to provide you with sufficient income to live on until other financial resources are available. If you don't have much saved in the way of financial assets and you would want to continue with the lifestyle supported by your current income, get enough disability coverage to replace your entire take-home (after-tax) monthly pay.

The benefits you purchase on a disability policy are quoted as dollars per month that you receive if disabled. So if your job provides you with a $2,000-per-month income after payment of taxes, then ask for a policy that provides a $2,000-per-month benefit.

If you pay for your disability insurance, the benefits are tax-free (but hopefully you won't ever have to collect them). If your employer picks up the tab, your benefits are taxable, so you need a higher amount of benefits.

In addition to the monthly coverage amount, you also need to select the duration of time you want a policy to pay you benefits. You need a policy that pays benefits until an age at which you become financially self-sufficient. For most people, that's age 65 or so. If you anticipate continuing to be dependent on your employment income past your mid-60s, you may want to obtain disability coverage that pays you until a later age.

On the other hand, if you've crunched some numbers (refer to Chapter 8) and see that you expect to be financially independent by age 55, you can get a policy that pays benefits up to that age — it'll cost you less than one that pays benefits until age 65. If you're within five years of being financially independent or able to retire, five-year disability policies are available, too. You might also consider such short-term policies because you're sure that someone (for example, a family member) can support you financially over the long term.

Other features you need in disability insurance

Disability insurance policies have many features that may be confusing to you. So that you can make an informed decision about purchasing disability insurance, we briefly go over these features.

✔ **Definition of disability.** An *own-occupation* or *regular-occupation* disability policy provides benefit payments if you can't perform the work you normally do. Some policies pay you only if you're unable to perform a job for which you are *reasonably trained*. Other policies revert to this definition after a few years of being own occupation.

Own-occupation policies are the most expensive because there's a greater chance that the insurer will have to pay you. The extra cost may not be worth it for you unless you're in a high income or specialized occupation and you'd have to take a big pay cut to do something else (and you wouldn't be happy about a reduced income and the required lifestyle changes).

✔ **Noncancellable and guaranteed renewable.** These features guarantee that your policy can't be cancelled because of poor health conditions. If you purchase a policy that requires periodic physical exams, you can lose your coverage just when you're most likely to need it.

✔ **Waiting period.** This is the "deductible" on disability insurance — the lag time between the onset of your disability and the time you begin collecting benefits. As with other types of insurance, you should take the highest deductible (longest waiting period) that your financial circumstances allow. This lag time significantly reduces the cost of the insurance and eliminates the hassle of filing a claim for a short-term disability. The minimum waiting period on most policies is 30 days, and the maximum can be up to one to two years. Try a waiting period of three to six months if you have sufficient emergency reserves.

✔ **Residual benefits.** This option pays you a partial benefit if you have a disability that prevents you from working full-time.

✔ **Cost-of-living adjustments (COLAs).** This feature automatically increases your benefit payment by a set percentage or in accordance with changes in inflation. The advantage of a COLA is that it retains the purchasing power of your benefits. A modest COLA, such as 4 percent, is worth having.

✔ **Future insurability.** A clause that many agents encourage you to buy, future insurability allows you to buy additional coverage, regardless of your health. For most people, paying for the privilege of buying more coverage later is not worth it because the income that you earn today fairly reflects your likely long-term earnings (except for cost-of-living increases). Disability insurance is sold only as a proportion of your income. Therefore, the only people who may benefit from the future insurability option are those whose income is artificially low now and who not only are confident of its rising significantly in the future but also need to protect it. (For example, you just got out of medical school and are earning a low salary while being enslaved as a resident.)

✔ **Insurer's financial stability.** As we discuss in Chapter 17, you should choose insurers that will be here tomorrow to pay your claim. But don't get too hung up on the safety of the company; benefits are often paid even if the insurer fails because the province or another insurer almost always bails the insurer out, and many policies are protected up to certain limits by CompCorp, an industry-run compensation scheme.

Where to buy disability insurance

The best place to check for buying disability insurance is through your employer or professional association. Unless these groups have done a lousy job shopping for coverage, group plans offer better value than you can purchase on your own. Just make sure that the plan that's offered meets the specifications discussed in the preceding section.

Don't trust an insurance agent to always be enthusiastic (or even honest) about the quality of a disability policy your employer or other group offers. Agents have a huge conflict of interest when they criticize these options, because your group insurance cuts them (and their commissions!) out of the picture.

If you don't have access to a group policy, check with your agent or a company you already do business with.

If you purchase disability insurance through a local agent, tread carefully. Some agents try to load down a policy with all sorts of extra bells and whistles to pump up the premium and their own commissions.

If you buy disability insurance through an agent, try to use a process called *list billing*. With list billing, you sign up for coverage with several others at the same time and are invoiced together. It can knock up to 15 percent off an insurer's standard prices. Ask your insurance agent how this works.

Other "insurance" to protect your income

Life insurance and disability insurance replace your income if you die or suffer a disability. But you could also see your income reduced or completely eliminated if you lose your job. Although no formal insurance policy exists to protect you against the forces that can cause this to happen, you can do a couple of things to reduce your exposure to this risk.

Make sure that you have an emergency reserve of money that you can tap into if you lose your job. (Chapter 8 offers specific guidelines for deciding how much money is right for you.)

Another form of "insurance" is to continually attend to your skills and professional development. Not only does upgrading your education and skills ensure that you are employable if you have to hit the streets to look for a new job, but it may also help you keep your old one and earn a higher income.

Out-of-Country Medical Insurance

Many people take extraordinary risks when they head out of the country on holiday, or even for work. No, we're not talking about running into rebels in some mountain kingdom. And we're not assuming that you'll hang-glide all day and helicopter ski at night. Just heading across the border to do some shopping in the States or flying to New York for a meeting for the day could prove disastrous to your finances if you don't have the proper medical insurance coverage.

If you belong to your provincial health care plan, you're covered by your province when you venture out of your home province, but only up to certain set levels. Each provincial plan has set amounts it will pay for various procedures and other medical costs. However, the amounts that the provincial plans pay are shrinking, and many represent only a small fraction of what an out-of-Canada medical emergency could cost. For example, Alberta, Saskatchewan, and Ontario have all slashed the daily hospital coverage from around $400 to $100.

If you have a premium credit card, don't blindly assume that you're adequately covered. The rules change all the time, and some of the eligibility requirements can be highly confusing. For example, the travel medical insurance with some premium cards covers you only for a certain number of days for each trip you make. You may be covered for 21 days, but if you're injured on the 22nd day, your card company won't foot any of the bill. More worrisome are programs that insure you up to a set trip length; if you're out of the country for longer than the allowable maximum, you aren't insured for any of your time away.

Another dangerous pitfall involves people travelling on company business. Although most corporations provide medical insurance for their employees when they're on the road, many policies have wrinkles that can cost you. For example, you may be covered during the week while you're on company business, but if you choose to stay over for the weekend to enjoy a little skiing at a nearby resort and break your leg, you may find you're responsible for any bills because the company policy doesn't cover injuries sustained on personal time.

You can buy travel medical insurance from most financial institutions and from associations such as the CAA. Compare rates and maximum payments before you buy. Consider getting at least $250,000 of coverage. Taking a higher deductible, say $750 or $1,000, often makes sense. Remember that you're insuring against the big losses. A higher deductible brings your premium down, and a medical bill of a few hundred dollars, although not enjoyable, won't be disastrous.

One other note: If you need medical care outside your own province but are still within Canada, your provincial plan generally covers your bills, thanks to interprovincial arrangements. The glaring exception is Quebec. Quebec residents may find that they're required to pay out-of-pocket medical costs when they're in another province. They then must submit a claim to the province in order to be paid back for their expenses.

The Most-Overlooked Form of Insurance

Many people buy all the right kinds of personal insurance, spending a small fortune over the course of their lives in the process. Yet they overlook the obvious, virtually free protection: taking care of themselves. If you work all day at a desk and use many of life's modern conveniences, you could end up being the Great Canadian Couch Potato. Odds are that you've heard of most of these forms of "life insurance," but if you're still on the couch, they apparently didn't sink in.

So, for you sofa spuds, we remind you of these seven healthful tips:

✔ Don't smoke.

✔ Drink alcohol in moderation, if you drink at all.

✔ Get plenty of rest.

✔ Exercise regularly.

✔ Eat healthfully (refer to Chapter 6 for diet tips that improve your health and save you money).

✔ Get regular health care checkups to detect medical, dental, and vision problems.

✔ Take time to smell the roses.

Chapter 19

Insuring Your Assets

· ·

In This Chapter

▶ Homeowner's/renter's insurance

▶ Automobile insurance

▶ Planning your estate

· ·

In Chapter 18, we discuss the importance of protecting your future income from the possibilities of death, disability, or large, unexpected medical expenses. But you also need to insure major assets that you acquire — your home, your car, your personal property — and that's what this chapter's all about.

You need to protect some of these assets for two reasons:

✔ **Your assets are valuable.** If you were to suffer a loss, replacing the assets with money out of your own pocket could be a financial catastrophe.

✔ **You have liability.** This reason is less well-known. If someone were injured or killed in your home or because of your car, a lawsuit could be even more financially devastating than an outright loss of the offending asset.

Homeowner's/Renter's Insurance

When you buy a home, most lenders require that you purchase homeowner's insurance. But even if they don't, you are wise to do so because your home and the personal property within it are worth a great deal and would cost a bundle to replace.

As a renter, damage to the building in which you live is not your financial concern, but you still have personal property that you may want to protect. And there's also the possibility, albeit remote, that you could be sued by someone who is injured in your rental unit.

Each insurance company prices its homeowner's and renter's policies based on its own criteria. You have to shop around at several companies to find the best rates. When shopping for a homeowner's or renter's policy, you should consider the important features that we cover in this section.

Dwelling coverage: The cost to rebuild

Neither the purchase price nor the size of your mortgage has anything to do with how much *dwelling coverage* you need. Ask yourself how much you would have to spend to *rebuild* your home if you lost it completely in a fire, an attack of locusts, or whatever. The cost to rebuild should be based on the size (square footage) of your home.

If you're a renter, rejoice that you don't need this coverage. If you're a condominium owner, check whether the coverage that the condo association has bought for the entire building is sufficient. (Likely, it won't cover the internal structures in your condominium units.)

Make sure that your homeowner's policy includes a *guaranteed replacement cost* provision. This nifty little feature ensures that the insurance company will rebuild the home even if the cost of construction is more than the policy coverage. If the insurance company underestimates your dwelling coverage, then *it* has to make up the difference.

Just to make your life more complicated, insurers define guaranteed replacement cost differently. Some companies pay for the full replacement cost of the home, no matter how much it ends up costing. Other insurers set limits. For example, the company may only pay up to 25 percent more than the dwelling coverage on your policy. Ask your insurer how it defines guaranteed replacement cost.

If you have an older property that has many costly-to-replace features that do not meet building codes, consider buying a rider that pays for code upgrades. This covers the cost of rebuilding your home to comply with building codes that are more stringent today than when your home was built. Ask your insurance company what your basic policy covers and what it doesn't cover. Some companies include a certain amount (for example, 10 percent of your dwelling coverage) for code upgrades in the base policy.

Personal property coverage

On a homeowner's policy, the amount of personal property coverage is typically derived from the amount of dwelling coverage you carry. Generally, you get personal property coverage of 50 to 75 percent of the dwelling coverage. This is usually more than enough.

We aren't big fans of riders that you can buy to cover jewelry, computers, furs, and other somewhat costly items that may not be fully covered by typical homeowner's policies. Ask yourself if your out-of-pocket expense from the loss of such items would constitute a financial catastrophe. Unless you have thousands of dollars worth of jewelry or computer equipment, for example, we'd skip such riders.

Some policies come with *replacement cost guarantees,* which pay you for the cost to replace an item. This payment can be considerably more than what a used item was worth before it was damaged or stolen. If this feature is not part of the standard policy sold by your insurer, you may want to purchase it as a rider, if available.

As a renter or condominium owner, you need to choose a dollar amount of the personal property that you want covered. Tally it up instead of guessing — the total cost of replacing all your personal property may surprise you.

Make a list — or even better, take pictures or make a video — of your belongings with an estimate of what they're worth. Keep this list updated; you need it if you have to file a claim. Keeping receipts for major purchases may also help your case. No matter how you document your belongings, don't forget to keep the documentation somewhere besides your home — otherwise, it could be destroyed along with the rest of your house in a fire or other disaster.

Liability insurance

Liability insurance protects you financially against lawsuits arising from bad things that happen to others on your property. At a minimum, you want enough insurance to cover your financial assets — covering two times your assets is better. Buying extra coverage is inexpensive and well worth the cost.

The probabilities of being sued are low, but if you *are* sued and lose, you could owe big bucks. If you have substantial assets to protect, you might consider an umbrella or excess liability policy (which we discuss later in this chapter).

Liability protection is one of the side benefits of purchasing a renter's policy — you protect your personal property and insure against lawsuits. (But don't be reckless with your banana peels now that you have liability insurance!)

Flood and earthquake insurance

As we discuss in Chapter 17, you want to purchase the broadest possible coverage when buying any type of insurance. The problem with homeowner's insurance is that it isn't broad enough — it doesn't typically cover losses due to earthquakes and floods. You must buy such disaster coverage piecemeal.

If an earthquake or flood strikes your area and your home is destroyed, you would be out tens, if not hundreds, of thousands of dollars without proper coverage. Yet, many people don't carry these important coverages, often due to misconceptions:

- ✔ **"Not in my neighbourhood."** Many people mistakenly believe that earthquakes occur only in California and Japan. But they can occur in many parts of Canada as well. Vancouver is built on a major fault line, and known (though not very active) fault lines lie in eastern Canada, including the Ottawa-Hull region. The cost of earthquake coverage is based on insurance companies' assessment of the risk of your area and property type, so you shouldn't decide whether to buy insurance based on how small you think the risk is. The risk is already built into the price.

  When the Rider River overflowed its banks and put much of Southern Manitoba underwater in the spring of 1997, it underscored just how ruinous a flood can be. In the last couple of years, floods have also caused extensive damage in many other parts of the country, including Quebec, Ontario, and Alberta. Like earthquakes, floods aren't a covered risk in standard homeowner's policies, so you need to purchase a flood insurance rider. Check with your current homeowner's insurer or with those recommended in this chapter. A flood insurance rider can be tough to find, though, as it's offered by few insurers.

- ✔ **"The government will bail me out."** Not true. The vast majority of government financial assistance is through no- or low-interest loans. Loans, unfortunately, need to be repaid, and the money comes out of your pocket.

- ✔ **"In a major disaster, insurers would go bankrupt anyway."** This is highly unlikely, given the reserves that insurers are required to keep and the fact that the insurance companies *reinsure* — that is, they buy insurance to back up the policies they write.

The only people who might consider not buying earthquake or flood coverage are people who have little equity in their property and who are willing to walk away from the property and the mortgage in the event of a major quake or flood. Keep in mind that doing so damages your credit report because you will have essentially defaulted on your loan.

You may be able to pay for much of the cost of earthquake or flood insurance by raising the deductibles on the main part of your homeowner's/renter's insurance and other insurance policies, such as those for autos. You can more easily afford the smaller claims, not the big ones. If you think flood or earthquake insurance is too costly, compare those costs with what you will incur to completely replace your home and personal property. Buy this insurance if you live in an area that has a chance of being affected by these catastrophes. To help keep the cost of earthquake insurance down, consider taking a 10 percent deductible. Most insurers offer deductibles of 5 or 10 percent of the cost to rebuild your home. Ten percent of the rebuilding cost is a good chunk of money. But what you want to insure against is losing the other 90 percent.

Deductibles

As we discuss in Chapter 17, you're better off with the highest deductibles you're comfortable with. You'll save on insurance premiums year after year, and you won't have to go through the hassle of filing small claims. The point of insurance is to protect against catastrophic losses, not the little losses.

Special discounts

You may qualify for special discounts. Companies and agents that sell homeowner's and renter's insurance don't always check to see if you're eligible for discounts. After all, the more you spend on policy premiums, the more money they make! If your property has a security system, if you are older, or if you have other policies with the same insurer, you may qualify for a lower rate. Don't forget to ask.

Where to buy homeowner's/ renter's insurance

Each insurance company prices its homeowner's and renter's policies based on its own criteria. So the lowest-cost company for your neighbour's property might not be so for yours. You have to shop around at several companies to find the best rates. A good starting place for quotes is the following list of companies that sell directly to the public:

- **Belair Direct** (800-268-8551)
- **Canada Trust Financial Insurance** (888-588-5999)
- **CIBC Insurance** (888-275-2422)

    ✔ **Direct Protect.** (800-810-4990)

    ✔ **Green Line Insurance Access** (888-982-0080)

    ✔ **Royal Bank Insurance.** Sold through Genco (800-769-2526)

    ✔ **Zenith.** Available only to Ontario residents (888-732-1330)

Don't worry that some of these companies require you to call an 800 number for a price quote. This doesn't mean they are unreachable. This process saves you money because these insurers don't have to pay commissions to local agents hawking their policies. These companies have local claims representatives to help you if and when you do have a claim.

Auto Insurance

Over the course of your life, you'll probably spend tens of thousands of dollars on auto insurance. You should look for the following important features when searching for an auto insurance policy.

Bodily injury/property damage liability

As with homeowner's liability insurance, auto liability insurance provides insurance against lawsuits. Especially in a car, accidents happen. Make sure that you have enough bodily injury liability insurance to cover your assets. (Coverage from double to five times your assets is preferable.)

Coping with teen drivers

If you have a teenage driver in your household, in addition to worrying a lot more, you're going to spend a lot more on auto insurance. Try to keep your teenager out of your car as long as possible. It's the best advice we can offer. If you're foolish enough to allow your teenager to drive (just kidding), you can take a number of steps to keep from spending all your take-home pay on auto insurance bills.

First, if you have more than one car in your household, don't let your teenager drive the more expensive one(s).

Second, make sure that your teen does well in school. Some insurers offer discounts if your child is a high academic achiever and has successfully completed a driver's education class.

And finally, have your teenager share in the costs of using the car. If you pay all the insurance, gas, oil changing, and maintenance bills, your teenager won't value the privilege of using your "free" car.

If you're just beginning to accumulate assets, don't mistakenly assume that you don't need any extra liability protection. Liability coverage is a provincial requirement, but the minimum amounts are low — usually in the tens or hundreds of thousands. Also, don't forget that your future earnings, which are an "asset," may be garnisheed in a lawsuit.

Property damage liability insurance covers damage done by your car to other people's cars and property. The amount of property damage liability coverage in an auto insurance policy is usually determined as a consequence of the bodily injury amount selected; $50,000 is a good minimum to shoot for.

Uninsured or underinsured motorist liability

If you're in an accident with another motorist and he doesn't carry his own liability protection or doesn't carry enough, *uninsured or underinsured motorist liability coverage* allows you to collect for lost wages, medical expenses, and pain and suffering incurred in the accident.

If you already have a comprehensive major medical plan and long-term disability insurance, then uninsured or underinsured motorist liability coverage is largely redundant; you only give up the ability to collect for general pain and suffering if you drop this coverage. But note that this coverage also insures passengers in your car who may lack adequate medical and disability coverage.

To provide a death benefit to those financially dependent on you in the event of a fatal auto accident, buy term life insurance (refer to Chapter 18).

Deductibles

To keep your auto insurance premiums down and to eliminate the need to file small claims, take the highest deductibles you are comfortable with (most people should consider $500 to $1,000). On an auto policy, two deductibles exist: *collision* and *comprehensive*. Collision applies to claims arising from collisions (note that you can bypass collision coverage when you rent a car if you have collision coverage on your own policy). Comprehensive applies to other claims for damages not caused by collision (for example, a window broken by vandals).

As your car ages and is worth less, you can eventually eliminate your comprehensive and collision coverages altogether. The point at which you do this is up to you. Remember that the purpose of insurance is to compensate you for financially catastrophic losses. For some people, this amount may be as high as $5,000 or more — others may choose $1,000 as their threshold point. But most insurance companies won't pay more than the book value of your car, regardless of what it costs to repair or replace it.

Where to buy auto insurance

You can use the same list presented in the homeowner's/renter's insurance section of this chapter to obtain quotes for auto insurance.

Special discounts

You may be eligible for special discounts on auto insurance. Don't forget to tell your agent or insurer if your car has a security alarm, air bags, or antilock brakes. If you're older or have other policies or cars insured with the same insurer, you may also qualify for discounts. And make sure that you're given appropriate "good driver" discounts if you've been accident- and ticket-free in recent years.

And here's another idea: *Before* you buy your next car, call your insurer and ask for insurance quotes for the different models that you're considering. The cost of insuring a car should factor into your decision as to which car you buy because the insurance costs will be a major portion of your car's ongoing operating expenses. And different insurers have differing pricing systems for particular car models.

Overlooked auto insurance: Safe driving

The real story about auto fatalities lies not in the who, what, and where of specific accidents but in the why. When we ask that question, we see how many of them are preventable.

No matter what kind of car you drive, you can and should drive safely. Stay within the speed limits and don't drive while intoxicated, tired, or in adverse weather conditions. And wear your seat belt!

You can also greatly reduce your risk of dying in an accident by driving a safe car. You don't need to spend buckets of money to get a car with air bags, reinforced sides, front and rear-impact resistance, and good visibility. *Consumer Reports'* annual auto buying guide has lots of good information on individual car model safety.

Little stuff: Coverage to skip

Auto insurers have dreamed up all sorts of riders, such as towing and rental car reimbursement, that cover small-dollar items that usually aren't worth insuring. On the surface, these riders appear to be inexpensive. But the riders are expensive given the little that you'd collect from a claim plus the hassle of filing. Riders that waive the deductible under certain circumstances make no sense, either. The point of the deductible is to reduce your policy cost and the hassle of filing small claims.

Umbrella Insurance

Umbrella or excess liability insurance is additional liability insurance that's added on top of the liability protection on your home and car(s). If you're fairly affluent and have, for example, $700,000 in assets, you can buy a $1 million umbrella liability policy for around $150 per year to add to the $300,000 liability that you have on your home and car. This is a small cost for big protection.

Umbrella insurance is generally sold in increments of $1 million. So how do you decide how much you need if you have a lot of assets? As we say with other insurance coverages, you should have at least enough liability insurance to protect your assets and preferably enough to cover twice the value of those assets. You can usually purchase umbrella insurance through your existing homeowner's or auto insurance company.

Estate Planning

Estate planning is the process of deciding what happens to your assets after you die. Thinking about this in the context of insurance may seem a bit odd, but the time and cost of various estate-planning manoeuvres is really nothing more than buying insurance: You insure that, after you die, everything will be taken care of as you wish and that taxes will be minimized. Thinking about it in this way can help you to better evaluate whether certain options make sense at particular points in your life.

Depending on your circumstances, you may eventually want to contact a lawyer who specializes in estate-planning matters. However, educating yourself first about the different options is worth a little bit of your time. More than a few lawyers have their own agendas (increased fees) about what you should do, so be careful. And most of the estate-planning strategies that you're likely to benefit from don't require hiring a lawyer.

Wills, living wills, and medical powers of attorney

If you have children who are minors (dependent), a *will* is a necessity. A will names the guardian to whom you entrust your children if both you and your spouse die. If you and your spouse both die without a will (called *intestate*), the province (courts and social service agencies) decides who will raise your children. Therefore, even if you can't decide at this time who would raise your children, you should *at least* appoint a trusted guardian who could decide for you.

If you don't have children who are still minors, a will makes good sense. It gives instructions on how to handle and distribute all your worldly possessions. If you die without a will, your province decides how to distribute your money and other property, according to provincial rules. Therefore, your friends, more-distant relatives, and favorite charities will probably receive nothing.

And without a will, your heirs are legally powerless, and the province may appoint a public executor to supervise the distribution of your assets at a fee of around 5 percent of your estate. A bond typically must also be posted at a cost of several hundred dollars.

Don't assume that if you're married and you die without a will your spouse automatically inherits everything. He or she won't! Under an intestate, your children receive a share of your estate (except in Manitoba). In some provinces, your spouse gets only a flat sum and must share the remainder of your assets with your children. If your children are under 18, they can't touch their share until they turn 18, even if the family needs the money to live on. The money is administered by the official guardian in your province, who in all likelihood won't earn anywhere near reasonable returns on the assets.

A medical power of attorney and a living will are useful additions to a standard will. A *medical power of attorney* grants authority to someone you trust to make decisions with a physician regarding your medical care options. A *living will* tells your doctor what, if any, life-support measures you would accept or would not accept. However, living wills still don't have full legal status. In some provinces, they're enforceable only as long as none of your living relatives disagrees with your wishes. Distribute copies of your living will to your close relatives and explain your decisions.

Nobody but you should be able to decide when to keep on fighting and when to accept death. Write to your provincial and federal MP and demand that living wills be given full legal standing.

Investment insurance

Insurance companies don't sell policies that protect the value of your investments. But you can shield your portfolio from many of the dangers of a fickle market through diversification.

If all your money is invested in bank accounts or bonds, you're exposed to the risks of inflation, which can erode the purchasing power of your money. Conversely, if the bulk of your money is invested in one high risk stock, your financial future could go up in smoke if that stock crashes and burns (remember Bre-X?).

Chapter 10 discusses the benefits of diversification and how to choose investments that do well under different conditions. Chapter 12 discusses how mutual funds are powerful investment vehicles that make diversification easy and cost-effective.

The simplest and least-costly way to prepare a will, a living will, and a medical power of attorney is to use one of the high-quality, user-friendly software packages recommended in Chapter 22. Be sure to give copies of these documents to the guardians and executors named in the documents. You can also use the programs to work out the basics of your estate plan, cutting down on the time and cost of using a lawyer to dot the *i*'s and cross the *t*'s.

You don't need a lawyer to make a legal will. Most lawyers, in fact, prepare wills and living trusts using software packages! What makes a will *valid* is that it is witnessed by two people (and signed by you, of course!).

If doing it all yourself seems overwhelming, another option (besides hiring an attorney) is to use a paralegal service to help you prepare the documents. These services generally charge 50 percent or less of what an attorney charges. In some provinces, holographic wills are valid — that is, handwritten by you, signed, and dated by you. A holographic will is a good temporary measure, but do a more formal will as soon as you can.

Probate and living trusts

Because of our quirky legal system, even if you have a will, some or all of your assets must go through a court process known as probate. *Probate* is the legal process for administering and implementing the directions in a will. Probate can be a lengthy, expensive hassle for your heirs — with fees ranging as high as 1.5 percent, depending on your province. In addition, your assets become a matter of public record as a result of probate.

Property and assets that are owned in joint tenancy generally pass to heirs without having to go through probate. If you have designated a beneficiary, proceeds from an RRSP, RRIF, an insurance policy, or pension plan also do not require probate. Assets such as your family home or joint bank account also avoid probate as long as you register their ownership as *"joint and survivor."*

A *living trust* effectively transfers assets into a trust. You control those assets and can revoke the trust whenever you desire. The advantage of a living trust is that upon your death, assets can pass directly to your beneficiaries without going through probate.

Living trusts are likely to be of greatest value to people who meet the following criteria:

- ✔ Age 60 and older
- ✔ Single
- ✔ Assets worth more than $1 million that must pass through probate (including real estate, nonretirement plans, and small business)

As with a will, you do *not* need a lawyer to establish a legal and valid living trust. (See the software recommendations in Chapter 22 and consider paralegal services that we mention in the previous section on wills.) Lawyer fees to establish a living trust can range from $700 to $2,000. A competent lawyer who charges reasonable fees is of greatest value to people with large estates (greater than $600,000) who don't have the time, desire, and expertise to maximize the value derived from estate planning.

Note: Living trusts keep assets out of probate but have nothing to do with minimizing capital gains taxes triggered when you die.

Part V
The Part of Tens

The 5th Wave — **By Rich Tennant**

"IT'S REALLY QUITE AN ENTERTAINING PIECE OF SOFTWARE. THERE'S ROLLER COASTER ACTION, SUSPENSE AND DRAMA, WHERE SKILL AND STRATEGY ARE MATCHED AGAINST WINNING AND LOSING. AND I THOUGHT MANAGING OUR BUDGET WOULD BE DULL."

In this part . . .

You encounter what might be called a diverse and valuable hodgepodge. Here you find the choicest information, ranging from financial strategies for ten life changes to the best financial software packages. Here you also find the all-important "Ten Questions to Ask Financial Advisers Before You Hire Them," which may save you a lot of heartache and money.

Chapter 20

Ten Questions to Ask Financial Advisors Before You Hire Them

• •

Don't consider hiring a financial advisor until you read the rest of this book. If you aren't educated about personal finance, how can you possibly evaluate the competence of someone you might hire to help you make important financial decisions?

We firmly believe that you're your own best financial advisor. However, we know that some people don't want to make financial decisions without getting assistance. Perhaps you're busy, or you simply can't stand making money decisions.

But recognize that when you hire a financial advisor, you have a lot at stake. Besides the cost of his or her services, which generally don't come cheap, you place a lot of trust in the advisor's recommendations. The more you know, the better the advisor you end up working with and the fewer services you need to buy.

These ten questions get to the core of an advisor's competence and professional integrity. Get answers to these questions *before* you decide to hire a financial advisor.

What percentage of your income comes from fees paid by your clients versus commissions from the products that you sell?

Asking this question first may save you the trouble and time of asking the next nine. The best answer is, "100 percent of my income comes from fees paid by clients." Anything less than 100 percent means the person you're speaking with is a salesperson with a vested interest in recommending certain strategies and product purchases.

Sadly, more than a few "financial advisors" don't tell the truth. In an undercover investigation done by *Money* magazine, nearly $1/3$ of advisors who claimed they were fee-only turned out to be brokers who sold investment and insurance products on a commission basis.

What percentage of fees paid by your clients is for ongoing money management versus hourly financial planning?

The answer to how the advisor is paid provides a big clue as to whether the planner has an agenda to convince you to hire him to manage your money. If what you want are objective and specific financial planning recommendations, you should seek advisors who derive their income from hourly fees. Many counsellors and advisors call themselves "fee-based," which usually means they make their living managing money for a percentage.

Some advisors don't tell you the truth. Also be aware that some advisors have been known to operate two separate companies. One company claims to give advice on a fee basis. However, the other (generally hidden) company sells products or manages money.

If you want a money manager, you can hire the best quite inexpensively through a mutual fund or, if you have substantial assets, you can hire an established money manager (see Chapter 11).

What is your hourly fee?

Rates, as with legal and tax advisors, vary all over the map. We've seen and heard of fees as low as $50 per hour all the way up to several hundred dollars per hour. If you shop around, you can find terrific planners who charge around $100 to $150 per hour.

Because good planners spend a reasonable portion of their time researching and running their business, don't assume they're getting rich at your expense at this rate. Running a business is costly, but you shouldn't pay hundreds of dollars per hour unless you're wealthy and want an advisor who works only with people like you. Also, be aware that a number of planners who manage money or sell products charge very high hourly rates because they don't really want to work with people on an hourly fee basis.

Do you also perform tax or legal services?

Be wary of someone who claims to be an expert beyond one area. The tax, legal, and financial fields are vast in and of themselves and are difficult for even the best and brightest advisor to cover simultaneously. One exception is the accountant who also performs some basic financial planning by the hour. Likewise, a good financial advisor should have a good grounding in tax and legal issues that relate to your personal finances. Larger firms may have specialists available in different areas.

What work and educational experience qualifies you to be a financial planner?

There's no one right answer here. Ideally, a planner should have experience in the business or financial services field. Some say to look for planners with at least five or ten years' experience. We've always wondered how planners earn a living their first five or ten years if folks won't hire them until they reach these benchmarks! A good planner should also be good with numbers, speak in plain language, and have good interpersonal skills.

Education is sort of like food. Too little leaves you hungry. Too much might leave you feeling stuffed and uncomfortable. And less of high quality is better than a lot of low quality.

Because investing decisions are a critical part of financial planning, take note of the fact that the most common designations of educational training among professional money managers are MBA (master of business administration) and CFA (chartered financial analyst). Refer to Chapter 3 for a complete explanation of the financial planning industry.

Have you ever sold limited partnerships? Options? Futures? Commodities?

The correct answers here are *no, no, no,* and *no.* If you don't know what these disasters are, refer to Chapter 10. Also, be wary of any financial advisor who once dealt in these areas but claims to have seen the light and reformed his ways.

Professionals with poor judgement may not repeat the same mistakes, but they're more likely to make some new ones at your expense. Our experience is that even advisors who have "reformed" are unlikely to be working by the hour. Most work on commission or want to manage your money for a hefty fee.

Do you carry liability insurance?

You wouldn't (or shouldn't) let contractors into your home to do work without knowing they have insurance to cover any mistakes they make, should they cause your home to look like the one in the movie *The Money Pit.* Likewise, you should insist on hiring a planner who carries protection in case she makes a major mistake for which she is liable. Make sure that she carries enough coverage given what she's helping you with.

Some counsellors may be surprised by this question or may think you're a problem customer looking for a lawsuit. On the other hand, accidents happen; that's why insurance exists. So if the planner doesn't have liability insurance, she missed one of the fundamental concepts of planning: Insure against risk. Don't make the same mistake by hiring her.

Can you provide references of clients with needs similar to mine?

Take the time to ask other people who have used the planner what the planner did for them. Inquire what the advisor's greatest strengths and weaknesses are. You can learn a bit about the planner's track record as well as style. And because you want to have as productive a relationship as possible with your planner, the more you learn about the planner, the easier it will be for you to hit the ground running if you hire him.

Some financial advisors offer a "free" introductory consultation. If this is offered to allow you to check out the advisor and it makes you feel more comfortable about hiring that planner, fair enough. But be careful: Often, "free" consultations are offered by planners who work on commission or who will try to sell you ongoing money management services. So the "free" consultation ends up being a big sales pitch for certain products or services offered through the advisor.

The fact that a planner doesn't offer a "free" consultation may be a good sign. Counsellors who work strictly by the hour and are busy can't afford to burn an hour of their time for an in-person "free" session. They also need to be careful of folks seeking "free" advice. Such advisors usually are willing to spend some time on the phone answering background questions. They should also be able to send background materials by mail and provide references if you ask.

Will you provide specific strategies and product recommendations that I can implement on my own if I choose?

This is an important question. Some advisors may indicate that you can hire them by the hour. But then they provide only generic advice without many specifics. Even worse is the troubling trend among planners who *double dip* — they charge an hourly fee to make you feel like you're not working with a salesperson. Then they try selling commission-based products. Also be aware that some advisors say you can choose to implement their recommendations on your own, but they then recommend financial products that carry commissions.

How is implementation handled?

Ideally, find an advisor who lets you choose whether you can hire him to help with implementation after the recommendations have been presented to you. If you know that you'll follow through on the advice and can do so without further discussions and questions, don't buy the planner's time to implement.

On the other hand, if you hired the counsellor in the first place because you lack the time, desire, and/or expertise to manage your financial life, building implementation into the planning work makes good sense. If you're the type of person who needs to tie a string around a finger to remember to do something but then forgets why the string is there, pay for the necessary hand-holding.

Chapter 21

Eric and Tony's Tips for Ten Life Changes

● ●

Many of life's changes come unexpectedly, like earthquakes. Others we can see coming when they're still far off on the horizon, like a big storm moving in off the ocean.

Ideally, it shouldn't matter. Whether a life change is predictable or not, our ability to navigate successfully through its challenges and to adjust quickly to its new circumstances depends largely on our degree of preparedness.

Perhaps you find our comparison of life changes to earthquakes and storms to be a bit negative. After all, some of the changes we discuss in this chapter should be occasions for joy, and here we are comparing them to natural disasters. But realize that what one defines as a "disaster" has everything to do with his or her preparedness. To the person who has stored no emergency rations in his basement, the big snowstorm that has trapped him in his home could mean a disaster. But to the prepared person with plenty of food and water, that same storm could mean a vacation from work and a relaxing week in the midst of a winter wonderland.

Before we discuss critical financial issues for you to deal with before and during major life changes, here are some general tips that apply to all life changes:

- ✓ **Stay in good financial shape.** An athlete is best able to withstand physical adversities during competition by training and eating well. Likewise, the more sound your finances are to begin with, the better able you'll be to deal with life changes.

- ✓ **Change requires change.** Even if your financial house is in order, a major life change — the birth of a child, buying a home, starting a business, getting a divorce, retiring — should prompt you to review your personal financial strategies. Why? Because life changes often affect your income, spending, need for insurance, and ability to accept financial risk.

- **Make changes sooner rather than later.** Being human, most of us procrastinate. But with a major life change on the horizon, procrastination could be costly. You (and your family) might overspend and accumulate high-cost debts, lack proper insurance coverage, or take other unnecessary risks. Early preparation can save you from these pitfalls.

- **Control stress and your emotions.** Life changes often are accompanied by stress and other emotional upheavals. Not only taking action but also doing so fully informed is vital during this period. Educating yourself is key, and you may want to hire experts to help (refer to Chapter 3), but avoid abdicating decisions and responsibilities to advisors.

Here, then, are the major life changes that you may have to deal with at some point in your life. We hope and wish you more of the good changes than the bad.

Starting your first job

If you've just graduated from university or some other program, or are otherwise entering the workforce, your increased income and reduction in educational expenses is usually a welcome relief. You would think then that more young adults wouldn't have financial trouble and challenges. But they do, largely because of poor financial habits picked up at home or from the world at large. Here's how to get on the path to financial success:

- **Don't abuse credit.** The use and abuse of credit can cause financial pain and hardship well into adult life. You'd like furniture, a new television, and lots of fun vacations, but all these things cost money. To get off on the right financial foot, young workers should avoid getting in the habit of making purchases on credit cards that they can't pay for in full when the bill arrives in the mail. The simple solution if you overspend and run up outstanding credit card balances: Don't carry a credit card. Cash and cheques worked fine for decades before credit cards arrived on the scene. If you need the convenience of making purchases with a piece of plastic instead of cash or cheques, get a debit card (refer to Chapter 5).

- **Get in the saving and investing habit.** If you hope to someday own a home and cease full-time work, you'll need to save over many years. Thinking about a home purchase or retirement is usually not in the active thought patterns of first-time job seekers. We're often asked, "At what age should a person start saving?" To us, that's similar to asking at what age you start brushing your teeth. Well, when you have teeth to brush! So we say you should start saving and investing money from your first pay cheque. Try starting to save 5 percent and then eventually 10 percent of every pay cheque. If you're having trouble saving money, track your spending and make cutbacks as needed (refer to Chapters 4 and 6).

Ideally, your savings should be directed into an RRSP or other retirement plan (refer to Chapter 9) that offers tax benefits. You might also want to accumulate down payment money to purchase a home.

✔ **Get insured.** Many people starting out are able to rationalize themselves out of buying insurance. When you're young and healthy, it's hard to imagine life otherwise. But because accidents and unexpected illnesses can strike at any age, forgoing coverage can be financially devastating. Buying disability coverage, which replaces income lost to a long-term disability, in a first full-time job with more limited benefits is wise. And as you begin to build your assets, consider making out a will to ensure that your assets go where you want in the event of your death.

✔ **Continue your education.** Once you're out in the workforce, you (like many other people) may realize how little you've learned in formal schooling that can be used in the real world and, conversely, how much you need to learn (like personal financial management) that school never taught you. Read, learn, and continue to grow. Continuing education helps you with your career; it also helps you enjoy the world around you.

Changing jobs or careers

During your adult life, you will almost surely change jobs — perhaps as often as several times a decade. We hope that most of the time you'll be changing by your own choice. But let's face it: Job security isn't what it used to be. Corporate downsizing has made victims of even the most talented workers.

Always be prepared for a job change. No matter how happy you are in your current job, knowing that your world won't fall apart if you aren't working tomorrow will give you an added sense of security and encourage an openness to possibility. Whether it's a job change by choice or necessity, the following financial manoeuvres will ease the transition:

✔ **Structure your finances to afford an income dip.** Spending less than you earn always makes good financial sense, but if you're coming up to a possible job change, this is even more important, particularly if you're entering a new field or starting your own company and you expect a short-term income dip. Many people view a lifestyle of thriftiness as restrictive, but ultimately those thrifty habits can give you *more* freedom to do what you want to do. Be sure to always keep your emergency reserve fund full (refer to Chapter 8).

✔ **If you're relocating, evaluate the total financial picture.** At some point in your career, you may have the option of relocating. But don't call the moving company until you understand the financial consequences of such a move. You can't simply compare salaries and benefits between the two jobs. Also compare the cost of living between the two areas — that includes housing, commuting, income and property taxes, food, utilities, and all the other major expenditure categories that we discuss in Chapter 4.

If you lose your job, batten down the hatches. Normally, when you lose your job through no choice of your own, you get little advance warning. That doesn't mean, however, that you can't do anything financially. Evaluating and slashing your current level of spending may be necessary. Everything should be fair game, from how much you spend on housing to how often you eat out to where you do your grocery shopping. Avoid at all costs the temptation to maintain your level of spending by accumulating consumer debt.

Getting married

If you're ready to tie the knot with the one you love, congratulations! We hope that you have a long, healthy, and happy life together. In addition to making emotional and moral commitments to one another, you and your spouse will probably merge many of your financial decisions and resources. It would be highly unusual for you and your spouse to have identical money personalities; after all, opposites often attract. Even if you're in complete agreement about your financial goals and strategies, managing as two is different than managing as one. Do the following *before* walking down the aisle:

✔ **Take a compatibility test.** Because so many marriages end in failure and some that stay together probably shouldn't, a good way to minimize your chances for heartache is to ensure you know what you're getting yourself into. Too many couples never discuss their goals and plans before marriage; failing to do so breaks up way too many of these marriages. Finances are just one of many issues to discuss; others include expectations for having and raising children, dealing with in-laws, career goals, and so on. Ministers, priests, and rabbis sometimes offer premarital counselling that can bring issues and differences to the surface. Don't let the euphoria of short-term romance blind you to important issues vital to the long-term health of your marriage.

✔ **Consider taxes.** Getting married presents a number of opportunities for cutting your tax bill, many of them through income splitting. For example, have the higher-income spouse pay for all household expenses. This leaves more money to be invested by the lower-earning spouse, which is taxed at a lower rate. A spousal RRSP helps move retirement income into the hands of the lower-earning spouse to lower your household's total tax bill when you start receiving your pension.

In addition, many tax credits and deductions can be claimed by either you or your spouse when you file your tax returns. Be sure to do your returns together to maximize your use of these credits and deductions.

✔ **Discuss and set joint goals.** Once you're married, you and your spouse should set aside time once a year or every few years to discuss personal and financial goals for the years ahead. If for no other reason, talking about where you want to go ensures that you aren't rowing your financial boat in opposite directions.

✔ **Separate but equal or jointly managed?** Some couples choose to keep separate financial accounts, whereas others pool resources. Philosophically, we like the idea of pooling better. After all, marriage is a partnership and shouldn't be a "his" versus "hers" affair. In some marriages, however, spouses choose to keep some money separate, particularly for spending purposes so that they don't feel the scrutiny of a spouse with different spending preferences. Spouses who have been through divorce may choose to keep the assets they bring into the new marriage separate in order to earmark and protect their assets in the event that they divorce again. As long as you jointly accomplish what you need to, some separation of money is okay. But for the health of your marriage, don't hide money from one another, and, if you're the higher-income spouse, don't try to assume power and control over your joint income. If you run your own business and hire your spouse, though, separate accounts are a must.

✔ **Coordinate and maximize employer benefits.** If one or both of you have access to a package of employee benefits through an employer, both of you should understand how best to make use of those benefits. Coordinating and using the best that each package has to offer is like giving yourselves a pay raise. For example, if you both have access to a drug plan, compare which has better benefits. Likewise, one of you may have a better retirement savings plan — one which matches and offers superior investment options. Unless you can afford to save the maximum through both your plans, saving more in the better plan will increase your combined assets. (*Note:* If you're concerned about what happens if you save more in one of your retirement plans and then divorce, in most provinces that money is considered part of your joint assets and can be divided equally.)

✔ **Discuss life and disability insurance needs.** If you and your spouse can make do without each other's income, you might not need any income-protecting insurance. However, if, like many husbands and wives, both spouses depend upon each other's incomes, or if one spouse depends fully or partly on the other's income, you might each need to have long-term disability and term life insurance policies (refer to Chapter 18). This also applies if either or both of you are supporting children.

✔ **Update your wills.** When you marry, you should update your wills. If you haven't gotten around to making a will, having a will is potentially more valuable when you're married, especially if you want to leave money to others in addition to your spouse, or if you have children for whom you should name a guardian. Refer to Chapter 19 for more information on wills.

✔ **Reconsider beneficiaries on RRSPs, investments, and life insurance.** With retirement plans and life insurance policies, you name beneficiaries to whom the money or value in those accounts goes in the event of your passing. When you marry, you probably want to rethink those beneficiaries.

Starting a small business

Many people aspire to be their own bosses, but far fewer people actually leave their jobs in order to achieve that dream. Psychologically and financially, giving up the apparent security of a job with benefits and a built-in network of coworkers is difficult for most people. Going into small business is not for everyone, but don't let inertia be the pin that deflates your dream. Here are some tips to help get you started and increase your chances for long-term success:

✔ **Prepare to ditch your job.** If you spend all or nearly all that you earn while employed and haven't banked a war chest, you're going to feel financially dependent on your pay cheque. Many people in such a situation never leave their jobs behind to pursue their entrepreneurial dreams. Live as spartan a lifestyle as you can while you're employed so that you maximize your ability to save money; you'll simultaneously develop thrifty habits that will help you weather the reduced income and increased expenditure period that comes with most small business start-ups. You might also consider easing into your small business if you can by working at it part time in the beginning, with or without cutting back on your normal job.

✔ **Develop a business plan.** If you research and think through your business idea, you'll not only reduce the likelihood of your business failing and increase its success if it thrives, but you'll also feel more comfortable taking the entrepreneurial plunge. A good business plan should be a blueprint for how you expect to build the business. It should describe in detail the business idea, the marketplace you'll be competing in, your marketing plans, and expected revenue and expenses.

✔ **Replace your insurance coverage.** Before you finally decide to leave your job, set the wheels in motion to get proper insurance coverage. With disability insurance, securing coverage before you leave your job is best so that you have income to qualify for coverage. If you have life insurance through your employer, you should secure new individual coverage as soon as you know you're going to leave your job (refer to Chapter 18 for more details).

✔ **Establish a retirement savings plan.** Once your business is up and making a profit, consider establishing an RRSP or other retirement savings plan. As we explain in Chapter 9 and 13, such plans allow you to shelter a good portion of your business income from taxation. When you're your own boss and don't have an employee benefits department to help look out for you, no one but you is going to be concerned about your financial future.

Buying a home

Most Canadians end up buying homes. To be a financial success, you need not own a home, but home ownership, if done right, certainly offers financial rewards. Over the course of your adult life, the real estate that you own should appreciate in value. Additionally, someday you should have your mortgage paid off, which will greatly reduce your housing costs. As a renter, on the other hand, your full housing costs increase over time because of inflation.

If you're considering buying a home

✔ **Get your overall finances in order.** Before you consider buying a home, you need to analyze your current budget, your ability to afford debt, and your future financial goals. Make sure that your expected housing expenses still allow you to save properly for retirement and other long- or short-term objectives. Don't buy a home based upon what lenders are willing to lend. Read and digest the relevant portions of this book to get your financial house in order before you buy.

✔ **Determine if now's the time.** Especially if you're a first-time home buyer, buying if you don't see yourself staying put three to five years rarely makes financial sense. Buying and selling a home gobbles up a good deal of money in transaction costs — you'll be lucky to recoup all those costs even within a five-year period. Also, if your income is likely to drop or you have other pressing goals, such as starting a business, you might wait to buy.

For more information about buying a home, be sure to read Chapter 16.

Having children

If you thought being a responsible adult, holding down a job, paying your bills on time, and preparing for your financial future was tough, wait 'til you add kids to the equation. Most parents find that, with kids in the family, the already precious commodities of time and money become even more precious — sometimes even extinct. The more efficiently you learn how to manage your time and money, the better able you'll be to have a sane, happy, and financially successful life as a parent.

Here are some key things to recognize and do both before and after you begin your family:

- ✔ **Set your priorities: You can't do it all and have it all.** As with many other financial decisions, starting or expanding a family requires that you financially plan ahead. Set your priorities and structure your finances and living situation accordingly. Is it more important to have a bigger home in a nice community, or would you rather have less pressure to work and spend more time with your family? Keep in mind that a less-hectic work life not only gives you more free time but also often reduces your cost of living by decreasing meals out, dry cleaning, day care expenses, and so on.

- ✔ **Take a hard look at your budget.** If you've had a hard time living within your means before children, then you definitely should take an honest look at how your income and spending will change after your family grows. In addition to diaper changes and less sleep at night, children mean increased spending. At a minimum, expenditures for food and clothing will increase. But you're also likely to spend more on housing, insurance, day care, and education. On top of that, if you want to play an active role in raising your children, working at a full-time job won't be possible. So while you consider the added expenses, you may also need to factor in a decrease in income.

  No simple rules exist for estimating how children will affect your household's income and expenses. On the income side, figure out how much you'll want to cut back on work. On the expense side, statistics show that the average household with school-age children spends about 20 percent more than those without. A more scientific approach would be for you to go through your budget category by category and estimate how kids will change your spending (use the worksheets in Chapter 4).

- ✔ **Boost insurance coverages *before* getting pregnant.** Before you try to have a baby, be sure that you have adequate disability insurance, as pregnancy is considered a preexisting condition. And most families-to-be should buy life insurance. Buying life insurance *after* the bundle of joy comes home from the hospital is a risky proposition — if Mom or Dad develops a health problem, she or he could be denied coverage. Also consider buying life insurance for a stay-at-home parent. Even though that parent doesn't bring in income, if he or she were to pass away, hiring assistance could cripple the family budget.

- ✔ **Check maternity leave with your employers.** Many larger employers offer extra maternity leave for women and, in rare but thankfully increasing cases, for men. Some employers also top up what you receive from the Employment Insurance system. Understand the options and the financial ramifications before you consider the leave and ideally before you get pregnant.

✔ **Update your will.** If you had a will before starting a family, you'll need to do a new one. If you don't have a will, make one now. With children in the picture, you must name a guardian in your will who will be responsible for raising your children should you and your spouse both pass away. Although choosing a guardian is a daunting decision, even more frightful is the thought of letting local courts decide who would raise your children.

✔ **Understand child care tax benefits.** For every one of your children, you get a monthly non-taxable payment, as long as your income is below certain limits. The basic amount is $1,020 for each child. If you have more than two children, that amount is increased by $75 for the third and each subsequent child. If you don't claim any child care expenses, you also get a additional $213 for each child under the age of 7. However, the Child Tax Benefit starts getting trimmed back once your household income gets over $25,921.

If you're a two-parent family, you can also claim a tax deduction for child care expenses, as long as they are incurred so that you or your spouse can work, carry on a business, or go to school full time. Usually the deduction must be claimed by the lower-earning spouse. A single parent can also claim the deduction. You can claim up to $7,000 for each child under the age of 7, and up to $4,000 for each child age 7 to 16. The total amount you claim also can't be larger than two-thirds of your *earned income* — basically, what you earn from your salary and your business. Some provinces also have an additional child care tax credit for lower income families.

✔ **Don't indulge the children.** Toys, art classes, sports, field trips, and the like can rack up big bills, especially if not controlled. Some parents exercise little control over children's programs. Most parents don't set guidelines or limits on extracurricular activities. Many are putting their children's desires ahead of all other financial needs and goals. Others are mindlessly following the example of the family that lives next door. Introspective parents have shared with us that they feel some insecurity about providing the best for their children. The parents (and kids) that seem happiest and most financially successful are those who clearly distinguish between material luxuries and family necessities.

As children get older and become indoctrinated into the world of shopping, all sorts of other purchases come into play. Consider giving your kids a weekly allowance and letting them learn how to spend and manage it. And when they're old enough, having your kids get part-time jobs helps teach financial responsibility as well.

Caring for aging parents

There comes a time for many of us when we reverse roles with our parents. Instead of being the one who is cared for, you become the caregiver or the caretaker. As your parents age, they may need help with a variety of issues and living tasks. Although it's unlikely that you'll have the time or ability to perform all these functions yourself, you may well end up being the coordinator of service providers who can.

Here are some things to do when caring for aging parents:

✔ **Take some time off.** Caring for an aging parent, particularly one who is having health problems, can be time-consuming and emotionally draining. If you were already juggling the responsibilities of a job, marriage, and parenthood before your parents needed help, you now may well feel completely overwhelmed. Do yourself and your parents a favour and use some vacation time to help get things in order. Although not the kind of vacation you probably envisioned, the time should reduce your stress and help you get more on top of things.

✔ **Get help where possible.** In most communities, a variety of nonprofit organizations offer information and sometimes even counselling to families grappling with caring for the elderly parents. You can find such resources through your province's department of health or through recommendations from local hospitals and doctors. You'll especially want to get assistance and information if your parents may need some sort of home care, nursing home care, or assisted-living arrangement.

✔ **Get involved in their health care.** Your aging parents may already have a lot on their minds or simply may not be able to coordinate and manage all the health care providers giving them medications and advice. Try to be their advocate. Speak with their doctor(s) to understand their current medical condition and need for various medications and to help coordinate caregivers. Visit nursing homes and speak with prospective care providers.

✔ **Understand tax breaks.** If you financially support a parent who is mentally or physically infirm, you may be able to claim a nonrefundable tax credit. If you're a single parent and supporting a parent, you can claim the Equivalent-to-Spouse Amount. In addition, you may be eligible for a new caregiver credit that can reduce your taxes by up to $400.

✔ **Discuss getting the estate in order.** Parents don't like talking and thinking about their demise and usually feel awkward discussing it with their children. But opening a dialogue between you and your folks about such issues can be healthy in many ways. Discussing wills, living wills, living trusts, and estate planning strategies (refer to Chapter 19) can not only make you aware of your folks' situation but can also improve their plans to both their benefit and yours.

Getting a divorce

Sadly, half of all marriages end in divorce. In most marriages destined to split up, there are early warning signs that both parties recognize; sometimes, however, one spouse surprises the other with an unexpected request for divorce.

Whether planned or unexpected, here are some key things to consider when getting a divorce:

- **Question the divorce.** Some say that divorcing is too easy, and we tend to agree. Although some couples are indeed better off to part ways, others give up too easily, thinking that the grass is greener elsewhere only to later discover that all lawns have weeds and crabgrass. Just as with a lawn that isn't watered and fertilized, relationships can wither without nurturing.

  Money and disagreements over money are certainly a contributing factor to marital unhappiness. Unfortunately, in many relationships, money is wielded as power by the spouse who earns more of it. Try talking things over, perhaps with a marital counsellor; invest in making your relationship stronger, and reap the dividends for years to come.

- **Separate your emotions from the financial issues.** Separating your feelings from your finances is easier said than done, but it's extremely important nonetheless. Feelings of revenge may be common in some divorces, but they probably only help to ensure that the lawyers get rich at your expense as the two of you butt heads. If you really want a divorce, work at doing it efficiently and harmoniously so that you can get on with your lives.

- **Detail resources and priorities.** Draw up a list of all the assets and liabilities that you and your spouse have. Be sure that you're getting the financial facts, including investment account records and statements. Once you know the whole picture, begin to think about what is and isn't important to you financially and otherwise.

- **Educate yourself about personal finance and legal issues.** Divorce sometimes forces non-financially oriented spouses to get a crash course in personal finance at a difficult emotional time. Hopefully, this book can help educate you financially. In terms of the legal issues of divorce, visit a bookstore and pick up a good legal guide or two about divorce.

- **Choose advisors carefully.** Odds are that you'll retain the services of one or more specialists to assist you with the many issues, negotiations, and concerns of your divorce. Legal, tax, and financial advisors can help, but recognize their limitations and conflicts of interest. Lawyers, unfortunately, have the conflict of benefiting financially the more complicated things become and the more you haggle with your spouse. Don't use your divorce lawyer for financial or tax advice — your lawyer probably knows no more than you do in these areas. Also, realize that you don't need a lawyer to get divorced. As for choosing tax and financial advisors, if you think you need that type of help, refer to Chapters 3 and 20 for how to find good advisors.

✔ **Analyze your spending needs.** When you're going back to being single, while your household expenses will surely be less, you'll probably be making do with less income. Many divorcees find themselves financially squeezed in the early years following a divorce. In addition to helping you adjust to a new budget, analyzing your spending needs pre-divorce will help you negotiate a fairer settlement with your spouse.

✔ **Review needed changes to insurance.** If you're covered under your spouse's employer insurance plans for any type of insurance, be sure to set the wheels in motion to get those coverages replaced (refer to Chapter 18). If you or your children will still be financially dependent on your spouse post-divorce, be sure that the divorce agreement mandates life insurance coverage. And you should revise your will (refer to Chapter 19).

✔ **Revise your retirement plan.** With changes to your income, expenses, assets, liabilities, and future needs, your retirement savings plan will surely need an overhaul after a divorce. Refer to Chapters 8 and 9 for a reorientation.

Receiving a windfall

Whether through inheritance, stock options, small business success, or lottery winnings, you may receive a financial windfall at some point in your life. Like many who are totally unprepared psychologically and otherwise for their sudden good fortune, you may well find that a flood of money can create more problems than it solves. If you're saying, "I should have such problems," fair enough. Who wouldn't rather be rich than poor?

Here are a few tips to help you make your windfall the financially pleasant experience that it should be:

✔ **Take the time to educate yourself.** If you've never had to deal with significant wealth, there's no reason that we'd expect you to know how to handle it. Don't rush and pressure yourself to invest it as soon as possible. Leaving the money where it is or stashing it in one of the higher-yielding money market funds recommended in Chapter 14 is a far better short-term solution than piling it into investments that you don't understand and haven't taken the time to research.

✔ **Beware the sharks.** You may begin to wonder if someone has posted your net worth, address, and home telephone number in the local newspaper and on the Internet. Brokers and financial advisors may flood you with marketing materials, telephone solicitations, and lunch date requests. Most of these folks who pursue you do so for a reason: They want to convert your money into their income either by selling you investment and other financial products or by managing your money. Stay away from these sharks, educate yourself, and take charge of your own financial moves. Decide on your own terms whom to hire, and seek them out. Most of the best advisors that we know don't have the time or philosophical orientation to chase after prospective clients.

✔ **Recognize the emotional side of coming into a lot of money.** One of the side effects of accumulating wealth quickly is that you may have feelings of guilt or otherwise be unhappy, especially if you expected money to solve your problems. Getting a big inheritance from your folks may make you feel guilty if you didn't invest in your relationship with them and now, with their passing, you regret how you interacted with them. As another example, if you poured endless hours into a business venture that finally paid off, all that money sitting in your investment accounts may leave you with a hollow feeling if you divorced and lost friends by neglecting your relationships.

✔ **Pay down debts.** One of the simplest and best investments you can make if you come into wealth is to pay off your debts. Eric had a counselling client who was frustrated because he didn't know how to invest several million dollars he had. Partly because he had worked so hard in his business to build his wealth, he was worried about losing money on investments. He had a decent-size home mortgage at 8 percent interest, which made complete sense for him to pay off. Money is generally borrowed to allow us to buy things that we otherwise couldn't buy in one fell swoop. When you have plenty of money on hand, getting rid of debts is an especially good move.

✔ **Diversify.** To protect your wealth, don't keep it all in one pot. Mutual funds (refer to Chapter 12) are an ideally diversified, professionally managed investment vehicle to consider. And if you want your money to continue growing, consider the wealth-building investments — stock mutual funds, real estate, and small business options — we discuss in Part III of this book.

✔ **Make use of the opportunity.** Most people spend their whole lives working for a pay cheque in order to pay a never ending stream of monthly bills. Although we're not advocating a hedonistic lifestyle, why not take some extra time to travel, spend time with your family, and do the hobbies you've long been putting off? And how about trying a new career that you'd find more fulfilling and that might make the world a better place? Most people never have the flexibility to choose how they spend their time. If you do, don't waste it.

Retiring

If you've spent the bulk of your adult life working, retiring can be a challenging life transition. Most Canadians have an idealized vision of how wonderful a retired life would be. No more irritating bosses and work deadlines. Unlimited time to travel, play sports, and lead the good life. Sounds good, huh? Well, the reality for most Canadians is far different, especially for those who don't plan ahead financially and otherwise.

Here are some tips to help you through retirement:

- **Plan both financially and personally.** Leaving a full-time job and career behind creates even bigger challenges — what to do with all your free time — the opposite problem new parents have. You can get too much of a good thing, which is why planning for your time and activities in retirement is even more important than planning financially. If your focus during your working years is solely on your career and saving money, you may lack interests, friends, and the ability to know how to spend money once you do retire.

- **Take stock of your resources.** Many people worry and wonder if they have sufficient assets to cut back on work or retire completely, yet they haven't crunched any numbers to see where they stand. Sometimes in life, ignorance can be blissful, but this is a case where ignorance might cause you to misunderstand how little or much you really have accumulated for retirement versus what you need. Start by reading the relevant portions of Chapter 8 and obtaining some of the recommended work booklets and software that can help you with retirement planning.

- **Reevaluate your insurance needs.** During your working years, you carry disability and perhaps some life insurance to protect you and your dependents should you not be able to earn an income. If you have sufficient assets to retire, you won't need to retain insurance to protect your employment income any longer. On the other hand, as your assets have grown over the years, you may be underinsured with regards to liability insurance (refer to Chapter 19).

- **Decide on health care/living options.** Medical expenses in your retirement years, particularly the cost of nursing home care, can be daunting. Which course of action you take — supplemental insurance, buying into a retirement community, or not doing anything — depends on your financial and personal situation. Early preparation increases your options. If you wait until you have major health problems, it may be too late to choose certain paths. Refer to Chapter 18 for more details.

- **Decide what to do with your retirement plan money.** When you're ready to retire, you may have to decide what to do with your retirement plan money and which of your employer's pension options you'd like. If you have money in a retirement savings plan, many employers offer you the option of leaving the money in the plan rather than rolling it over into your own retirement account. Brokers and financial advisors clearly prefer that you do the latter because it means more money for them. Read Part III of this book to learn about investing and evaluating the quality of your employer's retirement plan investment options.

✔ **Pick a pension option.** Selecting a pension option (plans that pay a monthly benefit during retirement) is similar to choosing a good investment — each pension option carries different risks, benefits, and tax consequences. Pensions are structured by actuaries based on reasonable life expectancies. The younger the age when you start collecting your pension, the less you get per month. Check to see if the amount of your monthly pension stops increasing past a certain starting age. You obviously wouldn't want to delay access to your pension benefits past that age because you receive no reward for waiting any longer, and you collect the benefit for fewer months.

If you know that you have a health problem that shortens your life expectancy, drawing your pension sooner is usually to your benefit. If you plan to continue working in some capacity and earning a decent income once you leave your employer, waiting for higher pension benefits when you'll be in a lower tax bracket is probably wise.

As for your other choices that affect what pension amount your surviving spouse receives should you die first, at one end of the spectrum you have the risky single-life option, which pays benefits until you pass away and provides no benefits thereafter for your spouse. This option maximizes your monthly take while you are alive. Only consider this option if your spouse could do without this income. The least-risky option and thus least financially rewarding while the pensioner is still living is the *100 percent joint and survivor option,* which pays your survivor the same amount that you received while still alive. The other joint-and-survivor options fall somewhere in between these two extremes and generally make sense for most couples who desire decent pensions early in retirement but want a reasonable amount to continue, should the pensioner die before his or her spouse.

✔ **Get your estate in order.** Confronting one's mortality is never a joy, but when you're considering retiring or are retired, getting your estate in order makes all the more sense. Learn about wills and trusts that might benefit you and your heirs. Also consider gifting if you have more than you need. You can't take it with you, and if you're worried about taxes, gifting money yearly to your heirs reduces probate fees and often taxes payable by your estate.

Chapter 22

Ten Tips for Using Your Computer for Your Personal Finances

• •

*S*oon everybody will own a computer. And every business will have a Website. So shouldn't you just buy a bunch of software, load it onto a personal computer, and join up with everyone else in the cyber-universe?

The short answer is no.

Although a computer may be able to assist you with your personal finances, it's simply one of many tools. Computers are really best at performing routine tasks faster: processing lots of bills or performing many calculations.

Computers aren't smart, and computers and all the accompanying paraphernalia certainly aren't cheap. And never assume that just because you access something financial through your computer the information you access is any good or that it's even information at all.

You can access three major repositories of personal finance stuff through your computer. Although the lines are sometimes a bit blurry among these three categories, they are roughly defined as software, commercial online services, and the Internet.

- ✔ *Software* is a computer program, typically packaged in a box about as big as a hardcover book the size of *War and Peace* and sold at a retail store (although our technogeek friends tell us that more and more software is sold online). Most of the mass-marketed financial software packages sell for under $100. If you've ever used a word-processing program such as Word or WordPerfect, or a spreadsheet program such as Lotus 1-2-3 or Excel, then you've used software.

- ✔ *Commercial online services* can be accessed through your computer via a modem. America Online and CompuServe are the two biggest commercial online services. For a monthly fee, such services offer you access to their information online.

> ✔ The *Internet* is a vast ocean of stuff that can generally be accessed via a modem, which allows your computer to talk with other computers over phone lines. To access the Internet, you need some sort of Web browser, which the previously mentioned commercial online services provide or which you can obtain through an Internet service provider. Most of the financial stuff on the Internet is supplied by companies marketing their wares and, hence, is available for free.

Note: Our recommendations for the *best* personal finance software packages and online sites appear are in **bold** type throughout this chapter. We mention the runners-up if they make sense for certain types of situations, but they aren't highlighted in bold. Unless otherwise stated, you can purchase the recommended software packages through most software sellers. To access the online sites, here are some useful phone numbers: America Online 888-265-4357; CompuServe 800-848-8990; and Sympatico 800-773-2121.

Focus on software

Although the number of personal finance software packages and online sites is mushrooming rapidly, quality is having a hard time keeping up, especially among the free Internet sites. Most of the best of what is financially out there for your computer falls into the software category.

> ✔ Good software can guide you to better organization and management of your personal finances.
>
> ✔ Good software can help you complete mundane tasks or complex calculations more quickly and easily and provide basic advice in unfamiliar territory.
>
> ✔ Good software can make you feel in control of your life.

Mediocre and bad software can make you feel stupid, however, or, at the very least, it make you want to tear your hair out. Lousy packages usually end up in the software graveyard.

Having reviewed many of the packages available, we can assure you that if you're having a hard time with some of the programs out there (even sometimes the more useful ones), you aren't at fault. Too many packages assume that you already know things such as your tax rate, your mortgage options, and the difference between stock and bond mutual funds. Much of what's out there isn't user-friendly and is too technically oriented. Some of it is even flawed in its financial accuracy.

A good software package, like a good tax or financial advisor, should be your partner in helping you better manage your finances. It should simply and concisely explain financial terminology and provide a road map to help you make decisions by offering choices and recommendations so that you can play with alternatives before following a particular course of action.

Although financial software packages are available that do more than one task or address more than one area of personal finances, no package covers the whole range of financial issues.

Tread carefully on the Web

"Go surfing!"

"Cool!"

No, you're not eavesdropping on a Southern California beach conversation. To hear promoters of companies with sites on the globe's largest computer network known as the Internet, you may think that the Internet is not only a hip place to be but *the* place to be.

We're increasingly asked questions like, "How do I research investments through the Internet?" or "How can I use the Internet to manage my personal finances?"

Our answer: "Very carefully."

Like information from any medium, you have to sift out the good from the bad. If you blindly navigate on the Internet and naively think that what's out there is useful "information," "research," or "objective advice," you may be in for a rude awakening.

Most personal finance sites on the Internet are free, which — guess what — means that these sites are basically advertising or are dominated and driven by advertising. If you're looking for written material by unbiased experts or journalists, well, you don't have much to pick from. So here are a few rules for Web surfing safety:

> ✔ **Consider the source.** *The Internet Report,* recently published by the investment banking firm Morgan Stanley, cites a short list of the "coolest" finance sites. On the list is the site of banking giant Bank of America (B of A). Because it's been a long time since we were in junior high school, we're not quite sure what cool means anymore. If cool can be used to describe a well-organized and graphically pleasing Web site, then we guess we could say that B of A's site is cool.

> However, if you're looking for sound information and advice, then B of A's site is decidedly "uncool." It steers you in a financial direction that benefits, not surprisingly, the bank and not you. For example, in the At Home section, users are asked to plug in their gross monthly income and down payment, which then is used to spit out the supposed amount that one can afford to spend on a home. No mention is given to other financial goals and concerns — such as saving for retirement — that affect one's ability to spend a particular amount of money on a home.

In the Credit Cards and Loans area, consider this advice: "Maybe you *can* have it now. When you don't have the cash on hand for important purchases, Bank of America can help you borrow what you need. From a new car, to that vacation you've been longing for, to new kitchen appliances, you can make these dreams real now." Click on a button on the bottom of this screen and presto, you're on your way to racking up credit card and auto debt. Why bother practising delayed gratification, living within your means, or buying something used if getting a loan is "easy" and comes with "special privileges"?

- **Watch out for "sponsored" content.** Another problem to watch out for on Internet sites is "sponsored" content, a euphemism for advertising under the guise of editorial content. Often buried in small print in an obscure part of the Web page or site, you'll usually find a disclaimer or note saying that an article is sponsored by (in other words, it's paid advertising by) the "author."

For example, The Mutual Fund Home Page, a U.S. site, states that its "primary purpose is to provide viewers with an independent guide that contains information and articles they can't get anywhere else." The "content" of the site suggests otherwise. In the Expert's Corner, viewers are treated to material reprinted from a newsletter that advocates frequent trading in and out of mutual funds to time market moves. It turns out that the "article" is "sponsored by the featured expert": In other words, it's a paid advertisement. (The track record of the newsletter's past recommendations, which isn't discussed, is poor.)

- **Financial planning or financial selling?** We also suggest skipping most of the financial-planning advice offered by financial service companies with financial products to sell. Such companies can't take the necessary objective, holistic view required to render useful advice. Investment companies, for example, will prod you into establishing mutual fund accounts with them without pointing out the benefits of paying off debt first. If you did that, though, you couldn't set up an account with them.

- **Short-term thinking and hot-tip touting.** Many financial Internet sites provide real-time stock quotes as a hook to some site that's cluttered with advertising. Our experience with individual investors is that the more short term they think, the worse they do, and checking your portfolio during the trading day certainly promotes short-termism. Some of these sites charge a nominal monthly fee and in return also throw in largely worthless content.

And finally, beware of tips offered around the electronic water cooler — message boards. As in the real world, chatting with strangers and exchanging ideas is fine. However, if you don't know the identity and competence of message board posters or chat room participants, why would you follow their financial advice or stock tips? Getting ideas from various sources is okay, but educate yourself and do your homework before making personal financial decisions.

If you want to best manage your personal finances and learn more, remember that there's a grain of truth in the old expression, "You get what you pay for." Free information on the Internet, especially that which is provided by companies in the financial services industry, is largely self-serving. Stick with information providers who have proven themselves in the printed world or who don't have anything to sell, except objective information and advice. Where appropriate in this chapter, we recommend useful Internet sites that meet these criteria.

Pay your bills and track your money

Every month, you write out by hand a bunch of cheques to the same organizations and people you wrote cheques to last month and the month before that. Chequebook software automates the process of paying your bills. When you have to make your monthly payment to the phone company, for example, your monthly cheque, already made payable to the phone company, pops up on-screen at your command. All you have to do is fill in the new amount that you have to pay. And your cheque gets printed on your computer's printer. (For a small monthly fee, you can even pay your bills electronically, completely eliminating the process of writing and mailing in cheques.) What's even better is that the program automatically tracks your cheque writing and prepares reports that detail your spending by category — so that you can get a handle on where the fat is in your budget.

- **Quicken** (available in Windows, DOS, and Macintosh versions) is an easy-to-use chequebook software program. In addition to offering the printed cheques and electronic bill-payment features, Quicken is a financial organizer. The program also allows you to track your investments and other assets and your loans and other financial liabilities.

- Although many small-business owners have used Quicken for their accounting needs, **QuickBooks** (available in Windows, DOS, and Macintosh versions) is a useful, straightforward software package specifically designed for keeping track of a small business's finances.

- In addition to Quicken, Microsoft Money is another good program that we've reviewed.

One drawback of using these programs to track your spending is that they only capture what you enter. So the amount and spending category of your individual credit card and cash purchases, which for most people are substantial, are omitted unless you enter such data (or you bank with a financial institution that allows you to download your credit card transactions using a modem).

Using chequebook software to plan for life changes

One thing is certain about life: It changes — marriage, buying a home, family expansion, starting a business, divorce, retirement, or death of a spouse. As we highlight in Chapter 21, although some life events bring joy and others sorrow, all bring financial change. If you don't manage this change, it may end up managing and ruling you.

We've witnessed the best of savers turn into deficit financiers due to the financial upheaval and shock waves from a major life event — even those events that were anticipated. One of the useful things that you can do with a chequebook software program is to use it to plan ahead for life changes.

For example, if you'd like to take the entrepreneurial plunge and leave your full-time job, you should know if you can afford to do that and what impact changed expenses and income would have on your ability to save money. Wannabe parents, likewise, should consider how increased expenses and a likely reduction in income would affect their monthly budget.

Chequebook software programs come with suggested categories for tallying your expenses — such as housing, clothing, auto, cable TV, furniture, insurance, telephone, other utilities, education, and so on. Useful for planning for change, the better programs that we recommend in this chapter also allow you to create your own categories. You can adjust and create new spending and income categories to match your personal financial situation. For example, if you're planning on having a baby, the program allows you to create a new major category, Baby, and then subcategories within it: diapers, clothing, child care, baby equipment, and so on. Before Junior arrives, you can plug in estimated spending numbers and compare the income and expense numbers to the ones in your current expense report without the baby expenditures.

Going through this exercise is a great way to estimate what impact a child or other significant life change will have on your financial situation. Eric once advised some nervous expectant parents to use their existing chequebook software as they were wondering what financial impact having a baby would have on their household finances. Their findings: Given their expected spending, the parents would go from saving 12 percent of their annual incomes to spending 5 percent more than they earned. But the lower-income spouse was also surprised to see that, by working half time rather than full-time, the couple's net savings would actually increase thanks largely to lower taxes, child care, and work-related expenses.

As you plan for your next life change, remember software's limitations. Even the best software can't factor in the nonfinancial considerations such as how you feel about working more or less because of a life change. Software may also mistakenly give you the illusion of control. Those expectant parents Eric worked with learned that they were having three new additions to their family and not just one!

Plan for retirement

Retirement planning software helps you to plan for retirement by crunching the numbers for you. But it can also teach you how particular changes — such as your investment returns, the inflation rate, or your savings rate — can affect when, and in what style, you can retire. The biggest time savings aspect of retirement planning software is that it lets you more quickly play with and see the consequences of changing the assumptions.

Some of the major investment companies that we profile in Part III of this book offer high-quality, low-cost retirement planning software.

Here are some good retirement planning programs to consider:

- **MoneyGuide** (Windows only) may be purchased at software retailers and bookstores for $39.95. Try the program or order it through the Internet at www.tefinancial.com

- **Retire! Personal Edition** (Windows only) may be ordered by calling 1-800-294-6622.

- **RRIFmetic For Windows** (Windows only) may be ordered by calling 1-800-663-4088, or by visiting the company's Web site at www.fimetrics.com.

The chequebook packages that we recommend earlier in this chapter have retirement-planning calculators that do a decent job of giving you a sense of where you stand with saving and planning for retirement.

Prepare your taxes

Tax-preparation software can save you time and money. Unlike most other personal finance software, this type of software is relatively easy to learn because you just have to enter data that the program specifically asks for. The program then plugs the data into the appropriate tax form. Good tax-preparation software contains all the forms needed to file your return. This feature reduces your chances of having to run to the post office for specialized forms that you didn't realize you'd need until April 30.

Among the better-tax preparation programs we've reviewed are **QuickTax** (Windows, Macintosh), **CanTax** (Windows, DOS), and **GriffTax** (Macintosh). These programs are easy to use. They "interview" you to gather the necessary information and select the appropriate forms based on your responses. More-experienced taxpayers can bypass the interview and jump directly to the forms they know they need to complete. These programs also help flag overlooked deductions and credits and identify other tax-reducing strategies.

If you're mainly after tax forms, you can download all sorts of tax forms without charge through the government Web site at www.revcan. ca/menu/EmenuLZZ.html.

Research investments

When you research investments with your computer, you can bypass the software and online worlds and not be at all left behind. Why? Well, much of what's out there is a watered-down version of better-printed publications, isn't very good, or is geared toward professional investors.

If you're an investing and mutual fund novice, you probably won't succeed using the major mutual fund software programs in the marketplace such as Portfolio Analytics' PAL*Trak,* Southam's Mutual Fund SourceDisk, and Globe HySales. Such programs don't offer enough guidance for beginners on mutual fund basics, such as how to analyze annual operating expense ratios, the merits of no-load versus load funds, how to construct a portfolio, and how to allocate assets. And they aren't cheap, costing around $400 for a year's worth of information and updates. If you know your way around the fund world, though (for basics on funds, see Chapter 12), these programs contain loads of information on performance, costs, and fund holdings that can be useful for choosing appropriate funds.

Much of the best information in the commercial online world is geared toward investing in individual stocks. So if you've given up on being the next Warren Buffett and have decided to use mutual funds, the online world will be of limited use to you.

The major commercial online services — which are set up to charge for information — offer a number of helpful resources for an individual stock investor.

The advantage of going online isn't that you profit from getting news sooner or from tapping into the latest predictions of yet more gurus, but that you can access useful resources quicker and cheaper than you could before (that is, if your modem is speedy and you know where to look). Rather than schlepping off to the library and fighting over the favourite investing reference manuals, ponying up hundreds of dollars to buy print versions for your own use, or slogging through voice mail hell when you call government agencies, you can access a variety of materials with your computer. You can also usually pay for just what you need.

To obtain access to contact information, as well as annual reports, financial statements, and other reports filed with securities authorities by Canadian companies, try SEDAR (System for Electronic Document Analysis and Retrieval) at www.sedar.com. You'll also find the bulk of publicly available documents filed by mutual funds here as well.

For a concise financial summary for a U.S. company that comes with links to the company's Web site, SEC filings, and a Web search for references, check out Hoover's Company Profiles on America Online. Because of these connections, Hoover's is a good starting point for researching individual companies.

Also on America Online (AOL), the Disclosure site supplies information from SEC filings and other sources on public U.S. companies. Like Hoover's, Disclosure is a useful place to start if you have particular stocks already in mind and want to learn more about the companies' businesses and financials. Disclosure holds your hand through the process of navigating and understanding the various documents. To sidestep the commercial online service's charges, you can access U.S. Securities and Exchange Commission (SEC) documents directly via the SEC's Web site (www.sec.gov) but be aware that navigating this site takes patience. All public U.S. corporations, as well as mutual funds, file with the agency.

Although we've always been leery of financial service company "educational" materials because of bias and self-serving advice, some companies have done a worthy job. Trimark's site (www.Trimark.com) offers a good overview of how funds work, along with a well-thought-out retirement planning program that you can download for free called Trimark Time Piece. The investor-friendly Green Line family of funds has an extensive site (www.tdbank.ca) that provides explanations of different investment strategies, as well as market updates and advice for beginners. For broader coverage of mutual funds, stocks, and investing, as well as other personal finance topics like insurance and mortgages, visit The Knowledge Centre at www.imoney.com. You'll find many articles on a wide number of topics, which Tony put together.

Tracking your investment returns often not worth the headache

Accurately tracking the return on your investments can be an extremely complicated, tedious, and time-consuming task — exactly the type of chore that computers were designed to relieve us of. Although one would think that a number of excellent investment tracking software packages would be on the market today, we feel that such available packages are . . . well . . . usually complicated, tedious, and time-consuming. At this point anyway, these programs often aren't any more efficient than the old-fashioned method of pencil, paper, and a calculator.

Our big gripe with the investment tracking software programs is that most of them don't allow you to determine your investment's total return. And the few programs that do require lots of your time to get to that point. Your effective or *internal rate of return* (IRR), which compares your original amounts invested to the current market value, is the best way to measure the success of your investments over time. Two of the packages that we discuss earlier in the chapter, Quicken and Microsoft Money, calculate IRR, but many other software packages that we've reviewed do not.

Most of the other packages calculate your *cost base,* which is your original investment plus reinvested dividends and capital gains, for which you would have already paid taxes outside of an RRSP. When you sell an investment that isn't tax-sheltered, you need to know the cost base for tax purposes (refer to Chapter 7). Cost base reports make your returns look less generous because reinvested distributions increase your original investment and

Fools and their money

In addition to research tools and publications, the online world is also home to pundits attempting to pick the next Microsoft or claiming to have a trading system to beat the market.

Although virtually unknown a few years ago when they had a few dozen subscribers to their printed stock-picking newsletter, AOL's Motley Fools have promoted themselves to prominence by flogging the market-beating returns of their Fool Portfolio. The chief Fools are David and Tom Gardner, who also now oversee AOL sites on such disparate topics as sports, movies, and contemporary culture.

The Gardners claim that with minutes of effort, novices can easily earn 25 to 35 percent per year investing in individual stocks and can handily beat mutual funds. But as is the case in the careers of so many stock-picking pundits, the Fools' rapid ascent to visibility in early 1996 has since been followed by less-than-stellar returns.

Two stocks, Iomega and America Online, which were entirely responsible for the Fool portfolio's short-term market-beating returns, were later knocked down by more than 65 percent from their early 1996 peaks. In fact, in the year after that peak, the Fool portfolio under-performed the market by a whopping 50 percent! The Fools also post the returns of two other model portfolios; both have under-performed the market averages. Like many other newsletters, the Fools also use trading methods developed by looking at historic data to claim propriety to market-beating trading systems. In their Investing for Growth area,

they make it seem as if they've actually been using this system since 1980 to generate 26+ percent annual returns. In the first full quarter after this system was published, their model portfolio plunged more than 25 percent while the stock market rose.

The Fools attribute the uniqueness of their investment philosophy to the phenomenon of electronic message boards. The theory behind these message boards is certainly admirable: Thousands of citizen investors are given a place to exchange hot new stock tips before the big guys on Wall Street even know what's going on. Although it's an appealing idea, the reality is uglier. Message boards are a Never-Never Land of accountability; identities, agendas, and the competence of message writers are usually a mystery. Any postings of true substance are buried in an avalanche of hype: owners of a given stock are cheerleading, and anyone with a dissenting viewpoint is often torn to shreds.

Other print newsletters, most with mediocre to dismal historic performance, are putting their wares online as well. Just as you shouldn't invest in a mutual fund without first examining its actual track record and that of its manager, do the same before following the advice of stock-picking pundits online.

If you decide to become a cyber-stock picker and take on the risks of individual stock-picking, remember the old expression about the parting of fools and their money. Do your homework and research before you buy. Don't buy a stock based only on a pundit's opinion.

seemingly reduce your returns. We know from direct experience that investors often look at the cost base reports — which are sometimes misleadingly named "investment performance" or "investment analysis" — and assume that these base reports tell them what their total investment returns are. Using software for cost base calculations generally isn't worthwhile because most investment companies provide cost base information for you upon request or when you sell an investment.

If you want to analyse your historic returns, you need to gather up all your old account statements (if you can find them) and enter in every investment you made as well as all reinvestments of dividends, interest, and capital gains distributions.

If you're a buy-and-hold mutual fund investor, investment tracking software has limited benefit given the time required to enter your data. Mutual funds and many other published resources tell you what the funds' total return was for the past year so you don't need to enter every dividend and capital gain distribution for yourself.

As for calculating the return of your overall portfolio with the old-fashioned method of paper and pencil mentioned above, simply weight the return of each investment by the portion of your portfolio invested in it. For example, with a simple portfolio equally divided between two investments, which returned 10 percent and 20 percent respectively, your overall portfolio return would be 15 percent.

Investment tracking software can be more useful for stock traders. In our experience, stock traders don't usually track their overall returns. If they actually used one of these programs, they could at least see how all their trading depresses their returns. (Rare is the stock picker who can go through this exercise and actually beat the market indexes over the long run.)

One of the greatest benefits of these packages is that using them can help get you organized. If you enter your investments into the package, they can help you make sure you don't lose track of your holdings. Of course, if your home burns to the ground and you don't have a backup copy of your files or software, you'll have to start from scratch. (And we hope you've got home/renter's insurance!)

Trading online

If you do your investing homework, trading securities online may save you money and perhaps some time. For years, discount brokers (which we discuss in Chapter 10) had been heralded as the low cost source for trading, and many of them offer online trading. They include Canada Trust (www.ctsecurities.com), Bank of Montreal's Investorline (www.investorline.com), CIBC's Investor's Edge (www.cibc.com/products/investments/invest_edge/), Royal Bank's Action Direct (www.royalbank.com/english/adirect), Scotia Discount Brokerage

Online (www.scotiacapital.com/SDB/), and TD Green Line (www.tdbank.ca/tdbank/Greenline/English/index.html). An added benefit of investing online through discount brokers is that many give you an additional discount on commissions, typically 10 percent.

You can also try Priority Brokerage (www.priority.com) and eTrade (www.canada.etrade.com). This second company, eTrade, in fact, has built its securities brokerage business around online trading. Without the overhead of branch offices, and by accepting and processing trades by computer, eTrade keeps its costs and brokerage charges to a minimum. Cut-rate electronic brokerage firms like these are for people who want to direct their own financial affairs and don't want or need to work with a personal broker.

Investment tracking and trading software can be helpful, but it can also encourage people to trade more than they should. Following investments on a daily basis encourages you to think short term. Remember that the best investments are bought and held for the long haul (see Part III for more information).

Reading and searching periodicals

The AOL Company News and the CompuServe News sites provide recent news from the major wire services. Prodigy has Dow Jones News Retrieval, but it only covers the past 21 days. All the services can search for information on specific subjects, but be forewarned that you usually get way more information than is relevant to you. On the Web, you can find most Canadian releases at Canada Newswire's site at www.newswire.ca.

For access to print publications online, a good starting point is the *Globe and Mail's* site at www.globefund.com. You can read many of the stories on mutual funds, as well as articles from the *Report on Business*'s popular weekend section, Investing. Over at Canoe (www.canoe.com) you can find useful articles from *The Financial Post.* Both sites offer tools that help you sift through the many funds available to find those that meet your needs (performance, type of fund, MER, and so forth).

The AOL Financial Newsstand has current issues of major business magazines and a host of major newspapers and other magazines. The CompuServe Business Database Plus is even more extensive: It contains five years of articles from 750 publications including industry and specialized business newsletters. The cost for this service is 25 cents U.S. per minute and $1.50 U.S. per downloaded article.

Many business and financial publications are going online to offer investors current news and financial market data. *The Wall Street Journal* offers an online personalized edition of the paper (update.wsj.com) that lets you tailor content to meet your specific needs. The cost is $49 U.S. per year ($29 U.S. if you're already a *Journal* subscriber).

EyeQ (www.datatimes.com) also offers an intelligent news search engine and value for the money. The service costs $39 U.S. per month, and $3 U.S. per article retrieved.

Preparing legal documents

Just as you can prepare a tax return with the advice of a software program, you can also prepare common legal documents. This type of software may save you from the often difficult task of finding a competent and affordable lawyer.

Using legal software is generally preferable to using fill-in-the-blank documents. Software has the built-in virtues of directing and limiting your choices and keeping you from making common mistakes. Quality software also incorporates the knowledge and insights of the legal eagles who developed the software. And these features can save you money.

If your situation isn't unusual, legal software may work well for you. As to the legality of documents that you create with legal software, remember that a will, for example, is made legal and valid by your witnesses; the fact that a lawyer prepares the document is *not* what makes it legal.

An excellent package for preparing your own will is **Quicken Family Lawyer** (Windows). In addition to allowing you to prepare wills, Family Lawyer can also help you prepare a *living will* and medical power of attorney (refer to Chapter 19).

Another good all-around package is **My Legal Assistant,** published by MLA Systems (Windows). The program includes a large number of forms, including legal templates for leases, powers of attorney, wills, and domestic agreements. The package also includes a number of business documents, including a bill of sale and a promissory note. My Legal Assistant is available at software retailers, or you can order it by calling 613-834-5164.

If you still want to have a lawyer review and complete your final documents to ensure that you've dealt with all eventualities and haven't left any loopholes, preparing a legal document like a will with a software program still makes sense. It can help focus you on matters you need to consider, prompt you to gather all the necessary bits of information, and educate you about the process. You'll help ensure that your will and other documents will have the results you expect, plus you'll spend less time with your lawyer, saving on legal fees.

Index

(continued)

•*L*•

(continued)

(continued)

(continued)

Notes

Notes

IDG BOOKS WORLDWIDE BOOK REGISTRATION

Register This Book and Win!

We want to hear from you!

Visit **http://my2cents.dummies.com** to register this book and tell us how you liked it!

- ✔ Get entered in our monthly prize giveaway.

- ✔ Give us feedback about this book — tell us what you like best, what you like least, or maybe what you'd like to ask the author and us to change!

- ✔ Let us know any other ...*For Dummies*® topics that interest you.

Your feedback helps us determine what books to publish, tells us what coverage to add as we revise our books, and lets us know whether we're meeting your needs as a ...*For Dummies* reader. You're our most valuable resource, and what you have to say is important to us!

Not on the Web yet? It's easy to get started with *Dummies 101*®: *The Internet For Windows*® *98* or *The Internet For Dummies*,® 5th Edition, at local retailers everywhere.

Or let us know what you think by sending us a letter at the following address:

...*For Dummies* Book Registration
Dummies Press
7260 Shadeland Station, Suite 100
Indianapolis, IN 46256-3945
Fax 317-596-5498

BESTSELLING BOOK SERIES FROM IDG